Celebrating Diversity

Third Edition

EDITED BY

CORA SARJEANT WILDER
AND JAMES SHERRIER

GINN PRESS

160 Gould Street
Needham Heights, MA 02194-2310

Printed in the United States of
America

10 9 8 7 6 5 4 3 2 1

ISBN 0–536–58378-1

BA 9454

GINN PRESS
160 Gould Street/Needham Heights, MA 02194
Simon & Schuster Higher Education Publishing Group

COPYRIGHT ACKNOWLEDGMENTS

CONTENTS

INTRODUCTION

WHY THIS TEXT

What follows is a collection of readings that were carefully selected to provide a resource for students engaged in a course designed to provide an overview of the existing and growing diversity in American society. The title, *Celebrating Diversity* was chosen to express the excitement and creativity that such diversity can bring to the American scene. It is also meant to emphasize the similarities that unite us far more than the diversities that all too often attract our attention.

Underneath all diversity lies commonality. This may seem to be a paradox; however, the fact is that all human organisms are fundamentally the same. The emphasis which some place on sex and skin color is more artificial than real. In reality, we are all condemned to live out our lives on the crust of this planet and therefore we all face the same basic human issues. All peoples, at all times and in all places, must develop responses to basic human realities such as birth, growth, education, sex, toil and death. Most of our responses to the basic human issues are directly influenced by the solution our particular culture has evolved to answer the question: what is the basic nature of mankind? Is Man essentially good, evil or neutral? In addition, by what criteria do we evaluate ourselves and each other? What is most important? Is it what one has accomplished, what one is, or what one is becoming? Different peoples living at different times and in different environments and facing different historical pressures, have evolved different responses to these and other life issues. Because these responses worked, or seemed to work, they became part of the social fabric and belief system of the given group. They were and are rarely questioned. Thus we develop cultural filters through which we view and compare our favorite responses with those of other groups. In homogeneous societies this may cause little difficulty; however, in a diverse nation like ours where the responses of other groups are all too visible, this often leads to contention. We, looking through our own cultural filters, tend to see other responses as outrageous, suspect and even harmful.

It is the purpose of this text, and the kind of course it is designed to support, to help and encourage the student to come out from behind his or her cultural filter and take a clear and realistic look at the other available responses to human issues which abound in our diverse society. No one group has evolved responses that work best at all times and in all situations. We can and should learn from each other. Human beings grow best when they allow themselves to experience different ideas and modes of living and then alter their existing models of reality to accommodate these new experiences.

The purpose of this text is to (truly) celebrate human diversity and to recognize the very natural desire to survive and thrive that lies under all human responses.

The Editors

The Changing Face of Immigration (1989)
Lydio F. Tomasi

By the turn of the century, immigrants will represent the largest proportionate increase in population and work force the United States has encountered since World War I.

Only 15 percent of those entering the U.S. labor force over the next 13 years will be native-born males, compared to the current 47 percent, according to a report by the Hudson Institute. (See Chart 1.)

Approximately 600,000 legal and illegal immigrants are projected to enter the U.S. annually through the remainder of the century. Two-thirds or more of these immigrants of working age are likely to join the labor force. In the South and West where immigrant workers are concentrated, these newcomers are likely to reshape local economies dramatically, prompting faster growth and labor surpluses. The number of foreign residents in the South grew by 120 percent from 1970-1980, and by 97 percent in the West.

Non-whites, women and immigrants will comprise more than five-sixths of the net additions to the work force between now and the year 2000. They currently account for only 50 percent.

This transformation in the composition of the work force is compounded by rapid changes in the nature of the job market. The fastest growing areas of employment will be in the professional, technical and sales fields, requiring the highest skills and levels of education. All but one of these employment categories require more than a median level of education.

Among new immigrants, educational levels pose a startling profile. Of those adults who entered the U.S. in the 1970s, 25 percent had less than five years of school, compared to 3 percent of native-born Americans. On the other hand, 22 percent were college graduates, as compared with 16 percent of the native population. To bring this growing share of immigrants into the general population and labor force poses serious problems and opportunities for policy-makers, business, labor, schools and state and local governments.

Despite fears to the contrary, it has been demonstrated that an annual influx of between 450,000-700,000 immigrants is economically beneficial to the country.

Chart 1

	1985 Labor Force	Net New Workers 1985–2000
Total	115,461,000	25,000,000
Native White Men	47%	15%
Native White Women	36%	42%
Native Non-white Men	5%	7%
Native Non-white Women	5%	13%
Immigrant Men	4%	13%
Immigrant Women	3%	9%

Studies in the Los Angeles labor market, where more than 1 million immigrants settled during the 1970s, demonstrate that during this period growth in the employment sector was well above the national average and unemployment levels were below the national average.

While manufacturing wages were depressed as a result of the immigrant influx, wages in the service industry sector, which bore the concentration of native-born Americans, rose faster than the national average. The service industry generally employs more native-born Americans because such jobs usually require education and skill levels not held by many immigrants.

Conclusions regarding the impact of immigration on the unemployment rate of native-born minorities are less certain. The results of one study suggest that the employment levels of native-born minorities are not adversely affected by immigration. A more thorough analysis is needed, however, before conclusions can be drawn.

Despite consistent evidence that the country benefits from immigrant labor, the public generally opposes immigration. Most polls show the majority favor less immigration, while 7 percent favor more.

Asian American Population: 1980 and Projected for 1990 and 2000

Rank	Ethnic Group	Number	Percent
	1980		
	Total	3,466,421	100.0
1	Chinese	812,178	23.4
2	Filipino	781,894	22.6
3	Japanese	716,331	20.7
4	Asian Indian	387,223	11.2
5	Korean	357,393	10.3
6	Vietnamese	245,025	7.1
	Other Asian	166,377	4.8
	1990		
	Total	6,533,608	100.0
1	Filipino	1,405,146	21.5
2	Chinese	1,259,038	19.3
3	Vietnamese	859,638	13.2
4	Korean	814,495	12.5
5	Japanese	804,535	12.3
6	Asian Indian	684,339	10.5
	Other Asian	706,417	10.8
	2000		
	Total	9,850,364	100.0
1	Filipino	2,070,571	21.0
2	Chinese	1,683,537	17.1
3	Vietnamese	1,574,385	16.0
4	Korean	1,320,759	13.4
5	Asian Indian	1,006,305	10.2
6	Japanese	856,619	8.7
	Other Asian	1,338,188	13.6

Source: Leon F. Bouvier and Anthony Agresta. "Projections of the Asian American Population, 1980-2030," in James T. Fawcett and Benjamin Carino (eds.), *Asian and Pacific Immigration to the United States*

Cultural Impacts

In the coming decade, America will become an increasingly diverse society as immigrants from all over the world enter in significant numbers.

Since 1965, the United States has experienced an immigration comparable in size, but of even greater diversity than the great migrations earlier in the century. In addition to a continuing stream from Europe, the source of most previous migration, 80 percent of new immigrants come from Asia and Latin America.

This new immigration will produce far-reaching social and economic changes:

- Texas, now nearly 23 percent Hispanic, is expected to contain no ethnic majority by 2015. Without counting undocumented aliens in the New York metropolitan area, New York City has been adding more than 75,000 legal immigrants annually. By 2000, only two of every three New Yorkers will be white.
- If present trends continue, Hispanics will grow to 47 million by 2020. In 1980, Hispanics numbered about 14 million. Asians, whose 1980 population was 3.4 million, are growing even faster; their total could triple this decade.

These changes mark a dramatic contrast from eight years ago when five out of six Americans were white, and one out of six was black, Hispanic or Asian.

Demographic Revolution

While Asian Americans are heavily concentrated in a few states in the West, they are beginning to spread throughout the nation.

In New York City, 35 percent of the population speaks a language other than English at home. In California, Asian Americans now outnumber blacks; by 2020, California's whites will account for only 40 percent of the population.

In sum, the United States is going through a demographic revolution. Every major institution in this society—government, communities, business, schools—faces the challenge of maximizing the gains newcomers promise while minimizing the conflicts that sometimes accompany diversity. By drawing on experience in responding to diversity and by planning carefully for the future, we can incorporate these new populations as successfully as we have the previous ones.

An advanced economy requires an educated work force. Because education is important to the immigrants' and the nation's future, we need to help school better deal with these new populations.

Teachers, administrators and students' curricula must adjust to the new reality of immigrant students. Language may be the most divisive issue raised by the new immigration, as testified by the recently passed "official English" referendum in Florida, Arizona and Colorado. The determination of sufficient funding, adequate staffing and bilingual curricula should remain in the hands of educators, not politicians or advocates.

However, the issue of language policy goes beyond the accepted goal that English literacy is an urgent national priority and beyond the controversial bilingual program. The increasing interdependence of nations demands the improvement of language proficiency of all Americans and should serve as a great motivation in foreign language education.

Heavy and continuing immigration patterns will create problems for the American social and economic systems and will require significant policy initiatives at the federal and state levels.

The country has sufficient resources to cope with these problems and the evidence suggests that the benefits newcomers bring far outweigh the costs. Also, powerful forces within the American society contribute to the speedy assimilation of immigrants into U.S. society and its democratic values.

From the beginning, the U.S. has absorbed immense numbers of people from many lands and the country has flourished. As one writer noted, "No other country has the courage to let its demographic mix change so quickly, and to bet that doing so will enrich it."

Dr. Lydio F. Tomasi is executive director of the Center for Migration Studies and editor of Migration World Magazine. *209 Flagg Place, Staten Island, N.Y. 10304.*

Beyond the Melting Pot (1990)

William A. Henry, III

Someday soon, surely much sooner, than most people who filled out their Census forms last week realize, white Americans will become a minority group. Long before that day arrives, the presumption that the "typical" U.S. citizen is someone who traces his or her descent in a direct line to Europe will be part of the past. By the time these elementary students of Brentwood Science Magnet School in Brentwood, Calif., reach mid-life, their diverse ethnic experience in the classroom will be echoed in neighborhoods and workplaces throughout the U.S.

Already 1 American in 4 defines himself or herself as Hispanic or nonwhite. If current trends in immigration and birth rates persist, the Hispanic population will have further increased an estimated 21%, the Asian presence about 22%, blacks almost 12% and whites a little more than 2% when the 20th century ends. By 2020, a date no further into the future than John F. Kennedy's election is in the past, the number of U.S. residents who are Hispanic or nonwhite will have more than doubled, to nearly 115 million, while the white population will not be increasing at all. By 2056, when someone born today will be 66 years old, the "average" U.S. resident, as defined by Census statistics, will trace his or her descent to Africa, Asia, the Hispanic world, the Pacific Islands, Arabia—almost anywhere but white Europe.

While there may remain towns or outposts where even a black family will be something of an oddity, where English and Irish and German surnames will predominate, where a traditional (some will wistfully say "real") America will still be seen on almost every street corner, they will be only the vestiges of an earlier nation. The former majority will learn, as a normal part of everyday life, the meaning of the Latin slogan engraved on U.S. coins—E PLURIBUS UNUM, one formed from many.

Among the younger populations that go to school and provide new entrants to the work force, the change will happen sooner. In some places an America beyond the melting pot has already arrived. In New York State some 40% of elementary- and secondary-school children belong to an ethnic minority. Within a decade, the proportion is expected to approach 50%. In California white pupils are already a minority. Hispanics (who, regardless of their complexion, generally distinguish themselves from both blacks and whites) account for 31.4% of public school enrollment, blacks add 8.9%, and Asians and others amount to 11%—for a nonwhite total of 51.3%. This finding is not only a reflection of white flight from desegregated public schools. Whites of all ages account for just 58% of California's population. In San Jose bearers of the Vietnamese surname Nguyen outnumber the Joneses in the telephone directory 14 columns to eight.

Nor is the change confined to the coasts. Some 12,000 Hmong refugees from Laos have settled in St. Paul. At some Atlanta low-rent apartment complexes that used to be virtually all black, social workers today need to speak Spanish. At the Sesame Hut restaurant in Houston, a Korean immigrant owner trains Hispanic immigrant workers to prepare Chinese-style food for a largely black clientele. The Detroit area has 200,000 people of Middle Eastern descent; some 1,500 small grocery and convenience stores in the vicinity are owned by a whole subculture of Chaldean Christians with roots in Iraq. "Once America was a microcosm of European nationalities," says Molefi Asante, chairman of the department of African-American studies at Temple University in Philadelphia. "Today America is a microcosm of the world."

History suggests that sustaining a truly multiracial society is difficult, or at least unusual. Only a handful of great powers of the distant past—Pharaonic Egypt and Imperial Rome, most notably—managed to maintain a distinct national identity while embracing, and being ruled by, an ethnic mélange. The most ethnically diverse contemporary power, the Soviet Union, is beset with secessionist demands and near tribal conflicts. But such comparisons are flawed, because those empires were launched by conquest and maintained through an aggressive military presence. The U.S. was created, and continues to be redefined, primarily by voluntary immigration. This process has been one of the country's great strengths, infusing it with talent and energy. The "browning of America" offers tremendous opportunity for capitalizing anew on the merits of many peoples from many lands. Yet this fundamental change in the ethnic makeup of the U.S. also poses risks. The American character is resilient and thrives on change. But past periods of rapid evolution have also, alas, brought out deeper, more fearful aspects of the national soul.

Politics: New and Shifting Alliances

A truly multiracial society will undoubtedly prove much harder to govern. Even seemingly race-free conflicts will be increasingly complicated by an overlay of ethnic tension. For example, the expected showdown in the early 21st century between the rising number of retirees and the dwindling number of workers who must be taxed to pay for the elders' Social Security benefits will probably be compounded by the fact that a large majority of recipients will be white, whereas a majority of workers paying for them will be nonwhite.

While prior generations of immigrants believed they had to learn English quickly to survive, many Hispanics now maintain that the Spanish language is inseparable from their ethnic and cultural identity, and seek to remain bilingual, if not primarily Spanish-speaking, for life. They see legislative drives to make English the sole official language, which have prevailed in some fashion in at least 16 states, as a political backlash. Says Arturo Vargas of the Mexican American Legal Defense and Educational Fund: "That's what English-only has been all about—a reaction to the growing population and influence of Hispanics. It's human nature to be uncomfortable with change. That's what the Census is all about, documenting changes and making sure the country keeps up."

Racial and ethnic conflict remains an ugly fact of American life everywhere, from working-class ghettos to college campuses, and those who do not raise their fists often raise their voices over affirmative action and other power sharing. When Florida Atlantic University, a state-funded institution under pressure to increase its low black enrollment, offered last month to give free tuition to every qualified black freshman who enrolled, the school was flooded with calls of complaint, some protesting that nothing was being done for "real" Americans. As the numbers of minorities increase, their demands for a share of the national bounty are bound to intensify, while whites are certain to feel ever more embattled. Businesses often feel whipsawed between immigration laws that punish them for hiring illegal aliens and anti-discrimination laws that penalize them for demanding excessive documentation from foreign-seeming job applicants. Even companies that consistently seek to do the right thing may be overwhelmed by the problems of diversifying a primarily white managerial corps fast enough to direct a work force that will be increasingly nonwhite and, potentially, resentful.

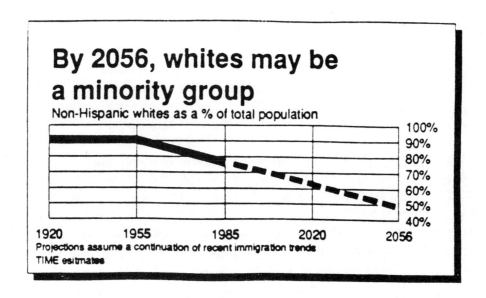

By 2056, whites may be a minority group

Non-Hispanic whites as a % of total population

Projections assume a continuation of recent immigration trends
TIME esitmates

Nor will tensions be limited to the polar simplicity of white vs. nonwhite. For all Jesse Jackson's rallying cries about shared goals, minority groups often feel keenly competitive. Chicago's Hispanic leaders have leapfrogged between white and black factions, offering support wherever there seemed to be the most to gain for their own community. Says Dan Solis of the Hispanic-oriented United Neighborhood Organization: "If you're thinking power, you don't put your eggs in one basket."

Blacks, who feel they waited longest and endured most in the fight for equal opportunity, are uneasy about being supplanted by Hispanics or, in some areas, by Asians as the numerically largest and most influential minority—and even more, about being outstripped in wealth and status by these newer groups. Because Hispanics are so numerous and Asians such a fast-growing group, they have become the "hot" minorities, and blacks feel their needs are getting lower priority. As affirmative action has broadened to include other groups—and to benefit white women perhaps most of all—blacks perceive it as having waned in value for them.

The Classroom: Whose History Counts?

Political pressure has already brought about sweeping change in public school textbooks over the past couple of decades and has begun to affect the core humanities curriculum at such élite universities as Stanford. At stake at the college level is whether the traditional "canon" of Greek, Latin and West European humanities study should be expanded to reflect the cultures of Africa, Asia and other parts of the world. Many books treasured as classics by prior generations are now seen as tools of cultural imperialism. In the extreme form, this thinking rises to a value-deprived neutralism that views all cultures, regardless of the grandeur or paucity of their attainments, as essentially equal.

Even more troubling is a revisionist approach to history in which groups that have gained power in the present turn to remaking the past in the image of their desires. If 18th, 19th and earlier 20th century society should not have been so dominated by white Christian men of West European ancestry, they reason, then that past society should be reinvented as pluralist and democratic. Alternatively, the racism and sexism of the past are treated as inextricable from—and therefore irremediably tainting—traditional learning and values.

While debates over college curriculum get the most attention, professors generally can resist or subvert the most wrong-headed changes and students generally have mature enough judgment to sort out the arguments. Elementary- and secondary-school curriculums reach a far broader segment at a far more impressionable age, and political expediency more often wins over intellectual honesty. Exchanges have been vituperative in New York, where a state task force concluded that "African-Americans, Asian-Americans, Puerto Ricans and Native Americans have all been victims of an intellectual and educational oppression. . . . Negative characterizations, or the absence of positive references, have had a terribly damaging effect on the psyche of young people." In urging a revised syllabus, the task force argued, "Children from European culture will have a less arrogant perspective of being part of a group that has 'done it all.'" Many intellectuals are outraged. Political scientist Andrew Hacker of Queens College lambastes a task-force suggestion that children be taught how "Native Americans were here to welcome new settlers from Holland, Senegal, England, Indonesia, France, the Congo, Italy, China, Iberia." Asks Hacker: "Did the Indians really welcome all those groups? Were they at Ellis Island when the Italians started to arrive? This is not history but a myth intended to bolster the self-esteem of certain children and, just possibly, a platform for advocates of various ethnic interests."

Values: Something in Common

Economic and political issues, however much emotion they arouse, are fundamentally open to practical solution. The deeper significance of America's becoming a majority nonwhite society is what it means to the national psyche, to individuals' sense of themselves and their nation—their idea of what it is to be American. People of color have often felt that whites treated equality as a benevolence granted to minorities rather than as an inherent natural right. Surely that condescension will wither.

Rather than accepting U.S. history and its meaning as settled, citizens will feel ever more free to debate where the nation's successes sprang from and what its unalterable beliefs are. They will clash over which myths and icons to invoke in education, in popular culture, in ceremonial speechmaking from political campaigns to the State of the Union address. Which is the more admirable heroism: the

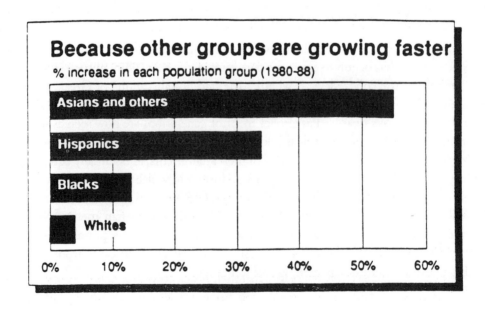

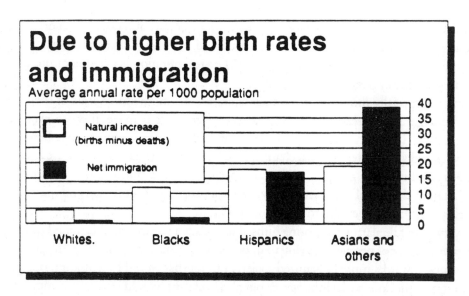

Due to higher birth rates and immigration
Average annual rate per 1000 population

- ☐ Natural increase (births minus deaths)
- ■ Net immigration

| | Whites. | Blacks | Hispanics | Asians and others |

courageous holdout by a few conquest-minded whites over Hispanics at the Alamo, or the anonymous expression of hope by millions who filed through Ellis Island? Was the subduing of the West a daring feat of bravery and ingenuity, or a wretched example of white imperialism? Symbols deeply meaningful to one group can be a matter of indifference to another. Says University of Wisconsin chancellor Donna Shalala: "My grandparents came from Lebanon. I don't identify with the Pilgrims on a personal level." Christopher Jencks, professor of sociology at Northwestern, asks, "Is anything more basic about turkeys and Pilgrims than about Martin Luther King and Selma? To me, it's six of one and half a dozen of the other, if children understand what it's like to be a dissident minority. Because the civil rights struggle is closer chronologically, it's likelier to be taught by someone who really cares.

Traditionalists increasingly distinguish between a "multiracial" society, which they say would be fine, and a "multicultural" society, which they deplore. They argue that every society needs a universally accepted set of values and that new arrivals should therefore be pressured to conform to the mentality on which U.S. prosperity and freedom were built. Says Allan Bloom, author of the best-selling *The Closing of the American Mind:* "Obviously, the future of America can't be sustained if people keep only to their own ways and remain perpetual outsiders. The society has got to turn them into Americans. There are natural fears that today's immigrants may be too much of a cultural stretch for a nation based on Western values."

The counterargument, made by such scholars as historian Thomas Bender of New York University, is that if the center cannot hold, then one must redefine the center. It should be, he says, "the ever changing outcome of a continuing contest among social groups and ideas for the power to define public culture." Besides, he adds, many immigrants arrive committed to U.S. values; that is part of what attracted them. Says Julian Simon, professor of business administration at the University of Maryland: "The life and institutions here shape immigrants and not vice versa. This business about immigrants changing our institutions and our basic ways of life is hogwash. It's nativist scare talk."

Citizenship: Forging a New Identity

Historians note that Americans have felt before that their historical culture was being overwhelmed by immigrants, but conflicts between earlier-arriving English, Germans and Irish and later-arriving

Italians and Jews did not have the obvious and enduring element of racial skin color. And there was never a time when the nonmainstream elements could claim, through sheer numbers, the potential to unite and exert political dominance. Says Bender: "The real question is whether or not our notion of diversity can successfully negotiate the color line."

For whites, especially those who trace their ancestry back to the early years of the Republic, the American heritage is a source of pride. For people of color, it is more likely to evoke anger and sometimes shame. The place where hope is shared is in the future. Demographer Ben Wattenberg, formerly perceived as a resister to social change, says, "There's a nice chance that the American myth in the 1990s and beyond is going to ratchet another step toward this idea that we are the universal nation. That rings the bell of manifest destiny. We're a people with a mission and a sense of purpose, and we believe we have something to offer the world."

Not every erstwhile alarmist can bring himself to such optimism. Says Norman Podhoretz, editor of *Commentary,* "A lot of people are trying to undermine the foundations of the American experience and are pushing toward a more Balkanized society. I think that would be a disaster, not only because it would destroy a precious social inheritance but also because it would lead to enormous unrest, even violence."

While know-nothingism is generally confined to the more dismal corners of the American psyche, it seems all too predictable that during the next decades many more mainstream white Americans will begin to speak openly about the nation they feel they are losing. There are not, after all, many non-white faces depicted in Norman Rockwell's paintings. White Americans are accustomed to thinking of themselves as the very picture of their nation. Inspiring as it may be to the rest of the world, significant as it may be to the U.S. role in global politics, world trade and the pursuit of peace, becoming a conspicuously multiracial society is bound to be a somewhat bumpy experience for many ordinary citizens. For older Americans, raised in a world where the numbers of whites were greater and the visibility of nonwhites was carefully restrained, the new world will seem ever stranger. But as the children at Brentwood Science Magnet School, and their counterparts in classrooms across the nation, are coming to realize, the new world is here. It is now. And it is irreversibly the America to come.

IRISH

POPULATION: 26 million	**PHYSICAL CHARACTERISTICS:** *Red hair* *Red cheeks* *Red noses*
RELIGION: *Bingo* **PRACTICING:** 91,683,082 (on March 17th)	**RACIAL TRAITS (GOOD):** *Always drunk* *Pray a lot* *Despise the English* **RACIAL TRAITS (BAD):** *Always drunk* *Religious hypocrite* *Hits women*
LOCATION: *Boston*	**DIET STAPLE:** *Whiskey*

CHAPTER 1

ACCULTURATION

Rediscovering Columbus, V: Under Indian Eyes (1991)

Peter Stanford

At dawn the little fleet headed in for the shore. Helms were put up and eager hands grabbed dew-furred halyards to hoist square foresails and then lateen mizzens, which had been stowed while the ships kept their offing under close-hauled mainsails after sighting land in the moonlight at 2 AM. Braces were tugged to haul yards around for the downwind run six miles to the low, sandy land before them.

We've lost track of what this land was, except that it was an island in the outer Bahamas. The leading candidates are Watling's Island (Samuel Eliot Morison's choice, now renamed San Salvador on the presumption that it is, in fact, Columbus's San Salvadore) and Samana Cay, just over 60 miles to the southeast. While these and other possibilities keep some very able minds engaged in debate, it seems enough for us to know that it was one of the sandy chain spreading southward from off Florida almost to Puerto Rico, like a scouting fleet disposed to catch intruders from overseas before they hit upon mainland America or the inner reaches of the Caribbean Sea.

These particular intruders had been wise to stand off during the dark hours and then come in by daylight. In their adventures among the islands, they were to find that most of the islands had outlying reefs of sharp coral, fit to tear out a ship's bottom if she stumbled upon them. The remarkably clear water made it possible to spot these underwater hazards, but only in daylight—a lesson that was to be brutally underlined later in their exploration of the islands.

For now, the voyagers skirted the reefs, which Columbus described as surrounding the whole of the island, and ran around to the leeward (downward) side, where the sea was calm and there was no danger of being set ashore, unless the wind changed and began to blow strongly from the opposite direction. Here they brought to and anchored off a beach.

The smell of land must have been intoxicating to these sailors, after their long days and anxious nights at sea, their doubts, their land sightings along the way that turned out not to be land after all. Columbus notes the greenness of things ashore, the "green and gracious trees, different from ours, covered by flowers and fruits of marvellous flavors, many types of fowl and small birds that sing with great sweetness." Later generations of intruders cut down the great hardwood forests, and intensive sugar cane cultivation impoverished the soil on these islands; but latter-day archaeology has recovered the bones of forest birds from islands that today are utterly denuded and barren.

And, of course, the islands had people. The Taino people, a branch of the Arawak family of peoples, inhabited all the islands Columbus saw on this first transatlantic journey.

Evidently they began gathering on the shore as Columbus, aboard the high-charged *Santa Maria*, prepared to go ashore in the ship's main boat. Fitting together the Las Casas and Ferdinand Columbus accounts (both based on Columbus's lost journal), Morison gives this picture of the Europeans' landing and first encounter with the natives:

> "Presently they saw naked people, and the Admiral went ashore in the armed ship's boat with the royal standard displayed. So did the captains of the *Pinta* and *Niña*, Martin Alonso Pinzón and Vicente Yáñez, his brother, in their boats, with the banners of the Expedition, on which were depicted a green cross with an F [Ferdinand] and a Y [Isabella] on the other, and over each his or her crown. And, all having rendered thanks to Our Lord kneeling on the ground, embracing it with tears of joy for the immeasurable mercy of having reached it, the Admiral arose and gave this island the name San Salvador."

A crowd of Indians gathered round and joined in the rejoicing. They were apparently considered by the Europeans to be part of the ceremony—the first, perhaps, of many misunderstandings to come, based on the native people's seeming to agree with vigorously asserted European assumptions. The absurdity of words being expected to convey understandings and agreements where there were no words in common persisted among the new arrivals. Indeed, the idea of Indians having their own picture of things seems to have been a long time breaking through to the European consciousness. For some Europeans, clearly, the breakthrough never came.

Columbus knew better than this. To him the Indians were people, always. Despite his crimes against the Indians—and they were recognized as crimes at the time, notably by his admirer and one-time shipmate, Las Casas—he never wavered in believing that they had their own immortal souls, their own ways of doing things and their own aspirations.

In these initial encounters, Columbus was charmed by the Indians' open friendliness and simple manners. "In order that we might win good friendship," he wrote, "because I knew that they were a people who could better be freed and converted to our holy faith by love than by force, I gave to some of them red caps and to some glass beads, which they hung on their necks, and many other things of slight value, in which they took much pleasure; they remained so much our friends it was a marvel . . ." And, they came back and "gave everything they had, with good will." That everything, he noted, was not very much.

He noted again and again how handsome these people were: "very well made, of very handsome bodies and very good faces . . . eyes very handsome and not small . . . no belly, but very well built." He noted their color, "not at all black, but the color of Canary Islanders," which, he said, was to be expected since they were on the same latitude as Ferro in the Canaries—which is approximately true.

He was, from very early on, aware of their existence as a people in another important dimension: They had a history. In his entry for that first day ashore, which may have been written a little later, he said:

> "I saw some who had marks of wounds on their bodies, and made signs to them to ask what it was, and they showed me how people of other islands which are near came there and wished to capture them, and they defended themselves. And I believed and now believe that people do come here from the mainland to take them as slaves."

Columbus pictured the mainland as being China. On later voyages he was to meet the Caribs in islands further south and east, who were systematically raiding the Tainos in the epoch when he happened on the scene.

But throughout this first voyage, he persisted in his belief that China, or perhaps Japan, was just around the corner. There he expected to find advanced civilizations of great wealth—gold-roofed houses in Japan, said the usually reliable Marco Polo—and ships larger than any built in Europe at this time (which was true). As latter-day historians laugh themselves silly over this error, let us ordinary mortals remember—please—that advanced European cartographers, working with the best available knowledge, continued to show China and Japan near the islands Columbus sailed among for years after this and other voyages to this part of the world.

Even Samuel Eliot Morison (whose superb biography of Columbus will be read long after these words are forgotten) permits himself an unseemly snicker at Columbus's foreshortened picture of the world. I have long been puzzled by this disdain and have come to the conclusion that Morison's own meticulous mind-set made it difficult for him to imagine the world as other than he knew it in fact to be.

But, let us imagine ourselves sailing among islands where the inhabitants, living very plain and simple lives, sport bits of gold ornament and tell (through sign language) of powerful domineering people living not far away. Would we not believe we were in the fabled Indies?

✳✳✳✳✳

The Taino Indians called the island Columbus and his men had hit upon *Guanahani,* meaning iguana, a creature now extinct on these islands. The Taino people themselves were thought until recently to be extinct, victims of the disease, warfare and conquest that fell calamitously upon them in the decades following the European incursion. But, according to a recent account, Taino ceremonial materials were transferred to western Cuba during the conquest, and there a few Indian communities have managed to survive, keeping their culture in living continuity with its pre-Columbian roots. The culture was also sustained through mixed marriages deliberately encouraged by some chiefs, notably Camagueybax in Cuba's Camaguey province. By this means, Spanish husbands got Indian land without fighting for it, and the Indian mothers knew that their children would not be enslaved or worked to death in the dread Spanish encomiendas—work camps run for the benefit of the Spanish conquistadores. This also produced children with built-in immunity to the European diseases, which were the worst killers of the Taino, as other Indians. Camagueybax clearly saw survival for his people in these mixed offspring, for whom he is said to have coined the Taino word *Guajiro,* or "one of us."

Other Tainos chose to battle the invading Spanish to the death—and sometimes, one feels, beyond. Las Casas records one noble example of ultimate resistance in his account of the execution of Hatuey, who left Hispaniola, where the Spanish had taken over, to organize resistance with the native Ciboneys in Cuba. This native warrior campaign lasted into the 1530s, more than a generation after Columbus's first landing in the islands. But, ultimately, Hatuey was captured. As he stood bound to a stake, a Spanish friar offered him baptism, which, he said, would cleanse his soul. Hatuey asked time to think about this. Then he asked where those thus saved would go after death, which for him was an imminent question. To heaven, he was told. And where do the Spanish go? Answer: To heaven. Then I don't want to go there, said Hatuey. With that, the torch was put to the brushwood piled around his feet.

A present-day student, José Barreiro, offers this comment:

> In the Taino culture, the dead are carried by the living and ongoing generations. They live in a parallel world and must be recognized and fed. A great deal of ceremonial attention is given this fundamental human responsibility by the Caribbean and Meso–American cultures. No doubt, a traditionalist such as Hatuey carried his own people's medicines and song into his final moment.[1]

Hispaniola was the center of the Taino culture, which spread out from there to Jamaica, Cuba and the Bahamas, including Guanahani. The men were much at home on the broad, often windy salt water highways that linked their islands. Columbus tells of great dugout canoes fashioned from the hardwood forests which then cloaked the now denuded islands, canoes capable of carrying forty men.

The Spanish who took an interest in Taino ways noted the absence of quarrelling in the organized Taino communities. A council of elders governed each village, and these old chiefs were noticed to speak with deliberation and evident authority. Villagers worked in gardens, in hunting or seafaring. They maintained fish ponds and irrigation works, played ball games and held dances for social and religious purposes. In these dances, called *areitos*, ancestors were honored and greeted, and ceremonial thanks rendered to the spirits of cultivated corn and wild food and game who fed the people.

Columbus missed the strong spiritual content of all this, and the religious awe that informed the Taino activities. The world around them was the creation of four brother gods (representing the four directions), who "walked on clouds and blue sky over the spirit world of the Caribbean," in José Barreiro's memorable phrase. A very navigational cosmogeny! And no wonder, for the Taino had come to the islands by canoe from South America, and the canoe remained the instrument that bound their culture together.

The Taino were part of a widespread and diverse Indian population that had arrived in the Americas in successive waves coming from Asia over the Siberian land bridge that existed in the waning millenia of the Ice Age, beginning perhaps as early as 40,000 BC. Agriculture based on cultivation of corn (maize) had been established in Central Mexico by 11,000 BC; by 7,000 BC this had diversified into cultivation of beans and squash as well. In the course of millenia, diverse cultures developed, including of 200 separate languages, some as different as Chinese is from German. In Central America, great empires rose and fell prior to the powerful Aztec empire overthrown by Cortes in 1521, or the Inca empire in South America, conquered by Pizarro a decade later. These boasted huge cities and societies bound together by a demanding religious system backed up by strong imperial armies.

The Taino existed outside the imperial orbit, but undoubtedly had contact with it. Their systems of government and social organization seem more uniform throughout their island realm than, for instance, the turbulent and warring tribes of the New England littoral, though the levels of technology were remarkably similar despite quite different terrain.

Trading networks were extensive, most undoubtedly carried out by coastal passages or inland lakes and rivers, but almost certainly not by long voyages. Goods were probably exchanged in what I call "concussive" barter between groups along the trade routes.

Hieroglyphic records were kept by the powerful Central American empires and, perhaps, by others, but not by writing as we know it. This placed some limits on conceptual development, though not on the depth, force or beauty of the concepts the Taino developed to explain their world and function in it.

No Indian learned to sail, though cotton cloth had been developed. Indians in Tierra del Fuego at the southern tip of South America seized a missionary ship in the mid-1800s but were unable to move her. They did not understand sailing. She was also too big to paddle and they did not know how to row, using big sweeps with lots of leverage. The same thing happened in North America on recorded occasions when Indians seized European ships. The natives of Vancouver Island, in the Pacific Northwest, have a magnificent seafaring culture, still flourishing today, based in coastal villages some of which were never conquered by the Europeans or their descendants. Their canoes were driven by paddle, not by sail, and moved on in time directly to the outboard motor. Across the continent in the Caribbean, the Caribs today build canoes and sail them—an innovation borrowed from the Europeans to cross between their islands on the steady, if boisterous, Trade Winds.

It's commonplace to say that similar sea conditions produce similar craft. But this is an excessively mechanistic view, surely. Why did the Norsemen who came to North America some 500 years before Columbus, have sails and oars—while the natives, who were strong enough to drive them out, had neither?

The truth would seem to be that such developments are produced by a culture, its values and aspirations, even its way of looking at things. The Ancient Greeks said Theseus taught them how to plow the water—and I think that is true. They became the great sailors of the Ancient world because it was in their story, their idea of their purposes on earth, to do so. So the Greeks had oars and, indeed, sailing ships 3,000 years before Columbus. And out of that Mediterranean culture Columbus sortied to encounter peoples who had no concept of the sailing ship.

Once you have an idea, of course, it is impossible to imagine being without it. Why, look at an autumn leaf being blown across a pond, and you see a sailing ship, progenitor of argosies. The Indian peoples looked and they saw no such thing.

But the things they did see, we are learning to see anew and value anew.

* * * * *

From the beginning, Columbus had intended to carry away a handful of Indians as interpreters for further encounters and to bring them into the mainstream of European civilization at the Spanish court. His journal entry for his first day ashore, as quoted directly by Las Casas, included this note:

"I, please Our Lord, will carry off six of them at my departure to Your Highnesses, so that they may learn to speak."

He meant, of course, learning to speak Spanish. And it is true that the Spanish language conveyed concepts unknown in the Arawak tongue of these Tainos, and facilitated operations, from sailing ships at sea to writing directions in books, which were beyond Taino thought or performance.

Just before stating this intention, Columbus wrote:

> "They ought to be good servants and of good skill, for I see that they repeat very quickly all that is said to them: and I believe that they would easily be made Christians, because it seemed to me that they belonged to no religion."

As we've seen, they did have a religion: Las Casas did not note this, but he chided Columbus for this "good servants" remark, which is repeated in different forms elsewhere in the journals. He said it opened the door to conquest and enslavement of the Indians, which he, as priest and later bishop, regarded as highly un–Christian acts. With this we may surely agree and salute Las Casas and a handful of others who stood up, defying sword and fire, to protest the subjugation of the Indian people.

The larger issue remains, and it is instructive to see it written into Columbus's account of his first day ashore in what he later was to call this "other world." That issue is, of course, how a culture functioning well in its environment is to deal with a more technologically developed culture.

Mankind's general progress is toward more advanced technologies and systems of knowledge and belief. Native peoples throughout the Americas and the South Pacific, even when not compelled to, tended to adopt European technology and strove to master thought systems more complex than those they had developed in the course of their own experience.

This process, compelled or voluntary, was often brutally destructive of native values, native persons and families, and native ethos and spirit. A few of Columbus's contemporaries saw this clearly, and a few later explorers, like Captain Cook in the Pacific, came to question the "benefits" of European culture brought to less developed peoples of the globe.

Various Indian cultures survived the terrible scenes of conquest and enslavement that followed upon the European incursion into the Americas, and indeed they may be said to be in renaissance today. This revival is based upon what we might call hearthstone values—the things which are transmitted from generation to generation to define a people and give it its sense of identity and worth. Do not the people—especially the young people—of the great cities of the West urgently need these things today?

Don't we all need as much of the human diversity we can get—all the hard-won strains which make up the heritage of earth's peoples? With mankind now brought face to face with itself everywhere as result of the voyaging that followed on Columbus's voyage 500 years ago, we may begin at least to ask such questions, which hung unspoken in the air as Columbus and his men first encountered the American Indians in the islands the Trade Winds had brought them to.

---

[1]José Barreiro, "A Note on Tainos: Whither Progress?" *Northeast Indian Quarterly* (Cornell University), Fall 1990, p.75.

Ethnic Families in America (1988)
Ethnic Diversity as the Criterion of Selection
Charles H. Mindel, Robert W. Habenstein, and Roosevelt Wright, Jr.

Although not randomly selected, the ethnic families presented in this book were chosen to represent a rather wide spectrum of distinguishable groups, ranging from the less than 100,000 Amish to the 26.5 million black people, whose ethnicity continues to be expressed through identifiable institutions and, significantly, the family. Nevertheless, there *are* large numbers of Americans who find it possible to trace descent to foreign nations and cultures such as Germany, Great Britain, and Canada, yet who retain little, if any, of an Old World cultural identity. Their lifestyles are largely indistinguishable from others of similar socioeconomic classes (except in certain enclaves here and there), and for this reason, they have been excluded from this work.

While the possession of an ethnic heritage that continues to be expressed in a distinctive family lifestyle is the common theme among all groups chosen in this work, the reasons for both the appearance in America (remembering that Native Americans had precedence!) and continued existence as an identifiable ethnic group remain to some extent unique. That groups migrating to America in great numbers in pre– and early– nineteenth century periods were responding to general social, economic, and class-oppressive pressures gave all immigrants of that time a measure of common status. Nevertheless, each has its own distinguishing features, contingencies, and value system to provide significantly different ethnic group life histories, and therefore, each has its own story to be told.

There is some justification, then for adopting the kaleidoscopic approach and simply jumbling all 17 family groups together without anything more ordered than what can be achieved by an alphabetical arrangement. Conversely, for those more compulsive about systemization, a set of formal ahistorical, all-inclusive categories might be constructed. We have chosen something less abstract through the pragmatically useful grouping of our ethnic families into five substantive categories: (1) European ethnic minorities, (2) Hispanic ethnic minorities, (3) Asian ethnic minorities, (4) historically subjugated ethnic minorities, and (5) socioreligious ethnic minorities.

These categories help sort out the groups, according to several dimensions, but they should in no way be taken as definitive, completely exclusive, or the only way to achieve a useful classification. The most important criterion in the minds of the editors has been that the categories appear to capture a particularly important contingency or group experience that has a continuing influence on its collective fate. In the following paragraphs, we briefly discuss the scheme that we have chosen:

1. European Ethnic Minorities
The four ethnic minorities in this category are the Polish, Irish, Italian, and Greek immigrants who arrived in the late nineteenth and early twentieth centuries. During a period extending from the early 1880s until the outbreak of World War I, almost 25 million European immigrants entered the United States. This influx represents the archetypal immigration to this country, and it is this period that we most often think of when we visualize immigrant life. It is from this wave of European immigration that most of today's non–Protestant white ethnics are descended.

2. Hispanic Ethnic Minorities

The three ethnic minorities in this category are the Mexicans, Cubans, and Puerto Ricans. Unlike other American ethnic groups, Hispanics have entered the United States in a variety of ways. Although Mexicans have come to this country in the nineteenth and twentieth centuries as voluntary immigrants, they retain a heritage of originally having been absorbed into American society as a conquered group. Puerto Ricans, too, are a group not clearly part of either voluntary immigration or conquest. Puerto Rico became a territory of the United States in 1898 following the Spanish American War, and in 1917, the inhabitants of the island were granted American citizenship. The greatest influx of Puerto Ricans to the United States was during the 1950s, when nearly 20 percent of the island's population moved to the mainland.

The movement of Cubans to the United States in the past two decades has been a voluntary immigration. Yet it differs from those of most past groups in that it was initially impelled mainly by political rather than economic motives. The problems that all of these groups have faced include economic integration and social assimilation into American society.

3. Asian Ethnic Minorities

The four ethnic minorities in this category are the Koreans, Chinese, Japanese, and Vietnamese. The Chinese and Japanese American ethnic minorities have been in this country in substantial numbers for 75 to 100 years. The Koreans and Vietnamese, however, are characterized by a sizeable number of recent, as well as continuing flow of, immigrants. Important questions for the study of all of these groups relate to the effects of time and generation on the cultural heritage but, more particularly, as they directly affect family life. The extent to which assimilation and acculturation has had an impact on ethnic identity and lifestyle remains one of the key problems encountered by these groups of people. In addition, the problems they have faced include adjusting to a modern business cycle and war-plagued industrialized society and to constant infusion of new representatives from their respective countries of origin.

4. Historically Subjugated Ethnic Minorities

The two groups, blacks and Native Americans, are categorized together because their identity and experience in this country have been the result of or strongly influenced by their respective race. These groups either preceded the arrival of the "Americans" or arrived later and were immediately or later placed in some form of bondage. Enslaved to the land, alienated from it, or bound in a latter-day peonage, blacks and Native Americans have in America the darkest and least savory group life histories from which to build viable ethnic cultures. In both of these groups, it will be noted that the role of the family, whether truncated or extended, becomes crucial for ethnic survival.

5. Socioreligious Ethnic Minorities

The four ethnic minorities in this category are the Amish, the Jews, the Arabs, and the Mormons. They are categorized together because their identity and experience have largely been the result of or strongly influenced, if not dominated, by their respective religions. They all sought in America a place to live that kind of social existence in which religion could continue to be vitally conjoined with all aspects of their life and livelihood.

References

Burgess, Ernest, Harvey J. Locke, and Mary M. Thomes. 1963. *The Family* (3rd ed.). New York: American Book.

Cavan, Ruth S. 1969. *The American Family* (4th ed.). New York: Thomas Y. Crowell.

Elkin, Frederick. 1970. *The Family in Canada: An Account of Present Knowledge and Gaps in Knowledge About Canadian Families.* Ottawa: The Vanier Institute of the Family.

Farber, Bernard. 1964. *Family Organization and Interaction.* San Francisco: Chandler.

Fuchs, Victor. 1968. *The Service Economy.* New York: National Bureau of Research. Distributed by Columbia University Press.

Geertz, Clifford. 1963. "The Integrated Revolution," in Clifford Geertz (ed.), *Old Societies and New Societies.* Glencoe, Il.: Free Press.

Glazer, Nathan. 1954. "Ethnic Groups in America: From National Culture to Ideology," in Morroe Berger, Theodore Abel, and Charles H. Page (eds.), *Freedom and Control in Modern Society.* New York: Van Nostrand.

———. 1973. "The Issue of Cultural Pluaralism in America Today," in Joseph Ryan (ed.), *White Ethnics: Their Life in Working Class America.* Englewood Cliffs, NJ: Prentice–Hall, pp. 168-177.

Glazer, Nathan, and Daniel P. Moynihan. 1970. *Beyond the Melting Pot* (2nd. ed.). Cambridge: MIT Press.

Gordon, Milton. 1964. *Assimilation in American Life.* New York: Oxford University Press.

Gouldner, Alvin. 1970. *The Coming Crisis in Western Sociology.* New York: Basic Books.

Greeley, Andrew M. 1969. *Why Can't They Be Like Us?.* New York: Institute of Human Relations Press.

———. 1974. *Ethnicity in the United States: A Preliminary Reconnaissance.* New York: John Wiley.

Ishwaran, K. (ed.). 1971. T*he Canadian Family: A Book of Readings.* Toronto: Holt, Rinehart and Winston of Canada.

Kephart, William M. 1972. *The Family, Society and the Individual* (3rd ed.). Boston: Houghton Mifflin.

Novak, Michael. 1973. "Probing the New Ethnicity," in Joseph Ryan (ed.), *White Ethnics: Their Life in Working Class America.* Englewood Cliffs, NJ: Prentice–Hall, pp. 158-167.

Nye, F. Ivan, and Felix Berardo. 1973. *The Family: Its Structure and Interaction.* New York: Macmillan.

Queen, Stuart, and Robert W. Habenstein. 1974. *The Family in Various Cultures* (4th ed.). Philadelphia: J. B. Lippincott.

Reiss, Ira. 1971. *The Family System in America.* New York: Holt, Rinehart and Winston.

Rose, Peter I. 1974. *They and We: Racial and Ethnic Relations in the United States* (2nd ed.). New York: Random House.

Wade, Mason (ed.). 1960. *Canadian Dualism.* Toronto: Toronto University Press.

The Two Worlds of Race: A Historical View (1965)

John Hope Franklin

I.

Measured by universal standards the history of the United States is indeed brief. But during the brief span of three and one-half centuries of colonial and national history Americans developed traditions and prejudices which created the two worlds of race in modern America. From the time that Africans were brought as indentured servants to the mainland of English America in 1619, the enormous task of rationalizing and justifying the forced labor of peoples on the basis of racial differences was begun; and even after legal slavery was ended, the notion of racial differences persisted as a basis for maintaining segregation and discrimination. At the same time, the effort to establish a more healthy basis for the new world social order was begun, thus launching the continuing battle between the two worlds of race, on the one hand, and the world of equality and complete human fellowship, on the other.

For a century before the American Revolution the status of Negroes in the English colonies had become fixed at a low point that distinguished them from all other persons who had been held in temporary bondage. By the middle of the eighteenth century, laws governing Negroes denied to them certain basic rights that were conceded to others. They were permitted no independence of thought, no opportunity to improve their minds or their talents or to worship freely, no right to marry and enjoy the conventional family relationships, no right to own or dispose of property, and no protection against miscarriages of justice or cruel and unreasonable punishments. They were outside the pale of the laws that protected ordinary humans. In most places they were to be governed, as the South Carolina code of 1712 expressed it, by special laws "as may restrain the disorders, rapines, and inhumanity to which they are naturally prone and inclined . . ." A separate world for them had [899] been established by law and custom. Its dimensions and the conduct of its inhabitants were determined by those living in a quite different world.

By the time that the colonists took up arms against their mother country in order to secure their independence, the world of Negro slavery had become deeply entrenched and the idea of Negro inferiority well established. But the dilemmas inherent in such a situation were a source of constant embarrassment. "It always appeared a most iniquitous scheme to me," Mrs. John Adams wrote her husband in 1774, "to fight ourselves for what we are daily robbing and plundering from those who have as good a right to freedom as we have." There were others who shared her views, but they were unable to wield such influence. When the fighting began General George Washington issued an order to recruiting officers that they were not to enlist "any deserter from the ministerial army, nor any stroller, negro, or vagabond, or person suspected of being an enemy to the liberty of America nor under eighteen years of age." In classifying Negroes with the dregs of society, traitors, and children, Washington made it clear that Negroes, slave or free, were not to enjoy the high privilege of fighting for political independence. He would change that order later, but only after it became clear that

Negroes were enlisting with the "ministerial army" in droves in order to secure their own freedom. In changing his policy if not his views, Washington availed himself of the services of more than 5,000 Negroes who took up arms against England.[1]

Many Americans besides Mrs. Adams were struck by the inconsistency of their stand during the War for Independence, and they were not averse to making moves to emancipate the slaves. Quakers and other religious groups organized antislavery societies, while numerous individuals manumitted their slaves. In the years following the close of the war most of the states of the East made provisions for the gradual emancipation of slaves. In the South, meanwhile, the anti-slavery societies were unable to effect programs of state-wide emancipation. When the Southerners came to the Constitutional Convention in 1787 they succeeded in winning some representation on the basis of slavery, in securing federal support of the capture and rendition of fugitive slaves, and in preventing the closing of the slave trade before 1808.

Even where the sentiment favoring emancipation was pronounced, it was seldom accompanied by a view that Negroes were the equals of whites and should become a part of one family of [900] Americans. Jefferson, for example was opposed to slavery; and if he could have had his way, he would have condemned it in the Declaration of Independence. It did not follow, however, that he believed Negroes to be the equals of whites. He did not want to "degrade a whole race of men from the work in the scale of beings which their Creator may *perhaps* have given them . . . . I advance it therefore, as a suspicion only, that the blacks, whether originally a distinct race, or made distinct by time and circumstance, are inferior to the whites in the endowment both of body and mind." It is entirely possible that Jefferson's later association with the extraordinarily able Negro astronomer and mathematician Benjamin Banneker, resulted in some modification of his views. After reading a copy of Banneker's almanac, Jefferson told him that it was "a document to which your whole race had a right for its justifications against the doubts which have been entertained of them."[2]

In communities such as Philadelphia and New York, where the climate was more favorably disposed to the idea of Negro equality than in Jefferson's Virginia, few concessions were made, except by a limited number of Quakers and their associates. Indeed, the white citizens in the City of Brotherly Love contributed substantially to the perpetuation of two distinct worlds of race. In the 1780's, the white Methodists permitted Negroes to worship with them, provided the Negroes sat in a designated place in the balcony. On one occasion, when the Negro worshippers occupied the front rows of the balcony, from which they had been excluded, the officials pulled them from their knees during prayer and evicted them from the church. Thus, in the early days of the Republic and in the place where the Republic was founded, Negroes had a definite "place" in which they were expected at all times to remain. The white Methodists of New York had much the same attitude toward their Negro fellows. Soon, there were separate Negro churches in these and other communities. Baptists were much the same. In 1809 thirteen Negro members of a white Baptist church in Philadelphia were dismissed, and they formed a church of their own. Thus, the earliest Negro religious institutions emerged as the result of the rejection by white communicants of their darker fellow worshippers. Soon there would be other institutions—schools, newspapers, benevolent societies—to serve those who lived in a world apart.

Those Americans who conceded the importance of education for Negroes tended to favor some particular type of education that would be in keeping with their lowly station in life. In [901] 1794, for example, the American Convention of Abolition Societies recommended that Negroes be instructed in "those mechanic arts which will keep them most constantly employed and of course, which will less subject them to idleness and debauchery, and thus prepare them for becoming good citizens of the United States." When Anthony Benezet, a dedicated Pennsylvania abolitionist, died in 1784 his will provided that on the death of his wife the proceeds of his estate should be used to assist in the establishment of a school for Negroes. In 1787 the school of which Benezet had dreamed was opened in Philadelphia, where pupils studied reading, writing, arithmetic, plain accounts, and sewing.

Americans who were at all interested in the education of Negroes regarded it as both natural and normal that Negroes should receive their training in separate schools. As early as 1773 Newport, Rhode Island, had a colored school, maintained by a society of benevolent clergymen of the Anglican Church. In 1798 a separate private school for Negro children was established in Boston; and two decades later the city opened its first public primary school for the education of Negro children. Meanwhile, New York had established separate schools, the first one opening its doors in 1790. By 1814 there were several such institutions that were generally designated as the New York African Free Schools.[3]

Thus, in the most liberal section of the country, the general view was that Negroes should be kept out of the main stream of American life. They were forced to establish and maintain their own religious institutions, which were frequently followed by the establishment of separate benevolent societies. Likewise, if Negroes were to receive any education, it should be special education provided in separate educational institutions. This principle prevailed in most places in the North throughout the period before the Civil War. In some Massachusetts towns, however, Negroes gained admission to schools that had been maintained for whites. But the School Committee of Boston refused to admit Negroes, arguing that the natural distinction of the races, which "no legislature, no social customs, can efface renders a promiscuous intermingling in the public schools disadvantageous both to them and to the whites." Separate schools remained in Boston until the Massachusetts legislature in 1855 enacted a law providing that in determining the qualifications of students to be admitted to any public school no distinction should be made on account of the race, color, or religious opinion of the applicant. [902]

Meanwhile, in the Southern states, where the vast majority of the Negroes lived, there were no concessions suggesting equal treatment, even among the most liberal elements. One group that would doubtless have regarded itself as liberal on the race question advocated the deportation of Negroes to Africa, especially those who had become free. Since free Negroes "neither enjoyed the immunities of freemen, nor were they subject to the incapacities of slaves," their condition and "unconquerable prejudices" prevented amalgamation with whites, one colonization leader argued. There was, therefore, a "peculiar moral fitness" in restoring them to "the land of their fathers." Men like Henry Clay, Judge Bushrod Washington, and President James Monroe thought that separation—expatriation— was the best thing for Negroes who were or who would become free.[4]

While the colonization scheme was primarily for Negroes who were already free, it won, for a time, a considerable number of sincere enemies of slavery. From the beginning Negroes were bitterly opposed to it, and only infrequently did certain Negro leaders, such as Dr. Martin Delany and the Reverend Henry M. Turner, support the idea. Colonization, however, retained considerable support in the most responsible quarters. As late as the Civil War, President Lincoln urged Congress to adopt a plan to colonize Negroes, as the only workable solution to the race problem in the United States. Whether the advocates of colonization wanted merely to prevent the contamination of slavery by free

Negroes or whether they actually regarded it as the just and honorable thing to do, they represented an important element in the population that rejected the idea of the Negro's assimilation into the main stream of American life.

Thus, within fifty years after the Declaration of Independence was written, the institution of slavery, which received only a temporary reversal during the Revolutionary era, contributed greatly to the emergence of the two worlds of race in the United States. The natural rights philosophy appeared to have little effect on those who became committed, more and more, to seeking a rationalization for slavery. The search was apparently so successful that even in areas where slavery was declining, the support for maintaining two worlds of race was strong. Since the Negro church and school emerged in Northern communities where slavery was dying, it may be said that the free society believed almost as strongly in racial separation as it did in racial freedom. [903]

II.

The generation preceding the outbreak of the Civil War witnessed the development of a set of defenses of slavery that became the basis for much of the racist doctrine to which some Americans have subscribed from then to the present time. The idea of the inferiority of the Negro enjoyed wide acceptance among Southerners of all classes and among many Northerners. It was an important ingredient in the theory of society promulgated by Southern thinkers and leaders. It was organized into a body of systematic thought by the scientists and social scientists of the South, out of which emerged a doctrine of racial superiority that justified any kind of control over the slave. In 1826 Dr. Thomas Cooper said that he had not the slightest doubt that Negroes were an "inferior variety of the human species; and not capable of the same improvement as the whites." Dr. S. C. Cartwright of the University of Louisiana insisted that the capacities of the Negro adult for learning were equal to those of a white infant; and the Negro could properly perform certain physiological functions only when under the control of white men. Because of the Negroe's inferiority, liberty and republican institutions were not only unsuited to his temperament, but actually inimical to his well-being and happiness.

Like racists in other parts of the world, Southerners sought support for their ideology by developing a common bond with the less privileged. The obvious basis was race; and outside the white race there was to be found no favor from God, no honor or respect from man. By the time that Europeans were reading Gobineau's *Inequality of Races,* Southerners were reading Cartwright's *Slavery in the Light of Ethnology.* In admitting all whites into the pseudonobility of race, Cartwright won their enthusiastic support in the struggle to preserve the integrity and honor of *the* race. Professor Thomas R. Dew of the College of William and Mary comforted the lower-class whites by indicating that they could identify with the most privileged and affluent of the community. In the South, he said, "no white man feels such inferiority of rank as to be unworthy of association with those around him. Color alone is here the badge of distinction, the true mark of aristocracy, and all who are white are equal in spite of the variety of occupation."[5]

Many Northerners were not without their own racist views and policies in the turbulent decades before the Civil War. Some, as Professor Louis Filler has observed, displayed a hatred of Negroes that [904] gave them a sense of superiority and an outlet for their frustrations. Others cared nothing one way or the other about the Negroes and demanded only that they be kept separate.[6] Even some of the abolitionists themselves were ambivalent on the question of Negro equality. More than one antislavery society was agitated by the suggestion that Negroes be invited to join. Some members thought it reasonable for them to attend, but not to be put on an "equality with ourselves." The New York abolitionist, Lewis Tappan, admitted "that when the subject of acting out our profound principles in treating men irrespective of color is discussed heat is always produced."[7]

In the final years before the beginning of the Civil War, the view that the Negro was different, even inferior, was widely held in the United States. Leaders in both major parties subscribed to the view, while the more extreme racists deplored any suggestion that the Negro could ever prosper as a free man. At Peoria, Illinois, in October 1854, Abraham Lincoln asked what stand the opponents of slavery should take regarding Negroes. "Free them, and make them politically and socially, our equals? My own feelings will not admit of this; and if mine would, we well know that those of the great mass of white people will not. Whether this feeling accords with justice and sound judgment, is not the sole question, if indeed, it is any part of it. A universal feeling, whether well or ill founded, cannot be safely disregarded. We cannot, then, make them equals."

The Lincoln statement was forthright, and it doubtless represented views of most Americans in the 1850's. Most of those who heard him or read his speech were of the same opinion as he. In later years, the Peoria pronouncement would be used by those who sought to detract from Lincoln's reputation as a champion of the rights of the Negro. In 1964, the White Citizens' Councils reprinted portions of the speech in large advertisements in the daily press and insisted that Lincoln shared their views on the desirability of maintaining two distinct worlds of race.

Lincoln could not have overcome the nation's strong predisposition toward racial separation if he had tried. And he did not try very hard. When he called for the enlistment of Negro troops, after issuing the Emancipation Proclamation, he was content not only to set Negroes apart in a unit called "U. S. Colored Troops," but also to have Negro privates receive $10 per month including clothing, while whites of the same rank received $13 per month plus clothing. Only the stubborn refusal of many Negro troops to accept discriminatory [905] pay finally forced Congress to equalize compensation for white and Negro soldiers.[8] The fight for union that became also a fight for freedom never became a fight for equality or for the creation of one racial world.

The Lincoln and Johnson plans for settling the problems of peace and freedom never seriously touched on the concomitant problem of equality. To be sure, in 1864 President Lincoln privately raised with the governor of Louisiana the question of the franchise for a limited number of Negroes, but when the governor ignored the question the President let the matter drop. Johnson raised a similar question in 1866, but he admitted that it was merely to frustrate the design of radical reformers who sought a wider franchise for Negroes. During the two years following Appomattox Southern leaders gave not the slightest consideration to permitting any Negroes, regardless of their service to the Union or their education or their property, to share in the political life of their communities. Not only did every Southern state refuse to permit Negroes to vote, but they also refused to provide Negroes with any of the educational opportunities that they were providing for the whites.

The early practice of political disenfranchisement and of exclusion from public educational facilities helped to determine subsequent policies that the South adopted regarding Negroes. While a few leaders raised their voices against these policies and practices, it was Negroes themselves who made the most eloquent attacks on such discriminations. As early as May 1865, a group of North Carolina Negroes told President Johnson that some of them had been soldiers and were doing everything possible to learn how to discharge the higher duties of citizenship. "It seems to us that men who are willing on the field of battle to carry the muskets of the Republic, in the days of peace ought to be permitted to carry the ballots; and certainly we cannot understand the justice of denying the elective franchise to men who have been fighting *for* the country, while it is freely given to men who have just returned from *four* years fighting against it." Such pleas fell on deaf ears, however; and it was not until 1867, when Congress was sufficiently outraged by the inhuman black codes, widespread discriminations in the South, and unspeakable forms of violence against Negroes, that the new federal legislation sought to correct the evils of the first period of Reconstruction.

The period that we know as Radical Reconstruction had no significant [906] or permanent effect on the status of the Negro in American life. For a period of time, varying from one year to fifteen or twenty years, some Negroes enjoyed the privileges of voting. They gained political ascendancy in a very few communities only temporarily, and they never even began to achieve the status of a ruling class. They made no meaningful steps toward economic independence or even stability; and in no time at all, because of the pressures of the local community and the neglect of the federal government, they were brought under the complete economic subservience of the old ruling class. Organizations such as the Ku Klux Klan were committed to violent action to keep Negroes "in their place" and, having gained respectability through sponsorship by Confederate generals and the like, they proceeded to wreak havoc in the name of white supremacy and protection of white womanhood.[9]

Meanwhile, various forms of segregation and discrimination, developed in the years before the Civil War in order to degrade the half million free Negroes in the United States, were now applied to the four million Negroes who had become free in 1865. Already the churches and the military were completely segregated. For the most part the schools, even in the North, were separate. In the South segregated schools persisted, even in the places where the radicals made a half-hearted attempt to desegregate them. In 1875 Congress enacted a Civil Rights Act to guarantee the enjoyment of equal rights in carriers and all places of public accommodation and amusement. Even before it became law Northern philanthropists succeeded in forcing the deletion of the provision calling for desegregated schools. Soon, because of the massive resistance in the North as well as the South and the indifferent manner in which the federal government enforced the law, it soon became a dead letter everywhere. When it was declared unconstitutional by the Supreme Court in 1883, there was universal rejoicing, except among the Negroes, one of whom declared that they had been "baptized in ice water."

Neither the Civil War nor the era of Reconstruction made any significant step toward the permanent elimination of racial barriers. The radicals of the post–Civil War years came no closer to the creation of one racial world than the patriots of the Revolutionary years. When Negroes were, for the first time, enrolled in the standing army of the United States, they were placed in separate Negro units. Most of the liberals of the Reconstruction era called for and worked for separate schools for Negroes. Nowhere was there any [907] extensive effort to involve Negroes in the churches and other social institutions of the dominant group. Whatever remained of the old abolitionist fervor, which can hardly be described as unequivocal on the question of true racial equality, was rapidly disappearing. In its place were the sentiments of the business men who wanted peace at any price. Those having common railroad interests or crop-marketing interests or investment interests could and did extend their hands across sectional lines and joined in the task of working together for the common good. In such an atmosphere the practice was to accept the realities of two separate worlds of race. Some even subscribed to the view that there were significant economic advantages in maintaining the two worlds of race.

III.

The post–Reconstruction years witnessed a steady deterioration in the status of Negro Americans. These were the years that Professor Rayford Logan has called the "nadir" of the Negro in American life and thought. They were the years when Americans, weary of the crusade that had, for the most part, ended with the outbreak of the Civil War, displayed almost no interest in helping the Negro to achieve equality. The social Darwinists decried the very notion of equality for Negroes, arguing that the lowly place they occupied was natural and normal. The leading literary journals vied with each other in describing Negroes as lazy, idle, improvident, immoral, and criminal.[10] Thomas Dixon's novels, *The Klansmen* and *The Leopard's Spots*, and D. W. Griffith's motion picture, "The Birth of A Nation," helped to give Americans a view of the Negro's role in American history that "proved" that he was unfit for citizenship, to say nothing of equality. The dictum of William Graham Sumner and his followers that "stateways cannot change folkways" convinced many Americans that legislating equality and creating one great society where race was irrelevant was out of the question.

But many Americans believed that they *could* legislate inequality; and they proceeded to do precisely that. Beginning in 1890, one Southern state after another revised the suffrage provisions of its constitution in a manner that made it virtually impossible for Negroes to qualify to vote. The new literacy and "understanding" provisions permitted local registrars to disqualify Negroes while permitting white citizens to qualify. Several states, including Louisiana, [908] North Carolina, and Oklahoma, inserted "grandfather clauses" in their constitutions in order to permit persons, who could not otherwise qualify, to vote if their fathers or grandfathers could vote in 1866. (This was such a flagrant discrimination against Negroes, whose ancestors could not vote in 1866, that the United States Supreme Court in 1915 declared the "grandfather clause" unconstitutional.) Then came the Democratic white primary in 1900 that made it impossible for Negroes to participate in local elections in the South, where, by this time, only the Democratic party had any appreciable strength. (After more than a generation of assaults on it, the white primary was finally declared unconstitutional in 1944.)

Inequality was legislated in still another way. Beginning in the 1880s many states, especially but not exclusively in the South, enacted statutes designed to separate the races. After the Civil Rights Act was declared unconstitutional in 1883 state legislatures were emboldened to enact numerous segregation statutes. When the United States Supreme Court, in the case of *Plessy v. Ferguson*, set forth the "separate but equal" doctrine in 1896, the decision provided a new stimulus for laws to separate the races and, of course, to discriminate against Negroes. In time, Negroes and whites were separated in the use of schools, churches, cemeteries, drinking fountains, restaurants, and all places of public accommodation and amusement. One state enacted a law providing for the separate warehousing of books used by white and Negro children. Another required the telephone company to provide separate telephone booths for white and Negro customers. In most communities housing was racially separated by law or practice.[11]

Where there was no legislation requiring segregation, local practices filled the void. Contradictions and inconsistencies seemed not to disturb those who sought to maintain racial distinctions at all costs. It mattered not that one drive-in snack bar served Negroes only on the inside, while its competitor across the street served Negroes only on the outside. Both were committed to making racial distinctions; and in communities where practices and mores had the force of law, the distinction was everything. Such practices were greatly strengthened when, in 1913, the federal government adopted policies that segregated the races in its offices as well as in its eating and rest-room facilities.

By the time of World War I, Negroes and whites in the South and in parts of the North lived in separate worlds, and the apparatus [909] for keeping the worlds separate was elaborate and complex. Negroes were segregated by law in the public schools of the Southern states, while those in the Northern ghettos were sent to predominantly Negro schools, except where their numbers were insufficient. Scores of Negro newspapers sprang up to provide news of Negroes that the white press consistently ignored. Negroes were as unwanted in the white churches as they had been in the late eighteenth century; and Negro churches of virtually every denomination were the answer for a people who had accepted the white man's religion even as the white man rejected his religious fellowship.

Taking note of the fact that they had been omitted from any serious consideration by the white historians, Negroes began in earnest to write the history of their own experiences as Americans. There had been Negro historians before the Civil War, but none of them had challenged the white historians' efforts to relegate Negroes to a separate, degraded world. In 1882, however, George Washington Williams published his *History of the Negro Race in America* in order to "give the world more correct ideas about the colored people." He wrote, he said, not "as a partisan apologist, but from a love for the truth of history."[12] Soon there were other historical works by Negroes describing their progress and their contributions and arguing that they deserved to be received into the full fellowship of American citizens.

It was in these post–Reconstruction years that some of the most vigorous efforts were made to destroy the two worlds of race. The desperate pleas of Negro historians were merely the more articulate attempts of Negroes to gain complete acceptance in American life. Scores of Negro organizations joined in the struggle to gain protection and recognition of their rights and to eliminate the more sordid practices that characterized the treatment of the Negro world by the white world. Unhappily, the small number of whites who were committed to racial equality dwindled in the post–Reconstruction years, while government at every level showed no interest in eliminating racial separatism. It seemed that Negro voices were indeed crying in the wilderness, but they carried on their attempts to be heard. In 1890 Negroes from twenty-one states and the District of Columbia met in Chicago and organized the Afro–American League of the United States. They called for more equitable distribution of school funds, fair and impartial trial for accused Negroes, resistance "by all legal and reasonable means" to [910] mob and lynch law, and enjoyment of the franchise by all qualified voters. When a group of young Negro intellectuals, led by W. E. B. Du Bois, met at Niagara Falls, Ontario, in 1905, they made a similar call as they launched their Niagara Movement.

However eloquent their pleas, Negroes alone could make no successful assault on the two worlds of race. They needed help—a great deal of help. It was the bloody race riots in the early years of the twentieth century that shocked civic minded and socially conscious whites into answering the Negro's pleas for support. Some whites began to take the view that the existence of two societies whose distinction was based solely on race was inimical to the best interests of the entire nation. Soon, they were taking the initiative and in 1909 organized the National Association for the Advancement of Colored People. They assisted the following year in establishing the National Urban League. White attorneys began to stand with Negroes before the United States Supreme Court to challenge the "grandfather clause," local segregation ordinances, and flagrant miscarriages of justice in which Negroes were the victims. The patterns of attack developed during these years were to become invaluable later. Legal action was soon supplemented by picketing, demonstrating, and boycotting, with telling effect particularly in selected Northern communities.[13]

IV.

The two world wars had a profound effect on the status of Negroes in the United States and did much to mount the attack on the two worlds of race. The decade of World War I witnessed a very significant migration of Negroes. They went in large numbers—perhaps a half a million—from the rural areas of the South to the towns and cities of the South and North. They were especially attracted to the industrial centers of the North. By the thousands they poured into Pittsburgh, Cleveland, and Chicago. Although many were unable to secure employment, others were successful and achieved a standard of living they could not have imagined only a few years earlier. Northern communities were not altogether friendly and hospitable to the newcomers, but the opportunities for education and the enjoyment of political self-respect were the greatest they had ever seen. Many of them felt that they were entirely justified in their renewed hope that the war would bring about a complete merger of the two worlds of race. [911]

Those who held such high hopes, however, were naive in the extreme. Already the Ku Klux Klan was being revived—this time in the North as well as the South. Its leaders were determined to develop a broad program to unite "native-born white Christians for concerted action in the preservation of American institutions and the supremacy of the white race." By the time that the war was over, the Klan was in a position to make capital of the racial animosities that had developed during the conflict itself. Racial conflicts had broken out in many places during the war; and before the conference at Versailles was over race riots in the United States had brought about what can accurately be described as the "long hot summer" of 1919.

If anything, the military operations which aimed to save the world for democracy merely fixed more permanently the racial separation in the United States. Negro soldiers not only constituted entirely separate fighting units in the United States Army, but, once overseas, were assigned to fighting units with the French Army. Negroes who sought service with the United States Marines or the Air Force were rejected, while the Navy relegated them to menial duties. The reaction of many Negroes was bitter, but most of the leaders, including Du Bois, counseled patience and loyalty. They continued to hope that their show of patriotism would win for them a secure place of acceptance as Americans.

Few Negro Americans could have anticipated the wholesale rejection they experienced at the conclusion of World War I. Returning Negro soldiers were lynched by hanging and burning even while still in their military uniforms. The Klan warned Negroes that they must respect the rights of the white race "in whose country they are permitted to reside." Racial conflicts swept the country, and neither federal nor state governments seemed interested in effective intervention. The worlds of race were growing further apart in the postwar decade. Nothing indicated this more clearly than the growth of the Universal Negro Improvement Association, led by Marcus Garvey. From a mere handful of members at the end of the war, the Garvey movement rapidly became the largest secular Negro group ever organized in the United States. Although few Negroes were interested in settling in Africa—the expressed aim of Garvey—they joined the movement by the hundreds of thousands to indicate their resentment of the racial duality that seemed to them to be the central feature of the American social order.[14]

More realistic and hardheaded were the Negroes who were [912] more determined than ever to engage in the most desperate fight of their lives to destroy racism in the United States. As the editor of the *Crisis* said in 1919, "We return from fighting. We return fighting. Make way for Democracy! We saved it in France, and by the Great Jehovah, we will save it in the U.S.A., or know the reason why." This was the spirit of what Alain Locke called "The New Negro." He fought the Democratic white primary, made war on the whites who consigned him to the ghetto, attacked racial discrimination in employment, and pressed for legislation to protect his rights. If he was seldom successful during the postwar decade and the depression, he made it quite clear that he was unalterably opposed to the un-American character of the two worlds of race.

Hope for a new assault on racism was kindled by some of the New Deal policies of Franklin D. Roosevelt. As members of the economically disadvantaged group, Negroes benefited from relief and recovery legislation. Most of it, however, recognized the existence of the two worlds of race and accommodated itself to it. Frequently bread lines and soup kitchens were separated on the basis of race. There was segregation in the employment services, while many new agencies recognized and bowed to Jim Crow. Whenever agencies, such as the Farm Security Administration, fought segregation and sought to deal with people on the basis of their needs rather than race they came under the withering fire of the racist critics and seldom escaped alive. Winds of change, however slight, were discernible, and nowhere was this in greater evidence than in the new labor unions. Groups like the Congress of Industrial Organizations, encouraged by the support of the Wagner Labor Relations Act, began to look at manpower resources as a whole and to attack the old racial policies that viewed labor in terms of race.

As World War II approached, Negroes schooled in the experience of the nineteen-twenties and thirties were unwilling to see the fight against Nazism carried on in the context of an American racist ideology. Some white Americans were likewise uncomfortable in the role of freeing Europe of a racism which still permeated the United States; but it was the Negroes who dramatized American inconsistency by demanding an end to discrimination in employment in defense industries. By threatening to march on Washington in 1941 they forced the President to issue an order forbidding such discrimination. The opposition was loud and strong. Some state governors denounced the order, and some manufacturers [913] skillfully evaded it. But it was a significant step toward the elimination of the two worlds.

During World War II the assault on racism continued. Negroes, more than a million of whom were enlisted in the armed services, bitterly fought discrimination and segregation. The armed services were, for the most part, two quite distinct racial worlds. Some Negro units had white officers, and much of the officer training was desegregated. But it was not until the final months of the war that a deliberate experiment was undertaken to involve Negro and white enlisted men in the same fighting unit. With the success of the experiment and with the warm glow of victory over Nazism as a backdrop, there was greater inclination to recognize the absurdity of maintaining a racially separate military force to protect the freedoms of the country.[15]

During the war there began the greatest migration in the history of Negro Americans. Hundreds of thousands left the South for the industrial centers of the North and West. In those places they met hostility, but they also secured employment in aviation plants, automobile factories, steel mills, and numerous other industries. Their difficulties persisted as they faced problems of housing and adjustment. But they continued to move out of the South in such large numbers that by 1965 one third of the twenty million Negroes in the United States lived in twelve metropolitan centers of the North and West. The ramifications of such large-scale migration were numerous. The concentration of Negroes in communities where they suffered no political disabilities placed in their hands an enormous amount of political power. Consequently, some of them went to the legislatures, to Congress, and to positions on the judiciary. In turn, this won for them political respect as well as legislation that greatly strengthened their position as citizens.

V.

Following World War II there was a marked acceleration in the war against the two worlds of race in the United States. In 1944 the Supreme Court ruled against segregation in interstate transportation, and three years later it wrote the final chapter in the war against the Democratic white primary. In 1947 the President's Committee on Civil Rights called for the "elimination of segregation based on race, color, creed, or national origin, from American life."[16] In the following year President Truman asked Congress to establish [914] a permanent Fair Employment Practices Commission. At the same time he took several steps to eliminate segregation in the armed services. These moves on the part of the judicial and executive branches of the federal government by no means destroyed the two worlds of race, but they created a more healthy climate in which the government and others could launch an attack on racial separatism.

The attack was greatly strengthened by the new position of world leadership that the United States assumed at the close of the war. Critics of the United States were quick to point to the inconsistencies of an American position that spoke against racism abroad and countenanced it at home. New nations, brown and black, seemed reluctant to follow the lead of a country that adhered to its policy of maintaining two worlds of race—the one identified with the old colonial ruling powers and the other with the colonies now emerging as independent nations. Responsible leaders in the United States saw the weakness of their position, and some of them made new moves to repair it.

Civic and religious groups, some labor organizations, and many individuals from the white community began to join in the effort to destroy segregation and discrimination in American life. There was no danger, after World War II, that Negroes would ever again stand alone in their fight. The older interracial organizations continued, but they were joined by new ones. In addition to the numerous groups that included racial equality in their over-all programs, there were others that made the creation of one racial world their principle objective. Among them were the Congress of Racial Equality, the Southern Christian Leadership Conference, and the Student Non–Violent Coordinating Committee. Those in existence in the 1950's supported the court action that brought about the decision against segregated schools. The more recent ones have taken the lead in pressing for new legislation and in developing new techniques to be used in the war on segregation.

VI.

The most powerful direct force in the maintenance of the two worlds of race has been the state and its political subdivisions. In states and communities where racial separation and discrimination are basic to the way of life, the elected officials invariably pledge themselves to the perpetuation of the duality. Indeed, candidates frequently vie with one another in their effort to occupy the most [915] extreme segregationist position possible on the race question. Appointed officials, including the constabulary and, not infrequently, the teachers and school administrators, become auxiliary guardians of the system of racial separation. In such communities Negroes occupy no policy-making positions, exercise no influence over the determination of policy, and are seldom even on the police force. State and local resources, including tax funds, are at the disposal of those who guard the system of segregation and discrimination; and such funds are used to enforce customs as well as laws to disseminate information in support of the system.

The white community itself acts as a guardian of the segregated system. Schooled in the specious arguments that assert the supremacy of the white race and fearful that a destruction of the system would be harmful to their own position, they not only "go along" with it but, in many cases, enthusiastically support it. Community sanctions are so powerful, moreover, that the independent citizen who would defy the established order would find himself not only ostracized but, worse, the target of economic and political reprisals.

Within the community many self-appointed guardians of white supremacy have emerged at various times. After the Civil War and after World War I it was the Ku Klux Klan, which has shown surprising strength in recent years. After the desegregation decision of the Supreme Court in 1954 it was the White Citizens' Council, which one Southern editor has called the "uptown Ku Klux Klan." From time to time since 1865, it has been the political demagogue, who has not only made capital by urging his election as a sure way to maintain the system but has also encouraged the less responsible elements of the community to take the law into their own hands.

Violence, so much a part of American history and particularly of Southern history, has been an important factor in maintaining the two worlds of race. Intimidation, terror, lynchings, and riots have, in succession, been the handmaiden of political entities whose officials have been unwilling or unable to put an end to it. Violence drove Negroes from the polls in the 1870's and has kept them away in droves since that time. Lynchings, the spectacular rope and faggot kind or the quiet kind of merely "doing away" with some insubordinate Negro, have served their special purpose in terrorizing whole communities of Negroes. Riots, confined to no section of the country, have demonstrated how explosive the racial situation can be in urban communities burdened with the strain of racial strife. [916]

The heavy hand of history has been a powerful force in the maintenance of a segregated society and, conversely, in the resistance to change. Americans, especially Southerners whose devotion to the past is unmatched by that of any others, have summoned history to support their arguments that age-old practices and institutions cannot be changed overnight, that social practices cannot be changed by legislation. Southerners have argued that desegregation would break down long-established customs and bring instability to a social order that, if left alone, would have no serious racial or social disorders. After all, Southern whites "know" Negroes; and their knowledge has come from many generations of intimate association and observation, they insist.

White Southerners have also summoned history to support them in their resistance to federal legislation designed to secure the civil rights of Negroes. At every level—in local groups, state governments, and in Congress—white Southerners have asserted that federal civil rights legislation is an attempt to turn back the clock to the Reconstruction era, when federal intervention, they claim, imposed a harsh and unjust peace.[17] To make effective their argument, they use such emotion-laden phrases as "military occupation," "Negro rule," and "black-out of honest government." Americans other than Southerners have been frightened by the Southerners' claim that civil rights for Negroes would cause a return to the "evils" of Reconstruction. Insecure in their own knowledge of history, they have accepted the erroneous assertions about the "disaster" of radical rule after the Civil War and the vengeful punishment meted out to the South by the Negro and his white allies. Regardless of the merits of these arguments that seem specious on the face of them—to say nothing of their historical inaccuracy—they have served as effective brakes on the drive to destroy the two worlds of race.

One suspects, however, that racial bigotry has become more expensive in recent years. It is not so easy now as it once was to make political capital out of the race problem, even in the deep South. Local citizens—farmers, laborers, manufacturers—have become a bit weary of the promises of the demagogue that he will preserve the integrity of the races if he is, at the same time, unable to persuade investors to build factories and bring capital to their communities. Some Southerners, dependent on tourists, are not certain that their vaunted racial pride is so dear, if it keeps visitors away and brings depression to their economy. The cities that see themselves [917] bypassed by a prospective manufacturer because of their reputation in the field of race relations might have some sober second thoughts about the importance of maintaining their two worlds. In a word, the economics of segregation and discrimination is forcing, in some quarters, a reconsideration of the problem.

It must be added that the existence of the two worlds of race has created forces that cause some Negroes to seek its perpetuation. Some Negro institutions, the product of a dual society, have vested interests in the perpetuation of that society. And Negroes who fear the destruction of their own institutions by desegregation are encouraged by white racists to fight for their maintenance. Even where Negroes have a desire to maintain their institutions because of their honest com-mitment to the merits of cultural pluralism, the desire becomes a strident struggle for survival in the context of racist forces that seek with a vengeance to destroy such institutions. The firing of a few hundred Negro school teachers by a zealous, racially-oriented school board forces some second thoughts on the part of the Negroes regarding the merits of desegregation.

VII.

The drive to destroy the two worlds of race has reached a new, dramatic, and somewhat explosive stage in recent years. The forces arrayed in behalf of maintaining these two worlds have been subjected to ceaseless and powerful attacks by the increasing numbers committed to the elimination of racism in American life. Through techniques of demonstrating, picketing, sitting-in, and boycotting they have not only harassed their foes but marshaled their forces. Realizing that another ingredient was needed, they have pressed for new and better laws and the active support of government. At the local and state levels they began to secure legislation in the 1940's to guarantee the civil rights of all, eliminate discrimination in employment, and achieve decent public and private housing for all.

While it is not possible to measure the influence of public opinion in the drive for equality, it can hardly be denied that over the past five or six years public opinion has shown a marked shift toward vigorous support of the civil rights movement. This can be seen in the manner in which the mass-circulation magazines as well as influential newspapers, even in the South, have stepped up their support of specific measures that have as their objective the elimination of at least the worst features of racism. The discussion of the [918] problem of race over radio and television and the use of these media in reporting newsworthy and dramatic events in the world of race undoubtedly have had some impact. If such activities have not brought about the enactment of civil rights legislation, they have doubtless stimulated the public discussion that culminated in such legislation.

The models of city ordinances and state laws and the increased political influence of civil rights advocates stimulated new action on the federal level. Civil rights acts were passed in 1957, 1960, and

1964—after almost complete federal inactivity in this sphere for more than three quarters of a century. Strong leadership on the part of the executive and favorable judicial interpretations of old as well as new laws have made it clear that the war against two worlds of race now enjoys the sanction of the law and its interpreters. In many respects this constitutes the most significant development in the struggle against racism in the present century.

The reading of American history over the past two centuries impresses one with the fact that ambivalence on the crucial question of equality has persisted almost from the beginning. If the term "equal rights for all" has not always meant what it appeared to mean, the inconsistencies and the paradoxes have become increasingly apparent. This is not to say that the view that "equal rights for some" has disappeared or has even ceased to be a threat to the concept of real equality. It is to say, however, that the voices supporting inequality, while no less strident, have been significantly weakened by the very force of the numbers and elements now seeking to eliminate the two worlds of race. [919]

John Hope Franklin (1915–   ) was born in Oklahoma, and is Professor of American History at the University of Chicago. Among his books are From Slavery to Freedom; Reconstruction after the Civil War; *and* The Emancipation Proclamation. *He is a member of the editorial board of the* Journal of Negro History.

[1]Benjamin Quales, *The Negro in the American Revolution* (Chapel Hill, NC, 1961), pp. 15-18

[2]John Hope Franklin, *Frome Slavery to Freedom: A History of American Negroes* (New York, 1956), pp.156-157.

[3]Carter G. Woodson, *The Education of the Negro Prior to 1861* (Washington, DC, 1919), pp. 93-97.

[4]P. J. Staudenraus, *The African Colonization Movement 1816-1865,* (New York, 1961), pp. 22-32.

[5]John Hope Franklin, *The Militant South, 1800-1861* (Cambridge, MA, 1956), pp. 83-86.

[6]Louis Filler, *The Crusade Against Slavery, 1830-1860* (New York, 1960), pp. 142-145.

[7]Leon F. Litwack, *North of Slavery: The Negro in the Free States, 1790-1860* (Chicago, 1961), pp. 216-217.

[8]Benjamin Quales, *The Negro in the Civil War* (Boston, 1953), p. 200.

[9]John Hope Franklin, *Reconstruction After the Civil War* (Chicago, 1961), pp. 154-158.

[10]Raylord W. Logan, *The Negro in American Life and Thought: The Nadir, 1877-1901* (New York, 1954), pp. 239-274.

[11]John Hope Franklin, "History of Racial Segregation in the United States, *Annals of the Academy of Political and Social Science,* Vol. 304 (March 1956), pp. 1-9.

[12]George W. Williams, *History of the Negro Race in America from 1619 to 1880* (New York, 1882), p. x

[13]Franklin, *From Slavery to Freedom,* pp.437-443.

[14]Edmund David Cronon, *Black Moses, The Story of Marcus Garvey and the Universal Negro Improvement Association* (Madison, WI, 1955), pp. 202-206.

[15]Lee Nichols, *Breakthrough on the Color Front* (New York, 1954), pp. 221-226.

[16]*To Secure These Rights, The Report of the President's Committee on Civil Rights* (New York, 1947), p. 166.

[17]John Hope Franklin, "As For Our History," in Charles G. Sellers (ed.), *The Southerner as American* (Chapel Hill, NC, 1960), pp. 1-18.

Comparing the Immigrant and
Negro Experience (1968)
National Advisory Commission on Civil Disorders

We have . . . surveyed the historical background of racial discrimination and traced its effect on Negro employment, on the social structure of the ghetto community, and on the conditions of life that surround the urban Negro poor. Here we address a fundamental question that many white Americans are asking today: why has the Negro been unable to escape from poverty and the ghetto like the European immigrants?

The Maturing Economy

The changing nature of the American economy is one major reason. When the European immigrants were arriving in large numbers, America was becoming an urban-industrial society. To build its major cities and industries, America needed great pools of unskilled labor. The immigrants provided the labor, gained an economic foothold, and thereby enabled their children and grandchildren to move up to skilled, white collar, and professional employment.

Since World War II, especially, America's urban-industrial society has matured; unskilled labor is far less essential than before, and blue-collar jobs of all kinds are decreasing in number and importance as a source of new employment. The Negroes who migrated to the great urban centers lacked the skills essential to the new economy; and the schools of the ghetto have been unable to provide the education that can qualify them for decent jobs. The Negro migrant, unlike the immigrant, found little opportunity in the city; he had arrived too late, and the unskilled labor he had to offer was no longer needed.

The Disability of Race

Racial discrimination is undoubtedly the second major reason why the Negro has been unable to escape from poverty. The structure of discrimination has persistently narrowed his opportunities and restricted his prospects. Well before the high tide of immigration from overseas, Negroes were already relegated to the poorly paid, low status occupations. Had it not been for racial discrimination, the North might well have recruited [287] Southern Negroes after the Civil War to provide the labor for building the burgeoning urban-industrial economy. Instead, Northern employers looked to Europe for their sources of unskilled labor. Upon the arrival of the immigrants, the Negroes were dislodged from the few urban occupations they had dominated. Not until World War II were Negroes generally hired for industrial jobs, and by that time the decline in the need for unskilled labor had already begun. European immigrants, too, suffered from discrimination, but never was it so pervasive as the prejudice against color in America, which has formed a bar to advancement, unlike any other.

Entry Into The Political System

Political opportunities also played an important role in enabling the European immigrants to escape from poverty. The immigrants settled for the most part in rapidly growing cities that had powerful and expanding political machines, which gave them economic advantages in exchange for political support. The political machines were decentralized; and ward-level grievance machinery, as well as personal representation, enabled the immigrant to make his voice heard and his power felt. Since the local political organizations exercised considerable influence over public buildings in the cities, they provided employment in construction jobs for their immigrant voters. Ethnic groups often dominated one or more of the municipal services—police and fire protection, sanitation, and even public education.

By the time the Negroes arrived, the situation had altered dramatically. The great wave of public building had virtually come to an end; reform groups were beginning to attack the political machines; the machines were no longer so powerful or so well equipped to provide jobs and other favors.

Although the political machines retained their hold over the areas settled by Negroes, the scarcity of patronage jobs made them unwilling to share with the Negroes the political positions they had created in these neighborhoods. For example, Harlem was dominated by white politicians for many years after it had become a Negro ghetto; even today, New York's Lower East Side, which is now predominantly Puerto Rican, is strongly influenced by politicians of the older immigrant groups.

This pattern exists in many other American cities. Negroes are still underrepresented in city councils and in most city agencies.

Segregation played a role here too. The immigrants and their descendants felt threatened by the arrival of the Negro [279] and prevented a Negro-immigrant coalition that might have saved the old political machines. Reform groups, nominally more liberal on the race issue, were often dominated by businessmen and middle-class city residents who usually opposed coalition with any low-income group, white or black.

Cultural Factors

Cultural factors also made it easier for the immigrants to escape from poverty. They came to America from much poorer societies, with a low standard of living, and they came at a time when job aspirations were low. When most jobs on the American economy were unskilled, they sensed little deprivation in being forced to take the dirty and poorly paid jobs. Moreover, their families were large, and many breadwinners, some of whom never married, contributed to the family income. As a result, family units managed to live even from the lowest paid jobs and still put some money aside for savings or investment, for example, to purchase a house or tenement, or to open a store or factory. Since the immigrants spoke little English and had their own ethnic culture, they needed stores to supply them with ethnic foods and other services. Since their family structures were patriarchal, men found satisfaction in family life that helped compensate for the bad jobs they had to take and the hard work they had to endure.

Negroes came to the city under quite different circumstances. Generally relegated to jobs that others would not take, they paid too little to be able to put money in savings for new enterprises. Since they spoke English, they had no need for their own stores; besides, the areas they occupied were already filled with stores. In addition, Negroes lacked the extended family characteristic of certain European groups—each household usually had only one or two breadwinners. Moreover, Negro men had fewer cultural incentives to work in a dirty job for the sake of the family. As a result of slavery and of long periods of male unemployment afterwards, the Negro family structure had become matriarchal; the man played a secondary and marginal role in his family. For many Negro men, then, there were few of the cultural and psychological rewards of family life. A marginal figure in the family, particularly when unemployed, Negro men were often rejected by their wives or often abandoned their homes because they felt themselves useless to their families.

Although most Negro men worked as hard as the immigrants to support their families, their rewards were less. The jobs did not pay enough to enable them to support their families, for prices and living standards had risen since the immigrants [280] had come, and the entrepreneurial opportunities that had allowed some immigrants to become independent, even rich, had vanished. Above all, Negroes suffered from segregation, which denied them access to the good jobs and the right unions, and which deprived them of the opportunity to buy real estate or obtain business loans or move out of the ghetto and bring up their children in middle-class neighborhoods. Immigrants were able to leave their ghettos as soon as they had the money; segregation has denied Negroes the opportunity to live elsewhere.

The Vital Element Of Time

Finally, nostalgia makes it easy to exaggerate the ease of escape of the white immigrants from the ghettos. When the immigrants were immersed in poverty, they too lived in slums, and these neighborhoods exhibited fearfully high rates of alcoholism, desertion, illegitimacy, and other pathologies associated with poverty. Just as some Negro men desert their families when they are unemployed and their wives can get jobs, so did the men of other ethnic groups, even though time and affluence has clouded white memories of the past.

Today, whites tend to exaggerate how well and how quickly they escaped from poverty, and contrast their experience with poverty-stricken Negroes. The fact is, among the many of the Southern and Eastern Europeans who came to America in the last great wave of immigration, those who came already urbanized were the first to escape from poverty. The others who came to America form rural backgrounds, as Negroes did, are only now, after three generations, in the final stages of escaping from poverty. Until the last 10 years or so, most of these were employed in blue-collar jobs, and only a small proportion of their children were able or willing to attend college. In other words, only the third, and in many cases, only the fourth generation has been able to achieve the kind of middle-class income and status that allows it to send its children to college. Because of favorable economic and political conditions, these ethnic groups were able to escape from lower-class status to working-class and lower-middle-class status, but it has taken them three generations.

Negroes have been concentrated in the city for only two generations, and they have been there under much less favorable conditions. Moreover, their escape from poverty has been blocked in part by the resistance of the European ethnic groups; they have been unable to enter some unions and to move into some neighborhoods outside the ghetto because descendants of the European immigrants who control these [281] unions and neighborhoods have not yet abandoned them for middle-class occupations and areas.

Even so, some Negroes have escaped poverty, and they have done so in only two generations; their success is less visible than that of the immigrants in many cases, for residential segregation has forced them to remain in the ghetto. Still, the proportion of nonwhites employed in white-collar, technical, and professional jobs has risen from 10.2 percent in 1950 to 20.8 percent in 1966, and the proportion attending college has risen an equal amount. Indeed, the development of a small but steadily increasing Negro middle class while the greater part of the Negro population is stagnating economically is creating a growing gap between Negro haves and have-nots.

This gap, as well as the awareness of its existence by those left behind, undoubtedly adds to the feelings of desperation and anger which breed civil disorders. Low-income Negroes realize that segregation and lack of job opportunities have made it possible for only a small proportion of all Negroes to escape poverty and the summer disorders are at least in part a protest against being left behind and left out.

The immigrant who labored long hours at hard and often menial work had the hope of a better future, if not for himself then for his children. This was the promise of the "American dream"—the society offered to all a future that was open-ended; with hard work and perseverance, a man and his family could in time achieve not only material well-being but "position" and status.

For the Negro family in the urban ghetto, there is a different vision—the future seems to lead only to a dead-end.

What the American economy of the late 19th and early 20th century was able to do to help the European immigrants escape from poverty is now largely impossible. New methods of escape must be found for the majority of today's poor. [282]

All jobs should be open to everybody, unless they actually require a penis or vagina.
Florence Kennedy

Attitudes Toward Acculturation in the English Fiction of the Jewish Immigrant, 1900–1917 (1991)

David M. Fine

When the Jewish immigrant began to write novels in the language of his adopted land, it was both natural and inevitable that his subject should have been his own adjustment to America. Having the leisure to write fiction meant having achieved some measure of success in America, and, as might be expected, the process the immigrant novelist characteristically described was one of assimilation and accommodation with the dominant culture. We are given most often an account of his own interpretation of "Americanization," a concept which could mean either the shedding of Old World customs and the absorption of native habits or the broader melting pot fusion of Old and New World culture. Rarely did cultural pluralism, or "cosmopolitanism"—the idea advanced by Horace Kallen that America existed as a confederation of culturally–distinct national and ethnic groups—play a part in the fiction written by the first generation immigrant, except as an idea to be rejected: the writer's own experience had moved in an opposite direction.

Like so many of the immigrant autobiographies which appeared during the period, the novels written by immigrant Jews had a hopeful message to preach. In a period characterized by the mounting distrust of foreigners and the suspicion that the newer arrivals from eastern Europe were unassimilable, these novels were optimistic affirmations of immigrant assimilability. There were exceptions, of course—among them Abraham Cahan's *The Rise of David Levinsky* and Sydney Nyburg's *The Chosen People*. We would like to contrast these two novels with others written by Jewish writers, particularly Elias Tobenkin, Ezra Brudno, and Edward Steiner, at the same time placing the immigrant novel within the larger cultural context of assimilation attitudes which prevailed in these years.

Although they were not the largest of the "new immigrant" groups, the Jews produced most of the period's immigrant fiction.[1] Like other large groups from southern and eastern Europe the Jews were motivated to emigrate for a variety of reasons, but to a greater extent than with the other groups, repression provided the spur. As a result, they brought a sizeable number of educated men with them and thus were able to achieve culturally in the first generation what other groups had to wait until the second and third generations to achieve. Moreover, since many were fleeing Czarist oppression, there were relatively few "birds of passage." In far greater proportion than other immigrants they planned to remain in America, so that the whole question of acculturation was a crucial one.

To some Jews acculturation meant sloughing off of Old World habits and embracing Christian American values. No better testament to this assimilation ideal exists than the autobiography of Mary Antin, *The Promised Land*, which created something of a literary sensation when it appeared in 1912. Her story tells of the girl who emigrated in 1894 at the age of thirteen from Polotsk, Russia, to Boston. In Russia she had been a stranger in her own land, a victim of Christian maliciousness and persecution. In America she is made to feel at home, and, encouraged to adopt the ways of her new land, she is reborn as an entirely new person: "I was born, I have lived, and I have been made over . . . . I am absolutely other than the person whose story I have to tell . . . . My life I still have to live; her life ended when mine began.²

To Danish–born journalist Jacob Riis, whose autobiography, *The Making of an American,* was written in much the same spirit as Miss Antin's, the clannishness of the recent immigrants stood as one of the chief stumbling blocks to acculturation. While he recognized that the tenement building and the sweat shop system were major factors which fostered the immigrant's cultural isolation, he pointed out to readers of *How the Other Half Lives* (1890) that some immigrant groups had risen from the ghettos rapidly, while others had stubbornly resisted Americanization. As the immigrant who made it in America, he had little patience with foreigners who were slow to adopt native ways. His sympathies diminished in proportion to the immigrants' obstinacy in clinging to Old World manners and traditions. The Russian Jews were to him among the most recalcitrant of the new immigrants, standing "where the new day that dawned on Calvary left them, stubbornly refusing to see the light."³

The immigrant novelist whose works came closest to advocating the kind of assimilation Mary Antin and Jacob Riis were recommending was Russian–born Elias Tobenkin. In *Witte Arrives* (1916), he describes the Americanization of Emile Witte (born Wittowski), who emigrates as a youth from Russia and after attending a Western university becomes a commercial and artistic success as a journalist, while his father remains a peddler in America, too rooted in Old World habits to become Americanized. So thoroughly has Witte been made over that his articles on domestic issues, we are told, have an "Emersonian flavor" and that most readers "would have placed the writer of such articles as none other than a scion of one of the oldest American families."⁴

Witte seals his "arrival" at the end of the novel by marrying a Gentile girl of wealthy, old New England stock, after his Jewish wife dies. His transformation from bewildered alien to successful citizen seems much too facile but for the fact that, like Tobenkin, Witte arrived in America as a young boy and grew up in the rural West and not in the urban ghetto. He became Americanized not as Mary Antin had, by erasing the stigmata of the past but as Jacob Riis had, by channeling his talents into the mainstream of the middle-class American reform movement, by putting his journalistic skills to the service of broad, native, democratic ideals.

The reviewers praised *Witte Arrives,* some likening it to *The Promised Land,* others reading it—or misreading it—as an affirmation of the melting pot, ignoring the implications of fusing contained in the metaphor. Typical of the latter view was the comment of H. W. Boynton, who wrote in *Bookman* that "the main picture of the ardent young alien becoming in a brief score of years a loyal thoroughgoing American is of a sort to stiffen our faith in the melting pot." A reviewer for *Nation,* commenting a year and a half later on Tobenkin's next novel, *The House of Conrad,* reminded readers of *Witte Arrives:* "It was the story of the melting pot, of a young Russian who came to this country in boyhood and made himself at least as American as the Americans."⁵

Such remarks illustrate the looseness with which the term "melting pot" was used during the period. As Philip Gleason has indicated in his essay on the melting pot in the *American Quarterly,* the term was employed in these years to denote almost any view toward assimilation favored by those using it.⁶ During the war years, with the fear of divided loyalties and the suspicion of all but "100 percent Americans," the traditional optimistic view that the melting pot was working to produce a stronger America by blending the best elements of Old and New World cultures lost ground to the view that the function of the pot was to purge the "foreign dross" and impurities" from the immigrant. In the popular mind the melting pot was identified more and more closely with indoctrination. As a result of this shift in the meaning of the term, those liberal critics who rejected narrow Americanization as a cultural ideal tended also to reject the melting pot, with its connotations of conformity and standardization. One of these critics was Randolph Bourne. Following the lead of Horace Kallen, Bourne rejected fusion altogether as either a realistic possibility of a desirable goal and called for an ethnically diverse, "Trans-National" America.[7] Writing in the *Dial* in 1918, Bourne sarcastically denounced what he called the "insistent smugness" of Tobenkin's *The House of Conrad,* which again emphasized the theme of assimilation and identified success with the absorption of native ideals.[8]

Acculturation in the novels of Elias Tobenkin and in the immigrant autobiography of Mary Antin presumes movement in one direction only: the immigrant sheds his past and adjusts to his adopted land. Missing from such statements is the traditional attitude that cultural blending is a two-way process, that Old World culture is needed to enrich the nation. This attitude found expression at the turn of the century in the settlement ideals of Jane Addams and in the journalistic sketches of Hutchins Hapgood. In her work at Chicago's Hull House and in her writing, Miss Addams, daughter of a prominent Midwestern family, concentrated on what the native American can gain from the "gifts" of the newcomers, and instead of premising her urban reform program on the rapid Americanization of the immigrants, as Riis was doing, she urged them to retain the rich folk traditions of their former lives and share them with Americans.[9] Hapgood, product of one of America's oldest families (his ancestors arrived at Massachusetts Bay in the 1640's), looked to the new immigrants to supply cultural and spiritual values to a nation caught up in getting and spending. Like his brother Norman, who became an authority on New York's Yiddish theater before taking over the editorship of *Collier's Weekly,* "Hutch" was infatuated with the Lower East Side ghetto which he came to know as a New York reporter, working alongside Abraham Cahan on Lincoln Steffans' *Commercial Advertiser. The Spirit of the Ghetto* (1902), a collection of Hapgood's journalistic pieces, remains a moving if sentimental tribute to the cultural richness of New York's Lower East Side. In contrast to Jacob Riis, whose concern for slum reform and Americanization led him to sketch the ghetto's derelicts, paupers, and street arabs, Hapgood sketched its artists, poets, and scholars. Riis examined its crowded tenements, saloons, and stale beer drives; Hapgood its theaters, schools, and coffee houses.

By addressing themselves not merely to what the immigrants could gain by becoming Americans but to what America could gain by keeping its immigrant ports open, Jane Addams and Hutchins Hapgood brought forward into the urban-industrial age the traditional belief that the New World is a place of new men, and that the national character would continue to be modified by those who chose to come here.

The term "melting pot," used to describe the fusing of Old and New World cultures on American soil, was given currency by the English novelist-playwright Israel Zangwill, who used it as the title of his successful 1908 play about immigrant life in New York. The play concerns a young musician who has fled form Kishinev to his uncle's flat in New York following the pogrom in which his parents had been massacred before his eyes. Dedicated to the ideal of the melting pot, he composes an "American Symphony" which will passionately proclaim his faith in his new life. He is never allowed to forget the past, however; he carries as a reminder a Russian bullet in his shoulder and is given to hysterical paranoiac outbursts. The play's conflict arises when, incredulously, he learns that his fiancée, a non-Jewish Russian immigrant, is the daughter of the Czarist officer who led the Kishinev massacre. By the end of the play, though, his love for Vera and his ecstatic vision of America as a land where ancient hatreds can be put aside, prove stronger than the anguish of the past. At the opposite extreme from David's almost neurotic obsession with the melting pot is the cultural pluralism of the boy's uncle, Mendel Quixano, who rigorously opposes his nephew's marriage to a Christian girl even before he learns of Vera's past. The Jews, he argues, have survived in captivity and in the Diaspora only because they have sustained a separate identity and have refused to merge with the dominant culture. Assimilation would spell the death of the Jewish people.

Mendel's position had considerable support among America's immigrant Jews. Those who had fled the pogroms of Russia came to America not to be fused into a different culture but in order to be free to retain old beliefs, customs, and cultural identity. Opposition to melting pot blending came not only from Orthodox Jews and Zionists, but from many of those immigrants who had reached maturity in eastern Europe during the eighties and who retained the vivid memory of Czarist persecution. Such elders of the immigrant community were unwilling to give up their loyalty to Old World traditions which satisfied social and emotional as well as religious needs.[10] *The American Hebrew*, an important organ of the older, more assimilated German Jews, voiced the feelings of at least part of the ghetto when it said of Zangwill:

> Certain it is that no man who has felt so distinctly the heart-beats of the great Jewish masses can be expected to be taken seriously if he proposes Assimilation as the solution of the Jewish problem. Not for this did prophets sing and martyrs die.[11]

Opinion among "arrived" Jews was divided. Louis Marshall, president of the American Jewish Committee and one of the most influential Jews in American life, wrote that "the melting pot, as advanced by Zangwill, produces mongrelization . . . our struggles should be not to create a hybrid civilization, but preserve the best elements that constitute the civilization we are still seeking, the civilization of universal brotherhood."[12] On the other hand, President Roosevelt's Secretary of Labor and Commerce, Oscar Straus, the highest ranking Jew in government, reportedly shared with the President an enthusiasm for the play's optimistic message of fusion.[13]

In the years just prior to the premier of Zangwill's play two novels, written by immigrants, Ezra Brudno's *The Fugitive* (1904) and Edward Steiner's *The Mediator* (1907), affirmed the melting pot credo in a manner quite similar to Zangwill's. The novels are remarkably alike and can conveniently be described together. Both tell of Russian-Jewish youths, victims of Old World persecution who come to America with apocalyptic visions of the reunification of Jew and Christian. The faith in the healing power of the New World both authors wrote into their novels had its roots in their own successful public careers in America. Brudno, born in Lithuania in 1879, attended Yale University and went on to a prominent legal career. Steiner, a convert to Christianity, was born in Vienna in 1866, taught theology and sociology at Grinnell College in Iowa, and authored several books on immigration.

The early chapters of both novels are devoted to the Old World childhood of the protagonists. Both young men are raised in Christian environments. Brudno's hero, Israel Rusakoff, the son of an Orthodox Jew falsely convicted of the ritual slaughter of a Christian girl, is adopted by a Russian landowner who it later turns out—in one of the ironic coincidences which plague this fiction—is the repentant betrayer of the boy's father. Steiner's hero, Samuel Cohen, has been raised by a Catholic nurse following the death of his mother. So awed is he by the beauty and pomp of Catholicism he enters a monastery to study for the priesthood, only to abandon his vocation when he witnesses a brutal pogrom perpetrated in the name of Christianity. Both youths conclude that Christianity is a false sanctuary, that they cannot escape their pasts, that their destinies have been shaped by their heritage. Yet to return to the Orthodoxy of their fathers is as impossible as to reject their birthright completely. Old World Judaism—particularly in Brudno's novel—is rendered in its most medieval, oriental, and reactionary aspects.

In both works the flight to America is a flight from forms of oppression imposed by both Jew and Christian, but in the ghetto of New York's Lower East Side, they find further oppression. To indicate the debasement of the European Jew in the New World ghetto, both Brudno and Steiner employ the device, so common to the immigrant novel, of allowing figures from the protagonists' Old World past to reappear: prominent Russian Jews, forced to flee following the 1881 assassination of the Czar, turn up as sweatshop workers; former Talmudic scholars become Yankee "dandies" or "allrightniks." The usual metamorphosis places the Jew behind a sewing machine, tyrannized by the German-Jewish "sweater." Conventionally, the Americanized "uptown" German Jew is the villain in the fiction of the ghetto, both in these novels produced by the immigrants and in the popular native-drawn sketches of immigrant life which were then appearing in the magazines. Between the poles of rigid Old World piety and traditionalism and New World secularism and materialism, the heroes of Brudno and Steiner seek to define their American and Jewish identities. To reconcile Old World and New, Russian and German, Jew and Gentile, becomes their mission.

Steiner's "mediator" assumes a more active role in bringing about the rapprochement of the two worlds. Having been raised in a monastery and having fled with the traumatic recognition of the gulf between Christian teaching and Christian practice, he became an evangelist on the East Side, proclaiming the true spirit of Christ to Jew and Gentile. He is aided by the patrician philanthropist Mr. Bruce, but the mission he sets for himself is a broader one than the simple conversion advocated by Bruce. The conflict between the two men, which dominates the later chapters of the novel, centers on the distinction between the rival interpretations of Americanization, that is, one-sided assimilation with the dominant population group as against the more liberal melting pot ideal. Bruce seeks to Americanize the Jewish immigrant by converting him to Christianity; Samuel Cohen seeks to fuse the two faiths, preserving the highest ideals of both.

The protagonists in both novels confirm their roles as cultural mediators by marrying Gentile women. Brudno's hero, like Zangwill's, marries the daughter of his Old World enemy. Thus the marriage which has been forbidden in the Old World is sanctioned in the New. Steiner's hero weds the daughter of the missionary with whom he has joined forces. As in *Witte Arrives*, *The Melting Pot*, and *The Fugitive*, the union of the Jewish male with the Gentile woman—either a native-born aristocrat or the daughter of the Jew's Old World betrayer—provides the symbolism for the reconciliation of Old and New World. Marriage to a Christian American is both the badge signifying the immigrant's successful "arrival" and the broader symbol of the possibilities for cultural fusion in America.

The most interesting comment on the solution Steiner's mediator presents comes from another novel about a self-styled mediator written ten years later. In *The Chosen People* (1917) Sydney Nyburg, a Baltimore lawyer and grandson of a Dutch Jewish immigrant, tells the story of Philip Graetz, rabbi of an affluent urban synagogue who conceives his divinely-appointed mission to be the mediator between the Americanized, "uptown" German Jews of his own congregation and the recently-arrived "downtown" Russian Jews of the city's ghetto. Steiner's mediator sought to bring together Jew and Gentile; Nyburg's wants to join the two worlds of Jews in America. In both novels the clash is between the values of the Old World and those of the New; in both the protagonist is a self-appointed "prophet of peace," who, upheld by a visionary melting pot credo, directs his rhetoric to the fusion of two diverse worlds. The difference is that not only is Graetz singularly unfit for his chosen task, but the task itself is shown to be beyond the possibility of attainment by any single man. What the world needs, Graetz learns, is not the prophet with his abstract plea for justice, but the pragmatic bargainer—the tough-minded realist, who, if he cannot make the uptown Jew love his downtown brothers, can, at least, keep him from exploiting their labor.

Graetz's teacher and foil in the novel is a cynical, Russian-born labor attorney, David Gordon. In the strike which serves in the novel as a focus for the struggle between uptown and downtown, the workers of the ghetto are able to achieve better working conditions not because Graetz has convinced the industrialists of his congregation of their selfishness, but because Gordon has marshalled an army of workers willing to challenge the Jewish plutocracy. To Gordon, the two worlds of Jews cannot be kept from fighting as long as they occupy opposite poles in a capitalistic, individualistic society. His own solution is Zionism, which he feels will bind all Jews together in the building of their own society. Like the cultural pluralists, he believes that the Jews can stay alive only by defining their identity outside the value system of America. At the other extreme are the German Jews of Graetz's congregation, who embrace their Americanization ardently and are embarrassed by the persistence of Old World habits in the Russian Jews. They live in fear that the vast presence of the newcomers will undermine their own hard-won position in Christian America, and yet because they rely on the cheap labor force supplied by the recent immigrant, they have a vested interest in perpetuating his ignorance.

The Chosen People was a needed antidote to the facile affirmations of assimilation and the melting pot offered by such immigrant writers as Tobenkin, Brudno, and Steiner. Labor warfare between uptown German and downtown Russian Jews in Baltimore served Nyburg well as a vehicle for examining the broader question of the cultural gulf between older and newer Americans in the early years of the twentieth century. Abraham Cahan's major novel, *The Rise of David Levinsky*, appeared within a few months of *The Chosen People* and a few reviewers, pairing the two in their columns, noted the thematic parallels.

Levinsky's "rise" in America is an ironic one, for it is achieved at the expense of what is deepest and truest in him. He has realized the American dream of material success, but the victory is hollow. His life has been a dismal failure, he recognizes from his millionaire's perspective, because his outer achievements fail to satisfy his inner hunger.

The Rise of David Levinsky restates the theme which occupied Cahan in his earlier, shorter fiction. Throughout his tales of Jewish immigrant life in New York City, the Diaspora, a central and definitive historical fact in the Jewish experience, dominates the consciousness of the immigrant protagonists. His heroes are painfully aware of their exile, and whatever outer success they achieve in America, they are never permitted to forget what they have lost. This is Cahan's reply to the novels of acculturation with their glib, optimistic generalizations about cultural reconciliation and fusion. Under the pressure of New World experience, Old World values totter but never collapse entirely, for his protagonists are both unable and unwilling to extricate themselves from the grip of the past. Yearning for the past becomes one of the inescapable conditions—and, indeed, positive forces—in their lives. "The gloomiest past is dearer than the brightest present," Levinsky confesses.[14] And even Jake Podkovnik, Cahan's "Yekl," the flashy "allrightnik" and the most vulgar of his Americanizers, sees his Old World past as "a charming tale, which he was neither willing to banish from his memory nor reconcile with the actualities of his American present."[15] As Cahan's heroes outwardly assimilate into American life, they become increasingly alienated from themselves. The outer self comes into conflict with the inner self, which cannot and will not be stilled.

The result is loneliness, ennui, and guilt. In the no-man's land in which Cahan's heroes reside, there are no enduring loves or happy marriages. There are no unions with native-born aristocratic Gentile women to symbolize the melting pot blending of Old and New World. Nor are marriages or friendships from the Old World permitted to continue in the New. Yekl divorces his Russian wife for the perfumed, gaudy Mamie Fein. Levinsky, despite his great wealth, is rejected by three women. The widowed Asriel Stroom in "The Imported Bridegroom" (1898) is denied the old-age dream of seeing his Americanized daughter married to a pious Talmudic scholar. In Cahan's many other stories which deal with love and marriage in the ghetto, only one, "A Ghetto Wedding'" seems to offer the prospect of a permanent, fulfilling liaison. Contacts with the past are always unnerving. Yekl sends to Russia for his family but is embarassed by his wife's appearance at Ellis Island and forces her to remove the traditional wig which identifies her as a "greenhorn." Levinsky is always uncomfortable in the presence of Old World figures. In one scene he is unable—or unwilling— to leave a street car to offer aid to a destitute man he sees and recognizes as a fellow student from his boyhood in Russia. In a mood of nostalgia near the end of the novel he arranges a reunion with a "ship brother" twenty-five years after he and the other man, a tailor, arrived from Europe, but the affair is spoiled by mutual distrust and embarrassment, and Levinsky is made to feel guilty for his success. Throughout the book when faces from the past reappear, he is unable to contend with his mixed feelings of hostility and compassion. The faces remind him of all that he has striven to eliminate from his mind—his near starvation, the brutal death of his mother, the bitter Czarist oppression—and yet he cannot help identifying with these people, and he yearns for their company.

The conditions of Levinsky's present life have made it impossible for him to bridge the gulf to the past he yearns for, yet, paradoxically, he is never far removed from the past. Loneliness, hunger, and alienation have been so firmly stamped on his character since his boyhood, they seem the most authentic parts of him. And while he cries on the one hand for an end to his sorrows, the sorrows seem to have their own kind of value. Through his meteoric rise his inner identity has remained essentially unchanged. Neither the thorough Americanization prescribed by Mary Antin, Jacob Riis, and Elias Tobenkin, nor the cultural fusion urged by Jane Addams, Ezra Brudno, and Edward Steiner are, in the end, realizable states in Cahan's fictional world. With *The Rise of David Levinsky* the novel of immigrant acculturation is no longer the story of easy faith. David Levinsky, immigrant and entrepreneur, finds emptiness at the end of the American dream.[16]

It seems appropriately ironic that 1917, the year America entered the war and passed its first major immigration restriction law, should mark the publication of the two most probing novels of immigration acculturation. At the height of the xenophobia engendered by the foreign crisis, Sydney Nyburg and Abraham Cahan, the one a third-generation and the other a first-generation American, wrote the period's most compelling fictional accounts of the Jewish immigrant in urban America. *The Chosen People* and *The Rise of David Levinsky* stand apart from and above the other novels of immigrant acculturation in having resisted ideological formulas and doctrinaire solutions and in having succeeded in portraying realistically the ironies, complexities, and dilemmas of cultural assimilation. The setting for the conflict between Old and New World in both works is the urban industrial arena because it was here that older and newer Americans so often clashed. The industrial conflict served as a metaphor for the broader, more fundamental cultural conflict. Rabbi Philip Graetz, ideologically linked with the affluent industrialists of his congregation, discovered a deeper identity with the exploited proletariat of the ghetto. David Levinsky, whose outer identity shifted with his changing fortunes, discovered that his inner identity was inescapable.

One of the conclusions to be drawn from a study of the immigrant novel is that it is dangerous to assume that the foreign-born writer, because he lived through the process of adjustment, would necessarily produce the most trenchant accounts of the process. Some immigrant writers seemed more to reflect what they had read than what they had experienced. Conventions which they absorbed from the popular ghetto melodramas appearing in the journals—stock figures like the malevolent German Jewish sweater and the fiery young ghetto idealist, for instance—and the ideological doctrines of the reformers and the social theorists proved irresistable. In the novels of Elias Tobenkin, Ezra Brudno, and Edward Steiner, the psychological complexities of acculturation are evaded in favor of overly-enthusiastic affirmations of Americanization. As immigrants who succeeded in America, they used the novel, as Mary Antin used the autobiography, to chant the praises of their adopted land. While all the immigrant novelists of the period described the disparity between the expectations and the actualities of America, between the "imagined" and the "real" America, only Cahan among them pursued the psychological implication of that disparity, its permanent cost to the psyche. Only Cahan, among the pre-World War I, first-generation Jewish American novelists, refused to turn his immigrant heroes into propagandists or preachers, refused to blink his eyes as he faced the chasm which lay between Old World values and New World experience.

David M. Fine is a professor of history at California State University at Long Beach. He has studied the history and literature of American immigrant groups for many years. His publications include The City, the Immigrant, and American Fiction, 1820–1920 (1977), *as well as articles in* American Studies, American Jewish Historical Quarterly, *and* American Literary Realism.

---

[1]Between 1881 and 1917 some four million Italians came to America as compared to two million East European Jews. Moses Rischin, *The Promised City: New York's Jews, 1990–1911* (Cambridge, Massachusetts: 1962), p. 20. Harvey Wish, *Society and Thought in Modern America: A Social and Intellectual History of the American People from 1865* (New York: 1962), pp. 242, 248. [Author's note]

[2]Mary Antin, *The Promised Land* (Boston: 1912), p. xi. [Author's note]

[3]Jacob Riis, *How the Other Half Lives: Studies Among the Tenements of New York* (New York: 1892), p. 112. [Author's note]

[4]Elias Tobenkin, *Witte Arrives* (New York: 1916), p. 293. [Author's note]

[5]H. W. Boynton, "Witte Arrives," *Bookman*, XLIV (October, 1916), 183; "Dreams and the Main Chance," *Nation*, CVI (March 14, 1918), 295–296. For other reviews of *Witte Arrives* see *New York Times Book Review*, August, 1916, 334; Edward Hale, "Recent Fiction," *Dial*, LXI (September 21, 1916), 194; and "Witte Arrives," *Nation*, CIII (September 28, 1916), 304–305. [Author's note]

[6]Philip Gleason, "The Melting Pot: Symbol of Fusion or Confusion?" *American Quarterly*, XVI (Spring, 1964), 20–46. [Author's note]

[7]Randolph Bourne, "Trans-National America," *Atlantic Monthly*, CXVIII (July 1916), 86–97. For Horace Kallen's position, see Democracy Versus the Melting Pot," *Nation*, C (1915), 217–220. A more recent statement by Kallen is contained in *Culture Pluralism and the American Idea: An Essay in Social Philosophy* (Philadelphia:1956). [Author's note]

⁸Randolph Bourne, "Clipped Wings," *Dial*, LXIV (April 11, 1918), 358–359. [Author's note]

⁹See, for instance, her address, "The Objective Value of a Social Settlement," in *Philanthropy and Social Progress: Seven Essays* (New York: 1893), pp. 27–40, and her *Twenty Years at Hull House* (New York: 1910), especially p. 246. [Author's note]

¹⁰Solomon Liptzin, *Generation of Decision* (New York: 1958), pp. 175–176. [Author's note]

¹¹Quoted in "Mr. Zangwill's New Dramatic Gospel," *Current Literature*, XLV (December, 1908), 672. [Author's note]

¹²Charles Reznikoff, ed., Louis Marshall: Champion of Liberty (New York: 1957) p. 809. [Author's note]

¹³*Current Literature*, loc. cit., p. 671. [Author's note]

¹⁴Abraham Cahan, *The Rise of David Levinsky* (New York: 1917), p. 526. [Author's note]

¹⁵Abraham Cahan, *Yekl, A Tale of the New York Ghetto* (New York: 1896), p. 54. [Author's note]

¹⁶Our discussion of *The Rise of David Levinsky* follows the general lines of Isaac Rosenfeld's essay, "America, the Land of the Sad Millionaire," *Commentary*, XIV (August, 1952), 131–135. For a different approach see David Singer, "David Levinsky's Fall: A Note on the Liebman Thesis," *American Quarterly*, XIX (Winter, 1967), 696–697. Beginning with the thesis of Professor Charles Liebman that East European Jewish immigrants to America were not, in the main, Orthodox Jews as is commonly assumed, Singer attempts to demonstrate that Levinsky had rejected his Old World piety long before emigrating and that such gestures as cutting his earlocks in America are not to be interpreted as signs of his loss of faith but of his desire for cultural assimilation and social acceptance. For a recent account of Cahan's career and a discussion of his fiction, including the earlier magazine version of Levinsky, see Ronald Sanders, *The Downtown Jews: Portraits of an Immigrant Generation* (New York: 1969). [Author's note]

If you live in New York, even if you're Catholic, you're Jewish.
                                            Lenny Bruce

NEGROES

POPULATION: *22 million plus* *2 million passing*	**PHYSICAL CHARACTERISTICS:** *Darker than white people*
RELIGION: *The numbers* **PRACTICING:** *22 million plus* *2 million passing*	**RACIAL TRAITS (GOOD):** *Poor* *Natural born athletes* *Great sense of rhythm* **RACIAL TRAITS (BAD):** *Think they're as good as you are.* *Starting to move into better neighborhoods* *Always muttering something about "Sheet"*
LOCATION: *Harlem and U.S. Highways*	**DIET STAPLE:** *Pot*

CHAPTER 2

CLASS

The New American Poverty (1984)
Michael Harrington

The poor are still there.

Two decades after the President of the United States declared an "unconditional" war on poverty, poverty does not simply continue to exist; worse, we must deal with structures of misery, with a new poverty much more tenacious than the old.

Structures of misery. The idea was a commonplace when one thought of Appalachia a generation ago. An economy controlled by absentee corporations neglected basic investments, which eroded the physical and social infrastructure as well as the tax base. People fled this impossible situation, so there were even fewer human resources, which made further investment unlikely. That in turn further eroded the physical and social infrastructure as well as the tax base. Under such conditions, poverty is not merely an episode or the fault of some heartless Scrooge, but the ongoing product of the organization of disorganization.

Now there are new structures of misery. In the winter of our national discontent in 1982–83, when there were more jobless Americans than at any other time in almost half a century, a young worker walked through the milling, sometimes menacing men on East Third Street in Manhattan and asked the City of New York for a bed at the Municipal Shelter. One of the reasons he was there was that there are steel mills in South Korea. That is, the poor—and the entire American economy— are caught up in a crisis which is literally global. Yet one cannot simply blame changes in the way the world is run for what is happening on East Third Street, or in the *barrios* of Los Angeles, the steel towns of the Monongahela Valley, and the backwoods of Maine.

The great, impersonal forces have indeed created a context in which poverty is much more difficult to abolish than it was twenty years ago. But it is not the South Koreans— or the Japanese, the

West Germans, or anyone else—who have decided that the human costs of this wrenching transition should be borne by the most vulnerable Americans. We have done that to ourselves.

One reason is that this economic upheaval did not simply strike at the poor. It had an enormous impact on everyone else and, among many other things, changed the very eyes of the society. In the sixties there was economic growth, political and social movement, hope. What was shocking was that poverty existed at all, and the very fact that it did was an incitement to abolish it. I simplify, of course. Even then, as I pointed out in *The Other America*, suburbanization was removing the middle class from daily contact with the poor. In our geography, as in our social structure, we were becoming two nations.

Moreover, the optimistic sixties often overlooked the systemic nature of its own poverty. I remember a quintessential political cocktail party of those times. It was during the 1964 Presidential campaign at the Dakota, perhaps the most chic apartment building in New York City. A leading trade unionist was talking to some of the intellectual elite. We are going to the moon, he said. Why can't we put an end to the slums? He, and almost everyone else there, knew that our capacities were boundless, that we could deal with ghettos as well as outer space. But there are no people on the moon, no landlords, no silk-stocking districts reluctant to welcome the ex-poor into affluent neighborhoods. Lunar exploration posed technical problems; abolishing poverty raised issues of power and wealth.

Few people realized this in 1964, so there was a social war without a human enemy. The opposing forces were abstractions: hunger, illiteracy, bad housing, inadequate motivation, and the like. It was innocently assumed that ending the outrage of poverty was in everyone's interest. It was not until the seventies, during the debate over Richard Nixon's Family Assistance Plan, that a Southern congressman bluntly stated the more complex truth. If the government provided a minimum income to everyone, "Who," he asked will iron my shirts and rake the yard?"

But even if there were more than a few illusions in the sixties, they facilitated some very real gains. There were many of the working poor who, in a decade of falling unemployment, fought their way out of poverty. The aging made dramatic gains through Medicare and increased, indexed social security benefits. Blacks successfully eradicated legal Jim Crow; Chicanos and Filipinos created a union in the fields; even Appalachia registered some gains. If the antipoverty program turned out to be a skirmish rather than an unconditional war, it nonetheless made some significant advances.

In the eighties it is not simply that structural economic change has created new poverties and given old poverties a new lease on life. That very same process has impaired the national vision; misery has simultaneously become more intractable and more difficult to see.

In the seventies and the early eighties, we had both inflation and recession, which subverted the established liberal wisdom; the highest unemployment rates since the Great Depression; and a consequent loss of political and social nerve. Crises, particularly at first, do not make people radical or compassionate. They are frightening, and most people concentrate on saving themselves. Thoughts of "brothers" or "sisters," who are moral kin but not one's blood relatives, are a luxury many cannot afford. It was not an accident that the Economic Opportunity Act of 1964 proclaimed that its goal was "to eliminate the paradox of poverty in the midst of plenty." It is somewhat more problematic to summon the average American to such a struggle in the midst of declining real wages and chronic unemployment. . . .

At the same time, the process of suburbanization, which puts the poor out of sight and mind, has proceeded apace over the past two decades. The central cities have become reservations for the marginalized, as distant from the everyday consciousness as are the Navajos in the empty reaches of the Southwest. In 1982 *The Economist* of London wrote that the security forces in the shopping malls of America were there "to insulate their clientele from the undesirable elements of the real world— and those elements are as likely to be the poor and unwashed as the snow and the sun." "With less physical community," the article went on, "street life in cities will diminish and become less varied, criminals will gain ascendancy, buildings will become like fortresses." That is not, of course, an exercise in futurism; it is a sober description of what is going on in the United States.

So the national vision has been impaired in a number of ways. As men and women turned inward to face their own relative deprivation, it became harder to see anyone else's absolute suffering; and the Balkanization of American social structure only made things worse. More broadly, where the sixties spoke of possibilities, the eighties were forced to become aware of limits, which some assumed, wrongly, were ugly necessities to be imposed on those at the bottom of the society. In the process, America has lost its own generous vision of what it might be. . . .

The Chinese ideograph for crisis is composed of the symbols for two words: danger and hope.

That accurately describes these times. The old poverty—the pace of social and economic time is accelerated and 1 am talking of the ancient days twenty and thirty years ago— seemed to be an exception to the basic trends of the society. Everyone was progressing steadily; a minority had been left behind. Therefore it would be a rather simple matter to deduct some few billions as they poured out of our industrial cornucopia and to use them to abolish the "pockets" of poverty. But the new poverty I have described in this book is quite different. It is, in complex ways, precisely the extreme consequence of tendencies that are transforming the entire society. To repeat, one reason why young men in the winter of 1983 had to ask New York City for beds for the night was that there were steel mills in South Korea, a fact that also menaced relatively well-paid trade unionists and even corporate executives.

This is the great danger confronting the new poor. If their plight is not an anomaly of the affluent society but the outcome of massive economic trends, why will the majority undertake the fairly radical changes that are needed in order to help a minority that is either not seen, despised, or feared? In the sixties, people thought that the struggle against poverty was going to be a lovely little war. But if, in the eighties, the poor and their friends explain that it is going to be a difficult and arduous struggle, who will respond, particularly when everyone is concerned about how it will affect him personally?

In that very real danger there is also hope. The majority of the people of the United States cannot possibly make themselves secure unless they also help the poor. That is, the very measures that will most benefit the working people and the middle class— the rich will take care of themselves, as they always have—will also strike a blow against poverty. That is by no means an automatic process; there are specific measures that have to be worked out to deal with particular problems of the poor. But basically the programs that are in the self-interest of the majority are always in the special interest of the poor.

Therefore, . . . I will not propose a politics based simply on morality and solidarity— not *simply* based on those values, but certainly based upon them. An increase in compassion and caring is essential, and for all of the simplifications of the early sixties, those were generous years, which does them credit. But in addition to affirming that we are indeed our sisters' and our brothers' keepers, it must also be said that the abolition of poverty requires programs—above all, full employment—that will probably do more for the nonpoor than for the poor. One is not asking men and women who have troubles enough of their own to engage in a noblesse oblige that is, in any case, patronizing. One appeals to both their decency and their interest. But how is it that justice and self-interest are, in this miraculous case, in harmony with each other?

Full employment is good for almost everyone. That is a critical reason.

In the sixties, one of the most significant accomplishments of the decade came not from the War on Poverty as such, but from the fact that unemployment declined, with one insignificant exception, in every year of the Kennedy and Johnson administrations. So it was that the working poor constituted one of the two groups (the aging were, of course, the other) who made the greatest progress in the struggle to get out of poverty. And the harmony of justice and self-interest being asserted here as a possible future was a fact then. In a mere ten years the real buying power of production workers went up by more than 15 percent. In 1980, by stark contrast, the weekly wage had declined in real buying power to 1962 levels.

Would these patterns of escape from poverty in the sixties still hold in the eighties? Not for everyone; poor women are, we shall see, a special and very important case. But blacks, Hispanics, and other minorities, whether members of a marginalized underclass or part of the working poor, would gain. So would immigrants, and the question of undocumented workers would be put into a context in which decency would be an economic possibility as well as a moral imperative. The newness of much of the new poverty is precisely a function of an occupational structure that has destroyed many of the rungs of social mobility, the traditional escape routes from poverty. If a full-employment economy would begin to restore some of those possibilities, it would have a major and positive impact on these groups of the new poor.

Moreover, a full-employment economy is probably more effective at job counseling than are some psychiatrists and social workers. When it becomes the norm for everyone to work, people who were "unemployable" only yesterday suddenly turn out to be quite useful. World War II demonstrated this when it took women, blacks, and the long-term unemployed and put them to work in the arms plants; so did the European postwar boom, which showed that Greek and Yugoslavian peasants could do useful work in a sophisticated West German economy. Motivation is often not a matter of individual will but of social atmosphere. Full employment motivates work.

Full employment would even help reduce the levels of crime and violence in America. I am not proposing a strawman here, i.e., I am not suggesting that we disband the police and wait for jobs to abolish crime. I am saying, to frightened people as well as to the conservative cynics who tend that strawman and think they have actually done serious intellectual work, that a radical drop in the jobless rate will appreciably lower the number of muggings and assaults. There are other things that have to be done to protect society from violence. But this is certainly the most humane way of fighting crime.

Full employment would help a great number of the new poor; and it would benefit the nonpoor as well.

When the official figures admitted to more than eleven million unemployed and almost two million "discouraged workers" driven out of the labor market in 1983. that was obviously disastrous for those who had lost their jobs. But it also made things much worse for those who were still at work. The existence of a huge pool of idle people makes those with jobs fearful and helps drive wages down. It also sets off that vicious cycle where people clutch at every possibility and take jobs for which they are overqualified, and those they replace do the same until the least qualified at the bottom suffer the most. As a result, a pervasive sense of insecurity saps any spirit of militancy. It was not an accident that members of the United Automobile Workers turned against concessions to the companies almost the minute the economy improved a bit in 1983. So it is that a full employment economy would not simply help the least paid, or the unemployed; it would set in motion a virtuous cycle that would improve the lot of everyone in the labor force.

This process would aid the successful members of minority groups as well as those in the underclass. The blacks and Hispanics who have risen in the occupational structure suffer from two contrasting problems: On the one hand, they are guilty because they have left behind so many despairing members of their own group; on the other hand, they suffer from that "statistical discrimination" which equates everyone in the group with its violent, and rather tiny, minority of criminals. Insofar as a full-employment economy would both reduce violence on the part of that minority and open up opportunities for the millions of the nonviolent poor who are black and Hispanic, it would improve the quality of life even for those who have already made it into the middle class.

In the case of women, these connections are even more obvious. Women and minorities in the seventies and eighties suffer from the same structural problem that is one of the main causes of the new poverty. There is no longer juridical racism and sexism in the United States; there is *occupational* racism and sexism. That is, minorities and women are paid the same for the same job (not, however, for equivalent jobs, where there is still a gap), but they hold many more bad jobs than do men or white Anglos. One of the consequences of the poverty of the underclass, of the immigrants and the undocumented workers, we have seen, is to remove any reason for business to modernize the bottom of the American economy. As long as there are plenty of frightened, hungry people willing to do dirty jobs for a song, dirty jobs will persist and sweatshops will thrive in the back alleys of the economy.

This situation has not simply hurt the people at the bottom; it has distorted and skewed the entire occupational structure. It has been one of the main reasons why there is a gap between the very bottom and the lower reaches of the stable working class. That is precisely the space that should be filled by people on their way up, but there is no incentive for business to create it. Women—and often minority immigrant women—are concentrated on the lower reaches. They are often the sweatshop and low-paid production workers. This is one of the major reasons for the "feminization" of poverty. But it is also a reason why so many of those intermediate jobs either do not exist or else are designed for low productivity and low wages. And there are even more women trying to fill that niche in the economy. . . .

I have located the new American poverty within an analysis of the sweeping changes in the world and national economies which cause it but threaten to disrupt the lives of the rest of America as well. So the program I summarize here is as radical as the problem I have defined.

In urging full employment to fight against that possibility, I am well aware that I am taking a position to the left of a good part of the Democratic Party and even of a stratum of ex-liberals who fought for the Humphrey-Hawkins bill in the seventies and are now somewhere in between a retreat and a rout. Moreover, there is an arguable case that my own ideas are "utopian." But what is unarguable is that if America accepts an official rate of 6–7 percent unemployment as necessary for the system, the problems of misery and social breakdown will increase in "good times" and become epidemic in bad times. My critics have a right to their point of view, but they should then come up with *their* solution. They might, for example, want to go back to Swift's "modest proposal" for dealing with the poverty of eighteenth-century Ireland: to kill and eat the babies of the poor.

My irony makes it clear, I hope, that the difficult program for full employment I outline here (and I stress the word *outline*) is both radical in American terms and the *only* realism if we are to confront the new American poverty.

Stir Crazy (1991)

Robert Scheer

Loved the Super Bowl but couldn't help noticing that most of the top players were black and that the fans were white. Then, as football season gave way to basketball and the Gulf war dragged on, I switched to old movies and caught *Spartacus*. Great flick. Slaves picked from Rome's colonies revolt under the leadership of gladiators, the only role models the slaves had back then.

Something gnawed at me, some connection, and I switched back to ESPN and CNN. That's one nice thing about sports mania and war—black men are allowed to become positive role models. Which is what George Bush must have been thinking when he vetoed the civil rights act last year—there's no further need to redress the historic wrongs of slavery, segregation and racism when black men seem to be doing so well.

So I mused until a report that had a stark statistic landed on my desk: "Nearly one in four black men in the age group 20-29 is under the control of the criminal–justice system—in prison or jail, on probation or parole." Which means the good old U.S. of A. incarcerates black men at four times the rate of racist South Africa.

Now, what's going on here? We cheer for our black guys on the playing field, we wave American flags for them in combat, but we send every fourth one off to prison. It's not just blacks, of course, who are being jailed at an unprecedented rate. The report, prepared by the reliable Washington–based research group The Sentencing Project, says we now have a higher percentage of our entire population in prison than any other country on earth. It documents that in the past few years, the U.S. has pulled past South Africa, which is now number two, while the Soviet Union struggles to keep its hold on third place in the Jail Your Own Sweepstakes. More than 1,000,000 Americas are currently incarcerated, double the figure of ten years ago. During a decade in which politicians of every political stripe attempted to outdo themselves in talking tough on crime, we have managed to place an entire colony of our population behind bars, without any serious public debate and with no appreciable impact on the crime rate.

The craze to jail has little to do with stopping the hard crime that frightens people. The evidence is overwhelming that there is no demonstrable correlation between having lots of people in jail and having a safe society. As the Sentencing Project report notes, "American murder rates are at least seven times as high as [those of] most [European countries]," which average less than one quarter our rate of incarceration.

At a cost of at least $50,000 to build a cell and $20,000 annually to house each prisoner, we have managed to spend tens of millions on this approach to crime busting, while starving any and all alternative programs that might prevent crime. Most people are in jail for crimes so petty that if the criminals had held even the most minimal jobs, the crime wouldn't have been cost effective. Yet we've all but abandoned job-training programs, other than the military, and have pulled the plug on inner-city schools, unleashing instead vast firepower against the ghetto.

The pathetic truth is that it is mostly crime committed by poor people that gets punished, and much of it, in dollar terms, is paltry. Incompetent criminals with inferior lawyers or overworked public defenders are the ones who go to jail. Only 20 percent of *reported* crimes end in arrest. And the bigger the fish, the less likelihood of his being caught. "The vast majority of inmates," reports the National Council on Crime and Delinquency, "are sentenced for petty crimes that pose little danger to public safety or significant economic loss to victims."

This is particularly true on the Federal level, despite the scary invocation of the Willie Horton example in the past Presidential race. As *Time* magazine—not a bastion of bleeding hearts—concluded in evaluating President Bush's ballyhooed crime–fighting proposals of a couple of years ago, "The President's proposals would have virtually no impact on the kinds of crime that Americans most fear: assault, robbery and rape, as well as virtually all murders and most drug offenses." Why? Because those crimes fall outside the Federal purview. *Time* noted that of 47,700 inmates held in Federal penitentiaries that year, "a mere 118" had been convicted of murder.

After taking a swipe at Bush for failing to move against assault weapons, *Time* pointed out the underlying practical problem: The money is just not there to build and maintain the prisons to accommodate ever larger numbers of convicts. Instead, prisoners are simply recycled through the system more quickly and in larger numbers, with little done to rehabilitate them while they are there. "Prison gates have become more like revolving doors: Nearly two thirds of all convicts are rearrested within three years of their release." Noting the six percent imprisonment rate, *Time* concluded, "Even doubling the current prison population, which would cost more than 43 billion dollars, would leave the chance of a prospective criminal's facing imprisonment at no more than ten percent."

Meaning that the zealots' drive to jail more people has little connection with a program to curtail crime. First, what is required, most experts in the field agree, is to sort out serious crime from all the junk charges that are now clogging the courts. In particular, the war on drugs has diverted our crime–fighting priorities from assaults on people and toward social engineering of the most myopic kind. It's amazing that we have the resources to hound casual drug users but can't make a serious dent in violent crimes against innocent bystanders.

Second, say many of these experts, we need to devote the same energies and finances to improving the lot of the people who commit the chicken–coop burglaries and holdups that land them in the can. If 43 percent of prisoners are black and another huge chunk is *Latino* and poor white, it ought to tell us something about the social causes of crime.

Uh-oh. Sounds like the old bleeding heart, doesn't it? But what's so hardheaded and realistic about telling a kid in Bedford–Stuyvesant that his only three choices in life are making the Knicks, joining the Army or committing crimes that have only a six percent chance of landing him in jail? And then the hardheads make the choice even niftier by unleashing a jihad against drugs, which, of course, just increases the huge profits of the narcotics trade, which in turn, makes drugs far and away the best ghetto job opportunity.

What *I* think, Romans and countrymen, is that the demagogs who started this lock–em–up craze should be held accountable. They've helped destroy almost half a generation of black youth in a mindless thrashing out at a problem requiring a calibrated response. It's time to stop hamming it up with showy theatrics. Enough with the circus barkers.

"Although the tragedy was real, the infamous Horton anecdote was hollow," John J. DiIulio, Jr., a leading criminal–justice expert, pointed out in a recent Brookings Institution study. "[More than] 99.5 percent of prison furloughs result neither in a violation of the terms of the furlough nor in a new crime."

On the other hand, parolees have a shockingly high recidivism rate. The point is that there is not a good "liberal" alternative to prison. In fact, the debate is not one of conservative or liberal idealogy.

→ in a longer period of time in office?

Liberal governor Mario Cuomo of New York has built more prisons and put more people in jail than his Republican predecessors. And conservative governor George Deukmejian of California presided over a system that had more than 200,000 convicted criminals released on probation to ease the pressure on its overcrowded prisons. The point is not political but practical: We must stop making cheap theater out of the evidence and begin to think clearly about what works and what doesn't as an alternative to hard time.

Why? Try this hardheaded reason: because we just don't have the money to keep expanding the prison population at the rate of the past ten years. Ten years ago, the total cost of all jail construction, services and operations was 2.5 billion dollars. Now it is 25 billion dollars, and no one knows where to easily find more.

The fact is, we are already forced by overcrowded prisons and limited Government budgets to use many alternatives to straight time. About 2,500,000 Americans are now walking the streets on parole or probation. Despite all the laws passed mandating stiffer sentences, actual time served has not increased over the past decade, because there is no room at the inn and early release is required to make room for fresh convicts. Bottom line, ma'am.

States such as Minnesota have excellent programs that sentence nonviolent criminals to probation at home, with close supervision, while the "prisoner" studies or holds a job. The alternative—locking up all of those people, and the millions coming after them, and throwing away the key—has been tried and doesn't work. Even the South Africans and the Soviets, heavy-handed though they are, are coming to their senses and accepting limits to just how many people they can lock up. We're not there yet.

What we seem to believe in is this neoapartheid society, where the inner city is abandoned and its black youth are ignored and shunned until they make enough noise to attract our attention either on football fields or in Arabia. Or, for one out of four, by committing crimes and getting thrown into jail.

Something is nagging at me again. What does it all remind me of? Colonies of black guys as gladiators, facing more or less the same choices: Go for the illegal bread or join the circuses. And, meanwhile, the Romans figure that if they keep cracking down on the misbeggoten and keep cheering for the few who become heroes, it will all be OK. They never pause to consider, using hardheaded accounting, that it would be cheaper to send a kid to college than to gladiator school. Or to prison.

Roll *Spartacus.*

First secure an independent income, then practice virtue.
                    Greek saying

Day Work in the Suburbs: The Work Experience of Chicana Private Housekeepers

Mary Romero (1991)

Introduction

Most research on domestic service begins with a set of assumptions based on the experience of European immigrant women. For these white, rural immigrant women, domestic service often represented a path to assimilation into the dominant American culture. As most foreign-born (and native-born) white domestics have historically been young and single, the occupation usually functioned as an interim activity between girlhood and marriage. Domestic service could also offer a first step toward employment in the formal sector and mobility into the middle class. Hence, domestic service became known as the "bridging occupation" (Broom and Smith 1963).

The experience of minority women differs radically. For women of color, domestic service has not resulted in social mobility but rather has trapped them in an occupational ghetto (Glenn 1981). Most minority women have not moved into other occupations as a result of their experience as domestics; instead, they have remained in domestic service throughout their lives. Minority women are usually married and work to support their families. Married black domestics have usually remained employed, whether they lived in or were day workers, and they have not experienced intergenerational mobility (Lerner 1972; Katzman 1981; Rollins 1985); married Japanese-American (Glenn 1981) and Chicana domestics (Romero 1987) who were primarily day workers experienced some intergenerational mobility. Examination of the work histories of minority women domestics has led several researchers to abandon the traditional emphasis on assimilation and mobility and to focus instead on the actual work experience, particularly the employer/employee relationship.

Several researchers have documented the caste-like situation faced by generations of black women workers in the United States (Chaplin 1964; Katzman 1981). Their limited job opportunities in the South can be inferred from the fact that black servants were found even in lower middle class and working class white families. Better working conditions and higher wages attracted black women to Northern households. As factory and other job opportunities outside the home opened up for foreign-born white women, black women began to dominate the domestic occupation in the North. For a short period during the Depression, black women found themselves replaced by white domestics; but, in general, there were not enough white domestics to offer serious competition and the white women's positions as servants was short-lived. In 1930, 20 percent of household workers were native-born white and 41 percent, foreign born white; by 1949, the proportion of foreign-born white had dropped to 11 percent. Moreover, while two-thirds of all black women were employed as domestics in 1930, this had only dropped to 50 percent by 1940. It was only after World War II that black women entered other fields in large numbers (Coley 1981).

The majority of Japanese-American women working in the Bay Area prior to World War II were employed as domestics, a disproportionate concentration that persisted for more than one generation.

Glenn's study (1986; 1981; 1980) of Japanese-American women in the San Francisco Bay Area identified several characteristics that made domestic service a port of entry into the labor market:

> The nonindustrial nature of the job, the low level of technology, and the absence of complex organization made it accessible; its menial status reduced competition from other groups who had better options; and the willingness of employers to train workers provided *issei* and *nisei* women with opportunities to acquire know-how and form connections outside the family and away from direct control of fathers and husbands (Glenn 1981: 381-82).

At the same time, successful generations of Japanese women became trapped by established pathways that provided access to the job in the beginning, but later separated them from other opportunities and resources. Consequently, Japanese women frequently continued to work as domestics even after marriage.

Because both domestic and mistress are women, their gender designates them as responsible for housework. In the case of white European domestics, the mistress frequently assumed a benevolent or even motherly role. However, this cannot be assumed with regard to minority women serving as domestics, as in this instance the mistress is in the position of delegating low–status work to women not only of a lower class but also of a different ethnic and racial group. In the case of black women, the domination/subordination pattern of the relationship grew out of attitudes developed during slavery that black servants were inferiors and nonpersons. Racism prevented white mistresses from assuming the surrogate mother role with their black domestics; instead, they adopted a benevolent role, treating the women as "childlike, lazy and irresponsible," hence requiring white governance (McKinley 1969).

In short, studies of black and Japanese-American women indicate that domestic service is not a "bridging occupation" offering transition into the formal sector. These studies have raised additional questions about minority women's experience as domestic workers. Rather than approaching domestic service in terms of acculturation and intergenerational mobility, researchers can approach the occupation from the worker's point of view. The following study explores domestic service as a serious enterprise with skills that have been either dismissed or ignored by previous researchers.

Method

This study is based on interviews with 25 Chicanas living in an urban western city. I conducted two- to three-hour open-ended interviews in the women's homes. I asked the women to discuss their work histories, particularly their experience as domestics. Detailed information on domestic work included strategies for finding employers, identification of appropriate and inappropriate tasks, the negotiation of working conditions, ways of doing housework efficiently, and the pros and cons of domestic work. The accounts included descriptions of the domestics' relationships to white middle class mistresses and revealed the Chicanas' attitudes toward their employers' lifestyles.

A snowball sampling method was used to identify Chicana domestic workers. Several current and former domestic workers I knew introduced me to other workers. Churches and social service agencies also helped to identify domestic workers in the community. In a few cases, community persons also assisted. The respondents ranged in age from 29 to 58. The sample included welfare recipients as well as working class women. All but one of the women had been married. Four were single heads of households; the other women were currently living with husbands employed in blue-collar occupations, such as construction and factory work. All of the women had children. The smallest family consisted of one child and the largest family had seven children. At the time of the interview, the women who were single heads of households were financially supporting no more than two children. Nine women had completed high school, and seven had no high school experience. One woman had never attended school at all. The remaining eight had at least a sixth–grade education.

Research Findings

Work Histories

The majority of the women had been employed in a variety of jobs over their lifetimes. They had been farm workers, waitresses, factory workers, sales clerks, cooks, laundresses, fast-food workers, receptionists, school aides, babysitters, dishwashers, nurse's aides, and cashiers. Almost half of the women had worked as janitors in hospitals and office buildings or as hotel maids. About one-fourth of the women had held semiskilled and skilled positions as beauticians, typists, medical record clerks, and the like. Six of the women had worked only as domestics.

Only three women had worked as domestics prior to marriage; each of those three had worked in live-in situations in rural areas of the Southwest. Several years later after marriage and children, these women returned as day workers. Most of the women, however, had turned to nonresidential day work in response to a financial crisis; in the majority of cases, it was their first job after marriage and children. Some of the women remained domestics throughout their lives, but others moved in and out of domestic work. Women who returned to domestic service after employment elsewhere usually did so after a period of unemployment. Because of the flexible schedule, most of the women preferred housework to other employment during their children's preadolescent years. Many of the older women had returned to domestic service because the schedule could be arranged around their family responsibilities and health problems. For all of the women, the occupation was an open door: they could always find work as a domestic. Their experience as domestics had lasted from 5 months to 30 years. Women 50 years and over had worked in the field from 8 to 30 years, while 4 of the women between the ages of 33 and 39 had 12 years experience.

The women's opportunities in the labor market were apparently not significantly improved by working as domestics. No matter how intimate the relationship between employee and employer, the domestic was never included in a broader social network that might provide other job opportunities. As long as community resources were limited to low-paying; low–status positions, the women found it difficult to obtain employment that offered benefits and a higher salary. Still, it is important to keep in mind that horizontal mobility can make significant differences in the quality of one's life. As Becker noted:

> All positions at one level of work hierarchy, while theoretically identical, may not be equally easy or rewarding places in which to work. Given this fact, people tend to move in patterned ways among the possible positions, seeking that situation which affords the most desirable setting in which to meet and grapple with the basic problems of their work. (Becker 1952, 470).

While the women I interviewed preferred factory position is because of their pay and benefits, many found themselves hired during the peak season and subsequently laid off. Women unable to obtain regular factory positions usually remained in domestic service until they retired or health problems emerged. Most of their clerical experience was in community-based organizations. Only when jobs increased in the Chicano community—for instance, through CETA or bilingual education programs—did the women have an opportunity to develop skills useful in applying for jobs elsewhere. These programs usually freed the women from daywork as a domestic. Only after retirement or periods of unemployment did these women again return to daywork to supplement the family income.

Finding Day Work

In acquiring most of these jobs, the women relied upon word of mouth. Their sources for information on job openings included husbands, sisters, cousins, friends, and neighbors. Thus, their networks were usually confined to the Chicano community. Women reported that family members usually assisted in obtaining employment as a domestic. For instance, one woman had been working in the fields with her family one day when her husband returned from the owner's home with a job offer to do housework. Sisters, cousins and in-laws frequently suggested housekeeping and willingly provided the contacts to obtain employers. Several women joined the ranks in response to a relative's need for a replacement during an illness, vacation, or family obligation. One woman started out with a cleaning agency. However, she quickly abandoned the agency, preferring to work independently. This pattern of using informal networks in job searches is consistent with other research findings on work (Reid 1972, Katz 1958).

Younger women's introduction to domestic service frequently began with an apprenticeship period in which they accompanied a relative or friend. Two women would work together for a certain period of time (several days or weeks) until the newcomer decided she was ready to take on her own employers on a regular basis. This training provided newcomers with an opportunity to acquire tips about cleaning methods, products, appliances, the going rate, advantages and disadvantages of charging by the house or the hour, and how to ask for a raise.

Most women found their first employers through the community network of other domestic workers. Later, new employers were added with the assistance of current employers who recommended their employees to friends and neighbors. Two women reported using ads and employment agencies along with relatives and friends. But most voiced a strong preference for the informal network. Recommendations and job leads from the informal network of family and friends provided women with a sense of security when entering a new employer's home.

In many ways these women demonstrated employment patterns similar to other working women in traditionally female occupations. Movement in and out of the labor market coincided with stages of family life. Husbands' unemployment, underemployment, or financial crisis were the major reasons for reentry into the work force. And, like most other women, domestic workers found employment in low-paying, low-status jobs. However, their ability to obtain immediate employment may distinguish them from other women who seek employment during times of financial crisis. These Chicana workers were unique in that they could always find employment as domestics. The challenge was to find a job *outside* domestic service.

Work Conditions of Day Work in the Suburbs

Most of the domestics interviewed for this study drove 20 to 60 minutes every morning to work. In two cases, the employer provided transportation. All of the women worked for non-Hispanic families. The usual arrangement was to work for one household per day; however, with an increase in the number of professional, middle class people living in smaller units, such as condominiums, cleaning two apartments a day had become a more common pattern. Exceptions in the present sample included two women working solely for parish priests and another woman working for one family five days a week. The average work week ranged from three to five days a week. Almost half of the women worked six- or seven-hour days, and the others worked half-days.

During the course of interviews, it became apparent that norms were changing regarding the type of tasks associated with general housekeeping. Older women with 20 or more years experience considered ironing, laundry, window cleaning, cooking, and babysitting as part of the job; however, none of the women currently employed as domestics identified such requests as the norm. Several current domestic workers and younger informants distinguished between "maid" work and "housekeeping" on the basis of these tasks. Glenn (1986) found similar trends. Twenty years ago, domestics service usually meant ten- to twelve-hour days and often included yard work and cleaning the cars or the garage. Today the work usually consists of vacuuming all the rooms (frequently moving the furniture), washing and waxing the floor, dusting, and cleaning the bathrooms and kitchen. Each home typically requires four to seven hours.

After the first two workdays in an employer's home, the women established a routine for housecleaning. For instance, the women would arrange a schedule to work around members of the employer's family who were at home. Domestics identified themselves as professional housekeepers with responsibility for maintaining the employer's home. Maintenance involved bringing the employer's house up to a standard that would then be maintained on a weekly basis. Domestics established a routine for incorporating extra tasks on a rotating schedule: for example, cleaning the refrigerator or oven once a month. The employer's cooperation in establishing a routine played an important part in the employee's decision to keep a particular job.

Most women earned between 30 and 65 dollars a day depending on the number of hours worked. Most women averaged 8 dollars an hour. Employers usually paid by cash or personal check each day the domestic came. A few paid by personal check once a month. Although none of the women received health care benefits, some employers offered other benefits. Four of the older women were paying into Social Security; this had been initiated by long-term employers who expressed concern over their employees' welfare. Paid vacations were another benefit obtained by women who had worked several years for the same employer. As with Social Security, a paid vacation was the exception rather than the norm. A few of the women received Christmas bonuses. None of the women received automatic annual raises. Because very few employers offered a raise, the women were forced to make the request. Since the only power the women had was to quit, the most common strategy was to pose an ultimatum to the employer—"Give me a raise or I'll quit." Sometimes a woman would announce to her employer that she had to quit because she faced a problem with transportation or childcare. In this instance, the hope was that the employer would offer a raise to keep the employee from quitting.

Most people clean house once or twice a week and assume the domestic's experience is comparable. However, the domestic's routine recurs everyday: carrying the vacuum up and down the stairs; vacuuming sofas and behind furniture; washing and waxing floors; scrubbing ovens, sinks, tubs, and toilets; dusting furniture; emptying wastebaskets; cleaning mirrors. Backaches from scrubbing and picking up toys, papers, and clothes are common. All of the work is completed while standing or kneeling. Beyond the physical demands of the job, many women faced the additional stress of having their work treated as non-work. Several domestics recalled occasions when employers' children or guests spilled drinks on the floor or messed up a room and expected the worker simply to redo her work. All of the women refused, pointing out that the work had already been completed. Although domestics are paid for housework, the job is treated no differently than housework done by housewives (Oakley 1974).

Maximizing Work Conditions

Housework itself offers few intrinsic rewards; therefore, women who choose domestic service over other low-paying, low-status jobs typically strive to maximize their working conditions. The women interviewed for this study put a great deal of thought into identifying ways to improve work conditions, and they had very clear goals in establishing conditions with employers.

Flexibility in their work time was the crucial factor for many of the women who wanted to be home with their children. As Mrs. Lopez* explains:

> I'd always try to be home when the children went to school and be home when they came home. . . . I would never leave my children alone. I always arranged with the ladies [employers]—always told them that I had children and that I had to come home early.

Domestic work allowed the women to arrange their own hours, adding or eliminating employers to lengthen or shorten the work week. Determining their own schedule allowed the women to get their children off to school in the morning and be back home when school was over. It also provided a solution for women with preschool age children:

> Most of the people I've worked for like kids, so I just take the kids with me. It's silly to have to work and pay a sitter; it won't work (Mrs. Montoya, age 33, 12 years' experience, mother of two).
>
> So that's mainly the reason I did it [domestic work], because I knew the kids were going to be all right and they were with me and they were fed and taken care of (Mrs. Cordova, age 30, 8 years' experience, mother of two).

Domestics were thus able to fulfill family obligations without major disruptions at home or work.

> You can change the dates if you can't go a certain day, and if you have an appointment, you can go later and work later, just as long as you get the work done. . . . I try to be there at the same time, but if I don't get there for some reason or another, I don't have to think I'm going to lose my job or something (Mrs. Sanchez, 54 years old, 18 years' experience, mother of six).
>
> That's one thing with doing daywork—if the children are sick or something, you just stayed home because that was my responsibility to get them to the doctor and all that (Mrs. Lopez, age 64).

Since the domestics worked alone and had a different employer each day, they could control the number of days and hours spent cleaning. Women who needed to attend to family responsibilities found employers for two or three days a week and arranged to clean the houses in five hours. In contrast, women whose major concern was money could work six days a week and clean two houses everyday. In order to control the number of days and hours worked, women established a verbal contract identifying what tasks constituted general housekeeping. This agreement was flexible and was adjusted to particular situations as they arose. As Mrs. Sanchez explained:

---

*I have changed the subjects' names to protect their anonymity.

> Suppose one day they [the employers] may be out of town, and that day you go to work. You won't have much work to do, but you'll get paid the same. And then maybe some other time they're going to have company and you end up working a little more and you still get paid the same. So it averages about the same, you know, throughout the month (Age 54, 18 years' experience).

Maintaining a routine for accomplishing necessary tasks allowed domestics to control the work environment and eliminated the need for employers to dictate a work schedule. Once an agreement was made, the workers determined how quickly or slowly they would work. Contract work provided employees with considerable autonomy, as well as recognition of their skills by employers.

On the other hand, a few women found contracts inadequate in controlling the amount of work requested. Instead, they clearly stipulated the number of hours they would work. Then they would do as much work, at their own pace, as the time allowed. By establishing a set number of hours, the domestic forced the employer to choose particular tasks to be rotated each week. Planning and organizing the work permitted the domestic to feel like her own boss. When the employer permitted, domestic work offered a variety of advantages not available in many other jobs. Key among these advantages was autonomy. Once the employee was no longer taking orders and receiving instructions about how to clean, she had the freedom to structure the day's work. Mrs. Portillo spoke about the importance of this job characteristic:

> Once the person learns that you're going to do the job, they just totally leave you to your own. It's like it's your own home. That's what I like. When you work like in a hospital or something, you're under somebody. They're telling you what to do or this is not right. But housecleaning is different. You're free. You're not under no pressure, especially if you find a person who really trusts you all the way. You have no problems (Age 68, 30 years' experience).

All of the informants preferred to work alone in the house. Women who achieved a degree of autonomy in their work environment were often able to substitute mental labor for physical labor. Planning and organization were essential for maintaining the house and arranging the work tasks in the most efficient manner. Several of the women were responsible for keeping an inventory of cleaning supplies as well as for maintenance of housekeeping equipment. It was not uncommon for the women to be called upon to rearrange furniture and fixtures. Therefore, autonomy in the work environment made it possible to unite the mental and manual labor involved in housework. Most of the women noted that this combination made the work more interesting and meaningful.

The Relationship between Mistress and Domestic

Class differences have always existed between mistresses and domestics; however, cultural differences are a relatively recent phenomenon in domestic service. Historically, mistresses have defined the employment of ethnic minority women as a benevolent gesture, offering to the less fortunate the opportunity to culturally and morally upgrade themselves. Mistresses frequently pry into or comment on domestics' personal lives without invitation. Sometimes they treat domestics like children. Racism is a reality of the job. Although many incidents are difficult to respond to, most women quit employers who make racist comments, such as "Chicanas have too many children" or "Chicanas lack ambition."

Several of the women in this study felt they were treated as cultural curiosities. Often mistresses would limit questions and discussion topics to Chicano culture and attempt to explain differences in their experiences as cultural. For instance, one woman recalled that an employer had decorated her house with Santcs purchased on her annual trips to northern New Mexico. The employer was quite shocked to realize the domestic did not own a large wooden statue of her patron saint. Most of the mistresses' inquiries were about ethnic food. Several employers asked the domestic to make tortillas or chile, but the women were very hesitant about sharing food. All of the women felt the request for Mexican food was inappropriate, except when they considered the employer a friend. Even though the women engaged in conversations about Chicano culture, history, or social issues, inquiries frequently created tension. Consequently, such discussions were avoided as much as possible.

In past research, researchers assumed that employers transmitted cultural values and norms to the employee, providing a "bridge" to a middle class lifestyle. However, the women interviewed for this study strongly expressed the opposite view. They found that domestic skills did not transfer to any other setting, nor did they provide the legitimate "work experience" needed to move upwards in the formal sector. Often the domestics felt a sense of being trapped because they lacked suitable job experience, opportunities, and education. Mrs. Fernandez spoke of her limited alternatives in an assessment of her job skills:

> I'm not qualified to do much, you know. I've often thought about going back to school and getting some kind of training. I don't know what I would do if I would really have to quit housework because that wouldn't be a job to raise a family on if I had to. So I would have to go back and get some training in something (Age 35, 9 years' experience, mother of 4, eleventh grade education).

The two oldest women interviewed (68 and 64 respectively) saw discrimination and racism limiting their job choices.

> There was a lot of discrimination, and Spanish people got just regular housework or laundry work.... There was so much discrimination that Spanish people couldn't get jobs outside of washing dishes—things like that (Mrs. Portillo, 30 years' experience, 68 years old, mother of two).

This study found the cultural exchange between domestic and employer to be much more diffuse than that described in research on domestics at the turn of the century (Katzman 1981) and in Third World countries (Smith 1971). However, I did find that material culture was frequently transmitted to the domestic who developed a need for particular appliances and products. Several women had acquired new appliances, such as microwave ovens, in the last few years. Some of the younger women had incorporated a "white middle class" decor and style of arranging furniture in their own homes. Many of the women acquired a taste for objects similar to those in the employer's home. However, it is difficult to attribute this interest solely to the work experience because of the substantial influence of the media. Younger women were more apt to incorporate new ways of doing things into their own homes. Although there was evidence of acculturation in the arrangement of furniture and wall decorations, certain traditional items remained, such as family pictures and religious art. I would argue that this readiness to incorporate material culture reflects class aspirations rather than assimilation to white American culture.

Cultural diffusion was not one way. Employers who turned over the control of the work process allowed workers to introduce new cleaning products and methods. A few of the older women became surrogate mothers to their employers and were called upon to discuss childrearing practices. The amount of cultural exchange was determined by the degree to which employers accepted domestics as experts in housekeeping.

Minimizing the Personal Cost of Being a Domestic

Many women found the stigma attached to domestic work painful. A few manifested embarrassment and anger at being identified as a house cleaner. Other women were very defensive about their work and attempted to point out all the benefits associated with flexible work schedule and autonomy.

The women used several strategies for coping with the personal pain of being a domestic. They attempted to eliminate the stigma attached to the occupation by making a distinction between the positions of maid and housekeeper, defining the former as involving personal service. The younger women, in particular sought to redefine the job. Mrs. Fernandez noted the distinction between maid and housekeeper in the following story:

> They [the employer's children] started to introduce me to their friends as their maid. "This is our maid Angela." I would say, "I'm not your maid. I've come to clean your house, and a maid is someone who takes care of you and lives here or comes in everyday, and I come once a week and it is to take care of what you have messed up. I'm not your maid. I'm your housekeeper." (Age 35, 9 years' experience).

By identifying themselves as professional housekeepers, the women emphasized their special skills and knowledge and situated their work among male-dominated jobs that are treated as semiskilled, such as carpet cleaning. This also served to define their relationships to their employers. Mrs. Montoya illustrated the relationship:

> I figure I'm not there to be their personal maid. I'm there to do their housecleaning— their upkeep of the house. Most of the women I work for are professionals, and so they feel it's not my job to run around behind them. Just to keep their house maintenance clean, and that's all they ask. (Age 33, 12 years' experience).

The women redefined their employers as clients, vendors, and customers. Defining themselves as professionals, these domestics no longer saw themselves as acting in the subordinate role of employee to the dominant role of employer. Without recognition of their authority, however, the domestics had to rely on mistresses' cooperation. This is similar to women's lack of authority in other female-dominated occupations such as nursing and teaching. (See Ritzer 1977 and chapters by Spencer and Corley and Mauksch in this volume.)

Another strategy women used to lessen the stigma of doing domestic work was to focus on the benefits to their families. By praising aspects of domestic service compatible with traditional mother and wife roles, the woman's social identity was shifted to family rather than work roles. Since the status of motherhood is much higher than that of domestic worker, identifying with the traditional family role served to minimize the stigma attached to the work role. Again this strategy was found particularly among younger and more educated women. Mrs. Montoya, a high school graduate and mother of two, stressed that domestic work was preferable to other jobs because it did not interfere with her role as a mother:

> I make my own hours so I can go to [school] programs when I'm needed. I go to conferences when I'm needed. When the kids are ill, I'm there. . . . It's one of the best jobs that I could find in my situation where I am home with my family before and after school. I'm always around.

The women were usually available to participate in school functions, and many played an active role in the community. The fact that these women identified primarily with traditional family roles is consistent with other research findings suggesting that jobs are not the central interest of workers' lives (Dublin 1956).

Women tended to deny that they were actually employed, as did their families. Many of the women remarked that their families did not consider them to be working outside the home; their employment was dismissed as "shadow work," the peculiarly nonwork status commonly given to housework (Oakley 1974; Illich 1982). Therefore, the women's families saw no reason to give them credit or to help out at home. A few husbands did not want their wives working and retaliated by becoming more demanding about housework, laundry, and meals. This attitude was particularly common in families where mothers worked part time. The women received little help from their husbands or their children in doing cooking, laundry, and housekeeping. Children occasionally helped with the housework, and retired husbands were described as sporadically cooking a meal, removing the laundry from the dryer, vacuuming the living room, or "telling the children what to do." Consequently, women working six–to seven–hour days, five days a week as domestics experienced the common "double day" syndrome known to many working mothers regardless of their occupation.

The women described their wages as providing "extras" not afforded by their husbands' incomes. The items listed as "extras" were: food, children's clothes, remodeling the house, savings, children's tuition, and payment of bills. Clearly, their contributions enhanced their family's subsistence and went beyond the stereotypical 'pin money.' The notion that their employment provided extras rather than subsistence for the family was part of these women's strategy for coping with the stigma of being a domestic worker. In essence, they maintained a social identity based on the family rather than on the work role. Since the status attached to being a mother and wife is much higher than that assigned to the domestic, women defined their work as adding to the fulfillment of their traditional female role.

Discussion

Chicana domestic workers share experiences similar to those of other minority women. Although a few of those interviewed worked on a live-in basis prior to marriage, they only worked on a nonresidential basis after marriage. This is quite similar to the pattern found among Japanese-American women (Glenn 1981). Chicana domestic workers also experience domestic service as an "occupational ghetto" as have so many Japanese-American and black women in the United States. Minority women have not moved into the formal work sector as a consequence of their experience as domestics, but have continued to have few options. The present investigation begins to explain why domestic service does not constitute a "bridging occupation" for minority women.

The use of informal networks to obtain daywork as described by Chicana domestics is also found in the Japanese-American community; while community resources provide Japanese-American women with immediate employment as a domestic, the residential and social segregation also "tend to insulate members from information about other occupations" (Glenn 1981, 380). This method of job searching has likewise been documented for various other workers, including professionals (Reid 1972; Katz 1958; Caplow and McGee 1958). It follows that potential for social mobility is related to expanding resources within the community rather than to simple assimilation into another community's norms and values. I would argue that domestic service serves as a bridging occupation only when employers make their informal networks available to domestics. Research on minority women in domestic service indicates that employers do not share these informal networks; that is, domestics do not become "just one of the family." As a result, domestics experience social segregation and do not gain access to other occupations.

Analysis of the work histories collected from Chicana domestic workers shows that they found their options limited in low-paying, low-status, dead end jobs. The women's choice of domestic service over another job (such as waitressing or farmwork) was most often based on the flexible schedule and potential for autonomy on the job. Selecting employers who worked outside the home and establishing verbal contracts were attempts to increase autonomy. The women also tried to modernize their occupation by redefining themselves as professional housecleaners. These strategies are all essentially individualistic. However, as unionization among housekeepers increases, these women will be able to pursue collective approaches to the struggle for better working conditions.

References

Becker, H.S. 1952. "The career of the Chicago public schoolteacher," *American Journal of Sociology* 57:470.

Broom, L., and J. H. Smith. 1963. "Bridging occupations," *British Journal of Sociology* 14:321-34.

Caplow, T., and R. McGee. 1958. *The Academic Marketplace.* New York: Basic Books.

Chaplin, D. 1964. "Domestic service and the Negro," In *Blue Collar World,* edited by A.B. Shoistak and WI. Gomberg, Englewood Cliffs, NJ.: Prentice-Hall. pp. 527-536.

Coley, S.M. 1981. "And Still I Rise: An Exploratory Study of Contemporary Black Private Household Workers" Ph.D. diss., Bryn Mawr College, Bryn Mawr, PA.

Dublin, R. 1956. "Industrial workers' world: A study of the central life interests of industrial workers," *Social Problems* 3:131-42.

Glenn, E.N. 1980. "The dialectics of wage work: Japanese-American women and domestic service, 1905-1940," *Feminist Studies* 6:432-71.

——. 1981. "Occupational ghettoization: Japanese-American women and domestic service, 1905-1970," *Ethnicity* 8:352-86.

——. 1986. *Issei, Nisei, War Bride: Three Generations of Japanese-American Women in Domestic Service.* Philadelphia: Temple University Press, University Press.

Illich, 1. 1982. *Gender.* New York: Pantheon Books.

Katz, F.E. 1958. "Occupational contract network," *Social Forces* 41:52-5.

Katzman, D.H. 1981. *Seven Days a Week: Women and Domestic Service in Industrializing America.* New York: Oxford University Press, 1978.

Lerner, G. 1972. *Black Women in White America: A Documentary History.* New York: Pantheon Books.

McKinley, G.E. 1969. "The stranger in the gates: Employer reactions toward domestic servants in America, 1825-1875." Ph.D. Diss., Michigan State University, East Lansing.

Oakley, A. 1974. *The Sociology of Housework.* New York: Pantheon Books.

Reid, G. 1972. "Job search and the effectiveness of job-finding methods," *Industrial and Labor Relations Review* 25:479-95.

Ritzer, G. 1977. *Working Conflict and Change.* Englewood Cliffs, NJ: Prentice-Hall.

Rollins, J. 1985. *Between Women: Domestics and Their Employers.* Philadelphia: Temple University Press.

Romero, M. 1987. "Domestic service in the transition from rural to urban life: The case of La Chicana,' *Women's Studies,* forthcoming.

Smith, M.L. 1971. "Institutionalized servitude: The female domestic servant in Lima, Peru." Ph.D. Diss., Indiana University, Bloomington.

The Organizer's Tale (1991)

César Chávez

It really started for me 16 years ago in San Jose, California, when I was working on an apricot farm. We figured he was just another social worker doing a study of farm conditions, and I kept refusing to meet with him. But he was persistent. Finally, I got together some of the rough element in San Jose. We were going to have a little reception for him to teach the *gringo* a little bit of how we felt. There were about 30 of us in the house, young guys mostly. I was supposed to give them a signal—change my cigarette from my right hand to my left, and then we were going to give him a lot of hell. But he started talking and the more he talked, the more wide-eyed I became and the less inclined I was to give the signal. A couple of guys who were pretty drunk at the time still wanted to give the *gringo* the business, but we got rid of them. This fellow was making a lot of sense, and I wanted to hear what he had to say.

His name was Fred Ross, and he was an organizer for the Community Service Organization (CSO) which was working with Mexican-Americans in the cities. I became immediately really involved. Before long I was heading a voter registration drive. All the time I was observing the things Fred did, secretly, because I wanted to learn how to organize, to see how it was done. I was impressed with his patience and understanding of people. I thought this was a tool, one of the greatest things he had.

It was pretty rough for me at first. I was changing and had to take a lot of ridicule from the kids my age, the rough characters I worked with in the fields. They would say, "Hey, big shot. Now that you're a *politico,* why are you working here for 65 cents an hour?" I might add that our neighborhood had the highest percentage of San Quentin graduates. It was a game among the *pachucos* in the sense that we defended ourselves from outsiders, although inside the neighborhood there was not a lot of fighting.

After six months of working every night in San Jose, Fred assigned me to take over the CSO chapter in Decoto. It was a tough spot to fill. I would suggest something, and people would say, "No, let's wait till Fred gets back," or "Fred wouldn't do it that way." This is pretty much a pattern with people, I discovered, whether I was put in Fred's position, or later, when someone else was put in my position. After the Decoto assignment I was sent to start a new chapter in Oakland. Before I left, Fred came to a place in San Jose called the Hole-in-the-Wall and we talked for half an hour over coffee. He was in a rush to leave, but I wanted to keep him talking; I was scared of my assignment.

There were hard times in Oakland. First of all, it was a big city and I'd get lost every time I went anywhere. Then I arranged a series of house meetings. I would get to the meeting early and drive back and forth past the house, too nervous to go in and face the people. Finally I would force myself to go inside and sit in a corner. I was quite thin then, and young, and most of the people were middle-aged. Someone would say, "Where's the organizer?" And I would pipe up, "Here I am." Then they would say in Spanish—these were very poor people and we hardly spoke anything but Spanish—"Ha! This *kid?*" Most of them said they were interested, but the hardest part was to get them to start pushing themselves, on their own initiative.

The idea was to set up a meeting and then get each attending person to call his own house meeting, inviting new people—a sort of chain letter effect. After a house meeting, I would lie awake going over the whole thing, playing the tape back, trying to see why people laughed at one point, or why they were for one thing and against another. I was also learning to read and write, those late evenings. I had left school in the 7th grade after attending 67 different schools, and my reading wasn't the best.

At our first organizing meeting we had 368 people: I'll never forget it because it was very important to me. You eat your heart out; the meeting is called for 7 o'clock and you start to worry about 4. You wait. Will they show up? Then the first one arrives. By 7 there are only 20 people, you have everything in order, you have to look calm. But little by little they filter in and at a certain point you know it will be a success.

After four months in Oakland, I was transferred. The chapter was beginning to move on its own, so Fred assigned me to organize the San Joaquin Valley. Over the months I developed what I used to call schemes or tricks—now I call them techniques—of making initial contacts. The main thing in convincing someone is to spend time with him. It doesn't matter if he can read, write or even speak well. What is important is that he is a man and second, that he has shown some initial interest. One good way to develop leadership is to take a man with you in your car. And it works a lot better if you're doing the driving; that way you are in charge. You drive, he sits there, and you talk. These little things were very important to me; I was caught in a big game by then, figuring out what makes people work. I found that if you work hard enough you can usually shake people into working too, those who are concerned. You work harder and they work harder still, up to a point and then they pass you. Then, of course, they're on their own.

I also learned to keep away from the established groups and so-called leaders, and to guard against philosophizing. Working with low–income people is very different from working with the professionals, who like to sit around talking about how to play politics. When you're trying to recruit a farmworker, you have to paint a little picture, and then you have to color the picture in. We found out that the harder a guy is to convince, the better leader or member he becomes. When you exert yourself to convince him, you have his confidence and he has good motivation. A lot of people who say OK right away wind up hanging around the office, taking up the workers' time.

During the McCarthy era in one Valley town, I was subjected to a lot of redbaiting. We had been recruiting people for citizenship classes at the high school when we got into a quarrel with the naturalization examiner. He was rejecting people on the grounds that they were just parroting what they learned in citizenship class. One day we had a meeting about it in Fresno, and I took along some of the leaders of our local chapter. Some redbaiting official gave us a hard time, and the people got scared and took his side. They did it because it seemed easy at the moment, even though they knew that sticking with me was the right thing to do. It was disgusting. When we left the building they walked by themselves ahead of me as if I had some kind of communicable disease. I had been working with these people for three months and I was very sad to see that. It taught me a great lesson.

That night I learned that the chapter officers were holding a meeting to review my letters and printed materials to see if I really was a Communist. So I drove out there and walked right in on their meeting. I said, "I hear you've been discussing me, and I thought it would be nice if I was here to defend myself. Not that it matters that much to you or even to me, because as far as I'm concerned you are a bunch of cowards." At that they began to apologize. "Let's forget it," they said. "You're a nice guy." But I didn't want apologies. I wanted a full discussion. I told them I didn't give a damn, but that they had to learn to distinguish fact from what appeared to be a fact because of fear. I kept them there till two in the morning. Some of the women cried. I don't know if they investigated me any further, but I stayed on another few months and things worked out.

This was not an isolated case. Often when we'd leave people to themselves they would get frightened and draw back into their shells where they had been all the years. And I learned quickly that there is no real appreciation. Whatever you do, and no matter what reasons you may give to others, you do it because you want to see it done, or maybe because you want power. And there shouldn't be any appreciation, understandably. I know good organizers who were destroyed, washed out, because they expected people to appreciate what they'd done. Anyone who comes in with the idea that farmworkers are free of sin and that the growers are all bastards, either has never dealt with the situation or is an idealist of the first order. Things don't work that way.

For more than 10 years I worked for the CSO. As the organization grew, we found ourselves meeting in fancier and fancier motels and holding expensive conventions. Doctors, lawyers and politicians began joining. They would get elected to some office in the organization and then, for all practical purposes, leave. Intent on using the CSO for their own prestige purposes, these "leaders," many of them, lacked the urgency we had to have. When I became general director I began to press for a program to organize farmworkers into a union, an idea most of the leadership opposed. So I started a revolt within the CSO. I refused to sit at the head table at meetings, refused to wear a suit and tie, and finally I even refused to shave and cut my hair. It used to embarrass some of the professionals. At every meeting I got up and gave my standard speech: we shouldn't meet in fancy motels, we were getting away from the people, farmworkers had to be organized. But nothing happened. In March of '62 I resigned and came to Delano to begin organizing the Valley on my own.

By hand I drew a map of all the towns between Arvin and Stockton—86 of them, including farming camps—and decided to hit them all to get a small nucleus of people working in each. For six months, I traveled around, planting an idea. We had a simple questionnaire, a little card with space for name, address and how much the worker thought he ought to be paid. My wife, Helen, mimeographed them, and we took our kids for two or three day jaunts to these towns, distributing the cards door-to-door and to camps and groceries.

Some 80,000 cards were sent back from eight Valley counties. I got a lot of contacts that way, but I was shocked at the wages the people were asking. The growers were paying $1 and $1.15, and maybe 95 percent of the people thought they should be getting only $1.25. Sometimes people scribbled messages on the cards: "I hope to God we win" or "Do you think we can win?" or "I'd like to know more." So I separated the cards with the pencilled notes, got in my car and went to those people.

We didn't have any money at all in those days, none for gas and hardly any for food. So I went to people and started asking for food. It turned out to be about the best thing I could have done, although at first it's hard on your pride. Some of our best members came in that way. If people give you their food, they'll give you their hearts. Several months and many meetings later we had a working organization, and this time the leaders were the people.

None of the farmworkers had collective bargaining contracts, and I thought it would take ten years before we got that first contract. I wanted desperately to get some color into the movement, to give people something they could identify with, like a flag. I was reading some books about how various leaders discovered what colors contrasted and stood out the best. The Egyptians had found that a red field with a white circle and a black emblem in the center crashed into your eyes like nothing else. I wanted to use the Aztec eagle in the center, as on the Mexican flag. So I told my cousin Manuel,

"Draw an Aztec eagle." Manuel had a little trouble with it, so we modified the eagle to make it easier for people to draw.

The first big meeting of what we decided to call the National Farm Workers Association was held in September 1962, at Fresno, with 287 people. We had our huge red flag on the wall, with paper tacked over it. When the time came, Manuel pulled a cord ripping the paper off the flag and all of a sudden it hit the people. Some of them wondered if it was a Communist flag, and I said it probably looked more like a neo-Nazi emblem than anything else. But they wanted an explanation. So Manuel got up and said, "When that damn eagle flies—that's when the farmworkers' problems are going to be solved."

One of the first things I decided was that outside money wasn't going to organize people, at least not in the beginning. I even turned down a grant from a private group—$50,000 to go directly to organize farmworkers—for just this reason. Even when there are no strings attached, you are still compromised because you feel you have to produce immediate results. This is bad, because it takes a long time to build a movement, and your organization suffers if you get too far ahead of the people it belongs to. We set the dues at $42 a year per family, really a meaningful dues, but of the 212 we got to pay, only 12 remained by June of '63. We were discouraged at that, but not enough to make us quit.

Money was always a problem. Once we were facing a $180 gas bill on a credit card I'd got a long time ago and was about to lose. And we *had* to keep that credit card. One day my wife and I were picking cotton, pulling bolls, to make a little money to live on. Helen said to me, "Do you put all this in the bag, or just the cotton?" I thought she was kidding and told her to throw the whole boll in so that she had nothing but a sack of bolls at the weighing. The man said, "Whose sack is this?" I said, well, my wife's, and he told us we were fired. "Look at all that crap you brought in," he said. Helen and I started laughing. We were going anyway. We took the $4 we had earned and spent it at a grocery store where they were giving away a $100 prize. Each time you shopped they'd give you one of the letters of M-O-N-E-Y or a flag: you had to have M-O-N-E-Y plus the flag to win. Helen had already collected the letters and just needed the flag. Anyway, they gave her the ticket. She screamed, "A flag? I don't believe it," ran in and got the $100. She said "Now we're going to eat steak." But I said no, we're going to pay the gas bill. I don't know if she cried, but I think she did.

It was rough in those early years. Helen was having babies and I was not there when she was at the hospital. But if you haven't got your wife behind you, you can't do many things. There's got to be peace at home. So I did, I think, a fairly good job of organizing her. When we were kids, she lived in Delano and I came to town as a migrant. Once on a date we had a bad experience about segregation at a movie theater, and I put up a fight. We were together then, and still are. I think I'm more of a pacifist than she is. Her father, Fabela, was a colonel with Pancho Villa in the Mexican Revolution. Sometimes she gets angry and tells me, "These scabs—you should deal with them sternly," and I kid her, "It must be too much of that Fabela blood in you."

The movement really caught on in '64. By August we had a thousand members. We'd had a beautiful 90-day drive in Corcoran, where they had the Battle of the Corcoran Farm Camp 30 years ago, and by November we had assets of $25,000 in our credit union, which helped to stabilize the membership. I had gone without pay the whole of 1963. The next year the members voted me a $40 a week salary, after Helen had to quit working in the fields to manage the credit union.

Our first strike was in May of '65, a small one but it prepared us for the big one. A farmworker from McFarland named Epifanio Camacho came to see me. He said he was sick and tired of how people working the roses were being treated, and he was willing to "go the limit." I assigned Manuel and Gilbert Padilla to hold meetings at Camacho's house. The people wanted union recognition, but the real issue, as in most cases when you begin, was wages. They were promised $9 a thousand, but they were actually getting $6.50 and $7 for grafting roses. Most of them signed cards giving us the right to bargain for them. We chose the biggest company, with about 85 employees, not counting the irrigators and supervisors, and we held a series of meetings to prepare the strike and call the vote. There would be no picket line; everyone pledged on their honor not to break the strike.

Early on the first morning of the strike, we sent out 10 cars to check the people's homes. We found lights in five or six homes and knocked on the doors. The men were getting up and we'd say, "Where are you going?" They would dodge, "Oh, uh . . . I was just getting up, you know." We'd say, "Well, you're not going to work, are you?" And they'd say no. Dolores Huerta, who was driving the green panel truck, saw a light in one house where four rose-workers lived. They told her they were going to work, even after she reminded them of their pledge. So she moved the truck so it blocked their driveway, turned off the key, put it in her purse and sat there alone.

That morning the company foreman was madder than hell and refused to talk to us. None of the grafters had shown up for work. At 10:30 we started to go to the company office, but it occurred to us that maybe a woman would have a better chance. So Dolores knocked on the office door, saying, "I'm Dolores Huerta from the National Farm Workers Association." "Get out!" the man said, "you Communist. Get out!" I guess they were expecting us, because as Dolores stood arguing with him the cops came and told her to leave. She left.

For two days the fields were idle. On Wednesday they recruited a group of Filipinos from out of town who knew nothing of the strike, maybe 35 of them. They drove through escorted by three sheriff's patrol cars, one in front, one in the middle and one at the rear with a dog. We didn't have a picket line, but we parked across the street and just watched them go through, not saying a word. All but seven stopped working after half an hour, and the rest had quit by mid-afternoon.

The company made an offer the evening of the fourth day, a package deal that amounted to a 120 percent wage increase, but no contract. We wanted to hold out for a contract and more benefits, but a majority of the rose-workers wanted to accept the offer and go back. We are a democratic union so we had to support what they wanted to do. They had a meeting and voted to settle. Then we had a problem with a few militants who wanted to hold out. We had to convince them to go back to work, as a united front, because otherwise they would be canned. So we worked—Tony Orendain and I, Dolores and Gilbert, Jim Drake and all the organizers—knocking on doors till two in the morning, telling people, "You have to go back or you'll lose your job." And they did. They worked.

Our second strike, and our last before the big one at Delano, was in the grapes at Martin's Ranch last summer. The people were getting a raw deal there, being pushed around pretty badly. Gilbert went out to the field, climbed on top of a car and took a strike vote. They voted unanimously to go out. Right away they started bringing in strikebreakers, so we launched a tough attack on the labor contractors, distributed leaflets portraying them as really low characters. We attacked one—Luis Campos—so badly that he just gave up the job, and he took 27 of his men out with him. All he asked was that we distribute another leaflet reinstating him in the community. And we did. What was unusual was that the grower would talk to us. The grower kept saying, "I can't pay. I just haven't got the money." I guess he must have found the money somewhere, because we were asking $1.40 and we got it.

We had just finished the Martin strike when the Agricultural Workers Organizing Committee (AFL-CIO) started a strike against the grape growers, DiGiorgio, Schenley liquors and small growers, asking $1.40 an hour and 25 cents a box. There was a lot of pressure from our members for us to join the strike, but we had some misgivings. We didn't feel ready for a big strike like this one, one that was sure to last a long time. Having no money—just $87 in the strike fund—meant we'd have to depend on God knows who.

Eight days after the strike started—it takes time to get 1,200 people together from all over the Valley—we held a meeting in Delano and voted to go out. I asked the membership to release us from the pledge not to accept outside money, because we'd need it now, a lot of it. The help came. It started because of the close, and I would say even beautiful relationship that we've had with the Migrant Ministry for some years. They were the first to come to our rescue, financially and in every other way, and they spread the word to other benefactors.

We had planned, before, to start a labor school in November. It never happened, but we have the best labor school we could ever have, in the strike. The strike is only a temporary condition, however. We have over 3,000 members spread out over a wide area, and we have to service them when they have problems. We get letters from New Mexico, Colorado, Texas, California, from farmworkers saying, "We're getting together and we need an organizer." It kills you when you haven't got the personnel and resources. You feel badly about not sending an organizer because you look back and remember all the difficulty you had in getting two or three people together, and here *they're* together. Of course, we're training organizers, many of them younger than I was when I started in CSO. They can work 20 hours a day, sleep four, and be ready to hit it again; when you get to 39 it's a different story.

The people who took part in the strike and the march have something more than their material interest going for them. If it were only material, they wouldn't have stayed on the strike long enough to win. It is difficult to explain. But it flows out in the ordinary things they say. For instance, some of the younger guys are saying, "Where do you think's going to be the next strike?" I say, "Well, we have to win in Delano." They say, "We'll win, but where do we go next?" I say, "Maybe most of us will be working in the fields." They say, "No, I don't want to go and work in the fields. I want to organize. There are a lot of people that need our help." So I say, "You're going to be pretty poor then, because when you strike you don't have much money." They say they don't care about that.

And others are saying, "I have friends who are working in Texas. If we could only help them." It is bigger, certainly, than just a strike. And if this spirit grows within the farm labor movement, one day we can use the force that we have to help correct a lot of things that are wrong in this society. But that is for the future. Before you can run, you have to learn to walk.

There are vivid memories from my childhood—what we had to go through because of low wages and the conditions, basically because there was no union. I suppose if I wanted to be fair I could say that I'm trying to settle a personal score. I could dramatize it by saying that I want to bring social justice to farmworkers. But the truth is that I went through a lot of hell, and a lot of people did. If we can even the score a little for the workers then we are doing something. Besides, I don't know any other work I like to do better than this. I really don't, you know.

I have just enough white in me to make my honesty questionable.
Will Rogers

ENGLISH*

POPULATION: *Never so few*	**PHYSICAL CHARACTERISTICS:** *Extremely stiff upper lips*
RELIGION: *Retreating* **PRACTICING:** *2 retired Colonels on pension*	**RACIAL TRAITS (GOOD):** *Make excellent butlers* *Appear on Ed Sullivan show* **RACIAL TRAITS (BAD):** *Speech affectation* *Drive on wrong side of road* *Universally despised*
LOCATION: *Old Blighty*	**DIET STAPLE:** *Tea*

(*NOTE: The English need not be bothered about)

CHAPTER 3

COMMUNICATING

The Language of Oppression (1990)
Haig A. Bosmajian

"Sticks and stones may break my bones, but words can never hurt me." To accept this adage as valid is sheer folly. "What's in a name? that which we call a rose by any other name would smell as sweet." The answer to *Juliet's* question is "Plenty!" and to her own response to the question we can only say that this is by no means invariably true. The importance, significance, and ramifications *of* naming and defining people cannot be over-emphasized. From *Genesis* and beyond, to the present time, the power which comes from naming and defining people has had positive as well as negative effects on entire populations.

The magic of words and names has always been an integral part of both "primitive" and "civilized" societies. As Margaret Schlauch has observed, "from time immemorial men have thought there is some mysterious essential connection between a thing and the spoken name for it. You could use the name of your enemy, not only to designate him either passionately or dispassionately, but also to exercise a baleful influence."[1]

Biblical passages abound in which names and naming are endowed with great power; from the very outset, in *Genesis,* naming and defining are attributed a significant potency: "And out of the ground the Lord God formed every beast of the field and every fowl of the air; and brought them unto Adam to see what he would call them: and whatsoever Adam called every living creature, that was the name thereof."[2] Amidst the admonitions in *Leviticus* against theft, lying, and fraud is the warning "And ye shall not swear my name falsely, neither shalt thou profane the name of thy God: I am the Lord."[3] So important is the name that it must not be blasphemed; those who curse and blaspheme shall be stoned "and he that blasphemeth the name of the Lord, he shall surely be put to death, and all the congregation shall certainly stone him."[4] So important is the name that the denial of it is considered a form of punishment: "But ye are they that forsake the Lord, that forget my holy mountain. . . . Therefore will I number you to the sword, and ye shall all bow down to the slaughter: because when I called, ye did not answer; when I spake, ye did not hear. . . . Therefore thus saith the Lord God, behold, my servants shall eat, but ye shall be hungry. . . . And ye shall leave your name for a curse unto my chosen: for the Lord God shall slay thee, and call his servants by another name."[5]

To be unnamed is to be unknown, to have no identity. William Saroyan has observed that "the word nameless, especially in poetry and in much prose, signifies an alien, unknown, and almost unwelcome condition, as when, for instance, a writer speaks of 'a nameless sorrow.'" "Human beings," continues Saroyan, "are for the fact of being named at all, however meaninglessly, lifted out of an area of mystery, doubt, or undesirability into an area in which belonging to everybody else is taken for granted, so that one of the first questions asked by new people, two-year-olds even, whether they are speaking to other new people or to people who have been around for a great many years, is *What is your name?*"[6]

To receive a name is to be elevated to the status of a human being; without a name one's identity is questionable. In stressing the importance of a name and the significance of having none, Joyce Hertzler has said that "among both primitives and moderns, an individual has no definition, no validity for himself, without a name. His name is his badge of individuality, the means whereby he identifies himself and enters upon a truly subjective existence. My own name, for example, stands for me, a person. Divesting me of it reduces me to a meaningless, even pathological, nonentity."[7]

In his book *What Is In A Name?* Farhang Zabeeh reminds us that "the Roman slaves originally were without names. Only after being sold they took their master's praenomen in the genitive case followed by the suffix—'por' (boy), e.g., 'Marcipor,' which indicates that some men, so long as they were regarded by others as cattle, did not need a name. However, as soon as they became servants some designation was called forth."[8] To this day one of the forms of punishment meted out to wrongdoers who are imprisoned is to take away their names and to give them numbers. In an increasingly computerized age people are becoming mere numbers—credit card numbers, insurance numbers, bank account numbers, student numbers, et cetera. Identification of human beings by numbers is a negation of their humanity and their existence.

Philologist Max Muller has pointed out that "if we examine the most ancient word for 'name,' we find it is *naman* in Sanskrit, *nomen* in Latin, *namo* in Gothic. This *naman* stands for gnaman and is derived from the root, *gna,* to know, and meant originally that by which we know a thing."[9] In the course of the evolution of human society, R. P. Masani tells us, the early need for names "appears to have been felt almost simultaneously with the origin of speech . . . personality and the rights and obligations connected with it would not exist without the name."[10] In his classic work *The Golden Bough* James Frazer devotes several pages to tabooed names and words in ancient societies, taboos reflecting the power and magic people saw in names and words. Frazer notes, for example, that "the North American Indian regards his name, not as a mere label, but as a distinct part of his personality, just as much as are his eyes or his teeth, and believes that injury will result as surely from the malicious handling of his name as from a wound inflicted on any part of his physical organism."[11]

A name can be used as a curse. A name can be blasphemed. Namecalling is so serious a matter that statutes and court decisions prohibit "fighting words" to be uttered. In 1942 the United States Supreme Court upheld the conviction of a person who had addressed a police officer as "a God damned racketeer" and "a damned Fascist." *(Chaplinsky v. New Hampshire, 315 U.S. 568).* Such namecalling, such epithets, said the Court, are not protected speech. So important is one's "good name" that the law prohibits libel.

History abounds with instances in which the mere utterance of a name was prohibited. In ancient Greece, according to Frazer, "the names of the priests and other high officials who had to do with the performance of the Eleusinian mysteries might not be uttered in their lifetime. To pronounce them was a legal offense."[12] Jörgen Ruud reports in *Taboo: A Study of Malagasy Customs and Beliefs* that among the Antandroy people the father has absolute authority in his household and that "children are forbidden to mention the name of their father. They must call him father, daddy. . . . The children may not mention his house or the parts of his body by their ordinary names, but must use other terms, i.e., euphemisms.'"[13]

It was Iago who said in *Othello:*

> Who steals my purse steals trash; 'tis something nothing;
> 'Twas mine, 'tis his, and has been slave to thousands;
> But he that filches from me my good name
> Robs me of that which not enriches him
> And makes me poor indeed.

Alice, in Lewis Carroll's *Through the Looking Glass,* had trepidations about entering the woods where things were nameless: "This must be the wood," she said thoughtfully to herself, "where things have no names. I wonder what'll become of my name when I go in? I shouldn't like to lose it at all—because they'd have to give me another, and it would almost certain to be an ugly one."

A Nazi decree of August 17, 1938 stipulated that "Jews may receive only those first names which are listed in the directives of the Ministry of the Interior concerning the use of first names." Further, the decree provided: "If Jews should bear first names other than those permitted . . . they must . . . adopt an additional name. For males, that name shall be Israel, for females Sara." Another Nazi decree forbade Jews in Germany "to show themselves in public without a Jew's star . . . [consisting] of a six-pointed star of yellow cloth with black borders, equivalent in size to the palm of the hand. The inscription is to read 'JEW' in black letters. It is to be sewn to the left breast of the garment, and to be worn visibly."

The power which comes from names and naming is related directly to the power to define others—individuals, races, sexes, ethnic groups. Our identities, who and what we are, how others see us, are greatly affected by the names we are called and the words with which we are labelled. The names, labels, and phrases employed to "identify" a people may in the end determine their survival. The word "define" comes from the Latin *definire,* meaning to limit. Through definition we restrict, we set boundaries, we name.

"When I use a word," said Humpty Dumpty in *Through the Looking Glass,* "it means just what I choose it to mean—neither more nor less." "The question is," said Alice, "whether you can make words mean so many different things." "The question is," said Humpty Dumpty, "which is to be master —that's all."

During his days as a civil rights-black power activist, Stokely Carmichael accurately asserted: "It [definition] is very, very important because I believe that people who can define are masters."[14] Self-determination must include self-definition, the ability and right to name oneself; the master-subject relationship is based partly on the master's power to name and define the subject.

While names, words and language can be and are used to inspire us, to motivate us to humane acts, to liberate us, they can also be used to dehumanize human beings and to "justify" their suppression and even their extermination. It is not a great step from the coercive suppression of dissent to the extermination of dissenters (as the United States Supreme Court declared in its 1943 compulsory flag salute opinion in *West Virginia State Board of Education v. Barnette); nor is it a large step from defining a people as non-human or sub-human to their subjugation or annihilation. One of the first acts of an oppressor is to redefine the "enemy" so they will be looked upon as creatures warranting separation, suppression, and even eradication.

The Nazis redefined Jews as "bacilli," "parasites," "disease," "demon," and "plague." In his essay "The Hollow Miracle," George Steiner informs us that the Germans "who poured quicklime down the openings of the sewers in Warsaw to kill the living and stifle the stink of the dead wrote about it. They spoke of having to 'liquidate vermin'. . . . Gradually, words lost their original meaning and acquired nightmarish definitions. *Jude, Pole, Russe* came to mean two-legged lice, putrid vermin which good Aryans must squash, as a [Nazi] Party manual said, like roaches on a dirty wall. 'Final solution,' *endgültige Lösung*, came to signify the death of six million human beings in gas ovens."[15]

The language of white racism has for centuries been used to keep the nigger in his place." Our sexist language has allowed men to define who and what a woman is and must be. Labels like "traitors," "saboteurs," "queers," and "obscene degenerates" were applied indiscriminately to students who protested the war in Vietnam or denounced injustices in the United States. Are such people to be listened to? Consulted? Argued with? Obviously not! One does not listen to, much less talk to, traitors and outlaws, sensualists and queers. One only punishes them or, as Spiro Agnew suggested in one of his 1970 speeches, there are some dissenters who should be separated "from our society with no more regret than we should feel over discarding rotten apples."[16]

What does it mean to separate people? When the Japanese-Americans were rounded up in 1942 and sent off to "relocation camps" they were "separated." The Jews in Nazi Germany were "separated." The Indians of the United States, the occupants of the New World before Columbus "discovered" it, have been systematically "separated." As "chattels" and slaves, the blacks in the United States were "separated"; legally a black person was a piece of property, although human enough to be counted as three-fifths of a person in computing the number of people represented by white legislators.

How is the forcible isolation of human beings from society at large justified? To make the separation process more palatable to the populace, what must the oppressor first do? How does he make the populace accept the separation of the "creatures," or, if not accept it, at least not protest it? Consideration of such questions is not an academic exercise without practical implications. There is a close nexus between language and self-perception, self-awareness, self-identity, and self-esteem. Just as our thoughts affect our language, so does our language affect our thoughts and eventually our actions and behavior. As Edward Sapir has observed, we are all "at the mercy of the particular language which has become the medium of expression" in our society. The "real world," he points out, "is to a large extent unconsciously built up on the language habits of the group. . . . We see and hear and otherwise experience very largely as we do because the language habits of our community predispose certain choices of interpretation."[17]

George Orwell has written in his famous essay "Politics and the English Language": "A man may take to drink because he feels himself to be a failure, and then fail all the more completely because he drinks. It is rather the same thing that is happening to the English language. It becomes ugly and inaccurate because our thoughts are foolish, but the slovenliness of our language makes it easier for us to have foolish thoughts."[18] Orwell maintains that "the decadence in our language is probably curable" and that "silly words and expressions have often disappeared, not through any evolutionary process but owing to the conscious action of a minority."[19] Wilma Scott Heide, speaking as president of the

National Organization for Women several years ago, indicated that feminists were undertaking this conscious action: "In any social movement, when changes are effected, the language sooner or later reflects the change. Our approach is different. Instead of passively noting the change, we are changing language patterns to actively effect the changes, a significant part of which is the conceptual tool of thought, our language."[20]

This then is our task—to identify the decadence in our language, the inhumane uses of language, the "silly words and expressions" which have been used to justify the unjustifiable, to make palatable the unpalatable, to make reasonable the unreasonable, to make decent the indecent. Hitler's "Final Solution" appeared reasonable once the Jews were successfully labelled by the Nazis as sub-humans, as "parasites," "vermin," and "bacilli." The segregation and suppression of blacks in the United States was justified once they were considered "chattels" and "inferiors." The subjugation of the "American Indians" was defensible since they were defined as "barbarians" and "savages." As Peter Farb has said, "cannibalism, torture, scalping, mutilation, adultery, incest, sodomy, rape, filth, drunkenness—such a catalogue of accusations against a people is an indication not so much of their depravity as that their land is up for grabs."[21] As long as adult women are "chicks," "girls," "dolls," "babes," and "ladies," their status in society will remain "inferior"; they will go on being treated as subjects in the subject-master relationship as long as the language of the law places them into the same class as children, minors, and the insane.

It is my hope that an examination of the language of oppression will result in a conscious effort by the reader to help cure this decadence in our language, especially that language which leads to dehumanization of the human being. One way for us to curtail the use of the language of oppression is for those who find themselves being defined into subjugation to rebel against such linguistic suppression. It isn't strange that those persons who insist on defining themselves, who insist on this elemental privilege of self-naming, self-definition, and self-identity encounter vigorous resistance. Predictably, the resistance usually comes from the oppressor or would-be oppressor and is a result of the fact that he or she does not want to relinquish the power which comes from the ability to define others.

[1]Margaret Schlauch, *The Gift of Language* (New York: Dover, 1955), p. 13.
[2]*Genesis*, 2:19.[3]*Leviticus*, 19:12
[4]*Leviticus*, 25:16.
[5]*Isaiah*, 66:11–12.
[6]William Saroyan, "Random Notes on the Names of People," *Names*, 1 (December 1953), p. 239.
[7]Joyce Hertzler, *A Sociology of Language* (New York: Random House, 1965), p. 271
[8]Farhang Zabeeh, *What Is In A Name?* (The Hague: Martinus Nijhoff, 1968), p. 66.
[9]Cited in Elsdon Smith, *Treasury of Name Lore* (New York: Harper and Row, 1967), p. vii.
[10]R. P. Masani, *Folk Culture Reflected in Names* (Bombay: Popular Prakashan, 1966), p. 6.
[11]James Frazer, *The Golden Bough* (New York: Macmillan, 1951), p. 284.
[12]*Ibid., p.* 302.
[13]Jörgen Ruud, *Taboo: A Study of Malagasy Customs and Beliefs* (Oslo: Oslo University Press, 1960), p.15.
[14]Stokely Carmichael, speech delivered in Seattle, Washington, April 19,1967.
[15]George Steiner, *Language and Silence* (New York: Atheneum, 1970), p. 100.
[16]*New York Times*, October 21,1969, p. 25.
[17]Cited in John Carroll (ed.), *Language, Thought and Reality: Selected Writings of Benjamin Lee Whorf* (Cambridge, Mass.: The M.I.T. Press, 1956), p. 134.

[18]George Orwell, "Politics and the English Language," in C. Muscatine and M. Griffith, *The Borzoi College Reader*, 2nd ed. (New York: Alfred A. Knopf, 1971), p. 88.

[19]*Ibid.*

[20]Wilma Scott Heide, "Feminism: The *sine qua non* for a Just Society," *Vital Speeches*, 38 (1971–72), p. 402.

[21]Peter Farb, "Indian Corn," *The New York Review*, 17 (December 16,1971), p. 36.

*Being a woman is a terribly difficult trade,
since it consists principally of dealing with men.*
Joseph Conrad

Language Barrier Isolates Euro-Americans (1985)
Carol Innerst

They've lived for decades in the melting pot of the world, but hundreds of thousands of aged European immigrants still speak little or no English, according to officials at a weekend national conference on the problems of the Euro-American elderly.

Christopher L. Hayes, acting director of Catholic University's Center for the Study of Pre-Retirement and Aging, told the gathering his immigrant Italian grandmother has lived in the same tenement building in New York City for the last 52 years.

"Even though the plaster is falling off the walls and the roof leaks, she clings to the apartment because of the memories of the 'Paisans' and the Italian Club, which provided activities that brought Italy just a little closer.

"Today, most of the 'Paisans' have moved or died and the Italian Club has closed due to lack of members. She relies exclusively on my mother to read all her mail because she cannot read English," he said.

Social researchers are examining the failure of immigrants to learn English, a phenomenon often coupled with strong family and community support systems within the Little Italys and other ethnic neighborhoods of America, according to Terrence G. Wiley, lecturer at California State University at Long Beach.

The growing awareness of the problem has been generated in part by the growth of Spanish as the second most popular language in the United States, and by the influx of refugees since 1975, he said.

The meeting was funded by a grant from the US. Department of Health and Human Services' Administration on Aging.

Americans assume that all immigrants will learn to speak English, Mr. Wiley said. But Americans' lack of patience with those who speak a foreign language or who speak in broken English deters many older immigrants from learning English, he said.

According to the 1981 Survey of Language Supplement to the July 1975 Population Survey, there are 1.6 million people in the United States who don't speak English, Mr. Wiley said.

Of these, Italians comprise the largest Euro-American group, totaling some 160,000 people.

Moreover, more than 1 million bilingual Italians age 50 and over indicated that they normally do not speak English at home.

Among Germans, nearly 650,000 over the age of 50 indicated that they normally do not speak English at home. More than 100,000 Greeks indicated the same, as did over 500,000 French and 90,000 Portuguese.

More than 16 percent of all Italian immigrants called their competence in English "low." Among those arriving since 1970, nearly 54 percent called their English competence "low."

Many better-educated immigrants learn English naturally on the job, Mr. Wiley said. For those whose work and social lives center around their ethnic neighborhoods, there is less need to learn English.

"If an attempt is made to profile Euro-Americans who are most likely not to speak English well or at all, typically we find elderly Greek, Polish and Italian immigrants who have immigrated since the 1970s," he said.

"In still rarer cases, it is possible to find U.S.-born Euro-Americans, who have lived in a predominantly non English-speaking environment, who also have low English competence, " he said. "For example, among U.S. born French-Americans whose mother tongue was French, more than 3 percent indicated low proficiency in English.

"Consequently, despite the general trend toward anglicization, linguistic diversity among Euro-Americans is much greater than is commonly presumed," he said.

Calling attention to the language barrier in obtaining health and social services, Mr. Wiley cited a 1979 study showing that between 71 percent and 85 percent of Estonian, Greek, Hungarian, Italian, Jewish, Latvian, Lithuanian and Polish subjects did not use any formal services at all. It was not known whether they had less need for the services preferred to rely on mutual assistance within the family or community or were hindered by the language barrier.

Euro-American Elderly and Social Services Reform* (1985)

John A. Kromkowski and Thaddeus C. Radzialowski

Although Carol Innerst's May 20 article, "Many Euro–Americans isolated by the persisting language barrier," correctly concluded "that the linguistic diversity among Euro-Americans is much greater than is commonly presumed," much else about the piece, including its headline and possibly the conference itself, was wrong. There was a curiously nativist cast which does not reflect our understanding of the persistence of ethnicity in America.

The article's tone suggests that the Euro-American elderly should change to fit the requirements and limitations of social services rather than voice the need for better support from agencies which serve them. Ethnic Americans are tired of academic recommendations that argue the case for "professional care providers." The social service establishment even shows a touch of pique that the Euroethnic elderly are not major consumers of its services. There is great irony in this claim in an era that stresses the need for fresh public approaches to social service and more private community care and community-based non-profit services.

The conference should have concentrated on uncovering alternative ways the Euro-American communities have found to serve the needs of its elderly and how those could be bolstered by private, public and community resources.

The report fails to note that most Euro-Americans live in some kind of community or are part of ethnic networks. Just because they are separated from English-speaking professional care givers doesn't mean they are "isolated." Exemplary social service projects based on community resources for the elderly in Milwaukee, Cleveland, Baltimore, Seattle, South Bend and elsewhere are thriving.

In addition, the meeting should also have focused on ways that social service agencies can use ethnic networks and groups to deliver services, such as enrolling ethnic senior citizens groups in an HMO and training social service professionals to understand the needs and cultures of the people they serve.

Euro-Americans hardly need patronizing academic juggling of pre-1980 census data and the self-serving theories of the aging establishment still mired intellectually in the '60s.

---

*Reprinted with permission from *The Washington Times*, May 21, 1985. p. 6A.

Are We Speaking the Same Language? (1989)
Dorothy C. Judd

If I had immigrated to New Jersey from a foreign-speaking country I would have anticipated the need to learn a new language to make myself understood. But after my moving here from Boston, which is, after all, part of the same country—no border check, no passport—it comes as a shock that I still need an occasional interpreter after nearly 30 years.

Of course I expected to make some regional adjustments and I did. I soon learned to ask for soda instead of tonic, to say I was going to the shore instead of the beach, and to report that my children went sledding, not coasting. I stopped looking for frappes on menus and ordered a shake instead and no longer took my shoes to the cobbler to be repaired.

Other changes were not as easy. As long as I live I will wait "in line" never "on line." When I need something from the basement. I will go "down cellar" to get it. "Ants" will always be insects, not my relatives.

Slowly, given time, I could say corn flakes not "con" flakes, and go to New York not New "Yok." In fact I did pretty well with relearning that o–followed–by–r sound. But after a weekend in Boston, I came back and said "It was so hot that even though it was October first, all the college kids were wearing shots" (shorts). My friends here looked at one another and said "Oh no, Guess where she's been!"

But the a-followed-by-r sound is just not a sound I can master. It probably has somethlng to do with the fact that when reciting the alphabet, a Bostonian will say "q, ah, s, t,. . ." That 18th letter is much like the sound the doctor instructs you to make when he depresses your tongue and looks down your throat. So first of all, my infant ear never heard the sound of "ar," which is considered standard, and then, through long disuse, whatever part of my vocal system should have been imitating it simply atrophied.

It is sometimes frustrating that I can't make myself understood, as when I ask if some item comes in a "dahk-ah" shade and a friend has to translate or I call a number and the person hangs up because when I say "Mahk" he thinks it's a kid making parrot noises.

On the other hand, I've had some amusing experiences as a result of my accent. Once plagued by mosquitoes, I went to the supermarket and asked where I could find the "Yahd Gahd." The manager looked at me strangely and asked me to repeat my question. After the third try he handed me a pencil and paper and asked me to write down my request. Once he understood, we both had a good laugh— as did several customers who were listening.

I made lifelong friends with the produce manager when I asked if he had any "payahs." Only after describing them as yellow and outlining their shape with my hand did I get my point across. Every week thereafter, he'd see me and call out The "pay-ahs are over hee-ah, dee-ah!"

My friends "Bah-bra" and "Mah-sha" tolerate my butchering their names, but I pray that my son is only kidding when he says he's going to name sons "Clahk" and "Mah shall." It would be awful not to be able to pronounce my own grandsons' names. I already avoid ever trying to tell anyone my father's first name Garner. On my lips it sounds like the country Ghana and I fare no better when I try to spell it: G-a-ah-n-e-ah.

In my job as an elementary-school teacher, my accent has created some strange situations. My first year here, I called the roll and a little boy named "Mahk" did not answer though I knew he was there. When I prompted him, he said. "But teacher, that's not my name." Apologizing but firm, I said. "This year when you hear me make that sound you know that's your name ."

Another year, on the first day of school a child went home and told his mother he had a foreign teacher. Surprised, she said "Oh I thought you had Ms. Judd." To which he replied, "I do, but she sure doesn't speak English!"

When I first left Boston I found myself homesick for the sound of that accent. Long distance calling was not the casual occurrence it is today, and I was on a very limited budget. I would call what was then information, free, and ask for something requiring a response with an obvious sound like "Jod-an Mahsh" "Chahls-town" or "Pahk" Street. In those days they even gave addresses, so I got to listen longer.

Later, I discovered that a poet who like myself is a native of Medford, Mass., had recorded some of his poems. When I played his poetry for students, they said, "He sounds funny, just like you."

So I sound funny. I've grown to accept it—sort of like a distinguishing birthmark. It is certainly more readily apparent than a triangular splotch of brown on the left hip and less easily removed than a mole below the right ear.

Besides, it has its advantages. I never have to think of ways to strike up a conversation with someone I meet for the first time, and, what's more, they always remember me.

Dorothy C. Judd lives in West Orange, New York.

There's no thief like a bad book.
Italian proverb

You Are What You Say (1991)

Robin Lakoff

"Women's language" is that pleasant (dainty?), euphemistic, never aggressive way of talking we learned as little girls. Cultural bias was built into the language we were allowed to speak, the subjects we were allowed to speak about, and the ways we were spoken of. Having learned our linguistic lesson well, we go out in the world, only to discover that we are communicative cripples—damned if we do, and damned if we don't.

If we refuse to talk "like a lady," we are ridiculed and criticized for being unfeminine. ("She thinks like a man" is, at best, a left–handed compliment.) If we do learn all the fuzzy–headed, unassertive language of our sex, we are ridiculed for being unable to think clearly, unable to take part in a serious discussion, and therefore unfit to hold a position of power.

It doesn't take much of this for a woman to begin feeling she deserves such treatment because of inadequacies in her own intelligence and education.

"Women's language" shows up in all levels of English. For example, women are encouraged and allowed to make far more precise discriminations in naming colors than men do. Words like *mauve, beige, ecru, aquamarine, lavender,* and so on, are unremarkable in a woman's active vocabulary, but largely absent from that of most men. I know of no evidence suggesting that women actually *see* a wider range of colors than men do. It is simply that fine discriminations of this sort are relevant to women's vocabularies, but not to men's; to men, who control most of the interesting affairs of the world, such distinctions are trivial—irrelevant.

In the area of syntax, we find similar gender–related peculiarities of speech. There is one construction, in particular, that women use conversationally far more than men: the tag-question. A tag is midway between an outright statement and a yes–no question; it is less assertive than the former, but more confident than the latter.

A *flat statement* indicates confidence in the speaker's knowledge and is fairly certain to be believed; a *question* indicates a lack of knowledge on some point and implies that the gap in the speaker's knowledge can and will be remedied by an answer. For example, if, at a Little League game, I have had my glasses off, I can legitimately ask someone else: "Was the player out at third?" A *tag question*, being intermediate between statement and question, is used when the speaker is stating a claim, but lacks full confidence in the truth of that claim. So if I say, "Is Joan here?" I will probably not be surprised if my respondent answers "no"; but if I say, "Joan is here, isn't she?" instead, chances are I am already biased in favor of a positive answer, wanting only confirmation. I still want a response, but I have enough knowledge (or think I have) to predict that response. A tag question, then, might be thought of as a statement that doesn't demand to be believed by anyone but the speaker, a way of giving leeway, of not forcing the addressee to go along with the views of the speaker.

Another common use of the tag question is in small talk when the speaker is trying to elicit conversation: "Sure is hot here, isn't it?"

But in discussing personal feelings or opinions, only the speaker normally has any way of knowing the correct answer. Sentences such as "I have a headache, don't I?" are clearly ridiculous but there are other examples where it is the speaker's opinions, rather than perceptions, for which corroboration is sought, as in "The situation in Southeast Asia is terrible, isn't it?"

While there are, of course, other possible interpretations of a sentence like this, one possibility is that the speaker has a particular answer in mind—"yes" or "no"—but is reluctant to state it badly. This sort of tag question is much more apt to be used by women than by men in conversation. Why is this the case?

The tag question allows a speaker to avoid commitment, and thereby avoid conflict with the addressee. The problem is that, by so doing, speakers may also give the impression of not really being sure of themselves, or looking to the addressee for confirmation of their views. This uncertainty is reinforced in more subliminal ways, too. There is a peculiar sentence intonation–pattern, used almost exclusively by women, as far as I know, which changes a declarative answer into a question. The effect of using the rising inflection typical of a yes–no question is to imply that the speaker is seeking confirmation, even though the speaker is clearly the only one who has the requisite information, which is why the question was put to her in the first place:

(Q) When will dinner be ready?
(A) Oh . . . around six o'clock. . . ?

It is though the second speaker were saying, "Six o'clock—if that's okay with you, if you agree." The person being addressed is put in the position of having to provide confirmation. One likely consequence of this sort of speech–pattern in a woman is that, often unbeknownst to herself, the speaker builds a reputation of tentativeness, and others will refrain from taking her seriously or trusting her with any real responsibilities, since she "can't make up her mind," and "isn't sure of herself."

Such idiosyncrasies may explain why women's language sounds much more "polite" than men's. It is polite to leave a decision open, not impose your mind, or views, or claims, on anyone else. So a tag question is a kind of polite statement, in that it does not force agreement or belief on the addressee. In the same way a request is a polite command, in that it does not force obedience on the addressee, but rather suggests something be done as a favor to the speaker. A clearly stated order implies a threat of certain consequences if it is not followed, and—even more impolite—implies that the speaker is in a superior position and able to enforce the order. By couching wishes in the form of a request, on the other hand, a speaker implies that if the request is not carried out, only the speaker will suffer; noncompliance cannot harm the addressee. So the decision is really left up to addressee. The distinction becomes clear in these examples:

Close the door.
Please close the door.
Will you close the door?
Will you please close the door?
Won't you close the door?

In the same ways as words and speech patterns used *by* women undermine her image, those used to *describe* women make matters even worse. Often a word may be used of both men and women (and perhaps of things as well); but when it is applied to women, it assumes a special meaning that, by implication rather than outright assertion, is derogatory to women as a group.

The use of euphemisms has this effect. A euphemism is a substitute for a word that has acquired a bad connotation by association with something unpleasant or embarrassing. But almost as soon as the new word comes into common usage, it takes on the same old bad connotations, since feelings about the things or people referred to are not altered by a change of name; this new euphemisms must be constantly found.

There is one euphemism for woman still very much alive. The word, of course, is *lady*. *Lady* has a masculine counterpart, namely gentleman, occasionally shortened to gent. But for some reason *lady* is very much commoner than gent *(leman)*.

The decision to use *lady* rather than *woman*, or vice versa, may considerably alter the sense of a sentence, as the following examples show:

(a) A woman (lady) I know is a dean at Berkeley.
(b) A woman (lady) I know makes amazing things out of shoelaces and old boxes.

The use of *lady* in (a) imparts a frivolous, or nonserious, tone to the sentence: the matter under discussion is not one of great moment. Similarly, in (b), using *lady* here would suggest that the speaker considered the "amazing things" not to be serious art, but merely a hobby or an aberration. If *woman is* used, she might be a serious sculptor. To say *lady doctor is* very condescending, since no one ever says *gentleman doctor* or even *man doctor*. For example, mention in the San Francisco *Chronicle* of January 31, 1972, of Madalyn Murray O'Hair as the *lady atheist* reduces her position to that of scatterbrained eccentric. Even *woman atheist is* scarcely defensible: sex is irrelevant to her philosophical position.

Many women argue that, on the other hand, *lady* carries with it overtones recalling the age of chivalry: conferring exalted stature on the person so referred to. This makes the term seem polite at first, but we must also remember that these implications are perilous: they suggest that a "lady" is helpless, and cannot do things by herself.

Lady can also be used to infer frivolousnss, as in titles of organizations. Those that have a serious purpose (not merely that of enabling "the ladies" to spend time with one another) cannot use the word *lady* in their titles, but less serious ones may. Compare the *Ladies' Auxiliary* of a men's group, or the *Thursday Evening Ladies' Browning and Garden Society* with *Ladies' Liberation* or *Ladies' Strike for Peace*.

What is curious about this split is that *lady* is in origin euphemism—a substitute that puts a better face on something people find uncomfortable—for *woman*. What kind of euphemism is it that subtly denigrates the people to whom it refers? Perhaps *lady* functions as a euphemism for *woman* because it does not contain the sexual implications present in *woman*: it is not "embarrassing" in that way. If this is so, we may expect that, in the future, *lady* will replace woman as the primary word for the human female, since *woman* will have become too blatantly sexual. That this distinction is already made in some contexts at least is shown in the following examples, where you can try replacing *woman* with *lady*:

(a) She's only twelve, but she's already a woman.
(b) After ten years in jail, Harry wanted to find a woman.
(c) She's my woman, see, so don't mess around with her.

Another common substitute for *woman* is *girl*. One seldom hears a man past the age of adolescence referred to as a boy, save in expressions like "going out with the boys," which are meant to suggest an air of adolescent frivolity and irresponsibility. But women of all ages are "girls": one can have a man—not a boy—Friday, but only a girl— never a woman or even a lady—Friday; women have girlfriends, but men do not—in a nonsexual sense—have boyfriends. It may be that this use of girl is euphemistic in the same way the use of *lady* is: in stressing the idea of immaturity, it removes the sexual connotations lurking in *woman*. *Girl* brings to mind irresponsibility: you don't send a girl to do a woman's errand (or even, for that matter, a boy's errand). She is a person who is both too immature and too far from real life to be entrusted with responsibilities or with decisions of any serious or important nature.

Now let's take a pair of words which, in terms of the possible relationships in an earlier society, were simple male-female equivalents, analogous to *bull: cow*. Suppose we find that, for independent reasons, society has changed in such a way that the original meanings now are irrelevant. Yet the words have not been discarded, but have acquired new meanings, metaphorically related to their original senses. But suppose these new metaphorical uses are no longer parallel to each other. By seeing where the parallelism breaks down, we discover something about the different roles played by men and women in this culture. One good example of such a divergence through time is found in the pair, *master: mistress*. Once used with reference to one's power over servants, these words have become unusable today in their original master-servant sense as the relationship has become less prevalent in our society. But the words are still common.

Unless used with reference to animals, *master* now generally refers to a man who has acquired consummate ability in some field, normally nonsexual. But its feminine counterpart cannot be used this way. It is pratically restricted to its sexual sense of "paramour." We start out with two terms, both roughly paraphrasable as "one who has power over another." But the masculine form, once one person is no longer able to have absolute power over another, becomes usable metaphorically in the sense of "having power over *something.*" *Master* requires as its object only the name of some activity, something inanimate and abstract. But *mistress* requires a masculine noun in the possessive to precede it. One cannot say: "Rhonda is a mistress." One must be *someone's* mistress. A man is defined by what he does, a woman by her sexuality, that is, in terms of one particular aspect of her relationship to men. It is one thing to be an *old master* like Hans Holbein, and another to be an *old mistress*.

The same is true of the words *spinster* and *bachelor*—gender words for "one who is not married." The resemblance ends with the definition. While *bachelor* is a neuter term, often used as a compliment, *spinster* normally is used pejoratively, with connotations of prissiness, fussiness, and so on. To be a bachelor implies that one has the choice of marrying or not, and this is what makes the idea of a bachelor existence attractive in the popular literature. He has been pursued and has successfully eluded his pursuers. But a spinster is one who has not been pursued, or at last not seriously. She is old, unwanted goods. The metaphorical connotations of *bachelor* generally suggests sexual freedom; of *spinster*, puritanism or celibacy.

These examples could be multiplied. It is generally considered a *faux pas*, in society, to congratulate a woman on her engagement, while it is correct to congratulate her fiancé. Why is this? The reason seems to be that it is impolite to remind people of things that may be uncomfortable to them. To congratulate a woman on her engagement is really to say, "Thank goodness! You had a close call!" For the man, on the other hand, there was no such danger. His choosing to marry viewed as a good thing, but not something essential.

The linguistic double standard holds throughout the life of the relationship. After marriage, bachelor and spinster become man and wife, not man and woman. The woman whose husband dies remains "John's widow"; John, however, is never "Mary's widower."

Finally, why is it that salesclerks and others are so quick to call women customers "dear," "honey," and other terms of endearment they really have no business using? A male customer would never put up with it. But women, like children, are supposed to enjoy these endearments, rather than being offended by them.

In more ways than one, it's time to speak up.

Robin Lakoff (1942–) is a professor of linguistics at the University of California, Berkely. She was educated at Radcliffe, the University of Indiana, and Harvard, and is the author of Language and Women's Place *(1975) and co–author of* Face Value: The Politics of Beauty *(1984). In the following essay (*Ms. *magazine, July 1974) Lakoff discusses language used by, about, and toward women. She demonstrates in detail how the English language contributes extensively to put-downs of the "weaker sex."*

Women, asses and nuts require strong hands.
Italian proverb

If Black English Isn't A Language, Then Tell Me, What Is? (1991)

James Baldwin

The argument concerning the use, or the status, or the reality, of black English is rooted in American history and has absolutely nothing to do with the question the argument supposes itself to be posing. The argument has nothing to do with language itself but with the role of language. Language, incontestably, reveals the speaker. Language, also, far more dubiously, is meant to define the other— and, in this case, the other is refusing to be defined by a language that has never been able to recognize him.

People evolve a language in order to describe and thus control their circumstances or in order not to be submerged by a situation that they cannot articulate. (And if they cannot articulate it, they are submerged.) A Frenchman living in Paris speaks a subtly and crucially different language from that of the man living in Marseilles; neither sounds very much like a man living in Quebec; and they would all have great difficulty in apprehending what the man from Guadeloupe, or Martinique, is saying, to say nothing of the man from Senegal— although the "common" language of all these areas is French. But each has paid, and is paying, a different price for this "common" language, in which, as it turns out, they are not saying, and cannot be saying, the same things: They each have very different realities to articulate, or control.

What joins all languages, and all men, is the necessity to confront life, in order, not inconceivably, to outwit death: The price for this is the acceptance, and achievement, of one's temporal identity. So that, for example, though it is not taught in the schools (and this has the potential of becoming a political issue) the south of France still clings to its ancient and musical Provençal, which resists being described as a "dialect." And much of the tension in the Basque countries, and in Wales, is due to the Basque and Welsh determination not to allow their languages to be destroyed. This determination also feeds the flames in Ireland for among the many indignities the Irish have been forced to undergo at English hands is the English contempt for their language.

It goes without saying, then, that language is also a political instrument, means, and proof of power. It is the most vivid and crucial key to identity. It reveals the private identity, and connects one with, or divorces one from, the larger, public, or communal identity. There have been, and are, times and places, when to speak a certain language could be dangerous, even fatal. Or, one may speak the same language, but in such a way that one's antecedents are revealed, or (one hopes) hidden. This is true in France, and is absolutely true in England: The range (and reign) of accents on that damp little island make England coherent for the English and totally incomprehensible for everyone else. To open your mouth in England is (if I may use black English) to "put your business in the street." You have confessed your parents, your youth, your school, your salary, your self-esteem, and, alas, your future.

Now, I do not know what white Americans would sound like if there had never been any black people in the United States, but they would not sound the way they sound. *Jazz*, for example, is a very specific sexual term, as in *Jazz me, baby,* but white people purified it into the Jazz Age. *Sock it to me,* which means, roughly, the same thing, has been adopted by Nathaniel Hawthorne's descendants with no qualms or hesitations at all, along with *let it all hang out* and *right on! Beat to his socks,* which was once the black's most total and despairing image of poverty, was transformed into a thing called the Beat Generation, which phenomenon was, largely, composed of *uptight,* middle-class white people, imitating poverty, trying to *get down,* to get *with it,* doing their *thing,* doing their despairing best to be *funky,* which we, the blacks, never dreamed of doing—we were funky, baby, like *funk* was going out of style.

Now, no one can eat his cake, and have it, too, and it is late in the day to attempt to penalize black people for having created a language that permits the nation its only glimpse of reality, a language without which the nation would be even more *whipped* than it is.

I say that the present skirmish is rooted in American history, and it is. Black English is the creation of the black diaspora. Blacks came to the United States chained to each other, but from different tribes. Neither could speak the other's language. If two black people, at that bitter hour of the world's history, had been able to speak to each other, the institution of chattel slavery could never have lasted as long as it did. Subsequently, the slave was given, under the eye, and the gun, of his master, Congo Square, and the Bible—or, in other words, and under those conditions, the slave began the formation of the black church, and it is within this unprecedented tabernacle that black English began to be formed. This was not, merely, as in the European example, the adoption of a foreign tongue, but an alchemy that transformed ancient elements into a new language: *A language comes into existence by means of brutal necessity, and the rules of the language are dictated by what the language must convey.*

There was a moment, in time, and in this place, when my brother, or my mother, or my father, or my sister, had to convey to me, for example, the danger in which I was standing from the white man standing just behind me, and to convey this with a speed and in a language, that the white man could not possibly understand, and that, indeed, he cannot understand, until today. He cannot afford to understand it. This understanding would reveal to him too much about himself and smash that mirror before which he has been frozen for so long.

Now, if this passion, this skill, this (to quote Toni Morrison) "sheer intelligence," this incredible music, the mighty achievement of having brought a people utterly unknown to, or despised by "history"—to have brought this people to their present, troubled, troubling, and unassailable and unanswerable place—if this absolutely unprecedented journey does not indicate that black English is a language, I am curious to know what definition of languages is to be trusted.

A people at the center of the western world, and in the midst of so hostile a population, has not endured and transcended by means of what is patronizingly called a "dialect." We, the blacks, are in trouble, certainly, but we are not inarticulate because we are not compelled to defend a morality that we know to be a lie.

The brutal truth is that the bulk of the white people in America never had any interest in educating black people, except as this could serve white purposes. It is not the black child's language that is despised. It is his experience. A child cannot be taught by anyone who despises him, and a child cannot afford to be fooled. A child cannot be taught by anyone whose demand, essentially, is that the child repudiate his experience, and all that gives him sustenance, and enter a limbo in which he will no longer be black, and in which he knows that he can never become white. Black people have lost too many black children that way.

And, after all, finally, in a country with standards so untrustworthy, a country that makes heroes of so many criminal mediocrities, a country unable to face why so many of the nonwhite are in prison, or on the needle, or standing, futureless, in the streets—it may very well be that both the child, and his elder, have concluded that they have nothing whatever to learn from the people of a country that has managed to learn so little.

Do not insult the mother alligator until you have crossed the river.
Haitian proverb

Public and Private Language (1982)

Richard Rodriguez

I remember to start with that day in Sacramento—a California now nearly thirty years past—when I first entered a classroom, able to understand some fifty stray English words.

The third of four children, I had been preceded to a neighborhood Roman Catholic school by an older brother and sister. But neither of them had revealed very much about their classroom experiences. Each afternoon they returned, as they left in the morning, always together, speaking in Spanish as they climbed the five steps of the porch. And their mysterious books, wrapped in shopping-bag paper, remained on the table next to the door, closed firmly behind them.

An accident of geography sent me to a school where all my classmates were white, many the children of doctors and lawyers and business executives. All my classmates certainly must have been uneasy on that first day of school—as most children are uneasy—to find themselves apart from their families in the first institution of their lives. But I was astonished.

The nun said, in a friendly but oddly impersonal voice, "Boys and girls, this is Richard Rodriguez." (I heard her sound out: *Rich-heard Road-ree-guess.*) It was the first time I had heard anyone name me in English. "Richard," the nun repeated more slowly, writing my name down in her black leather book. Quickly I turned to see my mothers's face dissolve in a watery blur behind the pebbled glass door.

Many years later there is something called bilingual education—a scheme proposed in the late 1960s by Hispanic-American social activists, later endorsed by a congressional vote. It is a program that seeks to permit non-English speaking children, many from lower-class homes, to use their family language as the language of school. (Such is the goal its supporters announce.) I heard them and am forced to say no: It is not possible for a child—any child—ever to use his family's language in school. Not to understand this is to misunderstand the public uses of schooling and to trivialize the nature of intimate life—a family's "language."

Memory teaches me what I know of these matters; the boy reminds the adult. I was a bilingual child, a certain kind—socially disadvantaged—the son of working-class parents, both Mexican immigrants.

In the early years of my boyhood, my parents coped very well in America. My father had steady work. My mother managed at home. They were nobody's victims. Optimism and ambition led them to a house (our home) many blocks from the Mexican south side of town. We lived among *gringos* and only a block from the biggest, whitest houses. It never occurred to my parents that they couldn't live wherever they chose. Nor was the Sacramento of the fifties bent on teaching them a contrary lesson. My mother and father were more annoyed than intimidated by those two or three neighbors who tried initially to make us unwelcome. ("Keep your brats away from my sidewalk!") But despite all they achieved, perhaps because they had so much to achieve, any deep feeling of ease, the confidence of 'belonging' in public was withheld from them both. They regarded the people at work, the faces in crowds, as very distant from us. They were the others, *los gringos*. That term was interchangeable in their speech with another, even more telling, *los americanos.*

I grew up in a house where the only regular guests were my relations. For one day, enormous families of relatives would visit and there would be so many people that the noise and the bodies would spill out to the backyard and front porch. Then, for weeks, no one came by. (It was usually a salesman who rang the doorbell.) Our house stood apart. A gaudy yellow in a row of white bungalows. We were the people with the noisy dog. The people who raised pigeons and chickens. We were the foreigners on the block. A few neighbors smiled and waved. We waved back. But no one in the family knew the names of the old couple who lived next door; until I was seven years old, I did not know the names of the kids who lived across the street.

In public, my father and mother spoke a hesitant, accented, not always grammatical English. And they would have to strain—their bodies tense—to catch the sense of what was rapidly said by *los gringos*. At home they spoke Spanish. The language of their Mexican past sounded in counterpoint to the English of public society. The words would come quickly, with ease. Conveyed through those sounds was the pleasing, soothing, consoling reminder of being at home.

During those years when I was first conscious of hearing, my mother and father addressed me only in Spanish; in Spanish I learned to reply. By contrast, English (*inglés*), rarely heard in the house, was the language I came to associate with *gringos*. I learned my first words of English overhearing my parents speak to strangers. At five years of age, I knew just enough English for my mother to trust me on errands to stores one block away. No more.

I was a listening child, careful to hear the very different sounds of Spanish and English. Wide-eyed with hearing, I'd listen to sounds more than words. First, there were English (*gringro*) sounds. So many words were still unknown that when the butcher or the lady at the drugstore said something to me, exotic polysyllabic sounds would bloom in the midst of their sentences. Often, the speech of people in public seemed to me very loud, booming with confidence. The man behind the counter would literally ask, "What can I do for you?" But by being so firm and so clear, the sound of his voice said that he was a *gringo;* he belonged in public society.

I would also hear then the high nasal notes of middle-class American speech. The air stirred with sound. Sometimes, even now, when I have been traveling abroad for several weeks, I will hear what I heard as a boy. In hotel lobbies or airports, in Turkey or Brazil, some Americans will pass, and suddenly I will hear it again—the high sound of American voices. For a few seconds I will hear it with pleasure, for it is now the sound of *my* society—a reminder of home. But inevitably—already on the flight headed for home—the sound fades with repetition. I will be unable to hear it anymore.

When I was a boy, things were different. The accent of *los gringos* was never pleasing nor was it hard to hear. Crowds at Safeway or at bus stops would be noisy with sound. And I would be forced to edge away from the chirping chatter above me.

I was unable to hear my own sounds, but I knew very well that I spoke English poorly. My words could not stretch far enough to form complete thoughts. And the words I did speak I didn't know well enough to make into distinct sounds. (Listeners would usually lower their heads, better to hear what I was trying to say.) But it was one thing for *me* to speak English with difficulty. It was more troubling for me to hear my parents speak in public: their high-whining vowels and guttural consonants; their sentences that got stuck with 'ch' and 'a' sounds; the confused syntax; the hesitant rhythm of sounds so different from the way *gringos* spoke. I'd notice, moreover, that my parents' voices were softer than those of *gringos* we'd meet.

I am tempted now to say that none of this mattered. In adulthood I am embarrassed by childhood fears. And, in a way, it didn't matter very much that my parents could not speak English with ease.

Their linguistic difficulties had no serious consequences. My mother and father made themselves understood at the country hospital clinic and at government offices. And yet, in another way, it mattered very much—it was unsettling to hear my parents struggle with English. Hearing them, I'd grow nervous, my clutching trust in their protection and power weakened.

There were many times like the night at a brightly lit gasoline station (a blaring white memory) when I stood uneasily, hearing my father. He was talking to a teenaged attendant. I do not recall what they were saying, but I cannot forget the sounds my father made as he spoke. At one point his words slid together to form one word—sounds as confused as the threads of blue and green oil in the puddle next to my shoes. His voice rushed through what he had left to say. And, toward the end, reached falsetto notes, appealing to his listener's understanding. I looked away to the lights of passing automobiles. I tried not to hear anymore. But I heard only too well the calm, easy tones in the attendant's rely. Shortly afterward, walking toward home with my father, I shivered when he put his hand on my shoulder. The very first chance that I got, I evaded his grasp and ran on ahead into the dark, skipping with feigned boyish exuberance.

But then there was Spanish. *Español:* my family's language. *Español:* the language that seemed to me a private language. I'd hear strangers on the radio and in the Mexican Catholic church across town speaking in Spanish, but I couldn't really believe that Spanish was a public language, like English. Spanish speakers, rather, seemed related to me, for I sensed that we shared—through our language— the experience of feeling apart from *los gringos*. It was thus a ghetto Spanish that I heard and I spoke. Like those whose lives are bound by a barrio, I was reminded by Spanish of my separateness from *los otros, los gringos* in power. But more intensely than for most barrio children—because I did not live in a barrio—Spanish seemed to me the language of home. (Most days it was only at home that I'd hear it.) It became the language of joyful return.

A family member would say something to me and I would feel myself specially recognized. My parents would say something to me and I would feel embraced by sounds of their words. Those sounds said: *I am speaking with ease in Spanish. I am addressing you in words I never use with* los gringos. *I recognize you as someone special, close, like no one outside. You belong with us. In the family.*
(Ricardo.)

At the age of five, six, well past the time when most other children no longer easily notice the difference between sounds uttered at home and words spoken in public, I had a different experience. I lived in a world magically compounded of sounds. I remained a child longer than most; I lingered too long, poised at the edge of language—often frightened by the sounds of *los gringos,* delighted by the sounds of Spanish at home. I shared with my family a language that was startlingly different from that used in the great city around us.

For me there were none of the gradations between public and private society so normal to a maturing child. Outside the house was public society; inside the house was private. Just opening or closing the screen door behind me was an important experience. I'd rarely leave home all alone or without reluctance. Walking down the sidewalk, under the canopy of tall trees, I'd warily notice the—suddenly—silent neighborhood kids who stood warily watching me. Nervously, I'd arrive at the grocery store to hear there the sound of the *gringo*—foreign to me—reminding me that in this world so big, I was a foreigner. But then I'd return. Walking back toward our house, climbing the steps from the sidewalk, when the front door was open in summer, I'd hear voices beyond the screen door talking in Spanish. For a second or two, I'd stay, linger there, listening. Smiling, I'd hear my mother call out, saying in Spanish (words): 'Is that you, Richard?' All the while her sounds would assure me: *You are home now; come closer; inside. With us.*

'*Sí,*' I'd reply.

Once more inside the house I would resume (assume) my place in the family. The sounds would dim, grow harder to hear. Once more at home, I would grow less aware of that fact. It required, however, no more than the blurt of the doorbell to alert me to listen to sounds all over again. The house would turn instantly still while my mother went to the door. I'd hear her hard English sounds. I'd wait to hear her voice return to soft-sounding Spanish, which assured me, as surely as did the clicking tongue of the lock on the door, that the stranger was gone.

Plainly, it is not healthy to hear such sounds so often. It is not healthy to distinguish public words from private sounds so easily. I remained cloistered by sounds, timid and shy in public, too dependent on voices at home. And yet it needs to be emphasized: I was an extremely happy child at home. I remember many nights when my father would come back from work, and I'd hear him call out to my mother in Spanish, sounding relieved. In Spanish, he'd sound light and free notes he never could manage in English. Some nights I'd jump up just at hearing his voice. With *mis hermanos* I would come running into the room where he was with my mother. Our laughing (so deep was the pleasure!) became screaming. Like others who know the pain of public alienation, we transformed the knowledge of our public separateness and made it consoling—the reminder of intimacy. *We are speaking now the way we never speak out in public. We are alone—together,* voices sounded, surrounded to tell me. Some nights, no one seemed willing to loosen the hold sounds had on us. At dinner, we invented new words. (Ours sounded Spanish, but made sense only to us.) We pieced together new words by taking, say, an English verb and giving it Spanish endings. My mother's instructions at bedtime would be lacquered with mock-urgent tones. Or a word like *sí* would become, in several notes, able to convey added measures of feeling. Tongues explored the edges of words, especially the fat vowels. And we happily sounded that military drum roll, the twirling roar of the Spanish *r*. Family language: my family's sounds. The voices of my parents and sisters and brothers. Their voices insisting: *You belong here. We are family members. Related. Special to one another. Listen!* Voices singing and sighing, rising, straining, then surging, teeming with pleasure that burst syllables into fragments of laughter. At times it seemed there was steady quiet only when, from another room, the rustling whispers of my parents faded and I moved closer to sleep.

Supporters of bilingual education today imply that students like me miss a great deal by not being taught in their family's language. What they seem not to recognize is that, as a socially disadvantaged child, I considered Spanish to be a private language. What I needed to learn in school was that I had the right—and the obligation—to speak the public language of *los gringos*. The odd truth is that my first-grade classmates could have become bilingual, in the conventional sense of that word, more easily than I. Had they been taught (as upper-middle-class children are often taught early) a second language like Spanish or French, they could have regarded it simply as that: another public language. In my case such bilingualism could not have been so quickly achieved. What I did not believe was that I could speak a single public language.

Without question, it would have pleased me to hear my teachers address me in Spanish when I entered the classroom. I would have felt much less afraid. I would have trusted them and responded with ease. But I would have delayed—for how long postponed?—having to learn the language of public society. I would have evaded—and for how long could I have afforded to delay?—learning the great lesson of school, that I had a public identity.

Fortunately my teachers were unsentimental about their responsibility. What they understood was that I needed to speak a public language. So their voices would search me out, asking me questions. Each time I'd hear them, I'd look up in surprise to see a nun's face frowning at me. I'd mumble, not really meaning to answer. The nun would persist, "Richard, stand up. Don't look at the floor. Speak up. Speak to the entire class, not just to me!" But I couldn't believe that the English language was mine to use. (In part, I did not want to believe it.) I continued to mumble. I resisted the teacher's demands. (Did I somehow suspect that once I learned the public language my pleasing family life would be changed?) Silent, waiting for the bell to sound, I remained dazed, diffident, afraid.

Because I wrongly imagined that English was intrinsically a public language and Spanish an intrinsically private one, I easily noted the difference between classroom language and the language of home. At school, words were directed to a general audience of listeners. ("Boys and girls.") Words were meaningfully ordered. And the point was not self-expression alone but to make oneself understood by many others. The teacher quizzed: "Boys and girls, why do we use that word in this sentence? Could we think of a better word to use there? Would the sentence change its meaning if the words were differently arranged? And wasn't there a better way of saying much the same thing?" (I couldn't say. I wouldn't try to say.)

Three months. Five. Half a year passed. Unsmiling, ever watchful, my teachers noted my silence. They began to connect my behavior with the difficult progress my older sister and brother were making. Until one Saturday morning three nuns arrived at the house to talk to our parents. Stiffly, they sat on the blue living room sofa. From the doorway of another room, spying the visitors, I noted the incongruity—the clash of two worlds, the faces and the voices of school intruding upon the familiar setting of home. I overheard one voice gently wondering, "Do your children speak only Spanish at home, Mrs. Rodriguez?" While another voice added, "That Richard especially seems so timid and shy."

That Rich-heard!

With great tact the visitors continued, "Is it possible for you and your husband to encourage your children to practice their English when they are home?" Of course, my parents complied. What would they not do for their children's well-being? And how could they have questioned the Church's authority which those women represented? In an instant, they agreed to give up the language (the sounds) that had revealed and accentuated our family's closeness. The moment after the visitors left, the change was observed, *"Ahora, speak to us en inglés,"* my father and mother united to tell us.

At first, it seemed a kind of game. After dinner each night, the family gathered to practice "our" English. (It was still then *inglés,* a language foreign to us, so we felt drawn as strangers to it.) Laughing, we would try to define words we could not pronounce. We played with strange English sounds, often overanglicizing our pronunciations. And we filled the smiling gaps of our sentences with familiar Spanish sounds. But that was cheating, somebody shouted. Everyone laughed. In school, meanwhile, like my brother and sister, I was required to attend a daily tutoring session. I needed a full year of special attention. I also needed my teachers to keep my attention from straying in class by calling out, *Rich-heard*—their English voices slowly prying loose my ties to my other name, its three notes, *Ri-car-do*. Most of all I needed to hear my mother and father speak to me in a moment of seriousness in broken—suddenly heartbreaking—English. The scene was inevitable: One Saturday morning I entered the kitchen where my parents were talking in Spanish. I did not realize that they were talking in Spanish however until, at the moment they saw me, I heard their voices change to speak English.

Those *gringo* sounds they uttered startled me. Pushed me away. In that moment of trivial misunderstanding and profound insight, I felt my throat twisted by unsounded grief. I turned quickly and left the room. But I had no place to escape to with Spanish. (The spell was broken.) My brother and sisters were speaking English in another part of the house.

Again and again in the days following, increasingly angry, I was obliged to hear my mother and father: "Speak to us *en inglés (Speak.)*" Only then did I determine to learn classroom English. Weeks after, it happened: One day in school I raised my hand to volunteer an answer. I spoke out in a loud voice. And I did not think it remarkable when the entire class understood. That day, I moved very far from the disadvantaged child I had been only days earlier. The belief, the calming assurance that I belonged in public, had at last taken hold.

Shortly after, I stopped hearing the high and low sounds of *los gringos.* A more and more confident speaker of English, I didn't trouble to listen to *how* strangers sounded, speaking to me. And there simply were too many English-speaking people in my day for me to hear American accents anymore. Conversations quickened. Listening to persons who sounded eccentrically pitched voices, I usually noted their sounds for an initial few seconds before I concentrated on what they were saying. Conversations became content-full. Transparent. Hearing someone's *tone* of voice—angry or questioning or sarcastic or happy or sad—I didn't distinguish it from the words it expressed. Sound and word were thus tightly wedded. At the end of a day, I was often bemused, always relieved to realize how "silent," though crowded with words, my day in public had been. (This public silence measured and quickened the change in my life.)

At last, seven years old, I came to believe what had been technically true since my birth: I was an American citizen.

But the special feeling of closeness at home was diminished by then. Gone was the desperate, urgent, intense feeling of being at home; rare was the experience of feeling myself individualized by family intimates. We remained a loving family, but one greatly changed. No longer so close; no longer bound tight by the pleasing and troubling knowledge of our public separateness. Neither my older brother nor sister rushed home after school anymore. Nor did I. When I arrived home there would often be neighborhood kids in the house. Or the house would be empty of sounds.

The silence at home, however, was finally more than a literal silence. Fewer words passed between parent and child, but more profound was the silence that resulted from my inattention to sounds. At about the time I no longer bothered to listen with care to the sounds of English in public, I grew careless about listening to the sounds family members made when they spoke. Most of the time I heard someone speaking at home and didn't distinguish his sounds from the words people uttered in public. I didn't even pay much attention to my parents' accented and ungrammatical speech. At least not at home. Only when I was with them in public would I grow alert to their accents. Though, even then, their sounds caused me less and less concern. For I was increasingly confident of my own public identity.

I would have been happier about my public success had I not sometimes recalled what it had been like earlier, when my family had conveyed its intimacy through a set of conveniently private sounds. Sometimes in public, hearing a stranger, I'd hark back to my past. A Mexican farmworker approached me downtown to ask directions to somewhere. *"¿Hijito . . .?"* he said. And his voice summoned deep longing. Another time standing beside my mother in the visiting room of a Carmelite convent, before the dense screen which rendered the nuns shadowy figures, I heard several Spanish-speaking nuns— their busy, singsong overlapping voices—assure us that yes, yes, we were remembered, all our family was remembered in their prayers. (Their voices echoed faraway family sounds.) Another day, a dark-faced old woman—her hand light on my shoulder—steadied herself against me as she boarded a bus. She murmured something I couldn't quite comprehend. Her Spanish voice came near, like the face of a never-beforeseen relative in the instant before I was kissed. Her voice, like so many of the Spanish voices I'd heard in public, recalled the golden age of my youth. Hearing Spanish then, I continued to be a careful, if sad, listener to sounds. Hearing a Spanish-speaking family walking behind me, I turned to look. I smiled for an instant, before my glance found the Hispanic-looking faces of strangers in the crowd going by.

Today I hear bilingual educators say that children lose a degree of "individuality" by becoming assimilated into public society. (Bilingual schooling was popularized in the seventies, that decade when middleclass ethnics began to resist the process of assimilation—the American melting pot.) But the bilingualists simplistically scorn the value and necessity of assimilation. They do not seem to realize that there are *two* ways a person is individualized. So they do not realize that while one suffers a diminished sense of *private* individuality by becoming assimilated into public society, such assimilation makes possible the achievement of *public* individuality.

The bilingualists insist that a student should be reminded of his difference from others in mass society, his heritage. But they equate mere separateness with individuality. The fact is that only in private—with intimates—is separateness from the crowd a prerequisite for individuality. (An intimate draws me apart, tells me that I am unique, unlike all others.) In public, by contrast, full individuality is achieved, paradoxically, by those who are able to consider themselves members of the crowd. Thus it happened for me: Only when I was able to think of myself as an American, no longer an alien in *gringo* society, could I seek the rights and opportunities necessary for full public individuality. The social and political advantages I enjoy as a man result from the day that I came to believe that my name, indeed, is *Rich-heard Roadree-guess*. It is true that my public society today is often impersonal. (My public society is usually mass society.) Yet despite the anonymity of the crowd and despite the fact that the individuality I achieve in public is often tenuous—because it depends on my being one in a crowd—I celebrate the day I acquired my new name. Those middleclass ethnics who scorn assimilation seem to me filled with decadent self-pity, obsessed by the burden of public life. Dangerously, they romanticize public separateness and they trivialize the dilemma of the socially disadvantaged.

Richard Rodriguez was born in California in 1944, attended Stanford and Columbia universities, and received his doctorate in English literature from the University of California, Berkeley. In addition to a number of articles, he has written his autobiography, Hunger of Memory *(1982), from which the following selection was taken.*

Bilingual education continues to be subject of controversy. Its advocates believe that children entering school with little or no English will progress better if they are taught most subjects in their own language while learning English. In most bilingual programs the use of the first language is diminished or discontinued when children have mastered English.

Richard Rodriguez, whose first language was Spanish, uses his own experience to argue against bilingual education. To him Spanish remains his private language, the one he used at home, and English the public language he had to master in school in order to make his way in life. He believes that this distinction has helped him and would have been blurred if he had been taught in Spanish.

The International Language of Gestures (1984)

Paul Ekman, Wallace V. Friesen, and John Bear

On his first trip to Naples, a well-meaning American tourist thanks his waiter for a good meal well-served by making the "A-Okay" gesture with his thumb and forefinger. The waiter pales and heads for the manager. They seriously discuss calling the police and having the hapless tourist arrested for obscene and offensive public behavior.

What happened?

Most travelers wouldn't think of leaving home without a phrase book of some kind, enough of a guide to help them say and understand "Ja," "Nein," "Grazie" and "Oú se trouvent les toilettes?" And yet, while most people are aware that gestures are the most common form of cross-cultural communication, they don't realize that the language of gestures can be just as different, just as regional and just as likely to cause misunderstanding as the spoken word.

Consider our puzzled tourist. The thumb-and-forefinger-in-a-circle gesture, a friendly one in America, has an insulting meaning in France and Belgium: "You're worth zero." In parts of Southern Italy it means "asshole," while in Greece and Turkey it is an insulting or vulgar sexual invitation.

There are, in fact, dozens of gestures that take on totally different meanings as you move from one country or region to another. Is "thumbs up" always a positive gesture? Absolutely not. Does nodding the head up and down always mean "Yes"? No!

To make matters even more confusing, many hand movements have no meaning at all, in any country. If you watch television with the sound turned off, or observe a conversation at a distance, you become aware of almost constant motion, especially with the hands and arms. People wave their arms, they shrug, they waggle their fingers, they point, they scratch their chests, they pick their noses.

These various activities can be divided into three major categories: manipulators, emblems and illustrators.

In a manipulator, one part of the body, usually the hands, rubs, picks, squeezes, cleans or otherwise grooms some other part. These movements have no specific meaning. Manipulators generally increase when people become uncomfortable or occasionally when they are totally relaxed.

An emblem is a physical act that can fully take the place of words. Nodding the head up and down in many cultures is a substitute for saying, "Yes." Raising the shoulders and turning the palms upward clearly means "I don't know," or "I'm not sure."

Illustrators are physical acts that help explain what is being said but have no meaning on their own. Waving the arms, raising or lowering the eyebrows, snapping the fingers and pounding the table may enhance or explain the words that accompany them, but they cannot stand alone. People sometimes use illustrators as a pantomime or charade, especially when they can't think of the right words, or when it's simply easier to illustrate, as in defining "zigzag" or explaining how to tie a shoe.

Thus the same illustrator might accompany a positive statement one moment and a negative one the next. This is not the case with emblems, which have the same precise meaning on all occasions for all members of a group, class, culture or subculture.

Emblems are used consciously. The user knows what they mean, unless, of course, he uses them inadvertently. When Nelson Rockefeller raised his middle finger to a heckler, he knew exactly what the gesture meant, and he believed that the person he was communicating with knew as well.

The three of us are working on a dictionary of emblems, a few of which are discussed and illustrated in this article. In looking for emblems, we found that it isn't productive simply to observe people communicating with each other, because emblems are used only occasionally. And asking people to describe or identify emblems that are important in their culture is even less productive. Even when we explain the concept clearly, most people find it difficult to recognize and analyze their own communication behavior this way.

Instead, we developed a research procedure that has enabled us to identify emblems in cultures as diverse as those of urban Japanese, white, middle-class Americans, the preliterate South Fore people of Papua, natives of New Guinea, Iranians, Israelis and the inhabitants of London, Madrid, Paris, Frankfurt and Rome. The procedure involves three steps:

Give a group of people from the same cultural background a series of phrases and ask if they have a gesture or facial expression for each phrase: "What time is it?" "He's a homosexual." "That's good." "Yes." And so on. We find that normally, after 10 to 15 people have provided responses, we have catalogued the great majority of the emblems of their culture.

Analyze the results. If most of the people cannot supply a "performance" for a verbal message, we discard it.

Study the remaining performances further to eliminate inventions and illustrators. Many people are so eager to please that they will invent a gesture on the spot. Americans asked for a gesture for "sawing wood" could certainly oblige, even if they had never considered that request before, but the arm motion they would provide would not be an emblem.

To weed out these "false emblems," we show other people from the same culture videotapes of the performances by the first group. We ask which are inventions, which are pantomimes and which are symbolic gestures that they have seen before or used themselves. We also ask the people to give us their own meanings for each performance.

The gestures remaining after this second round of interpretations are likely to be the emblems of that particular culture. Using this procedure, we have found three types of emblems:

First, popular emblems have the same or similar meanings in several cultures. The side-to-side head motion meaning "No" is a good example.

Next, unique emblems have a specific meaning in one culture but none elsewhere. Surprisingly, there seem to be no uniquely American emblems, although other countries provide many examples. For instance, the French gesture of putting one's fist around the tip of the nose and twisting it to signify "He's drunk," is not used elsewhere. The German "good luck" emblem, making two fists with the thumbs inside and pounding an imaginary table, is unique to that culture.

Finally, multi-meaning emblems have one meaning in one culture and a totally different meaning in another. The thumb inserted between the index and third fingers is an invitation to have sex in Germany, Holland and Denmark, but in Portugal and Brazil it is a wish for good luck or protection.

The number of emblems in use varies considerably among cultures, from fewer than 60 in the United States to more than 250 in Israel. The difference is understandable since Israel is composed of recent immigrants from many countries, most of which have their own large emblem vocabularies. In addition, since emblems are helpful in military operations where silence is essential, and all Israelis serve in the armed forces, military service provides both the opportunity and the need to learn new emblems.

The kind of emblems used, as well as the number, varies considerably from culture to culture. Some are especially heavy on insults, for instance, while others have a large number of emblems for hunger or sex.

Finally, as Desmond Morris documented in his book, *Gestures.* there are significant regional variations in modern cultures. The findings we describe in this article apply to people in the major urban areas of each country: London, not England as a whole; Paris, not France. Because of the pervasiveness of travel and television, however, an emblem is often known in the countryside even if it is not used there.

The reverse side also has a reverse side.
Japanese proverb

SCOTS

POPULATION: *Lessening*	**PHYSICAL CHARACTERISTICS:** *Dour, tone-deaf,* *bony knees* *Despise the English*
RELIGION: *Saving grace*	**RACIAL TRAITS (GOOD):** *Economical* *Distill whiskey* *Taciturn* *Despise the English*
PRACTICING: *One 89-year old woman* *and her four bachelor sons*	**RACIAL TRAITS (BAD):** *Stingy* *Drink whiskey* *Boring*
LOCATION: *Low rent districts*	**DIET STAPLE:** *Mush*

CHAPTER 4

CUSTOMS

Don't Show a Sole in Arabia (1989)

Paul St. Pierre

There is nothing wrong with being offensive to some people. Telephone solicitors come readily to mind. Offending them might improve their characters and in any case couldn't worsen them. Giving offense is a well-established custom; in Western societies the people form teams, called political parties, so they can trade mean-spirited behavior back and forth.

Being offensive in a foreign country is quite different. It can cost you money and inconvenience. If your behavior poisons a few wells, fellow citizens who follow your route later will pay for it. Nobody gains, everybody loses and the pity is that all too frequently offense is given unintentionally by tourists who are, in real life, sober, decent and kindly folk.

There is a good Mexican example of the trouble they can make without trying. If you lift your left forearm vertically and hit the bottom of the elbow with the palm of the other hand—precisely the action you might take to swat a mosquito—you can deliver one of the more deadly of all insults. It's doubtful that many Mexicans could explain how this gesture acquired its meaning. Possibly there is no living Mexican who knows. But of its meaning, there is no doubt: It is a way of urging someone to have an incestuous relationship with his mother.

In Guadalajara the Tapatio Hotel, alert to such matters, has a leaflet for tourists with cars, warning them that tapping out "Shave and a Haircut, Two Bits" on the car horn carries the same message and must be rated dangerous. That is thoughtful service.

In Arabia, to cross your legs in such a way that you display the sole of your foot to your host is a grievous affront. In Spain it is grossly insulting to offer to split the bill in a restaurant. In Japan, don't sneeze in public even if you have to. In Mexico, never come straight to the point in a business discussion, instead engage in social chitchat and pick up the subject incidentally. But these are among gaffes that will occur rarely and will usually be perceived as ignorance rather than bad manners, the one being better than the other.

More pervasive harm is done subtly. Americans, Canadians and Germans have a reputation for loud talk. Those of us whose hearing is failing may see nothing wrong with clear, resonant speech but many other nationalities perceive it as arrogance and boorishness. Before they took the cure recently in the rearrangement of international exchange rates, Americans aroused distaste when abroad by waving handfuls of dollars in the air. The filthy filthy stuff was exactly what the natives were after, but quietly, please. Some nationalities, like the British, feel that paying money for goods or services is like some of the body functions which, although fundamental to good health, should be conducted in private and without comment.

When taking a taxi in parts of Arabia, it is not advisable to say, "Take me to the airport." Rather, one suggests that a trip to the airport might be pleasant. What does the driver say to such a thought?

The driver knows you want to go to the airport and nowhere else and that he is going to earn a fare by driving you there and nowhere else. But it chafes him to receive an order when a suggestion can serve just as well.

The logic does not matter. Always keep repeating to yourself, "I am not in my own country." Say it whenever you brush your teeth, provided you brush after every meal. Also, say it, three times, whenever you become irritated by some foreigners' habits.

The asking of directions often leads to irritation. There are only a few countries where people give good directions. One is Britain, where the bobbies are trained to do it without ever lifting an arm and pointing. (If they pointed, it is thought that traffic might be halted or misdirected.)

In Japan, Latin America, the Mediterranean countries and many others, a tourist who is lost must make a conscious effort to avoid being misdirected. This is done by never signaling the kind of answer you would like to get. Say, "Could you direct me to the post office?" but never say "The post office is straight, isn't it?"

The second question invites a yes or no answer and since it is rude to say no you will be told yes, even though you are walking directly away from the place you want to be. This compulsion to be polite instead of helpful encourages crankiness in a weary traveler but bite your tongue. It is their country and their custom, not yours. Somehow, they have got along all these years with a prohibition on the word no.

Clothing, and particularly the lack of it, is a constant cause of irritation and dismay. Some reactions in other countries are predictable, or should be. Where women use their dress as a hiding place, there may be toleration for foreign women in clothes that fit them. That toleration seldom extends to places of worship. But clothing taboos are no longer clear-cut. In some conservative states such as Greece, nude beaches have been established where foreigners may follow their peculiar custom by looking only at one another.

Sex, of course, rears its lovely, foolish head. Poets and other people prone to error are wrong about the language of love being universal. Many women have ended a happy day in a sad dispute with a highly insulted native at the hotel room door. She may not be conscious of it but she has been giving the wrong signals about their relationship all day.

It occurs in reverse, too. Liberated women of the English-speaking world who believe Europeans and others to be more sophisticated than men at home sometimes find they are not. More than one young man, a guide, a misguided guide who cannot distinguish between dalliance and alliance, has forsaken his nation's thousand years of culture and traveled to such places as Bismarck, N.D., where his one true love has spoken in this way: "Juan, what a wonderful surprise. We must grab a bite of lunch some day before you go home."

Anybody can understand that foreigners resent tourists with attitudes of superiority. It is not always easy to recognize how easy it is to appear condescending, particularly in third world countries where so many public services are, to put it bluntly, inferior.

On a recent visit to Yemen, I was assured by a tourist official that under the new republican government all education was free, including education at university level, and that hospital care was also available to all. Whatever the speed of the present government's programs, it is painfully obvious that there are so few schools, so few schoolteachers, so few universities and hospitals that his statement was preposterous. But why say so?

I responded by saying that this seemed excellent government policy. This enabled him to dispose of the matter honorably by commenting that, of course, not all the new policies had yet been implemented. Amity was preserved. A decade or two ago, I didn't think as quickly as that.

As we near the year 2000, tens of millions of people of a hundred nations travel abroad, if not for fun then to work. Everyone knows some of the errors because he has already made them himself. Also, most people know that tourists mean profits. That always helps. And there is not that much unconscious offensiveness that won't yield to the treatment of a little more knowledge beforehand, a little less haste in acting and speaking the genuine expressions of curiosity and joy in your new surroundings and the good old simple smile.

Finally, man being an experimenting animal, he is apt to welcome the new and the strange in his life, and even when not new, tourists are strange.

Once in Quebec City, when I was attending a changing of the guard of the Royal 22d Regiment, the scarlet-coated regimental band fell silent for one of the more heavy moments of that solemn function and a proper hush descended on us. Then there floated overhead a clear, cornfed female voice out of Kansas: "Do they change the orchestra too?"

Was any Canadian insulted? Hardly. Bless the woman; she offered us that day a delightfully different perspective on a custom we had been allowing to petrify for a century or so. I remember her better than the ceremony.

Hospitals Bend Some Rules to Accommodate Gypsy Customs (1985)

Mary Kay Quinlan

Gannett News Service

WASHINGTON—When Dr. James D. Thomas began his internship at Boston's Massachusetts General Hospital four years ago, one of his patients was a 45-year-old Gypsy woman with severe health problems—a history of heart attacks and kidney failure among others.

The woman and her extended network of Gypsy family and friends, whom he eventually treated, intrigued him, even though it often meant bending hospital rules to the breaking point to accommodate Gypsy customs.

Thomas found, for example, that the best way to prevent a riot when a 47-year-old Gypsy man lay dying—a victim of 10 heart attacks, numerous strokes and diabetes—was to perform cardiopulmonary resuscitation while wheeling his bed from intensive care to a room where he could die by an open window with a candle under the bed to light his spirit's way to heaven.

The 60 to 80 friends and relatives standing by then engaged in a 15-minute "anguished ritual" of pulling out their hair and wailing, Thomas said, "and then it was over."

The candle ritual at a Gypsy's death is "non-negotiable," and hospitals that have tried to prevent it have pandemonium, he said.

"They're sort of a people you read about but never really believe they exist," said Thomas, now a cardiologist at the Medical Center Hospital of Vermont in Burlington.

Thomas is one of the few American doctors to try to systematically study the health of this little-known minority. He has been welcomed into Gypsy homes and invited to Gypsy rituals, like death feasts.

Two Gypsy families he became acquainted with in Boston even moved to Burlington so he could continue to treat them, renting fortune-telling space in a prime commercial location downtown.

"They're a tight cultural group that have resisted integration into our society fiercely," he said.

One of the least known of the nation's ethnic minorities, Gypsies, who speak an unwritten language called Romani, trace their ancestors to northern India.

Scholars believe they began migrating west more than 1,000 years ago. Europe is now home to an estimated 5 million Gypsies, and an estimated 500,000 live in the United States, mostly in urban areas. The largest concentrations of Gypsies are believed to be in Los Angeles, Chicago, Boston and New York, as well as communities in Virginia, Texas and West Coast states.

Gypsy culture restricts contact with non-Gypsies. Illiteracy is high, and children attend school irregularly, often dropping out altogether as teen-agers to marry, with mates usually arranged by the parents.

Thomas said Gypsies make frequent use of the medical system, partly because of a lifestyle that is not "heart-healthy" and probably also because of hereditary characteristics that cause 90 percent to have diabetes by age 50.

But at the same time, they seem very frightened by illness and "often can't distinguish between (the severity of) a sprained ankle and a heart attack," he added.

Gypsies generally start smoking regularly as young children, shun exercise and eat foods high in salt, spices and fat—except during Lent, when, as Orthodox Catholics, they eat a strict diet of vegetables and fish.

"They could do this for their religion," Thomas said, "but they couldn't do it the rest of the year."

He said his Gypsy patients "can tell you why they should stop smoking, exercise and lose weight, but they say, 'I wouldn't be a Gypsy if I did that.'"

Thomas said he soon learned the only way to deal with his Gypsy patients was to respect their customs, deal with health problems that he could correct and not get frustrated by the rest.

From Pocho (1959)

José Antonio Villareal

He had been asking her questions again, and she was a little angry. She always became quiet when he asked her things. Suddenly she sat down and pulled him onto her lap. She held his head against her breasts, and her heart was beating through her dress loudly. She talked but she would not let him move his head to see her face.

"Look, little son," she said. "Many times I do not answer you when you ask me things, and other times I simply talk about something else. Sometimes this is because you ask things that you and I should not be talking about, but most of the time it is because I am ashamed that I do not know what you ask. You see, we are simple people, your father and I. We did not have the education because we came from the poorest class of people in México. Because I was raised by Spanish people, I was taught to read and write. I even went to school for a time, but your father did not, and it was only because, from the time he was a small boy, he decided he would never be a peón, that he taught himself to read and write. But that is all we can do, read and write. We cannot teach you the things that you want us to teach you. And I am deeply ashamed that we are going to fail in a great responsibility—we cannot guide you, we cannot select your reading for you, we cannot even talk to you in your own language.

"No, let me finish telling you. Already I can see that books are your life. We cannot help you, and soon we will not even be able to encourage you, because you will be obliged to work. We could not afford to spare you to go to school even if there was a way for you to do it, and there is a great sadness in our hearts."

"But my father wants me to go to school. Always he tells me that, and he never takes me out of school to work, the way the other men do with their children," said Richard.

"I know. But he talks aloud to drown out the thoughts in his head and the knowledge in his heart. Inside, he knows that it is inevitable that you will have to go to work soon, for you are the only boy in the family, and when you are in the secondary school, maybe it will be the end of your education."

Her words frightened him, because she was so sure of what she was saying, and he knew that she was telling him this to save him from heartbreak at some later time; then he thought of a thing that gave him hope. "I will finish the secondary, Mamá. Of that I am sure—as long as we live in town. My father cannot take me out of school until I become of age, and I will be too young. Then, after that, things might be different and I can continue on. Anyway, the girls can help out."

"What you say is true about the secondary school, but we cannot expect help from the girls much longer. They are growing up, and soon they will begin to marry. Their business and their responsibility will be with their husbands and their husbands' families."

"But they are young girls yet." He refused to be discouraged. "They will not possibly marry soon."

"Young? I was carrying your sister Concha when I was younger than she is now. No, my son, I know what I am telling you is true. Your father talks about you being a lawyer or a doctor when we return to México, but he knows that you will be neither and that he will never leave this place."

"But that was in México," he said. "In México, women marry young, but here we are Americans and it is different. Take the case of my teachers who are twenty-five or almost thirty years old and they have not married!"

"That is different," she explained patiently, "for they are cotorronas and will never marry. Here in your country, teachers are all cotorronas. They are not allowed to marry."

"Why?"

"I do not know. Maybe it is because parents do not want married women to have such intimate relationships with their children. I do not know."

How silly! he thought. *Mothers* are married, and what is more intimate than a child and its mother? But he did not say this to her, because his thoughts suddenly switched into English, and it occurred to him that his mother always followed rules and never asked why of them. He had known this but had never honestly accepted it, because it seemed such a loss to him to accept the fact that his mother was not infallible. And yet in a sense she was right, for Miss Crane and Miss Broughton and two or three others were close to seventy and were still called "Miss."

Back in Spanish, he remembered what she had just said about the professions, and knew that she wanted that for him and the family more than any other thing, with the possible exception of the priesthood, and, of course, that was impossible, because he was the only son and his father would undoubtedly shoot himself if his only son became a priest. He could almost hear his father say, when she timidly sought his reaction to such a possibility, "Make nuns of all the females if that will make you happy—let the boy be, for he is on earth for other things!" And Richard smiled that he would be spared that, at least. Then he suddenly felt a responsibility so heavy as to be a physical pressure, and first he became sad that his lot was a dictate and that his parents believed so strongly in the destiny, and then he was angry that traditions could take a body and soul—for he had a soul; of that he was certain—and mold it to fit a pattern. He spoke out then, but not in anger, saying things he sensed but did not really understand, an uncomprehending child with the strong desire to have a say in his destiny, with the willfull words of a child but with the knowledge and fear that his thoughts could not possibly come true.

"Then perhaps it is just as well that I cannot go on to school," he said. "For I do not intend to be a doctor or a lawyer or anything like that. If I were to go to school only to learn to work at something, then I would not do it. I would just work in the fields or in the cannery or something like that. My father would be disappointed in me if I did get an education, so it does not matter. When the time comes, I will do what I have to do."

She was surprised at his words, and she knew then that though she could understand him better than most people, she would never really get to know him.

"But all this reading, my son," she asked. "All this studying—surely it is for something? If you could go to the university, it would be to learn how you could make more money than you would make in the fields or the cannery. So you can change our way of living somewhat, and people could see what a good son we had, and it would make us all something to respect. Then, when you married and began your family, you would have a nice home and could be assured that you would be able to afford an education for your children."

He was disappointed and tried to keep the bitterness from his voice, but could not quite succeed. "And I am supposed to educate my children so they can change my way of living and they theirs, and so on? Ah, Mamá! Try to understand me. I want to learn, and that is all. I do not want to be something—I *am*. I do not care about making a lot of money and about what other people think and about the family in the way you speak. I have to learn as much as I can, so that *I* can live . . . learn for *me*, for *myself*—Ah, but I cannot explain to you and you would not understand me if I could!

Whatever bond they had shared for a while was now gone. The magic of the moment was broken, and she talked to him once again as his superior, and her voice had that old trace of impersonal anger. "But that is wrong, Richard," she said. "That kind of thinking is wrong and unnatural—to have that kind of feeling against the family and the custom. It is as if you were speaking against the Church.

They were standing now, and she moved to the table where the masa was, and began to roll out tortillas. He tried to make her see him in his way. "Mamá, do you know what happens to me when I read? All those hours that I sit, as you sometimes say, 'ruining my eyes'? If I do ruin them, it would be worth it, for I do not need eyes where I go then. I travel, Mamá. I travel all over the world, and sometimes out of this whole universe, and I go back in time and again forward. I do not know I am here, and I do not care. I am always thinking of you and my father except when I read. Nothing is important to me then, and I even forget that I am going to die sometime. I know that I have so much to learn and so much to see that I cannot possibly have enough time to do it all, for the Mexican people are right when they say that life is only a breath. I do not know that I will find time to make a family, for the important thing is that I must learn, Mamá! Cannot you understand that?"

"I have told you I understand very little. I know only that you are blasphemous and you want to learn more in order to be more blasphemous still—if that is possible. I know that we cannot live in a dream, because everything else around us is real."

"But that is exactly what I mean, Mamá. Everything does not necessarily have to be real. Who said that everything has to be real, anyway?"

She was perplexed, because she had got into a discussion in spite of her ignorance, yet she was intelligent enough to find her only answer. "I do not know, but I would say God said so. Yes, God must have said so, because He says everything. When you think of Him in the way you should, you will find the answers to any question you might have."

"It is too late for that, because I cannot believe everything that He says or said." He was deeply sorry that he must hurt her. He tried to ease her feelings, but was certain that in the end he would hurt her more. "You know, Mamá, it is partly because of that that I need to learn. I believe in God, Mamá—I believe in the Father, the Son, and the Holy Ghost, but I do not believe everything I am told about Him. Last year I tried to reach Him, to talk to Him about it. I used to go out into the orchards or the meadows and concentrate and concentrate, but I never saw Him or heard His voice or that of one of His angels. And I was scared, because if He willed it so, I knew that the earth would open and it would swallow me up because I dared to demand explanations from Him. And yet I wanted so desperately to know that I found courage to do it. Then, after a long time that I did this, I stopped and tried to find Him in church, because I would be safer there; He would not destroy a churchful of people just because of me. But I never saw Him or heard Him. Then, one day, I knew that indeed He *could* destroy the church, because if He could do the best thing in the world, He could also do the most evil thing in the world. Who am I, I thought, to dare bring out that which is cruel in Him? He *is* cruel, you know Mamá, but I believe in Him just the same. If I learn enough, I may sometime learn how to talk to Him. Some people do. You yourself have told me of miracles."

His mother looked at him as if he were not her son. She was frightened, and he thought she wanted to send him away, but she was his mother and loved him, and therefore she conquered her fear and held him and cried, "I have really lost you, my son! You are the light of my life and I have already lost you," she said. In spite of himself, his mother's tears always made him cry, and they rocked in each other's arms. For a moment, I thought that I had given birth to the Devil in a little angel's body, and

I knew that I could not bear the child I carry now in my womb. It will be born dead, I thought to myself—but only for a moment did I think that, my son. Forgive me, little one! Forgive me!"

His fear made him half believe that he was the Devil incarnate. Later, when his new sister was delivered stillborn and his mother almost died, he was griefstricken with the knowledge that he was to blame.

So now I have added murder and almost matricide to my evilness, he thought in his heart, but his mind knew that the tragedy had in no way been his fault. The senile midwife who worked the neighborhood was as much to blame as his mother, who obstinately refused to go to the hospital because of a certainty the doctor would be a man and would look at her private parts.

It is unpleasant to go alone, even to be drowned.
Russian proverb

Puerto Rican Paradise (1967)

Piri Thomas

Poppa didn't talk to me the next day. Soon he didn't talk much to anyone. He lost his night job—I forget why, and probably it was worth forgetting—and went back on home relief. It was 1941, and the Great Hunger called Depression was still down on Harlem.

But there was still the good old WPA. If a man was poor enough, he could dig a ditch for the government. Now Poppa was poor enough again.

The weather turned cold one more time, and so did our apartment. In the summer the cooped-up apartments in Harlem seem to catch all the heat and improve on it. It's the same in the winter. The cold, plastered walls embrace that cold from outside and make it a part of the apartment, till you don't know whether it's better to freeze out in the snow or by the stove, where four jets, wide open, spout futile, blue-yellow flames. It's hard on the rats, too.

Snow was falling. "My *Cristo*," Momma said, "*qué frio*. Doesn't that landlord have any *corazón*?[1] Why don't he give more heat?" I wondered how Pops was making out working a pick and shovel in that falling snow.

Momma picked up a hammer and began to beat the beat-up radiator that's copped a plea from so many beatings. Poor steam radiator, how could it give out heat when it was freezing itself? The hollow sounds Momma beat out of it brought echoes from other freezing people in the building. Everybody picked up the beat and it seemed a crazy, good idea. If everybody took turns beating on the radiators, everybody could keep warm from the exercise.

We drank hot cocoa and talked about summertime. Momma talked about Puerto Rico and how great it was, and how she'd like to go back one day, and how it was warm all the time there and no matter how poor you were over there, you could always live on green bananas, *bacalao*,[2] and rice and beans. "*Dios mío*," she said, "I don't think I'll ever see my island again."

"Sure you will, Mommie," said Miriam, my kid sister. She was eleven. "Tell us, tell us all about Porto Rico."

"It's not Porto Rico, it's Puerto Rico," said Momma.

"Tell us, Moms," said nine-year-old James, "about Puerto Rico."

Yeah, Mommie," said six-year-old José.

Even the baby, Paulie, smiled.

Moms copped that wet-eyed look and began to dream-talk about her *isla verde*,[3] Moses' land of milk and honey.

"When I was a little girl," she said, "I remember the getting up in the morning and getting the water from the river and getting the wood for the fire and the quiet of the greenlands and the golden color of the morning sky, the grass wet from the *lluvia*[4] . . . *Ai, Dios*, the *coquís*[5] and the *pajaritos*[6] making all the *música* . . ."

"Mommie, were you poor?" asked Miriam.

"*Sí, muy pobre*, but very happy. I remember the hard work and the very little bit we had, but it was a good little bit. It counted very much. Sometimes when you have too much, the good gets lost within and you have to look very hard. But when you have a little, then the good does not have to be looked for so hard."

"Moms," I asked, "did everybody love each other—I mean, like if everybody was worth something, not like if some weren't important because they were poor—you know what I mean?"

"*Bueno hijo,* you have people everywhere who, because they have more don't remember those who have very little. But in Puerto Rico those around you share *la pobreza*[7] with you and they love you, because only poor people can understand poor people. I like *los Estados Unidos,* but it's sometimes a cold place to live—not because of the winter and the landlord not giving heat but because of the snow in the hearts of the people."

"Moms, didn't our people have any money or land?" I leaned forward, hoping to hear that my ancestors were noble princes born in Spain.

"Your grandmother and grandfather had a lot of land, but they lost that."

"How come, Moms?"

"Well, in those days there was nothing of what you call *contratos,*[8] and when you bought or sold something, it was on your word and a handshake, and that's the way your *abuelos*[9] bought their land and then lost it."

"Is that why we ain't got nuttin' now?" James asked pointedly.

"Oh, it—"

The door opened and put an end to the kitchen yak. It was Poppa coming home from work. He came into the kitchen and brought all the cold with him. Poor Poppa, he looked so lost in the clothes he had on. A jacket and coat, sweaters on top of sweaters, two pairs of long johns, two pairs of pants, two pairs of socks, and a woolen cap. And under all that he was cold. His eyes were cold; his ears were red with pain. He took off his gloves and his fingers were stiff with cold.

"Como está?"[10] said Momma. "I will make you coffee."

Poppa said nothing. His eyes were running hot frozen tears. He worked his fingers and rubbed his ears, and the pain made him make faces. "Get me some snow, Piri," he said finally.

I ran to the window, opened it and scraped all the snow on the sill into one big snowball and brought it to him. We all watched in frozen wonder as Poppa took that snow and rubbed it on his ears and hands.

"Gee, Pops, don't it hurt?" I asked.

"*Sí,* but it's good for it. It hurts a little first, but it's good for the frozen parts."

I wondered why.

"How was it today?" Momma asked.

"Cold. My God, ice cold."

Gee, I thought, *I'm sorry for you, Pops. You gotta suffer like this.*

"It was not always like this," my father said to the cold walls. "It's all the fault of the damn depression."

"Don't say 'damn,'" Momma said.

"Lola, I say 'damn' because that's what it is—*damn.*"

And Momma kept quiet. She knew it was "damn."

My father kept talking to the walls. Some of the words came out loud, others stayed inside. I caught the inside ones—the damn WPA, the damn depression, the damn home relief, the damn poorness, the damn cold, the damn crummy apartments, the damn look on his damn kids, living so damn damned and his not being able to do a damn thing about it.

And Momma looked at Poppa and at us and thought about her Puerto Rico and maybe being there where you didn't have to wear a lot of extra clothes and feel so full of damns, and how when she was a little girl all the green was wet from the *lluvias*.

And Poppa looking at Momma and us, thinking how did he get trapped and why did he love us so much that he dug in damn snow to give us a piece of chance? And why couldn't he make it from home, maybe, and keep running?

And Miriam, James, José, Paulie and me just looking and thinking about snowballs and Puerto Rico and summertime in the street and whether we were gonna live like this forever and not know enough to be sorry for ourselves.

The kitchen all of a sudden felt warmer to me, like being all together made it like we wanted it to be. Poppa made it into the toilet and we could hear everything he did, and when he finished, the horsey gurgling of the flushed toilet told us he'd soon be out. I looked at the clock and it was time for "Jack Armstrong, the All-American Boy."

José, James, and I got some blankets and, like Indians, huddled around the radio digging the All-American Jack and his adventures, while Poppa ate dinner quietly. Poppa was funny about eating— like when he ate, nobody better bother him. When Poppa finished, he came into the living room and stood there looking at us. We smiled at him, and he stood there looking at us.

All of a sudden he yelled, "How many wanna play 'Major Bowes' Amateur Hour'?"

"Hoo-ray! Yeah, we wanna play," said José.

"Okay, first I'll make some taffy outta molasses, and the one who wins first prize gets first choice at the biggest piece, okay?" "Yeah, hoo-ray, *chevere.*"

Gee, Pops, you're great, I thought, *you're the swellest, the bestest Pops in the whole world, even though you don't understand us too good.*

When the candy was all ready, everybody went into the living room. Poppa came in with a broom and put an empty can over the stick. It became a microphone, just like on the radio.

"Pops, can I be Major Bowes?" I asked.

"Sure, Piri," and the floor was mine.

"Ladies and gentlemen," I announced, "tonight we present 'Major Bowes' Amateur Hour,' and for our first number—"

"Wait a minute, son, let me get my ukelele," said Poppa. "We need music."

Everybody clapped their hands and Pops came back with his ukelele.

"The first con-tes-tant we got is Miss Miriam Thomas."

"Oh, no not me first, somebody else goes first," said Miriam, and she hid behind Momma.

"Let me! Let me!" said José.

Everybody clapped.

"What are you gonna sing, sir?" I asked.

"Tell the people his name," said Poppa.

"Oh yeah. Presenting Mr. José Thomas. And what are you gonna sing, sir?"

I handed José the broom with the can on top and sat back. He sang very well and everybody clapped.

Everyone took a turn, and we all agreed that two-year-old Paulie's "gurgle, gurgle" was the best song, and Paulie got first choice at the candy. Everybody got candy and eats and thought how good it was to be together, and Moms thought it was wonderful to have such a good time even if she wasn't in Puerto Rico where the grass was wet with *lluvia*. Poppa thought about how cold it was gonna be tomorrow, but then he remembered tomorrow was Sunday and he wouldn't have to work, and he said so and Momma said, "*Sí,* "and the talk got around to Christmas and how maybe things would get better.

The next day the Japanese bombed Pearl harbor.

"My God," said Poppa. "We're at war."

"*Dios mío,*" said Momma.

I turned to James. "Can you beat that," I said.

"Yeah," he nodded. "What's it mean?"

"What's it mean?" I said. "You gotta ask, dopey? It means a rumble is on, and a big one, too."

I wondered if the war was gonna make things worse than they were for us. But it didn't. A few weeks later Poppa got a job in an airplane factory. "How about that?" he said happily. "Things are looking up for us."

Things *were* looking up for us, but it had taken a damn war to do it. A lousy rumble had to get called so we could start to live better. I thought, *How do you figure this crap out?*

I couldn't figure it out, and after a while I stopped thinking about it. Life in the streets didn't change much. The bitter cold was followed by the sticky heat; I played stickball, marbles, and Johnny-on-the-Pony, copped girls' drawers and blew pot. War or peace—what difference did it really make?

Piri Thomas, born in Spanish Harlem in 1928, began writing while in prison for armed robbery. His books include Down These Mean Streets *(1967);* Savior, Savior Hold My Hand *(1972);* Seven Times Long *(1974); and* The View from El Barrio *(1978).*

---

[1]heart
[2]codfish
[3]green island
[4]rain
[5]small treetoads
[6]little birds
[7]poverty
[8]contracts
[9]grandparents
[10]How are you?

Japanese-American Cultural Clash (1990)
Deborah L. Jacobs

John Artise's frequent tip to Japanese managers—"Don't ask a job applicant personal questions."—is often greeted with surprise. Without information on employees' religion, upbringing or home life, Japanese managers ask him, "How are we going to know them and trust them?"

As a vice president of Drake Beam Morin Inc., a New York career counseling firm, Mr. Artise conducts seminars for Japanese managers about the American workplace. Along with lawyers, other consultants and corporate officials, he says that clashes in custom, culture and management style have been a growing source of legal embroilments for Japanese companies doing business here.

Although litigation on employment issues also plagues their American counterparts, Japanese managers in the United States may be less sensitive to a multiracial society and unfamiliar with the legal constraints on employment practices, lawyers say. While many cases—among them claims of discrimination based on sex, age, and national origin—are legitimate, others stem from cultural misunderstandings or different philosophies about promotion and advancement.

Japanese firms commonly have at least one employment lawsuit pending against them, said Yoshihiro Tsurumi, a professor of international business at Baruch College, City University of New York, and a consultant. When a company loses a case, it can expect to pay at least $20 million in damages and litigation costs, he said.

To minimize the risk, Japanese companies have taken a variety of pre-emptive measures, issuing handbooks and videotapes and giving seminars on American employment law. Many are "making a concerted effort to bring in senior-level Americans," said Christine R. Houston, a recruiter with TASA Inc., a New York executive search firm.

But "even if you manage well, you have a chance of being sued," said Jiro Murase, a partner at Marake, Murase & White, a New York law firm with many Japanese clients.

The legal foundation for employment lawsuits against Japanese companies is the United States Supreme Court's 1982 decision in a case brought by female secretaries who alleged they were discriminated against in promotions at Sumitomo Shoji America Inc. . . . The Court held that a wholly owned American subsidiary of a Japanese company is technically an American corporation, and therefore bound by American law.

Under a consent decree that expired in June, Sumitomo was required to help non-Japanese employees achieve positions of responsibility in the company, said Ronald Green, a lawyer at Epstein, Becker & Green, who represents Sumitomo. As part of that "localization" effort, the company has installed a performance evaluation system comparable to those used at American companies, said Thomas Stirpay, Sumitomo's vice president for human resources.

Other recent cases include a suit against NEC Electronics Inc. brought by two American executives who alleged that the company had denied them retirement and other benefits. Thomas McDonald, vice president of administration and a board member, and Edward A. Neubauer, senior vice president of sales and marketing, said NEC officials induced them to stay at the company and then deprived them of the authority they had been promised. Seeking more than $62 million in damages between them, the managers contended they were the victims of "anti-American bias," and that the company retaliated against them when they expressed concern about personnel practices that might violate United States law. NEC denied the allegations. The case was settled in December for an undisclosed sum.

The most frequent complaint in employment suits against Japanese companies is that American personnel—particularly women—are treated unfairly. "The idea of giving women really equal treatment is still foreign for a lot of Japanese men," said Robert Christopher, author of "The Japanese Mind."

Carolyn York, hired as a secretary five years ago by Canon U.S.A. Inc., said she decided to sue the company after her requests for advancement were repeatedly denied. In her $3.8 million suit, scheduled for trial next month in Federal District Court in Dallas, Ms. York alleges she was sexually harassed by two supervisors and that the company favored Japanese men for managerial positions.

"They dragged me along for the ride, with me thinking I would get promoted and then they decided I was not going to be promoted," said Ms. York. An attorney for Canon said the company would have no comment.

Although class action lawsuits have declined in recent years, as judges more strictly apply the rules for bringing these cases, courts have allowed pending suits against both C. Itoh & Company (America), and the Mitsubishi Bank Ltd. to go forward as class actions. In the C. Itoh case, the court defined the class as all past and present female employees in the company's New York office who have suffered sex discrimination since December 1981. The court in the Mitsubishi case defined class even more broadly, to cover non-Oriental employees in the company's New York office denied promotions "on the basis of ancestry, race, or ethnic background" since March 1985.

Advice on handling the American legal system is increasingly easy to come by. Rita Risser, a San Jose, Calif., employment lawyer whose practice once included cases against Japanese companies, now advises American and Japanese firms on employment law. Lawyers at the firm of O'Melveny & Myers have written a book for Japanese clients about doing business in the United States, including a chapter on labor law issues, said Charles G. Bakaly, a partner.

At Mitsui & Company (U.S.A.), managers can view a videotape about American employment law and attend "acculturation," seminars, said William Manfredi, general manager of human resources.

The Mitsubishi International Corporation has put in place what it calls a long-range career path for its American managers, including periodic promotion reviews and rotation of staff to Japan. The program is designed "to retain employees of high potential," said Tsuginari Ono, the company's personnel director. And in part, he added, to "avoid lawsuits by local people."

Deborah L. Jacobs, based in Brooklyn, writes on business issues.

JEWS

POPULATION: 2.2 million	**PHYSICAL CHARACTERISTICS:** *Fixed noses, capped teeth, mink coats*
RELIGION: *3 branches: Litigation, Wholesale, Fund raising* **PRACTICING:** 2.2 million	**RACIAL TRAITS (GOOD):** *Rich* *Stay with own kind* *Despise the English* **RACIAL TRAITS (BAD):** *Christ Killer (Archaic)*
LOCATION: *New York City and this year's Miami Beach hotel*	**DIET STAPLE:** *Chicken Chow Mein*

CHAPTER 5

FAMILY

The Well-Baked Man (1984)
[Pima]

The Magician had made the world but felt that something was missing. "What could it be?" he thought. "What could be missing?" Then it came to him that what he wanted on this earth was some beings like himself, not just animals. "How will I make them?" he thought. First he built himself a *horno*, an oven. Then he took some clay and formed it into a shape like himself.

Now, Coyote was hanging around the way he usually does, and when Magician, who was Man Maker, was off gathering firewood, Coyote quickly changed the shape of that clay image. Man Maker built a fire inside the *horno*, then put the image in without looking at it closely.

After a while the Magician said: "He must be ready now." He took the image and breathed on it, whereupon it came to life. "Why don't you stand up?" said Man Maker. "What's wrong with you?" The creature barked and wagged its tail. "Ah, oh my, Coyote has tricked me," he said. "Coyote changed my being into an animal like himself."

Coyote said, "Well, what's wrong with it? Why can't I have a pretty creature that pleases me?"

"Oh my, well, all right, but don't intefere again." That's why we have the dog; it was Coyote's doing.

So Man Maker tried again. "They should be companions to each other," he thought. "I shouldn't make just one." He shaped some humans who were rather like himself and identical with each other in every part.

"What's wrong here?" Man Maker was thinking. Then he saw. "Oh my, that won't do. How can they increase?" So he pulled a little between the legs of one image, saying: "Ah, that's much better." With his fingernail he made a crack in the other image. He put some pleasant feeling in them somewhere. "Ah, now its good. Now they'll be able to do all the necessary things." He put them in the *horno* to bake.

"They're done now," Coyote told him. So Man Maker took them out and made them come to life.

"Oh my, what's wrong?" he said. "They're underdone; they're not brown enough. They don't belong here—they belong across the water someplace." He scowled at Coyote. "Why did you tell me they were done? I can't use them here."

So the Magician tried again, making a pair like the last one and placing them in the oven. After a while he said: "I think they're ready now."

"No they aren't done yet," said Coyote. "You don't want them to come out too light again; leave them in a little longer."

"Well, all right," replied Man Maker. They waited, and then he took them out. "Oh my. What's wrong? These are overdone. There burned too dark." He put them aside. "Maybe I can use them some other place across the water. They don't belong here."

For the fourth time Man Maker placed his images inside the oven. "Now, don't interfere," he said to Coyote, "you give me bad advice. Leave me alone."

This time the Magician did not listen to Coyote but took them out when he himself thought they were done. He made them come to life, and the two beings walked around, talked, laughed, and behaved in a seemly fashion. They were neither underdone nor overdone.

"These are exactly right," said Man Maker. "These really belong here; these I will use. They are beautiful." So that's why we have the Pueblo Indians.

Based on fragments recorded in the 1880s.

An Ecological Model of Ethnic Families (1982)

John Spiegel

This chapter will describe an ecological approach to ethnic families. We think it is important at the outset to provide you with a map of the field of family therapy within which to place this approach. Therefore, we believe it will be useful to sketch an outline of the similarities and differences among various approaches into which we may plug the ecological, or, in our terminology, the transactional field approach. Of course, a map is not an exhaustive nor an in-depth analysis but rather a quick survey of the landscape.

Commonalities

All family therapies hold in common three basic ideological assumptions. They may differ in the degree to which the assumptions are articulated or held at the center of attention, but they can be located at either the explicit or implicit level in their approach to theory, diagnosis, and treatment. They are as follows.

The Systems Approach

Family therapists pay as much attention to the family (whether nuclear or extended) as a system of interactive processes as they do the individual who happens to be the identified patient or client. It is assumed that in order to help the identified patient, the family will have to change some of the habitual—or ritual—ways in which it interacts and produces insoluble problems for the patient.

However, any variation or deviation from the basic routines of family interaction will be countered by a reaction among the members to restore the previous balance, no matter how pathological its effects for one or more family members. Such resistance is expected during the course of therapy and is usually ascribed to a homeostatic mechanism within the family system.

In addition, it is thought that the way the identified patient gets trapped in dysfunctional interactions is of greater concern than the particular psychopathological label that others have attached to the patient. While the clinician may focus on diagnostic terminology for particular purposes of research or epidemiology, when he or she is seeing a family, the attention goes to family process.

The Structural Approach

In general, family therapists, of whatever persuasion, are structuralists in the tradition of Levi-Strauss (1963) and Chomsky (1965), backed up by the long tradition of psychoanalysis. The observed behavior of family members is thought to be a surface phenomenon, generated by deeper and unobservable layers of structure that must be inferred.

Family theorists conceptualize these deeper structures in various ways, but all of them look for hidden patterns: distorted or disguised interactions, disqualifications, metamessages operating at a level opposite to the message conveyed, unappreciated ego masses, undiscovered coalitions, triads, rubber boundaries, pseudomutualities, schisms and skews, cultural value systems, or whatever. The task of the therapist, then, is to bring these deeper layers to the surface so that family members can change them.

The Interdisciplinary Approach

As a rule, family therapists bring their professional or disciplinary training into their understanding of family processes not as a rigid set of guidelines but as their contribution to the pooled effort involved in the treatment process. Cotherapists, for example, are usually from different disciplines since it is believed that each profession has something to give and to learn from the others.

Despite the tendencies of psychiatrists to consider themselves *primus inter pares,* theoretical and pragmatic contributions to the therapeutic process have frequently—as in the cases of Haley (1976) and Bateson (1972)—emanated from outside the helping professions. This openness to outside influences is more characteristic of family therapy than of any other treatment technology.

Divergences

The differences among the models emerge from two sets of dichotomies: (1) theoretical concepts borrowed from one field and then applied to family therapy versus a theoretical approach growing out of the direct experience with family therapy and (2) strict focus on the family itself versus inclusion of wider institutional contexts.

With respect to the first dichotomy, some family therapists have based their work on psychoanalytic or psychodynamic theory arising from work with individuals. They have simply broadened their theoretical approach to include the different family members. This approach grew out of child psychiatry, where the therapist always looked at mother-child interactions and sometimes saw one or the other parent as a part of the therapeutic process, as exemplified in the early work of Ackerman (1958). It also emerged from work with schizophrenic patients represented in the writings of Framo (1965) and Boszormenyi-Nagy (1962).

The theory of small group psychotherapy, such as the work of Bell (1961), has also been transferred and modified for application to the family as a group. Similarly, learning theory and behavior modification techniques (frequently with the addition of cognitive theoretical components), have been applied to family therapy (Mash, Hamerlynck, & Handy, 1975). Some borrowing of theory and technique is inevitable since we all stand on the shoulders of our predecessors. What is significant here is that the borrowed technique, as for the example in the behavioral approaches, is made the clinical focus.

These techniques stand in contrast to the theories and approaches that have grown out of direct experience with families, such as Bowen's Systems Therapy (1978) that grew out of work with schizophrenics and their families; the structural approach developed by Minuchin (1974) and his coworkers at the Philadelphia Child Guidance Clinic that grew out of work with Hispanic and Black families; and the problem-solving approach developed by Watzlawick, Beavin, and Jackson (1967), Haley (1976), and others in Palo Alto, California, that grew out of work, at least at first, with schizophrenics. The fundamental differences are so basic that they cannot be seen as equivalent to each other.

For example, the innovative aspects of the structural and problemsolving approaches are often so at odds with both common sense and traditional psychodynamic theory as to require a 180-degree switch in the mind set of the therapist. They both require, often from the first interview, a direct and sometimes dramatic intervention by the therapist that bypasses the surface phenomenon to get to the deeper structures activating the family interactions. This is clearly in contrast to the wait-and-see minimal interpretive techniques of the psychodynamically oriented therapists. Where the issue is "common sense," the intervention is more complex since it frequently features a paradoxical form of communication that is alien both to the logic of ordinary communications and to the interpretive procedures of the psychodynamic approach. Similarly, both the structural and problem-solving approaches tend to focus on the here and now of dysfunctional family transactions, while waiting for the past influences on current behavior (e.g., developmental childhood experiences of family members), to appear as a matter of course. However, in order to facilitate the exposure of these hidden interactions, therapists may borrow techniques, such as family sculpting or guided fantasy, from other more psychodynamic approaches.

The point we wish to make here is that we could not have predicted the emergence of these innovative approaches from a knowledge of the prior history of the field. By the same token, we cannot, at this stage, predict their relevance in the future. For example, it is not yet apparent how the technique of paradoxical communication can be useful to the human services generally.

The Institutional Context

The models discussed so far have been concerned primarily with the family as a system in its own right. The relationships between the family and wider institutional contexts stay in the background or emerge only as a context for symptomatic behavior, such as a child with a school problem or a couple involved in a court battle because of divorce proceedings. In such instances attention may be focused for a time on the characteristics of the school or the behavior of lawyers.

There are three interrelated approaches, however, that take a different, more varied, and more flexible position with respect to family systems or subsystems and that make an effort to deal with the interface between the family and the wider social system.

The first is the ecological approach proposed by Auerswald (1968, 1972, 1974). Based on a sweeping indictment of Western ideology and cognitive styles that are compared unfavorably with Eastern belief systems, his ecological program attributes the fragmentation and specialization of our service delivery institutions to the hierarchical, linear thinking about space and time in which we have all been educated. In its place, this program proposes a more complex and flexible thought structure that examines relationships. Ecological analysis has been a small but long-standing topic in the field of experimental psychology. For a review of this topic, see Berry (1980).

Where service delivery is concerned, this means transcending the firm boundaries and the associated intake policies of agencies to make the connections that individuals and families need in order to modify the dysfunctional ways in which they are maintaining (or failing to maintain) themselves in their environmental situation. For example, we all know of and complain about the inefficiencies caused by the organizational structure and work habits of social service agencies. But after a period of time, most attempts at innovative solutions of these problems get washed away by withdrawal of funding or burnout of leadership. Often according to Auerswald (1974), it is the implicit Western thought ways that cause the counterproductive fragmentation and specialization that requires attention first.

The second of these broader approaches is network therapy, as proposed by Speck and Attneave (1973) and Pattison (1977), among others. While still entailing an ecological principle, network therapy is more pragmatic and less ideological. This model assumes that any dysfunctional stalemate in the nuclear family may well be reinforced by the extended family or by friends or significant others in the neighborhood or community, or even by relatives living at a distance.

In therapy, attempts are made to assemble components from the wider systems, to reveal whatever pathological structures are being maintained by means of the network, to identify key persons involved in the reinforcing process, and to bring others into the network who may be able to provide a more benevolent, supportive function. Attention is paid to possible support systems wherever they are located and to the cultural and ethnic issues inherent in any environmental niche occupied by the family.

The third of these broader models, the transactional field approach, is associated with my own work (Spiegel, 1971; Papajohn & Spiegel, 1975). We took the word "transactions" (which is now coming into popular usage in the professional literature) from the philosopher John Dewey and the political scientist Arthur Bentley. Looking at the whole of Western civilization, Dewey and Bentley (1950) identified two principal explanatory thought ways and then proposed a third to make up for the deficiencies of the first two.

The first, "self-action," describes an entity as operating under its own internal powers or disposition. Aristotle's explanation of gravity—that a stone falls to earth because it is disposed to go back to its natural resting place—is a prototypical self-action concept. Contemporary child development studies, which are increasingly concerned with innate qualities of the human organism, are examples of this type of thinking.

The second mode of explanation, "interaction," involves thing acting upon thing acting upon thing. The origin of interactional thinking can be traced to Newton's theory of gravity, which posits a force of attraction exerted by objects upon each other over a distance of space. All stimulus-response observations and therapeutic procedures (e.g., behavior modification) grow out of interactional thinking.

Both self-actional and interactional thinking proceed in a straight line in time and space, from first to final causes. Perhaps more importantly, they suggest dependent or independent relationships rather than systems or processes; and when applied to human relations they create "blame systems" or pejorative labels. Thus, we get schizophrenogenic mothers, passive or immature fathers, delinquents, and so on, all acting or reacting in their roles as victims or victimizers in linear (or developmental) time.

To transcend these limitations, Dewey and Bentley proposed the term "transaction," which denotes system in process with system, where no entity can be located as first or final cause. In the case of the identified patient, whatever behavior is displayed is viewed within the context of the patient's ecological niche, or—in my terms—the transactional field (see Figure 2.1).

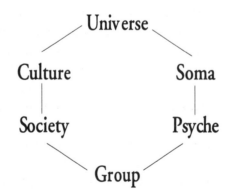

FIGURE 2.1 Organization of the transactional field.

The Universe is concerned with the nonliving world in general, all the way from the cosmos to the atomic nucleus. It includes the house or dwelling in which a family lives; the land on which that house is built; the surrounding terrain, urban or rural; the quality of the air a family breathes; and the food resources it consumes. Processes included in Universe are in transaction with processes in Soma, the anatomical structures and physiological processes within the human organism. The next focus, Psyche, takes in cognition, perception, problem-solving, conflict elaboration and reduction, emotional arousal, habit formation, and communication. Personality results from the integration of processes within Psyche, and from its transactions, on the one side, with Soma and, on the other, with the focus called Group. It is in groups such as the family, that behavior receives situational definitions and role attributions. However, groups do not exist in isolation from each other. They receive their forms and functions in accordance with their place in the larger network of social systems that we label Society. Finally, the family as a social institution, along with the other religious, educational, economic, legal, governmental, recreational, and voluntary institutions that make up Society, are anchored in a set of beliefs and values about the nature of the world and human existence known as Culture. Culture in turn contributes to the survival of a society in its ecological niche, as well as forming the basis of a people's beliefs about the nature of the Universe, thereby completing the circling of the transactional field.

Value Orientation Theory and Its Application: The United States Case

Therapeutic interventions are usually conceived as being directed at the process of conflict, anxiety, and defense systems within the individual or the family (or preferably both). The ecological approach keeps in mind that imbalance and conflict may arise from any focus in the transactional field. For example, it may begin with Society during times of economic depression, war, or rapid social change; or from Universe, as in the case of hurricanes or other natural disasters. Thus, illness, including mental illness, becomes only one aspect of destabilization, an aspect that gets overemphasized in the medical model. Making pathologies out of our imbalances and role conflicts within the family is not very helpful and may be, in fact, harmful; but making pathologies out of our value conflicts and cultural misunderstandings within ethnic or minority families can be even more harmful. Therefore, the ecological approach suggests that in families undergoing acculturation, Culture is the focus from which to begin the therapeutic process. It also recognizes that in addition to dealing with the clash of cultural norms, therapy needs to take into account the strengths within ethnic families—those cultural values that have facilitated survival in the ecological niche.

Again, the therapist working with an individual ethnic family needs to have a way to contrast his or her middle-class standards and beliefs and the values of different ethnic minorities. Table 2.1 is based on the theory of variation in cultural value orientations proposed by Kluckhohn (Kluckhohn & Strodtbeck, 1961). According to Kluckhohn, orientations are distinguished from concrete values by their levels of generality. "A value orientation is a generalized and organized conception, influencing behavior of time, of nature, of man's place in it, of man's relation to man, and of the desirable and undesirable aspects of man-environment and inter-human transactions" (Kluckhohn, 1951).

Operating within the Psyche focus of the transactional field, value orientations have three distinguishing qualities: (1) directional—they provide a program for selecting behaviors between more or less favored alternative behaviors; (2) cognitive—they provide a view of the nature of the world and of human affairs; and (3) affective—they are never taken lightly—people are ready to bleed and die for them—and they are the main reason why people and organizations become so resistant to change.

The classification of value orientations set forth in Table 2.1 is based on the following assumptions:

1. There are a limited number of common human problems for which all people in all places must find some solutions. These are:
   a. Time—the temporal focus of human life
   b. Activity—the preferred pattern of action in interpersonal relations
   c. The Relational Orientation—the preferred way of relating in groups
   d. The Man-Nature Orientation—the way people relate to the natural or the supernatural environment
   e. The Basic Nature of Man—the attitudes held about the innate good or evil in human behavior.

2. Although there is variability in the solutions to these problems, this variability is neither limitless nor random but occurs within a range of three possible solutions for each of these problems.
   a. Time—Past, Present, Future
   b. Activity—Doing, Being, Being-in-Becoming
   c. Relational—Individual, Collateral, Lineal
   d. Man-Nature—Harmony-with-Nature, Mastery-over-Nature, Subjugated-to-Nature
   e. Basic Nature of Man—Neutral/ Mixed, Good, Evil.

3. All possible solutions are in varying degrees present in the total cultural structure of every society, and every society will be characterized not only by a dominant profile of first-order value choices but also by substitute second- and third-order choices. Differences among various cultures are based on the pattern of preferences for each of these solutions in a dominant-substitute profile of values.

However, in the process of sociocultural change, second-order choices may be moved into the first order and vice versa. This is often the key to understanding generational problems between parents and children or marital difficulties, either in a cross-cultural marriage or in a marriage where one spouse is adapting faster than the other.

TABLE 2.1 Comparison of Value Orientation Profiles

	American middle class	**Italian**	**Irish**
Time	Future > Present > Past	Present > Past > Future*	Present > Past > Future
Activity	Doing > Being > Being-in-Becoming	Being > Being-in-Becoming > Doing	Being > Being-in-Becoming > Doing
Relational	Individual > Collateral > Lineal	Collateral > Lineal > Individual	Lineal > Collateral > Individual
Man–Nature	Dominant over > Subjugated > Harmony	Subjugated > Harmony > Dominant over	Subjugated > Harmony > Dominant over
Basic Nature of Man	Neutral > Evil > Good	Mixed > Evil > Good	Evil > Mixed > Good

In Table 2.1, U.S. middle-class preferences are compared with those of Southern Italian and rural Southern Irish families. Since the rank-ordered patterns for the American middle class exert the pull toward which ethnic groups move, let us begin with these mainstream values.

It is probably no great surprise that the American middle class places the Future orientation in the first-order position to the dimension of Time in human affairs. Americans plan their families, as well as their educational and occupational careers. They cut up their days and weeks into small time segments that they keep track of in little black appointment books.

Anything new becomes better than anything old, whether it be a new car, a new style, or a new idea. No one wants to be old-fashioned, left behind, or outmoded in the inexorable push for change. Youth is highly regarded as the representative of the future, while the elderly have so little future left to them they tend to take a back seat and are frequently neglected.

Mainstream Americans do take time out to live in the Present, their second-order choice. A Present-time orientation occurs in recreational situations, when people are supposed to have fun and forget about the Future. Even then, they may be so aware of taking time out they start looking at their watches, thinking, "I have to go home because I have to get up early tomorrow."

The Past is in a weak third-order position. Independence Day, Thanksgiving, and other Past-time oriented holidays are used for Present-time enjoyment, not for serious reenactment of a highly valued past. Nostalgia kicks notwithstanding, we are pro progress and anti tradition.

In the Activity dimension, the Doing orientation is at the core of the U.S. life-style. The competitiveness, the striving for upward mobility in jobs and social contacts are all associated with Doing. The first question asked of a stranger is, "What do you do?" and self-esteem depends as much (if not more) on how the world views our accomplishments than on internal standards.

Whereas Doing often involves controlling our feelings to get the job done properly and thus gain recognition, the Being alternative refers to the spontaneous expression of our inner feelings in any given situation. The second-order position of Being in the U.S. pattern is the consequence of its restriction to a limited number of contexts, such as family and recreational situations.

The Being-in-Becoming orientation shares with Being a concern with what the human being is rather than what he or she can accomplish. However, it stresses the development of different aspects of the person in a rounded and integrated fashion, which distinguishes it from the nose to the grindstone quality of Doing. We recall Leonardo da Vinci who might start an engineering project, switch to painting, and then, without having finished either, turn to anatomical dissection. Developing different interests was more important to him than getting the job done within a time frame, an alien concept to most mainstream Americans.

In the Relational dimension, the first choice of the Individual orientation reflects the preference for autonomy versus responsibility to any collectivity. Children are trained from infancy to be independent and to articulate their own needs and opinions. The separation-individuation process not only begins early, but is also continuously reinforced as the children are entrusted to baby sitters, go to nursery school, sleep over at the homes of friends, go off to summer camps, and then go away to college. Adults pursue their self interests, and if a better job beckons elsewhere a family member may just take off with a minimum of goodbye ceremony.

Every society, however, requires some responsibility to a collectivity, and the second-order choice—the Collateral orientation—in mainstream American values reflects the democratic ethos on which the nation was founded. Everyone is on the same level, and ideally power is distributed equally. At home, fathers prefer not to be strong authority figures but rather to have decisions arrived at through a family consensus. At work, the boss may assume a position of authority with an air of apologetic informality, as if to neutralize the inevitable hostility.

The Lineal or hierarchical orientation is theoretically in a weak, third-order position, but there are many ways in which it strongly intrudes itself, casting the shadow of hypocrisy upon our democratic principles. Racism is a prime example of the bias and prejudice fostered by the Lineal orientation. The bureaucratic institutions that are found in government and industry, with their tables of organization and flowcharts that channel communication from the top down (but not vice versa), are set up in lineal fashion.

Two conditions within the ecological niche require and justify the operations of the Lineal orientation (1) under conditions of material scarcity, when a strong authority is required to control aggression and competition for the scarce resources and to prevent the war of all against all and (2) in emergency situations characterized by great danger when time pressures require the leader to count on instant and unquestioned obedience. In the history of the world these two conditions have been combined and mutually reinforcing, most of the time. Western "civilized" empires and Oceanic "primitive" tribes have fought each other for the control of scarce resources. Democracy, a relative newcomer, has made its appearance only when technology, transportation, and the sharing of raw materials has reduced the scarcity and increased the availability of material goods and possessions.

The first-order choice of the Man-Nature category, Mastery-over–Nature, is based on the assumption that there are few (if any) problems that cannot be solved with the help of technology and the expenditure of vast sums of money. We have conquered infectious diseases, gone to the moon, and split the atom. Although we still have not mastered chronic illness, especially cancer and long-term mental illness, there is hope. And while a few imbalances, like war and weather, are more elusive, they are not impossible to control. Problem solving is where it is at. If parents have problems with children, husbands with wives, wives with husbands, then let us get to work. No need to suffer.

The problem is that some problems will not go away, at least not at the wave of the human hand. In that case, we switch to the second-order choice, Subjugated-to-Nature. If the experts and specialists have been unable to help, particularly with personal problems, then an appeal is likely to be made to the Deity. Or else the trouble simply has to be endured until it goes away due to the benevolence of God or natural forces.

The Mastery-over-Nature and Subjugated-to-Nature orientations are especially dichotomous, but the latter is not quite as removed from the third-order choice, Harmony-with-Nature. This assumes that there is not necessarily a clash between humans and nature but that there are many forces and influences both in the heavens and on earth (e.g., gods, demons, angels, saints, spirits, ghosts, wee folk). Human problems are thought to arise when we have not attended properly to or kept our lives in balance with all these sources of influence. So it may be that since it has not rained, the rain god may be angry, and a rain dance may help the situation. Even though many people may secretly believe in some aspects of this orientation, Harmony-with-Nature is likely to be put down as superstition or magical by mainstream Americans.

The final category, Basic Nature of Man, has undergone a change in the course of our country's short history. The position of the Puritan settlers was that people were born evil but perfectable. But, following the lead of 19th-century Humanism, the growth of secular colleges and universities, and the popularization of psychology and the social sciences during the 20th century, the concept of original sin has been displaced by the Neutral orientation. This assumes that we are born neither good nor evil, but more like a blank slate upon which the environment, the parents, the neighborhood, and the school leave their imprint during the course of growth and development. The Neutral position generates moral pragmatism as well since punishment is no longer expected from God for sins. Although it is felt that we should avoid hurting others when possible, there are no absolute prescriptions other than those legislated into law or our own inner sense of decency.

Innate Evil, in the second-order position, is, however, a continuous possibility. Fundamentalist sects have always promoted it, and born-again Christians are attempting to resurrect it. Also, large segments of the population may experience a heightened awareness of evil in periods of national stress. For example, under the stress of post World War II recovery, many Americans became convinced that government, the motion picture industry, and the media in general, had been infiltrated by Communists.

In the third-order position is the Good-but-Corruptible orientation, a view put forth by Rousseau after contemplating the noble savages described in the reports of early South Sea voyagers. It is a view held today by only a few "flower children," most of whom have disappeared into rural settings where they can cultivate goodness far from wicked civilization.

The dominant American choices in each dimension fit together nicely. Thus, if the personal achievement implied by Doing is to be facilitated, then it is good to be able to plan for the Future, as an Individual not too constrained by family or group ties, with the optimism supplied by the Mastery-over-Nature orientation, and the pragmatic morality, with which such self-interest is justified, afforded by the Neutral view of the Basic Nature of Man.

Unfortunately, this pattern also represents something of a pressure cooker, full steam ahead with little opportunity for relaxation without guilt or lowered self-esteem. It fosters a narcissistic self-involvement and allows no room for tragedy. If an airplane crashed killing hundreds of people, somebody "goofed" or the technology is to blame, and loved ones are compensated with money. Grieving ceremonies are weak or absent, and those who have suffered a loss may need the help of a therapist to undergo the separation process. Furthermore, the dominant choices have, at least in the past, applied only to men. Women have been socialized for inferior second-order alternatives—taking care of day-to-day affairs (Present), dealing with children's and husband's feelings (Being), attending to relatives and keeping in touch with friends (Collateral). The effort of the women's movement to correct this split in sex roles has been only partially successful.

Finally, there has been some resistance to the compulsive planning for the Future and the complete ignoring of the Past. Some middle class Americans refuse to wear watches or worry about the Future, while others connect with the Past by reading historical novels or biographies, collecting antiques, or keeping track of their family tree in the family Bible. Teenagers no longer feel they must postpone sexual experience until marriage, and, supported by moral pragmatism, there has been increased acceptance of both premarital and extramarital sex as well as homosexuality.

The Value Orientations of Italians and Irish

In the Time dimension, Italians and Irish are similar, both placing Present time in the first-order position. This is characteristic of most rural peoples for whom Time goes around in large cycles of anniversaries and holidays, seasons for sowing or reaping. The hours are marked by the position of the sun or the bell in the church steeple; and whether one looks back into the past or forward into the future, there is little evidence of, or expectation for, change. Only if there is an unusual problem will there be an appeal to the Past, usually by getting the advice of the elder generation.

The Future is last in both of these cultures, and one might wonder how such people could undertake the gigantic step of emigrating. The answer is that the rural economies of Southern Italy and Southern Ireland were depressed, and America was seen as a place of greater economic opportunities where one might live out a similar life-style with greater ease. Although many immigrants gave up farming, people from the same villages and families tended to go to the same cities in this country, forming "Little Italys" and Irish neighborhoods where, except for the shift from rural to urban settings, there was no need to undergo rapid sociocultural change.

In the Activity dimension, we again find similar profiles between the two ethnic groups. The Being orientation comes first, followed by Being-in–Becoming and then by Doing. The verbal emotionality of the Italians is well known; the Irish, on the other hand, are somewhat more restrained with strangers. Even with family members, the Irish often convey feelings more by subtle cues or by teasing than by words or direct confrontation.

Being-in-Becoming has an aesthetic quality for the Italians, an appreciation for physical qualities. For example, one Italian mother told us her children were doing very well in school. A mainstream American might surmise that they were getting good grades, but when asked why she thought this, the Italian mother said, "Because they have such beautiful eyes. All the teachers love them." For the Irish, the Being-in-Becoming orientation is more likely to find expression in appreciation for idiosyncrasies of character.

The fact that Doing occupies a last position for both Italians and Irish does not mean that there is any disposition to avoid hard work. However, when they come home, they talk very little about their work, unless they have a complaint or some scandal to share that will make food for gossip with the neighbors.

Gossip is the principal form of social control in rural communities or neighborhood enclaves where everyone knows everyone else.

In the Relational category, Italians prefer the Collateral orientation. Lateral relations are very important, and loyalty to the extended family system is demanded, as is both physical and emotional closeness. There is anguish over separation, which is to be avoided if at all possible. Italian husbands and fathers take the second-order Lineal position of authority only if there is strong disagreement within the family. Actually, because of the absence of a strong, superordinate authority, family (or neighborhood) arguments are apt to provoke collateral fission, a split that lends to protracted feuding.

The Individual orientation is not at all encouraged. If a child becomes too independent, he or she is scolded for being "willful" or for "having a big head." If the child persists he or she may be physically punished. But the next minute, acting out of the Being orientation, the parent is likely to pick up and hug and kiss the child.

Among the Irish, the first-order position is the Lineal orientation, which presents a unique problem. Husbands and fathers are supposed to be "the boss," but in rural Ireland the socialization of young men did not provide adequate reinforcement for this role. The farms were cut into such small pieces that the property could not be distributed to all the male children. Also, there was no system of primogeniture. It was up to the father to decide which of his sons would inherit the land; and he was in no hurry to make this decision as it would require him to retire to the "west room." Young men, with no source of stable income, were kept on pocket money and were unable to marry. The restless sons moved to the city or emigrated. Unable to marry, with no sexual outlets but prostitutes, the young men congregated in the pub. Thus drinking became "a good man's weakness," a forgivable and understandable indiscretion. When marriage finally occurred, the wife was likely to be the stronger person, ruling the family from behind the throne in order not to expose publicly the weakness of her husband. The men tended to overcompensate for this weakness through impulsive pugnacity. Sons were closer to their mothers than to their fathers, thus perpetuating the strain in the male role.

Since the Roman Catholic Church is the official religion for both groups, the Subjugated-to-Nature orientation holds the first-order position in the Man-Nature category. Suffering is expected as a part of our fate in this world. But where the Italians are pessimistic or resigned, the Irish tend to be stoical and tough-minded.

For Italians, the influence of the second-order Harmony-with-Nature orientation is still very strong. It has been partially assimilated into the church through the powers attributed to the local saint. There is also a fear of evil spirits, particularly of the power of the evil eye. The *Mal Ocho* is believed to be possessed by only certain people, and Italians are careful not to arouse their envy, especially where their children are concerned. Even second- and third-generation Italian Americans may continue to fear the evil eye, seeing it as the cause of family problems despite preliminary protests that they no longer subscribe to such superstitions.

Among the Irish, Harmony-with-Nature is manifested more by fanciful or mystical views of the powers in nature—elves, bog creatures, wee folk, and so on. It contributes to the Gaelic predilection for fantasy that is often so strong it interferes with the ability to distinguish fantasy from reality.

Few Italians or Irish take the Mastery-over-Nature orientation seriously. Even after exposure to American technology and problem solving, the optimism and hope associated with this view takes a long time to sink in.

In the Basic Nature of Man dimension, Italians hold a Mixed orientation in first place. They consider people to be born with the capacity to do good or evil, though some have more of one, some more of the other. No matter how the child turns out, it is not the fault of the parents but of fate. However, the Italians are aware of the potential for evil, particularly where male sexuality is concerned. Unmarried women are not allowed to date or be in the company of men without a chaperone. The Mixed orientation is also associated with a relaxed sense of morality. People will steal if given the opportunity, as guilt is not internalized and the only shame is to be caught.

For the Irish, the Evil orientation features a sharp awareness of sin and of the possibilities of yielding to temptation, which is always just around the corner. The harsher morality of the Irish Catholic Church as compared to the Italian led to this characteristic internalization of guilt. The Irish are also very reluctant to complain about pain or illness. This is associated not only with the tough-minded stoicism mentioned above but also with the notion that pain and illness may be God's punishments for sinful thinking or behavior.

Both Italians and Irish find mental illness in the family painful to acknowledge, but for different reasons. For Italians it is a blot on the family honor, a sign of bad blood lines. Or it may be a sign of witchcraft. For the Irish, it is another sign of punishment for sin. Both groups tend to somatize their emotional problems, thus seeming to lack insight.

In concluding this section, it may be helpful to point out the great cultural gap that Italians and Irish must traverse in order to accommodate to mainstream American value patterns. American first-order choice is in last place for these two groups. If accommodation is to occur without too much strain, it must be done slowly, over several generations.

Implications for Therapy

While ethnic families are attempting to understand and learn to implement the dominant value orientation patterns, those patterns themselves are undergoing change. The resulting confusion increases the stress of the acculturation process. This makes it very important for the family therapist to keep track of three acculturation issues: (I) the value patterns characteristic of the family's culture of origin; (2) where the family is in the acculturation process—that is, what values have been or are being changed at the time of intervention; and (3) the family's understanding or misunderstanding of mainstream American values. In the case of cross-cultural marriages, there is, of course, a fourth issue: (4) what conflicts have occurred or what compromises are being made to compensate for the differences between the two native value patterns.

Middle-class therapists, no matter what their ethnic origins, have been socialized in terms of mainstream values. The therapist will be Future oriented, expecting clients to be motivated and to keep appointments punctually. He or she will also expect families to be willing to work on therapeutic tasks (Doing), over reasonable periods of time (Future), with the prospect of change before them (Mastery-over-Nature). All this is to be done while taking a pragmatic view of moral issues (Neutral), and at the very least the therapist will expect to help clients to distance themselves from any overwhelming moral burden or intense feelings of shame. And clients will be expected to separate themselves from enmeshment in the family structure and to develop increased autonomy (Individual).

If these assumptions are open to questions, then it is very important for the therapist to be aware of the differences between his or her values and those of the ethnic families and to work out a way to resolve them (Giordano & Giordano, 1977). The principal therapeutic technique employed in our ecological approach is what we are calling the "culture broker." This is a concept borrowed from Weidman (Weidman, 1973,1975), with some modifications. The function of the culture broker also somewhat resembles Bowen's concept of the "coach" (Bowen, 1978). In this role, the therapist determines the family's value conflicts and confusions and then tries to help the family resolve them. While the therapist suggests pathways for accommodation, this is done without imposing his or her own values on the family. This requires a real effort on the part of the therapist to accept the family where it is and to respect and validate its value positions. Prior knowledge of the dominant values of the ethnic group in question is almost indispensable in such situations.

Assessment is first directed at two points: evaluating the clinical situation of the identified patient and determining his or her ethnic background and that of the spouse, as well as the characteristics of the patient's ecological niche or neighborhood. We do not take the view, subscribed to by some family therapists, that diagnosis is irrelevant. We are interested in the total transactional field and are therefore obliged to first investigate the intrapsychic processes of the identified patient and later those of other family members. Furthermore, we must maintain a liaison with other hospital departments (e.g., outpatient clinics or emergency rooms) and community mental health centers, for whom diagnosis and prognosis are important issues. However, at times we may be dealing with behavior or symptoms, such as the Puerto Rican *ataque* or the Portuguese pseudohallucination, neither of which are considered psychopathological in the eyes of the ethnic community. The following example illustrates such a case:

> A young Portuguese female whose family had been in this country for five years had
> made a suicide attempt. She had been depressed following the death of her mother the
> year before and had frequent visual and auditory hallucinations of her mother

appearing and speaking to her. The patient had jumped out a first-story open window believing that she had seen and heard her mother beckoning from the street.

Among the Portuguese such visual and auditory hallucinations are considered normal after the death of a loved one. The spirit of the deceased is considered to be active, hovering around, and interested in the affairs of family members. In fact, failure to encounter the spirit is often considered to be characteristic of an unfeeling or unloving child. But was jumping out a window considered reasonable in this context? As we did not know, we decided to ask the family and neighbors. There was a general agreement that jumping out a window was beyond the expected behavior, especially after a year from the time of death. This confirmed the clinical assessment we had arrived at on other grounds.

Determining the cultural and ethnic background can be simple or complex, depending upon the time since emigration, the number of generations in this country, and the number of intermarriages that has occurred. This determination should be included as routine in all family therapy, even though it may not be considered necessary with WASP families or those thoroughly acculturated into the middle class. Its routine absence is an indication of our cultural blindness—an insensitivity based in part on our false melting-pot ideology and in part on the therapist's wish to deny or ignore his or her own ethnicity.

Once we ask for ethnic or national background information, it is surprising how relevant it becomes, especially in the development of a genogram. However, it should be noted that it takes a long time to gather all the necessary information for a genogram. Many minorities are so involved in the Present and with their current difficulties, they do not want to spend much time talking about their ancestors. They want their problems fixed right now or as soon as possible. Also, people with a Present-time orientation often forget to keep appointments. Thus, it helps to make home visits as soon as possible, for many reasons. There are apt to be some family portraits, which helps with the genogram, and it is easier to see how roles are assigned in the family when observing them in their natural environment rather than in the artificial setting of an office. Furthermore, the therapist is likely to meet some family members who resist coming to the medical setting or who are suspicious of the intentions of the therapist. Such people are likely to find a reason to be absent on the first few visits but tend to get drawn in as family tensions begin to decrease.

For many of our ethnic and minority patients, their problems appear first as somatic symptoms, and such patients are often resentful about being referred for therapy, feeling let down by the doctors. Generally, we take the position that the complaints are real, and see to it that medical treatment is provided. We usually find that as we ask about the situation in which the symptoms appear or get worse, the information about family conflicts will gradually surface. After a while we will hear more about the family and less about the complaint, until we get to the point of being able to see the family. On the other hand, there are some families that can be seen sooner because of their concern about the identified patient.

Patients who are strongly oriented to Harmony-with-Nature, may believe that the symptoms or problems derive from an evil spirit, a family curse, the evil eye, or the ingestion of a magical substance (usually white powder surreptitiously placed in food or wine). In some cases these patients may simply not know where to find a native healer in this country. We will then make an attempt to locate such a person and to bring him or her into the treatment situation. Or, for example, if a Puerto Rican patient is already seeing a spiritist, he will attempt in some way to collaborate. Since native healers, root workers, spiritists, *curanderos,* and shamans are generally quite concerned with family relationships, it may be possible to work out an innovative (if unorthodox) form of family therapy. This kind of experimentation with alternative therapists has not happened too often in our work because many of them do not trust anyone connected with the medical establishment.

As is usually the case in therapy, the therapeutic contract develops out of the assessment procedure. Here we take a somewhat different tack—or so we believe—from most other family therapies. Because we are dealing with families based on Lineal or Collateral orientation, it is important to line ourselves up with the head of the family. This is normally the father, but in his absence it can be the mother or grandmother. Since the head of the family holds culturally sanctioned power, we would not be able to gain entree into the family without sincerely respecting that power and the objectives he or she has in mind for the family. Thus, we would not be able to get very far if we indicated that one of our goals was to obtain autonomy or individuation for a wife or daughter. However, we can identify with the values and goals of the head of the family, while offering a better way of implementing them, as in the case below:

> A Puerto Rican family had recently moved into a mixed neighborhood, and the father was terribly worried about his 15-year-old daughter's virginity. He insisted that the mother drive the daughter to and from school and would not let her date or attend school dances or other social affairs or leave the house unaccompanied by a family member. He felt that no woman could protect herself in the unsupervised presence of an attractive or seductive boy who wanted to have sex with her. He saw American sexual permissiveness and dating patterns as a disgusting and dangerous life-style.
>
> Meanwhile the daughter, though bright, had been doing poorly in school and was complaining of severe headaches—the reasons for the referral. In an individual interview she appeared depressed and acknowledged anger toward her father. However, she was afraid to confront him for fear of his violent anger at any sign of disobedience. The mother agreed with the daughter, thought the father was "crazy," but was also afraid to confront him openly.
>
> The therapist considered all the possible intrapsychic dynamics in the case: incestuous attachment of the father to the daughter; his hysterical personality formation; the daughter's repressed rage and sexual attachment to the father; and the mother's envy of the daughter and her implicit use of the daughter to retaliate against the father (triangulation).
>
> The therapist intervened through an individual interview with the father so as not to expose him to any loss of respect in front of the family— respect for the male role being of prime importance in Puerto Rican families. In the interview the therapist agreed with the father's view about the importance of maintaining control over his daughter's activities and preserving her virginity. He agreed that American dating patterns are quite permissive and that sexual intercourse under these circumstances is always a possibility, validating the father's fears. But he also pointed out that American girls usually have a great deal of unsupervised experience with boys from an early age, and that they have been trained not only how to protect themselves but also how to control their own feelings and behavior. Then the therapist explained the position of the daughter. She had been "grounded" prior to any misconduct, and it was suggested that this undeserved punishment was likely to bring out the very behavior it was designed to prevent. He then suggested to the father that it might be better to allow her some experience so that she could learn how to handle herself in these circumstances. It was further pointed out that she could come home and talk to him about it afterward.

> To condense this account quite a bit, the father finally permitted the daughter to go to a church dance with her girlfriends. Nothing untoward happened, but she gave him a vivid account of the dance, and he in turn gave her some advice. Gradually the father gained confidence in her good judgment and allowed her a little more freedom. The daughter's depression lifted, and her school work improved. At this point, with the father's increased confidence in his ability to solve problems, the therapy turned to the conflict between the husband and wife.

Undoubtedly, this outcome could be explained in terms of various theories of family therapy, to which we would have no objection. For us what is important is that the family took a small step toward accommodation to mainstream American values. This small step in the process of acculturation reconciled the peer-group values working upon the daughter without undermining the Puerto Rican values important to the father's sense of selfworth and dignity.

Did we impose our own American values on this family? We would say, "No." It is true that the range of choice was increased for the family by supplying information and suggesting possibilities that were in the direction of American values. But the family adopted the direction, after giving it a trial, because it worked. There was positive reinforcement supplied by the external situation not from the therapist. Thus, a therapeutic relationship can be solidified without alienating other family members by seeming to side too much with the power holder. Such small steps can lead to a considerable reduction in tension between conflicting value systems, and, by reverberating around the transactional field, to interpersonal and intrapersonal tension.

References

Ackerman. N. *The Psychodynomics of Family Life.* New York: Basic Books, 1958.

Auerswald, E. Interdisciplinary versus Ecological Approach. *Family Process* 7(2), 202-215, 1968-

Auerswald, E. Families, Change, and the Ecological Perspective. In A. Ferber, M. Mendelsohn, & A. Napier (Eds.), *The Book of Family Therapy.* New York: Science House, 1972.

Auerswald, E. Thinking about/Thinking about Health and Mental Health. In S. Arieti (Ed.), *American Handbook of Psychiatry* (2nd ed.). New York: Basic Books, 1974.

Bateson, G. *Steps to an Ecology of Mind.* New York: Ballantine, 1972.

Bell, J.E. *Family Group Therapy* (Public Health Monograph No. 64). Washington, D.C.: Department of Health, Education and Welfare, 1961.

Berry, J.W. Ecological Analyses for Cross-Cultural Psychology. In N. Warren (Ed.), *Studies in Cross-Cultural Psychology.* New York: Academic Press, 1980.

Boszormenyi-Nagy, I. The Concept of Schizophrenia from the Perspective of Family Treatment. *Family Process 1(1)* 103-113, 1962.

Bowen, M. *Family Therapy in Clinical Practice.* New York: Jason Aronson, 1978.

Chomsky, N. *Aspects of a Theory of Syntax* Cambridge: M.l.T. Press, 1965.

Dewey, J., & Bentley, A.F. *Knowing and the Known.* Boston: Beacon, 1950.

Framo, J.L. Rationale and Techniques of Intensive Family Therapy. In I. Boszormenyi-Nagy & J.L. Framo (Eds.), *Intensive Family Therapy.* New York: Harper & Row, 1965.

Giordano, J. & Giordano, G.P. *The Ethno-Cultural Factor in Mental Health: A Literary Review and Bibliography.* New York: Committee on Pluralism and Group Identity, American Jewish Committee, 1977.

Haley, J. *Problem-Solving Therapy: New Strategies for Effective Family Therapy.* San Francisco: Jossey-Bass, 1976.

Kluckhohn, C. Values and Value Orientations. In T. Parsons & E. Shils, *Toward A General Theory of Action.* Cambridge, Mass.: Harvard University Press, 1951.

Kluckhohn, F.R., & Strodtbeck, F.L. *Variations in Value Orientations* Evanston, Ill.: Row, Peterson, 1961.

Levi-Straus, C. *Structural Anthropology.* Boston: Beacon, 1963.

Mash, E.J., Hamerlynck, L.A., & Handy, L.C. (Eds.). *Behavior Modification and Families.* New York: Brunner/ Mazel. 1975.

Minuchin, S. *Families and Family Therapy.* Cambridge: Harvard University Press, 1974.

Papajohn, J., & Spiegel, J.P. *Transactions in Families: A Modern Approach for Resolving Cultural and Generational Conflict.* San Francisco: Jossey-Bass, 1975.

Pattison, E.M. A Theoretical-Empirical Base for Social System Therapy. In E.F. Foulks *et al.* (Eds.), *Current Perspectives in Cultural Psychiatry.* Jamaica, N.Y.: Spectrum, 1977.

Speck, R., & Attneave, C. *Family Networks.* New York: Vintage Books, 1973.

Spiegel, J. Transactions Inquiry: Description of Systems. In J. Papajohn (Ed.), *Transactions: The Interplay between Individual, Family and Society.* New York: Science House, 1971.

Watzlawick, P., Beavin, J.H., & Jackson, D.D. *Pragmatics of Human Communication.* New York: Norton, 1967.

Weidman, H.H. *Implications of the Culture Broker Concept for the Delivery of Health Care.* Paper presented at the Annual Meeting of the Southern Anthropological Society, Wrightsville Beach, S.C., 1973.

Weidman, H.H. Concepts as Strategies for Change. In J.N. Sussex (Ed.), *Psychiatry and the Social Sciences, Psychiatric Annals* (special Miami edition), 5(8), 17-19, 1975.

John Spiegel. Florence Heller School for Advanced Studies in Social Welfare, Brandeis University, Waltham, Massachusetts.

The Black American Family (1988)

Robert Staples

Introduction

As the United States' largest visible minority, the black population has been the subject of extensive study by behavioral scientists. Its family life has been of particular concern because of the unique character of this group, as a result of a history that is uncharacteristic of other ethnic groups. There are four cultural traits of the black group that distinguish it from other immigrants to the United States: (1) blacks came from a country with norms and values that were dissimilar to the American way of life; (2) they were from many different tribes, each with its own language, culture, and traditions; (3) in the beginning, they came without women; and, most importantly, (4) they came in bondage (Billingsley, 1968).

The study of black family life has, historically, been problem-oriented. Whereas the study of white families has been biased toward the middle–class family, the reverse has been true in the investigation of black family patterns. Until relatively recently, almost all studies of black family life have concentrated on the lower-income strata of the group, ignoring middle-class families and even stable, poor black families. Moreover, the deviation of black families from middle-class norms has resulted in them being defined as pathological. Such labels ignore the possibility that although a group's family forms may not fit into the normative model, it may instead have its own functional organization that meets the needs of the group (Billingsley, 1970).

One purpose of this description of black family life-style is to demonstrate how it has changed in the decade of the 1970s. Additionally, the forces that black families encounter, which create the existence of large numbers of "problem" families, must be carefully examined. Out of this systematic analysis of black family adaptations may come a new understanding of the black family in contemporary American society.

Historical Background

The Preslavery Period

There are several historical periods of interest in the evaluation of black family life in the United States. One era is the precolonial period of the African continent from which the black American population originated. The basis of African family life was the kinship group, which was bound together by blood ties, common interests, and mutual functions. Within each village, there were elaborate legal codes and court systems that regulated the marital and family behavior of individual members (Brown and Forde, 1967).

The Slave Family

In attempting to accurately describe the family life of slaves, one must sift through a conflicting array of opinions on the subject. Reliable empirical facts are few, and speculation has been rampant in the absence of data. Certain aspects of the slave's family life are undisputed. Slaves were not allowed to enter into binding contractual relationships. Because marriage is basically a legal relationship that imposes obligations on both parties and exacts penalties for the violation of those obligations, there was no legal basis for any marriage between two individuals in bondage. Slave marriages were regulated at the discretion of the slaveowners. As a result, some marriages were initiated by slaveowners and just as easily dissolved (Genovese, 1975).

Hence, there were numerous cases in which the slaveowner ordered slave women to marry men of his choosing after they reached the age of puberty. The slave owners preferred marriages between slaves on the same plantation, because the primary reason for slave unions was the breeding of children who would become future slaves. Children born to a slave woman on a different plantation were looked on by the slaveholder as wasting his man's seed. Yet, many slaves who were allowed to get married preferred women from a neighboring plantation. This allowed them to avoid witnessing the many assaults on slave women that occurred. Sometimes, the matter was resolved by the sale of one of the slaves to the other owner (Blassingame, 1972).

Historians are divided on the question of how many slave families were involuntarily separated from each other by their owners. Despite the slaveholder's commitment to keeping the slave families intact, the intervening events of a slaveholder's death, his bankruptcy, or lack of capital made the forceable sale of some slave's spouse or child inevitable. In instances where the slavemaster was indifferent to the fate of slave families, he would still keep them together simply to enforce plantation discipline. A married slave who was concerned about his wife and children, it was believed, was less inclined to rebel or escape than would an unmarried slave. Whatever their reasoning, the few available records show that slaveowners did not separate a majority of the slave couples (Blassingame, 1972).

This does not mean that the slave family had a great deal of stability. Although there are examples of some slave families living together for 40 years or more, the majority of slave unions were dissolved by personal choice, death, or the sale of one partner by the master. Although individual families may not have remained together for long periods of time, the institution of the family was an important asset in the perilous era of slavery. Despite the prevalent theories about the destruction of the family under slavery, it was one of the most important survival mechanisms for African people held in bondage (Blassingame, 1972; Fogel and Engerman, 1974).

In the slave quarters, black families did exist as functioning institutions and as models for others. The slave narratives provide us with some indication of the importance of family relations under slavery. It was in the family that the slave received affection, companionship, love, and empathy with his sufferings under this peculiar institution. Through the family, he learned how to avoid punishment, cooperate with his fellow slaves, and retain some semblance of his self-esteem. The socialization of the slave child was another important function for the slave parents. They could cushion the shock of bondage for him, inculcate in him values different than those the masters attempted to teach him, and represent another frame of reference for his self-esteem besides the master (Abzug, 1971).

Much has been written about the elimination of the male's traditional functions under the slave system. It is true that he was often relegated to working in the fields and siring children rather than providing economic maintenance or physical protection for his family, but the father's role was not as insignificant as presumed. It was the male slave's inability to protect his wife from the physical and sexual abuse of the master that most pained him. As a matter of survival, few tried, because the consequences were often fatal. However, it is significant that tales of their intervention occur frequently in the slave narratives. There is one story of a slave who could no longer tolerate the humiliation of his wife's sexual abuse before his eyes by the master. The slave choked him to death with the knowledge that it also meant his own death. He said he knew it would mean his death, but he was unafraid of death, so he killed him (Abzug, 1971:29).

One aspect of black family life frequently ignored during the slave era is the free black family. This group, which numbered about one-half million, was primarily composed of the descendants of the original black indentured servants and the mulatto offspring of slaveholders. For this minority of black families, the assimilation and acculturation process was, relatively, less difficult. They imitated the white world as closely as possible. Because they had opportunities for education, owning property, and skilled occupations, their family life was quite stable. Some of them even owned slaves, although the majority of black slaveholders were former slaves who had purchased their wives or children. It is among this group that the early black middle-class was formed (Frazier, 1932).

After Emancipation

There has been a prevailing notion that the experience of slavery weakened the value of marriage as an institution among black Americans. Yet, the slaves married in record numbers when the right to the freedom to marry was created by governmental decree. A legal marriage was a status symbol, and weddings were events of great gaiety. In a careful examination of census data and marriage licenses for the period after 1860, Gutman, (1976) found that the typical household was a simple nuclear family headed by an adult male. Further evidence that black people were successful in forming a dual-parent family structure is the data that show that 90 percent of all black children were born in wedlock by the year 1917.

The strong family orientation of the recently emancipated slaves has been observed by many students of the reconstruction era. One newspaper reported a black group's petition to the state of North Carolina asking for the right "to work with the assurance of good faith and fair treatment, to educate their children, to sanctify the family relation, to reunite scattered families, and to provide for the orphan and infirm" (Abzug, 1971:34). Children were of special value to the freed slaves, whose memories were fresh with the history of their offspring being sold away.

It was during the late nineteenth century that the strong role of women emerged. Men preferred their wives to remain at home, because a working woman was considered a mark of slavery. However, during the period, which has been described as the most explicitly racist era of American history (Miller, 1966), black men found it very difficult to obtain jobs and, in some instances, found work only as strikebreakers. Thus, the official organ of the African Methodist Episcopal church exhorted black families to teach their daughters not to avoid work, because many of them would marry men that would not make on the average more than 75 cents per day (Abzug, 1971:39). In 1900, approximately 41 percent of black women were in the labor force, compared with 16 percent of white women (Logan, 1965).

What was important, then, was not whether the husband or wife worked, but the family's will to survive in an era when blacks were systematically deprived of educational and work opportunities. Despite these obstacles, black families achieved a level of stability based on role integration. Men shared equally in the rearing of children; women participated in the defense of the family. As Nobles (1972) comments, a system in which the family disintegrates because of the loss of one member would be in opposition to the traditional principles of unity that defined the African family. These principles were to be tested during the period of the great black migration from the rural areas of the South to the cities of the North.

The rise of black illegitimately born children and female-headed households are concomitants of twentieth century urban ghettos. Drastic increases in these phenomena strongly indicate that the condition of many lower-class black families is a function of the economic contingencies of industrial America. Unlike the European immigrants before them, blacks were disadvantaged by the hard lines of northern segregation along racial lines. Furthermore, families in cities are more vulnerable to disruptions from the traumatizing experiences of urbanization, the reduction of family functions, and the loss of extended family supports.

In the transition from Africa to the American continent, there can be no doubt that African culture was not retained in any pure form. Blacks lacked the autonomy to maintain their cultural traditions under the severe pressures to take on American standards of behavior. Yet, there are surviving Africanisms that are reflected in black speech patterns, esthetics, folklore, and religion. They have preserved aspects of their old culture that have a direct relevance to their new lives. Out of the common experiences they have shared, a new culture has been forged that is uniquely black American. The elements of that culture are still to be found in their family life.

The Modern Black American Family

Among the principal variables that undergird family life are education, employment, and income. Looking at the 1980 census, one can find some absolute progress in certain areas for black families, little change in their status vis-à-vis white families, and the general problems of poverty and unemployment unchanged overall for many black families. In education, for example, the percentage of blacks graduating from high school increased slightly, but blacks were still more likely than whites to be high-school dropouts. The median number of school years completed by black Americans over 24 years of age was 12.0, in contrast to 12.3 for white Americans (U. S. Bureau of the Census, 1983).

There are two important aspects of the education situation to consider in assessing its relevance to blacks. First, black women tend to be slightly more educated than black men at all levels. In the past decade, the educational level of white men increased to reach the average of white women, whereas black men continued to lag behind black women (U. S. Bureau of the Census, 1983). Hence, an increase in the educational level of the black population will not automatically mean a rise in income or employment opportunities. The fact that much of that increase in education belongs to black women reduces the mobility level for blacks because black women, even educated ones, tend to be concentrated in lower-paying jobs than black men. Another significant factor is the sexual discrimination that women in our society face in the labor force (Bianchi, 1981; Collier and Williams, 1982).

The second important aspect of education is that it does not have the same utility for blacks as it does for whites. Although the incomes of black college graduates and whites who have completed only elementary school are no longer the same, the equal educational achievements of blacks and whites still are not reflected in income levels. The 1980 census reveals that blacks are still paid less for comparable work than whites. These figures lend substance to the argument by Jencks et al. (1972) that education alone will not equalize the income distribution of blacks and whites. In fact, the relative unemployment gap between blacks and whites increases with education. Although both blacks and whites incur difficulties because of a low level of education, college-educated whites face fewer barriers to their career aspirations. In analyzing the unemployment rate of black college graduates, they were unemployed as frequently as white males who had not graduated from high school (U. S. Civil Rights Commission, 1982).

During the past decade, the yearly median family income for blacks decreased at a faster rate than the median income for the population as a whole. Black family income is only 56 percent of white family income. The annual median income for white families in 1981 was $23,520, and for black families only $14,460. Even these figures are misleading because they do not show that black family incomes must be used to support more family members and that their family income is more often derived from the employment of both the husband and the wife. Also, according to the Labor Department, the majority of the female-headed black families are not earning the $9,284 a year needed to maintain themselves at a non-poverty standard of living (U. S. Bureau of the Census, 1983).

Furthermore, more than one-third of the nation's black population is still officially living in poverty. Approximately one-fourth of them are receiving public assistance. The comparable figures for whites were 10 percent and 4 percent. More than 70 percent of these black families living in poverty are headed by women. Approximately 41 percent of all black children are members of these families who exist on an income of less than $7,510 a year. Less than 15 percent of white children live in households that are officially defined as poor (U. S. Bureau of the Census, 1983).

The unemployment rate for blacks in 1982 was at its highest level since 1945. Overall, 18.9 percent of blacks were officially unemployed, compared with 8.6 percent for whites. In the years 1972-1982, black unemployment increased from 10.3 percent to 18.9 percent. Furthermore, this increase in unemployment during that 10-year period was highest among married black men who were the primary breadwinners in their household. Just as significant is the unemployment rate of black male teenagers. Approximately 50 percent of that group was unemployed, compared with 20.4 percent of white male teenagers. The highest unemployment rates in the country are among black male teenagers in low-income areas of central cities. Their unemployment rate is approximately 65 percent and has risen as high as 75 percent (U. S. Bureau of the Census, 1983).

What the recent census figures indicate is that the decade of the 1970s saw little significant change in the socioeconomic status of black families. An increase in educational achievements has produced little in economic benefits for most blacks. Based on the rate of progress in integrating blacks in the labor force in the past decade, it will take 9.3 years to equalize the participation of blacks in low-paying office and clerical jobs and a period of 90 years before black professionals approximate the proportion of blacks in the population (Staples, 1982).

Changing Patterns of Black Family Life

Recent years have brought about significant changes in the marital and family patterns of many Americans. Americans have witnessed an era of greater sexual permissiveness, alternate family lifestyles, increased divorce rates, and reductions in the fertility rate. Some of these changes have also occurred among black families and have implications for any public policy developed to strengthen black family life.

The sexual revolution has arrived, and blacks are very much a part of it (Staples, 1981). By the age of 19, black women were twice as likely as white women to have engaged in intercourse. Although the percentage for white females was lower, they were engaging in premarital coitus more often and with a larger number of sexual partners. However, a larger number of sexually active black females were not using reliable contraceptives, and 41 percent had been, or were, pregnant (Zelnik and Kantner, 1977).

One result of this increased premarital sexual activity among blacks is the large number of black children born out of wedlock. More than one half of every 1,000 black births were illegitimate in the year 1980. Moreover, the rate was higher in this period for blacks than in the most recent earlier periods. The racial differences in illegitimacy rates also narrowed in the last 20 years (U. S. Bureau of the Census, 1983). One reason for the continued racial differential is the greater use by white women of low-cost abortions. In one study, 26 percent of pregnant black women received an abortion, compared with 41 percent of white women (Cummings, 1983). In all probability, the black out-of-wedlock birth rate will continue to increase as a higher percentage of black children are born to teenage mothers.

When blacks choose to get married, the same economic and cultural forces that are undermining marital stability in the general population are operative. In the last decade, the annual divorce rate has risen 120 percent. For white women under the age of 30, the chances are nearly two out of four that their marriage will end in divorce. Among black women, their chances are two out of three. In 1981, 30 percent of married black women were separated or divorced, compared with 14 percent for white women. The divorce rate of middle-class blacks is lower, because the more money that a family makes and the higher their educational achievements, the greater are their chances for a stable marriage (U. S. Bureau of the Census, 1983).

A combination of the aforementioned factors has increased the percentage of black households headed by women. The percentage of female-headed families among blacks increased 130 percent in the last decade, from 21 percent to 47 percent. One-third of these female household heads worked and had a median annual income of only $7,510 in 1981. The percentage of black children living with both parents declined in the last decade, and currently, only 42 percent of children in black families are residing with both parents. It is apparently the increasing pressures of discrimination, urban living, and poverty that cause black fathers to leave their homes or never marry. At the income level of $20,000 and over, the percentage of black families headed by a man is similar to that for white families (U. S. Bureau of the Census, 1983).

The fertility rate of black women is hardly a factor in the increase of female-headed households among blacks. Between 1970 and 1980, the total birth rate for black women decreased sharply. The fertility rate of black women (2.3 children per black woman) is still higher than the 1.7 birth rate for white women. However, the average number of total births expected by young black wives (2.6) and young white wives (2.4) are very similar. As more black women acquire middle-class status or access to birth control and abortion, one can expect racial differentials in fertility to narrow (U. S. Bureau of the Census, 1983). The birth rate of college-educated black women is actually lower than their white counterparts.

This statistical picture of marital and family patterns among blacks indicates a continued trend toward attenuated nuclear families caused by the general changes in the society and the effects of the disadvantaged economic position of large numbers of black people. An enlightened public policy would address itself to the needs of those families rather than attempt to mold black families into idealized middle-class models, which no longer mean much, even for the white middle class. What is needed is a government policy that is devoid of middle-class puritanism, the protestant ethic, and male-chauvinist concepts about family leadership.

Sex Roles

In recent years the issue of sex roles and their definition has received much attention. Although the debate has centered on the issue of female subordination and male dominance and privilege, blacks have considerably different problems in terms of their sex-role identities. They must first overcome certain disabilities based on racial membership—not gender affiliation. However, that does not mean that sex-role identities within the black community do not carry with them advantages and disadvantages. In many ways they do, but instead of fighting over the question of who is the poorest of the poor, blacks must contend with the plaguing problem of an unemployment rate that is as high as 45 percent among black men. Factors correlating to that central problem are the declining life-expectancy rate of black men and rises in drug abuse, suicide, crime, and educational failures. These facts do not warrant much support for a movement to equalize the condition of men and women in the black community (Staples, 1982).

Along with the economic conditions that impinge on their role performance, black men are saddled with a number of stereotypes that label them as irresponsible, criminalistic, hypersexual, and lacking in masculine traits. Some of these stereotypes become self-fulfilling prophecies because the dominant society is structured in a way that prevents many black men from achieving the goals of manhood. At the same time, the notion of the castrated black male is largely a myth. Although mainstream culture has deprived many black men of the economic wherewithal for normal, masculine functions, most function in a way that gains the respect of their mates, children, and community.

Along with all the dynamic changes occurring in American society are slow but perceptible alterations in the role of black women. The implications of these changes are profound in light of the fact that they are central figures in the family life of black people. Historically, the black woman has been a bulwark of strength in the black community. From the time of slavery onward, she has resisted the destructive forces that she has encountered in American society. During the period of slavery, she fought and survived the attacks on her dignity by the slave system, relinquished the passive role ascribed to members of her gender to ensure the survival of her people, and tolerated the culturally induced irresponsibility of her man in recognition of this country's relentless attempts to castrate him.

Too often, the only result of her sacrifices and sufferings have been the invidious and inaccurate labeling of her as a matriarch, a figure deserving respect but not love. The objective reality of the black woman in America is that she occupies the lowest rung of the socioeconomic ladder of all sex-race groups and has the least prestige. The double burden of gender and race has put her in the category of a super-oppressed entity. Considering the opprobrium to which she is subjected, one would expect her to be well-represented in the women's liberation movement. Yet, that movement remains primarily white and middle class. This is in part the result of the class-bound character of the women's movement—it being middle class whereas most black women are poor or working class. Their low profile in that movement also stems from the fact that many of the objectives of white feminists relate to psychological and cultural factors such as language and sexist behavior whereas the black woman's concerns are economic.

There is a common ground on which blacks and women can and do meet—on such issues as equal pay for equal work, child care facilities, and female parity in the work force. Instead of joining the predominantly white, middle-class women's movement, many black women have formed their own organizations such as the Welfare Rights Organization, Black Women Organized for Action, and the Black Feminist Alliance. There is little question that there is a heightened awareness among black women of the problems they face based on their sex-role membership alone. Whether the struggle of black women for equal rights will come into conflict with the movement for black liberation remains to be seen. It is fairly clear that black women must be freed from both the disabilities of race and sex.

Male-Female Relationships

Relationships between black men and women have had a peculiar evolution. Unlike the white family, which was a patriarchy and sustained by the economic dependence of women, the black dyad has been characterized by more equalitarian roles and economic parity in North America. The system of slavery did not permit black males to assume the superordinate role in the family constellation because the female was not economically dependent on him. Hence, relationships between the sexes were ordered along social-psychological factors rather than economic compulsion to marry and remain married. This fact, in part, explains the unique trajectory of black male-female relationships.

Finding and keeping a mate is complicated by a number of social–psychological factors, as well as structural restraints. Social structure and individual attitudes interface to make male-female relationships ephemeral rather than permanent. The imbalance in the sex ratio will continue to deny large numbers of black women a comparable mate. Furthermore, there are only a limited number of ways to deal with that irreversible fact of life. At the same time, there exists a pool of black males who are available to this group of women, and the tension between them builds barriers to communicating and mating. This is a complex problem, and there is no easy solution. Although there are some black men who are threatened by the successful black woman, further investigation reveals other underlying forces. Men are torn between the need for security and the desire for freedom, the quest for a special person to call their own and the temptation of sexual variety. They see marriage as a way of establishing roots but are seduced by the enticement of all the attractive, possibly "better" women in their midst.

Given the advantage he has as a male in a sexist society and a high prestige in short supply in the black community, there is little incentive for him to undertake the actions needed to meet the needs of women. The women who feel that their emotional needs are not being met begin to recoil and adopt their own agenda based on a conception of self-interest. Some recognition must be made of the changing relations between men and women. The old exchange of feminine sexual appeal for male financial support is in a declining state. Women, increasingly, are able to define their own status and are economically independent. What they seek now is the satisfaction of emotional needs, not an economic cushion. Whereas men must confront this new reality, women must realize that emotional needs can be taken care of by men in all social classes. Although a similar education and income can mean greater compatibility in values and interests, it is no guarantee of compatibility nor of personal happiness. Common needs, interests, and values are more a function of gender than class.

One should not be deluded by the ostensible reluctance of many black single adults to enter the conjugal state. When a person has not been able to develop a lasting, permanent relationship with a member of the opposite sex, he or she must play it off and make the best of whatever it is they have at the moment. Although the industrial and urban revolution has made the single life more a viable way of life, it has also made the need for belonging more imperative. The tensions of work and the impersonality of the city have created a need to escape the depersonalization by retreating into some sort of an intimate sanctum. This is especially imperative for blacks in the middle class who have their selfhood tested daily by a racist society and who must often work and live in isolation. In modern society, individuals are required to depend on each other for permanence and stability, which is a function previously served by a large familial and social network.

It is the fear that even marriage no longer provides that permanence and stability that causes people to enter and exit their relationships quickly. It is the fear of failure that comes from failure. Until black single adults develop a tenacity to work as hard at a relationship as they did at their schooling and jobs, we will continue to see this vicious cycle repeated again and again. Marriage and the family continue to be the most important buffer for blacks against racism and depersonalization. When one looks at the strongest predictors of happiness in America, it is inevitably such social factors as marriage, family, friends, and children. Across the board, married people tend to be happier than those who are unmarried. The best confirmation of this fact is that most people who divorce eventually remarry. Before anyone can find happiness in a marriage, they must form a strong basis for marriage. It is that task that continues to perplex black single adults.

There is a growing trend toward single life among American blacks. A majority of black women over the age of 18 years are no longer married and living with a spouse (Staples, 1981). Although the institutional decimation of black males is the primary factor in this unprecedented number of singles, other sociocultural forces have an impact on the relationships between black men and women. Among them are the changes in black institutions and values. Franklin (1984) traces the conflict between black men and women to incompatible role enactments by the two sexes. The societal prescription that women are to be passive and men dominant is counteracted by black women who resist black men's dominance and black men who wish to be accorded the superior male role but cannot fulfill the economic provider role, which supports the dominance of men in American society.

Husbands and Wives. Marriages are very fragile today. Fewer people are getting married, and the divorce rate in the United States is at an all-time high. There are many forces responsible for this changing pattern including changing attitudes and laws on divorce, changing and conflicting definitions of sex roles and their functions in the family, economic problems, and personality conflicts. Although divorce is on the rise and its increase cuts across racial and class lines, it is still more pronounced among blacks. Only one out of every three black couples will remain married longer than 10 years.

It is not easy to pinpoint unique causes of black marital dissolution because they are very similar to those of their white counterparts. In some cases, it is the severity of the problems they face. Economic problems are a major factor in marital conflict and there are three times as many blacks as whites with incomes below the poverty level. The tensions blacks experience in coping with the pervasive incidents of racism often have their ramifications in the marital arena. One peculiar problem blacks face is the imbalanced sex ratio, which places many women in competition for the available males. Too often, the males they compete for are not available, and this places serious pressure on the marriages of many blacks.

At the same time, many blacks are involved in a functional marriage at any given point in time. Many adult blacks are married and have positive and loving relationships with their spouses. Unfortunately, practically no research exists on marital adjustment and satisfaction among blacks. What little research does exist indicates that black wives are generally less satisfied with their marriages than white wives. However, the source of their dissatisfaction is often associated with the problems of poverty and racism.

The last decade witnessed a significant increase in interracial dating and marriage. Among the reasons for this change in black-white dating and marriage was the desegregation of the public school system, the work force, and other social settings. In those integrated settings, blacks and whites met as equals, which facilitated homogenous mating. There were, of course, other factors such as the liberation of many white youth from parental control and the racist values they conveyed to them.

Not only has the incidence of interracial relations increased but their character has changed as well. Over 25 years ago, the most typical interracial pairing was a black male and a white female with the male partner generally being of a higher status. This pattern was so common that social theorists even developed a theory of racial hypergamy. In essence, it was assumed that the higher-status black male was exchanging his socioeconomic status for the privilege of marrying a woman who belonged to a racial group that was considered superior to all members of the black race. Contemporary interracial relations are much more likely to involve people with similar educational background and occupational status.

Although no research studies have yet yielded any data on the subject, there appears to be a change in interracial unions toward a decline in black male/white female couples and an increase in black female/white male pairings. Several factors seem to account for this modification of the typical pattern. Many black women are gravitating toward white men because of the shortage of black men and disenchantment with those they do have access to. In a similar vein, some white men are dissatisfied with white women and their increasing vociferous demands for sex-role parity. At the same time, there is a slight but noticeable decrease in black male/ white female unions. One possible reason is that it is no longer as fashionable as it was a few years ago. Also, much of their attraction to each other was based on the historical lack of access to each other and the stereotype of black men as superstuds and white women as forbidden fruit. Once they had had extensive interaction, the myths exploded and the attraction consequently diminished (Poussaint, 1983).

We should be fairly clear that there are relatively normal reasons for interracial attractions and matings. At the same time, it would be naive to assume that special factors are not behind them in a society that is stratified by race. Given the persistence of racism as a very pervasive force, many interracial marriages face rough sledding. In addition to the normal problems of working out a satisfactory marital relationship, interracial couples must cope with social ostracism and isolation. One recent phenomenon is the increasing hostility toward such unions by the black community, which has forced some interracial couples into a marginal existence. Such pressures cause the interracial-marriage rate to remain at a very low level. Less than 5 percent of all marriages involving a black person are interracial (Poussaint, 1983).

Childhood and Childrearing

One of the most popular images of black women is that of "Mammy," the devoted, affectionate nursemaids of white children who belonged to their slavemaster or employer. This motherly image of black women probably has some basis in fact. Motherhood has historically been an important role for black women, even more meaningful than their role as wives (Bell, 1971). In the colonial period of Africa, missionaries often observed and reported the unusual devotion of the African mother to her child. The slave mother also developed a deep love for, and impenetrable bond to, her children (Ladner, 1971). It would appear that the bond between the black mother and her child is deeply rooted in the African heritage and philosophy that places a special value on children because they represent the continuity of life (Brown and Forde, 1967).

Many studies have conveyed a negative image of the black mother because she does not conform to middle-class modes of childrearing. Yet, black mothers have fulfilled the function of socializing their children into the multiple roles they must perform in this society. They prepare them to take on not only the appropriate sex and age roles but also a racial role. Children must be socialized to deal with the prosaic realities of white racism that they will encounter daily. Black females are encouraged to be independent rather than passive individuals because many of them will carry family and economic responsibilities alone (Iscoe et al., 1964). Taking on adult responsibilities is something many black children learn early. They may be given the care of a younger sibling, and some will have to find work while still in the adolescent stage. The strong character structure of black children was noted by child psychiatrist Robert Coles (1964) who observed their comportment under the pressure of school integration in the South during a very volatile era.

The black mother's childrearing techniques are geared to prepare her children for a kind of existence that is alien to middle-class white youngsters. Moreover, many white middle-class socialization patterns may not be that desirable for the psychological growth of the black child. The casual upbringing of black children may produce a much healthier personality than the status anxieties associated with some rigid middle-class childrearing practices (Green, 1946). Using threats of the withdrawal of love if the child fails to measure up to the parent's standards is much more common among white parents than black parents of any class stratum. One result of the black child's anxiety-free upbringing is a strong closeness to his parents (Nolle, 1972; Scanzoni, 1971).

Although black parents are more likely to use physical rather than verbal punishment to enforce discipline than white parents, this technique is often buttressed by the love they express for their children. Moreover, as Billingsley (1969:567) has noted, "even among the lowest social classes in the Black community, families give the children better care than is generally recognized, and often the care is better than that given by white families in similar social circumstances." One indication of the decline in this attitude is found in the statistics, which show that child abuse has become more common in black families than in white families (Gil, 1971). Some of the racial differences can be attributed to reporting bias, but much of it reflects the effect of poverty and racism on black parent-child relationships.

The most undesirable aspect of the black child's life is reputed to be the absence of a positive male figure (Moynihan, 1965; Rainwater, 1966). A plethora of studies have found that the black child has low self-esteem because of his "blackness" and the fact that many children grow up in homes without a male role model. A number of studies have emerged that are in opposition to the theories of low self-esteem among blacks. In reviewing the literature on black self-esteem, some have concluded that much of it is invalid, and others have concluded that blacks are less likely to suffer from low self-esteem because of such countervailing influences as religion, reference groups, group identification, and positive experiences in the extended family (Staples, 1976:82-84).

Problems in child development are alleged to be a function of the father's absence or ineffectiveness. There has yet to be found a direct relationship between the father's absence and child maladaption (Hare, 1975; Rubin, 1974). In part, the black child continues to have male role models among the male kinsmen in his extended family network, and the mother generally regards her children's father as a friend of the family who she can recruit for help rather than as a father failing his parental duties. However, one must be careful not to overromanticize the single-parent family as a totally functional model. They are the poorest families in the United States and are overrepresented among the society's failures in education, crime, and mental health.

The ineffective black father has been assumed to be pervasive among black families. Much of the more recent literature suggests that black fathers have warm, nurturing relationships with their children and play a vital role in their children's psychology and social development (Lewis, 1975; Scanzoni, 1971). How well they carry out the paternal role may be contingent on the economic resources available to them. Hence, we find better patterns of parenting among middle-class black fathers who have the economic and educational resources, and, consequently, participate more in child care, are more child-oriented, and view their role as different from the mother's (Cazanave, 1979; Daneal, 1975). As far as the male child's sexual identity is concerned, Benjamin (1971) discovered that black male youth had a better conception of the male role when their father had one or more years of college education, indicating a strong relationship between the opportunity to play a role and the actual playing of that role.

The Aged

As a result of the declining fertility rate among blacks, the elderly represent a larger percentage of the total black population than in previous times. By 1979, blacks over the age of 65 years constituted 8 percent of the black population, in contrast to half the corresponding percentage in 1910. Increasingly, the black elderly population is disproportionately female. As a result of the growing gap in mortality rates between black men and women, widowhood occurs at an earlier age for black than white women. For example, during the years 1939-1941, there was only a difference of two years in the life-expectancy rate of black men and women. As of 1979, that gap had widened to 12 years (U. S. Bureau of the Census, 1983). Based on his calculations from 1975 fertility and mortality data, Sutton (1977) estimated that the chances of becoming a widow among married black women prior to age 65 are nearly one out of two. Those who become widows could expect to have a tenure of nine years in that status before their 65th birthday. Their chances of remarriage are undermined by the extremely low sex ratio among blacks 65 years of age and over. For every 100 black females in that age category, there were only 72 males in 1976 (U. S. Bureau of the Census, 1983).

Compounding the problems of early widowhood among the black elderly is the lingering problem of poverty. Approximately 36 percent of the black elderly were poor in 1977, compared with only 12 percent of elderly whites. Moreover, while the percentage of poor elderly decreased from 13 percent to 12 percent between 1975-1977, the number of poor black persons 65 years of age and over increased by 110,000 during the same period, maintaining the same percentage in poverty in 1975. One result of this overwhelming poverty is that a much larger percentage of elderly black wives continue to work after reaching the age of 65 years than their white counterparts (U. S. Bureau of the Census, 1983).

Despite their poverty, the extended-kin network manages to buttress the problems attendant to aging among its elderly members. When Hutchinson (1974) compared black and white low-income elderly, his results indicated that blacks and whites were identical in their expectations for the future, feelings of loneliness, amount of worrying, perception of others, and general life satisfaction. Moreover, the black elderly were more likely to describe themselves as being happier. One of the reasons the black elderly do not experience previous adjustment problems with growing old is that they continue to play a vital role in the extended family. Very few, for instance, are taken into the households of younger relatives. Only 4 percent of black families have relatives 65 years of age and over living with them. Instead, young black children often are taken into the households of elderly relatives, usually a grandmother. This process of informal adoption is so common that half of all black families headed by elderly women have dependent children, not their own, living with them (Hill, 1977).

Change and Adaptation

The last 30 years have culminated in the gradual disintegration of the black nuclear family. Changes in the black family structure are in tune with the changes in American families. A number of social forces account for the increase in the number of single adults, out-of-wedlock births, divorces, and single-parent households. As women have become economically and psychologically independent of men, they have chosen to remain single or leave marriages they regarded as not satisfying their needs. Simultaneously, the growing independence of women and the sexual revolution of the 1960s and 1970s have allowed many men to flee from the responsibility attendant to the husband and father roles (Ehrenreich, 1983).

Although these sociocultural forces have an impact on the marriage and family patterns of many Americans, they are more pronounced among blacks because of one critical etiological agent: the institutional decimation of black males. As an Urban League report concluded, "the attrition of Black males . . . from conception through adulthood finally results in an insufficient number of men who are willing and able to provide support for women and children in a family setting" (Williams, 1984). Thus, many black women are denied a real choice between monogamous marriage or single life. Most do choose to bear and raise children because that is deemed better than being single, childless, and locked into dead-end, low-paying jobs. Although many would prefer a monogamous marriage, that is no longer possible for the majority of black women. The same forces that drive many black men out of social institutions also propel them out of the family.

Those forces have their genesis in the educational system. Black women are more educated than black men at all levels except the doctoral level. This, again, is in the overall direction of change in American society. White men have also been losing ground to white women in educational achievements. The reasons for the ascendancy of women in the school system are unclear. Some speculate that because teachers are disproportionately female, the behaviors tolerated and most encouraged are those that are more natural for girls (Hale, 1983). The higher educational level of black women endows them with educational credentials and skills that make them more competitive in the job market. The changing nature of the economy has placed women at an advantage. While the industrial sector has been declining, the service and high-technology sectors of the economy have been expanding. Black women are more highly concentrated in the expanding sector of the economy whereas black men are overrepresented in the shrinking industrial jobs.

One consequence of the aforementioned factors is the attrition of black men in the labor force. According to a study by Joe and Yu (1984) almost 46 percent of the black men of working age were not in the labor force. As a rule, unemployed males are not good marriage prospects. The percentage of black women heading families alone in 1982 (42 percent) corresponds closely to the percentage of black males not in the labor force. Along with the number of black males not gainfully employed is the imbalance in the sex ratio, especially in the marriageable age ranges (18-35 years). Guttentag and Secord (1983) have shown that imbalanced sex ratios have certain predictable consequences for relationships between men and women. They give rise to higher rates of single adults, divorce, out-of-wedlock births, and female-headed households in different historical epochs and across different societies. Another analysis by Jackson (1971) revealed that among blacks, the percentage of female-headed households increases as the supply of males decreases. On the other hand, the percentage of female-headed households decreases when the supply of black males increases.

The crisis of the black family is, in reality, the crisis of the black male and his inability to carry out the normative responsibilities of husband and father in the nuclear family. The family's disintegration is only a symptom of the larger problem, that problem being the institutional decimation of black males. One should be clear that the institutional decimation of black males represents the legacy of institutional racism. The implications of this problem extend beyond the family. A majority of black children live in one-parent households today, and the median income available to those families is less than $7,500 per year. Although many children rise out of poor families to become successful adults, the odds are against them. Large numbers of them, especially the males, will follow their biological fathers to an early grave, prison, and the ranks of the unemployed. Only by resolving the problems of the black male can we restore the black family to its rightful place in our lives. The future of the race may be at stake.

References

Abzug, Robert H. 1971. "The Black Family During Reconstruction," in Nathan Huggins, et al. (eds.), *Key Issue in the Afro-American Experience.* New York: Harcourt, Brace and Jovanovich, 26-39.

Adams, Bert N. 1970. "Isolation, Function and Beyond: American Kinship in the 1960s," *Journal of Marriage and the Family,* 32(November):575-598.

Bell, Robert. 1971. "The Relative Importance of Mother and Wife Roles Among Negro Lower-Class Women," in *The Black Family: Essays and Studies.* Belmont, CA: Wadsworth, 248-256.

Benjamin, R. 1971. *Factors Related to Conceptions of the Black Male Familial Role by Black Male Youth.* Mississippi State University Sociological-Anthropological Press Series.

Bianchi, Suzanne. 1981. *Household Composition and Racial Inequality.* New Brunswick, NJ: Rutgers University Press.

Billingsley, Andrew. 1968. *Black Families in White America.* Englewood Cliffs, NJ: Prentice-Hall.

——. 1969. "Family Functioning in the Low-Income Black Community," *Social Casework,* 50(December):563-572.

——. 1970. "Black Families and White Social Science," *Journal of Social Issues,* 26(November): 127-142.

Blassingame, John. 1972. *The Slave Community.* New York: Oxford University Press.

Brown, A. R. Radcliffe, and Darryle Forde. 1967. *African Systems of Kinship and Marriage.* New York: Oxford University Press.

Brown, Prudence, et al. 1977. "Sex Role Attitudes and Psychological Outcomes for Black and White Women Experiencing Marital Dissolution," *Journal of Marriage and the Family,* 39(August):549-562.

Cazanave, Noel. 1979a. "Middle-Income Black Fathers: An Analysis of the Provider Role," *The Family Coordinator,* 28(November).

——. 1979b. "Social Structure and Personal Choice in Intimacy, Marriage and Family Alternative Lifestyle Research," *Alternative Life Styles,* 2(August):33 1- 358.

Chavis, William M., and Gladys Lyles. 1975. "Divorce Among Educated Black Women." *Journal of the National Medical Association,* 67(March): 128- I34.

Clayton, Richard R., and Harwin L. Voss. 1977. "Shacking: Cohabitation in the 1970s," *Journal of Marriage and the Family,* 39(May):273-284.

Coles, Robert. 1964. "Children and Racial Demonstrations," *The American Scholar,* 34(Winter):78-92.

Collier, Betty, and Louis Williams. 1982. "The Economic Status of the Black Male: A Myth Exploded," *Journal of Black Studies,* 12(June):487-498.

Cummings, Judith. 1983. "Breakup of Black Family Imperils Gains of Decades," *New York Times* (November 20):1-2.

Daneal, Jealean Evelyn. 1975. "A Definition of Fatherhood as Expressed by Black Fathers." Ph.D. diss., University of Pittsburgh.

Davis, George. 1977. *Black Love.* Garden City, NY: Doubleday.

Ehrenreich, Barbara. 1983. *The Hearts of Men: American Dreams and the Flight from Commitment.* Garden City, NY: Doubleday.

Fogel, William, and Stanley Engerman. 1974. *Time on the Cross.* Boston: Little, Brown.

Franklin, Clyde W. 1984. "Black Male-Female Conflict: Individually Caused and Culturally Nurtured," *Journal of Black Studies,* 15(December): 139-154.

Frazier, E. Franklin. 1932. *The Free Negro Family.* Nashville, TN: Fisk University Press.

Genovese, Eugene. 1975. *Roll, Jordan, Roll.* New York: Pantheon.

Gil, David. 1971. Violence Against Children. *Journal of Marriage and the Family,* 33(November): 637- 648.

Green, Arnold. 1946. "The Middle-Class Male Child and Neurosis," *American Sociological Review,* 11(February):31-41.

Gutman, Herbert. 1976. *The Black Family in Slavery and Freedom, 1750-1925.* New York: Pantheon.

Guttentag Marcia, and Paul Secord. 1983. *Too Many Women: The Sex Ratio Question.* Beverly Hills, CA: Sage.

Hale, Janice. 1983. *Black Children.* Provo, UT: Brigham Young University Press.

Hare, Bruce R. 1975. "Relationship of Social Background to the Dimensions of Self-concept." Ph.D. diss., University of Chicago.

Hays, William and Charles Mindel. 1973. "Extended Kinship Relations in Black and White Families," *Journal of Marriage and the Family,* 35(February).

Hill, Robert. 1977. *Informal Adoption Among Black Families.* Washington, DC: National Urban League Research Department.

Hill, Robert B., and Lawrence Shackleford. 1975. "The Black Extended Family Revisited, *Urban League Review,* 1(Fall): 18 -24.

Hutchinson, Iran. 1974. "Life Satisfaction of Lower Income Black and White Elderly." Paper presented at the National Council on Family Relations Meeting, St. Louis, MO.

Iscoe, Ira, Martha Williams, and Jerry Harvey. 1964. "Age, Intelligence and Sex as Variables in the Conformity Behavior of Negro and White Children," *Child Development,* 35:451-460.

Jackson, Jacqueline. 1971. "But Where Are the Men?" *The Black Scholar,* 4(December):34-41.

———. 1972. "Comparative Life Styles and Family and Friend Relationships Among Older Black Women," *The Family Coordinator,* 21(October):477-486.

Jencks, Christopher. 1972. *Inequality: A Re-Assessment of the Effect of Family and Schooling in America.* New York: Basic Books.

Joe, Tom, and Peter Yu. 1984. *The "Flip-Side" of Black Families Headed by Women; The Economic Status of Black Men.* Washington, DC: The Center for the Study of Social Policy.

Ladner, Joyce. 1971. *Tomorrow: The Black Woman.* Garden City, NY: Doubleday.

Lewis, Diane R. 1975. "The Black Family: Socialization and Sex Roles," *Phylon,* 36(Fall):221-237.

Logan, Rayford. 1965. *The Betrayal of the Negro.* New York: Collier.

Miller, Elizabeth. 1966. *The Negro in America: A Bibliography.* Cambridge: Harvard University Press.

Moynihan, Daniel Patrick, 1965. "Employment, Income, and the Ordeal of the Negro Family," *Daedalus,* 94(Fall):745-770.

Nobles, Wade. 1972. "African Root and American Fruit: The Black Family," *Journal of Social and Behavioral Sciences,* 20(Spring):52-64.

———. 1973. "Psychological Research and the Black Self-Concept: A Critical Review," *Journal of Social Issues,* 29(Winter):11–31.

Nolle, David. 1972. "Changes in Black Sons and Daughters: A Panel Analysis of Black Adolescent's Orientation Toward Their Parents," *Journal of Marriage and the Family,* 34(August):443-447.

Peters, Marie, and Cecile de Ford. 1978. "The Solo Mother" in R. Staples (ed.) *The Black Family: Essays and Studies* (2nd ed.), Belmont, CA: Wadsworth, pp. 192-200.

Poussaint, Alvin. 1983. "Black Men-White Women: An Update," *Ebony,* 38(August): 124-131 .

Rubin, Roger H. 1974. "Adult Male Absence and the Self-Attitudes of Black Children," *Child Study Journal,* 4:33-44.

Scanzoni, John. 1971. *The Black Family in Modern Society.* Boston: Allyn and Bacon.

Schulz, David. 1969. "Variations in the Father Role in Complete Families of the Negro Lower-Class," *Social Science Quarterly,* 49(December):651-659.

Scott, Joseph W. 1976. "Polygamy: A Futuristic Family Arrangement for AfricanAmericans," *Black Books Bulletin,* 4(Summer).

Smith, Marie. 1978. "Black Female's Perceptions on the Black Male Shortage." Master's thesis, Howard University.

Staples, Robert. 1976. *Introduction to Black Sociology.* New York: McGraw-Hill.

———. 1978. *The Black Family: Essays and Studies, Volume 2.* Belmont, CA: Wadsworth.

———. 1978a. "Race and Masculinity: The Black Man's Dual Dilemma," *Journal of Social Issues,* 34(Winter):169-183.

———. 1979. "Beyond the Black Family: The Trend Toward Singlehood," *Western Journal of Black Studies,* 3(Fall):150-157.

———. 1981. *The World of Black Singles: Changing Patterns of Male/Female Relations.* Westport, CT: Greenwood Press.

———. 1982. *Black Masculinity: The Black Male's Role in American Society.* San Francisco: Black Scholar Press.

Sutton, Gordon F. 1977. "Measuring the Effects of Race Differentials in Mortality upon Surviving Family Members," *Demography,* 14(November):419-429.

U. S. Bureau of the Census. 1983. *America's Black Population, 1970 to 1982: A Statistical View, July 1983.* Series P10/POP83. Washington, DC: U. S. Government Printing Office.

U. S. Civil Rights Commission. 1982. *Unemployment and Underemployment Among Blacks, Hispanics and Women.* Washington, DC: U. S. Government Printing Office.

Williams, Juan. 1984. "Black Male's Problems Linked to Family Crises," *The Washington Post,* August 1, p. A-6.

Zelnick, Melvin, and John Kantner. 1977. "Sexual and Contraceptive Experience of Young Unmarried Women in the United States, 1976 and 1971," *Family Planning Perspectives,* 9(May/June):55-59.

I never believed in Santa Claus because I knew no white dude would come into my neighborhood after dark.
Dick Gregory

The Puerto Rican Family (1987)

Joseph P. Fitzpatrick

The Puerto Ricans now constitute one of the major minority groups in the Eastern part of America. They come from a small island in the Caribbean, one of the Greater Antilles, about a thousand miles southeast of Florida. Puerto Rico was a Spanish colony from the time of its discovery by Columbus on his second voyage, 1493, until 1898 when it was ceded by Spain to America after the Spanish-American war. The ingenious peoples, now generally called Tainos, disappeared soon after the Spanish conquest either by death, flight, or absorption. The first African slaves in the Western world were brought to Puerto Rico in 1511. As a result the population of Puerto Rico is a mixture of Tainos, Caucasoid Europeans, and Blacks.

Puerto Ricans were granted American citizenship in 1917. In 1948 they were granted the right to elect their own island governor. In 1952, the present political status was approved by the U.S. Congress and inaugurated; this is the constitution of the island known as the *Estado Libre Asociado*, the Free Associated State of Puerto Rico, officially identified in English as the Commonwealth of Puerto Rico. Puerto Ricans enjoy most of the rights of American citizens, including that of completely free movement between the island and the American mainland. They do not vote for the President, nor do they have elected representatives in Congress. They pay no federal taxes.

A small colony of Puerto Ricans lived in New York City in the last century, mostly political leaders active in the movement for independence for the island. After 1898 a small but steady migration of Puerto Ricans began. This increased during the 1920s, diminished during the Depression of the 1930s and World War II, and increased to sizable proportions in the late 1940s, which has continued to the present. Many Puerto Ricans now return to the island; the migration is a two-way phenomenon of people migrating from the island to the mainland and others migrating back to the island.

The 1970 Census reported 1,454,000 Puerto Ricans living on the American mainland: 811,000 of these were born in Puerto Rico, 636,000 were born on the mainland of Puerto Rican parentage, 7,000 were born elsewhere. Approximately 60 percent (872,471) reside in New York State, the great majority in New York City; close to 10 percent (135,676) live in New Jersey, with sizable numbers in Connecticut, Massachusetts, Pennsylvania, and Ohio.

Puerto Ricans are the ethnic minority with the lowest income of all groups in New York City. As a result, many of them must seek public assistance, a source of income but a source of problems that complicate their lives enormously. As a people, they are a mixture of many colors, from completely Negroid to completely Caucasoid and face the difficult problem of adjusting to racial prejudice. Their children find it difficult to achieve well on the standardized English and Math tests in the schools; many drop out before finishing high school. There is a high rate of drug addiction among Puerto Rican youths; and the community faces many complicated problems in the area of health and mental health. Although most are baptized Catholics, it is estimated that less than 30 percent are in effective contact with any religious group in New York City, Catholic or Protestant. Many of them are attracted to the small, neighborhood Pentecostal sects.

Nevertheless, the Puerto Rican community continues to struggle for stability and development. It now has one elected representative in Congress, two in the New York City Council, one member of the New York State Senate, and two in the State General Assembly. Effective agencies are developing strength and influence: Aspira in the area of education, the Puerto Rican Forum in the area of community affairs, the Puerto Rican Family Institute in social service, the Puerto Rican Merchants Association in commerce, the Association of Home Town Clubs in the area of social and community life, and many others. In their migration and adjustment to New York City, they face the experience of millions of newcomers who preceded them into a city that has been formed by the continued migration of people; they face the conflict and collaboration, the strain and satisfaction, the frustration and achievement, that results from stranger meeting stranger in the most complicated city in the world.

In this experience, the family is the institution that faces the most direct shock of cultural change; it is also the institution that provides the greatest strength for its members in the process of change. Puerto Ricans bring with them a style and structure of family life that has been formed by four centuries of tradition on the island. In order to understand this family as it faces the adjustment to the mainland, the family as it exists on the island must be clearly understood. Many features of the family continue as the context of Puerto Rican life on the mainland. The consequences of cultural transition will be explained after a detailed description of the family in the tradition of Puerto Rico.

Historical Background

Four major influences have contributed to the structure of family life, kinship patterns, and the patterns of family living of the Puerto Ricans:*

(1) The culture of the Borinquen Indians, now generally referred to as the Tainos, the natives on the island when it was discovered; (2) the influence of Spanish colonial culture; (3) slavery; (4) the American influence and economic development.

Very little is known about the culture of the Borinquen Indians. Unlike those in other areas of the Spanish empire, the indigenous people in Puerto Rico seem to have disappeared as an identifiable group early in the history of the colony. Some speculations are available about their culture and family life, but little of it is reliable. New studies are now in progress.

---

*The literature on the Puerto Rican family is extensive and uneven. Steward (1957) is one of the best presentations of varied types of Puerto Rican families. Mintz (1960) is a life history that is really a study of family life in a small barrio on the southern coast of Puerto Rico in an area in which rates of consensual union have been high. It is probably the finest single book on this kind of Puerto Rican family. Landy (1959) is a study of socialization and life cycle among poor families in a town in the northeast section of the island. It is an excellent study of family life and socialization. Roberts and Stefani (1940) is out of date, but it has detailed descriptions of many family habits and practices that are still common among the poor and rural families of the island. Stycos (1955) was part of a study of attitudes toward birth control but actually presents extensive information about the Puerto Rican family, particularly in attitudes toward marriage, children, and sex. Rogler and Hollingshead (1965) is a study of the causes of schizophrenia in Puerto Rico, but it provides an excellent and detailed analysis of family experience, especially among poor Puerto Ricans. Lewis (1965) is a vivid and detailed picture of the day-to-day experiences of a family with a history of prostitution in a slum area of San Juan. The introduction, which presents a lengthy analysis of what Lewis calls the "culture of poverty," is important as a setting for the rest of the book. Fernandez–Marina (1961) is an analysis of a form of hysteria common among Puerto Ricans, but the analysis involves a study of the changes in the values of Puerto Rican families under the influence of the mainland. Hill (1955) and Stanton (1956) are also studies of family change.

Spanish Colonial Culture

The great influence in the past and present on all levels of Puerto Rican family life was the Spanish colonial culture, the important features of which will now be discussed.

Pre-Eminence of the Family. As in most cultures of the world, the individual in Latin America has a deep consciousness of his membership in a family. He thinks of his importance in terms of his family membership. This is not a matter of prestige (as in belonging to the Ford or Rockefeller family), but a much more elemental thing, and it is as strong among the families of the very poor as it is among those of the very wealthy. The world to a Latin consists of a pattern of intimate personal relationships, and the basic relationships are those of his family. His confidence, his sense of security and identity, are perceived in his relationship to others who are his family.

This is evident in the use of *names,* the *technonomy* of Puerto Rican and Latin families. The man generally uses two family names together with his given name, for example, José Garcia Rivera. Garcia is the name of José's father's father; Rivera is the family name of José's mother's father. Thus, the name indicates that Jose comes from the family of Garcia in his father's line and from the family of Rivera in his mother's father's line. In Spanish-speaking areas, if the man is to be addressed by only one family name, the first name is used, not the second. José would be called Mr. Garcia, not Mr. Rivera. The mixing of these names by Americans is a source of constant embarrassment to Spanish-speaking people. The former governor of Puerto Rico, Luis Muñoz Marin was regularly referred to in American publications as Governor Marin. It should have been Governor Muñoz. Referring to Muñoz Marin as Governor Marin would be similar to referring to John Fitzgerald Kennedy as President Fitzgerald.

On some formal occasions, Puerto Ricans, like other Spanish speaking people, will use the names of all four families from which they come. If José were announcing his wedding, or an important official appointment, he might write his name: José Garcia Diaz y Rivera Colon. By this he is telling the world that he comes from the families of Garcia and Diaz on his father's side, and Rivera and Colon on his mother's side. The Puerto Ricans are not as familiar and informal with their public figures as Americans are. They may refer to a person as Don* Luis, Señor Muñoz, Señor Muñoz Marin, or as Muñoz, but they would not refer to him with the equivalent of "Louie" the way Americans refer to Ike and Dick and Jack or Harry. Americans are more sensitive to the importance of the individual—it is Harry who is important, or Ike, or Dick—but Puerto Ricans emphasize the importance of presenting themselves in the framework of the family of which they are a part.

The wife of José writes her name Maria Gonzalez de Garcia. She retains the family name of her father's father, Gonzalez, and she adopts, usually with the *"de,* the first name of her husband, Garcia. She may use both his names and present herself as Maria Gonzalez de Garcia Rivera. On formal occasions she may retain both her family names and would then present herself as Maria Gonzalez Medina de Garcia Rivera. The children of José and Maria would be Juan Garcia Gonzalez, the daughter Carmen Garcia Gonzalez; in formal situations, they would be Juan or Carmen Garcia Rivera y Gonzalez Medina.

The family is much more involved in the process of courtship than would be the case with an American family. In America boys and girls mingle freely, date each other, fall in love, and by various

---

*Don is a title of respect used generally in direct speech toward a man (Doña for a woman). It has no class implication. Very poor and humble people use it of their own family members or friends as a sign of respect. It is generally used with the first name (Don Luis or Doña Maria) never without it (Don Louis Muñoz, perhaps, but never Don Muñoz).

means ask each other to marry. If they agree to marry, they will advise their parents. If the parents agree, the marriage proceeds happily; if the parents disagree with the couple, they may go ahead and get married regardless. In Puerto Rico, intermingling and dating is much more restricted. A young man interested in a young woman is expected to speak to the parents of the girl, particularly the father, to declare his intentions. A serious courtship may never get started if the families disapprove. As one Puerto Rican sociologist explained personally to the author: In America courtship is a drama with only two actors; in Puerto Rico, it is a drama of two actors, but the families are continually prompting from the wings. Marriage is still considered much more a union of two families than it would be in America.

Finally, Puerto Ricans have a deep sense of family obligation. One's primary responsibilities are to family and friends. If a person advances in public office or succeeds in business enterprises, he has a strong sense of obligation to use his gains for the benefit of his family. Americans also have a sense of family loyalty, but to a much larger degree, they expect to make it on their own. Success does not make them feel obliged to appoint family members to positions, share their wealth with relatives, or use their position for the benefit of the family. They expect selection in business and government to be on the basis of ability and effort, not personal or family relationships. This is an oversimplification, since family influence operates in America and people in Puerto Rico are increasingly chosen on the basis of ability and effort. But in Puerto Rico the sense of family is much deeper. As economic development proceeds on the island, or as its citizens adjust to American life, the need increases to sacrifice family loyalty and obligation to efficiency. The Puerto Rican finds this a very difficult thing to do.

Superior Authority of the Man. A second feature of the Puerto Rican family is the role of superior authority exercised by the man. This is not peculiar to Latin cultures; it is the common situation in most cultures of the world. The man expects to exercise the authority in the family; he feels free to make decisions without consulting his wife; he expects to be obeyed when he gives commands. As a larger middle class emerges in Puerto Rico, the role of the woman is in the process of being redefined. But in contrast to the characteristics of cooperation and companionship of American families, the woman in Puerto Rico has a subordinate role.

This must not be interpreted as meaning that women do not have subtle ways of influencing men. The influence of mother over son is particularly strong in the culture of the Puerto Ricans. Furthermore, women have played an unusually important role in public and academic life. In 1962, of the 76 *municipios* in Puerto Rico, 10 had women as mayors, the most famous being Doña Felisa Rincon de Gautier, who was mayoress of the capital city of San Juan for 20 years. Women are department chairmen of many of the departments of the University of Puerto Rico. Oscar Lewis (1965) found the Puerto Rican women among the families he studied to be much more aggressive, outspoken, and even violent than the women in the Mexican families he had studied. Nevertheless, the role is culturally defined and ordinarily maintained as subordinate to the authority of the husband. Until recently, and still to a surprising extent, women will not make such decisions as consultation of a doctor or sending children for medical treatment without seeking permission of the husband.

The superior position of the man is also reflected in what Americans call a double standard of morality in reference to sexual behavior (Stycos, 1955).* In Latin cultures, as in most cultures of the

---

*See reference to *machismo* in Stycos (1955).

world, a very clear distinction is made between the "good" woman, who will be protected as a virgin until marriage, and then be protected as a wife and mother, and the "bad" woman, who is available for a man's enjoyment. Puerto Ricans are concerned about their girls, and fathers and brothers feel a strong obligation to protect them. On the other hand, a great deal of freedom is granted to the boys. It is rather expected, sometimes encouraged, that a boy have sexual experiences with women before marriage. After marriage he may feel free to engage in what Puerto Ricans sometimes jokingly refer to as "extracurricular activities." These patterns of protection of the woman and freedom for the man are changing, but they are still quite different from patterns of sexual behavior on the mainland. It is also true that patterns of sexual behavior that are going through a revolution to greater sexual freedom in America involve boys and girls equally and thus draw us even further away from the style of life in Puerto Rico.

   Compadrazgo. Another consequence of the influence of Spain on the Puerto Rican family has been *compadrazgo,*† or the institution of *compadres.* These are people who are companion parents, as it were, with the natural parents of the child; the man is the *compadres,* the woman is the *comadre.* Sponsors at Baptism, for example, become the godparents *(padrinos)* of the child, and the *compadres* of the child's parents; this is also true of sponsors at Confirmation. Witnesses at a marriage become *compadres* of the married couple. Sometimes common interests or the intensification of friendship may lead men or women to consider themselves *compadres* or *comadres.* The *compadres* are sometimes relatives, but often they are not. They constitute a network of ritual kinship, as serious and important as that of natural kinship, around a person or a group. *Compadres* frequently become more formal in their relationships, shifting from the familiar "Tu" to the formal "Usted" in speech. They have a deep sense of obligation to each other for economic assistance, support, encouragement, and even personal correction. A *compadre* may feel much freer to give advice or correction in regard to family problems than a brother or sister would. A *compadre* is expected to be responsive to all the needs of his *compadre,* and ideally, he supplies assistance without question. When Sidney Mintz was doing his anthropological study of a *barrio* of Santa Isabel, Puerto Rico, his principal informant was a remarkable man, Taso Zayas, a farm worker who cut sugar cane. Mintz reached a degree of close friendship with Taso and later decided to do his life history. Mintz describes the relationship that had developed between himself and Taso. Taso had reached a point at which he felt free to ask Mintz for money. "In his own words he would not 'dare ask' if he were not sure I would respond; and failure to do so, if it were a matter of free choice would end our friendship" (Mintz, 1960). In other words, Mintz and Taso had become *compadres.*

Slavery

Another influence on family life in Puerto Rico was that of slavery. Slavery was a milder institution in Puerto Rico than in America. But slavery in the Western world has had a devastating effect on family life. Little effort was made to provide for the stability and permanence of the slave family; men and women, relatives, children, were bought, sold, exchanged, and shifted with little or no regard for permanent family union. Slave women were defenseless before the advances of free men.

---

†There is some evidence that *compadrazgo* may have existed among the indigenous people. Some traces of it have beeen found among the Mayans. But it definitely was a significant Spanish institution that the colonizers either implanted or reinforced when they arrived.

The usual consequences of slavery in the broken family life of Blacks have been as evident in Puerto Rico as elsewhere. A number of features of Spanish culture modified the effects to some extent. Consorting with a woman who was not one's wife was a practice of upper-class men in the Spanish colonial tradition and was not confined to Black women. Therefore, the extramarital relationships of white men and Black women tended to follow a pattern similar to that of white men with white women. Cultural patterns formed around these relationships that provided some advantages to the women and children involved in them. However, the mother-based family—the family with children of a number of fathers and no permanent male consort—has been a common phenomenon in Puerto Rican history.

America and Economic Development

Within recent years, two other major influences have become important: (1) the influence of America has affected the island through the educational system, which for many years after annexation was in the hands of Americans and conducted on the American model; (2) religious influence from the mainland. Most of the Catholic priests, brothers, and nuns working among Puerto Ricans during the past 50 years have come from America. Protestant denominations have been established on the island since the turn of the century, and Pentecostal sects have preached a strong and effective gospel among the poor. Finally, and most important, Puerto Ricans returning from the mainland either to visit or to stay bring with them a strong and direct influence of mainland culture in relation to the family. The consequences, particularly of this last influence, will be indicated later.

The Modern Puerto Rican Family

As a consequence of the above influences, a fourfold structural typology can be identified among Puerto Rican families.

1. EXTENDED FAMILY SYSTEMS. These are families in which there are strong bonds and frequent interaction among a wide range of natural or ritual kin. Grandparents, parents, and children may live in the same household, or they may have separate households but visit frequently. The extended family is evident regardless of the type of marriage (regularized or consensual), and it is a source of strength and support. Traditionally, this was by far the most common pattern of family life.
2. THE NUCLEAR FAMILY. With the rise of the middle class, the conjugal unit of father, mother, and children, not living close to relatives and with weak bonds to the extended family, is becoming more common. It is difficult to get reliable evidence on the number of these families, but observant Puerto Ricans are noticing that with migration and upward mobility their number is rapidly increasing. This is an expected response to social and economic development.
3. FATHER, MOTHER, THEIR CHILDREN, AND CHILDREN OF ANOTHER UNION OR UNIONS OF HUSBAND OR WIFE. This is not an uncommon phenomenon among Puerto Rican families. New Yorkers have complained about the difficulty of understanding the differing names of children in some Puerto Rican households. In places on the island in which this phenomenon is common, children will identify themselves accordingly. If a visitor asks a boy if the girl with him is his sister, he may respond: "Yes, on my father's side," or "Yes, on my mother's side."
4. THE MOTHER-BASED FAMILY, WITH CHILDREN OF ONE OR MORE MEN, BUT WITH NO PERMANENT MALE CONSORT IN THE HOME. According to the 1970

census, 18.5 per cent of families in Puerto Rico were of this type. These four types of family structure are evident among Puerto Ricans on the mainland.

Consensual Unions

Important in relation lo family structure is the phenomenon of consensual unions,* which in former years have been common on the island but have been rapidly declining. A consensual union is a relatively stable union of a man and a woman who have gone through a religious or civil marriage ceremony. They begin living together and raising their family, and may live this way throughout their lives. At some later date they may regularize the union in a civil or religious ceremony.

This is not the "common law" marriage, which is an institution in English common law. The Roman law tradition, which has prevailed in Puerto Rico, never recognized a union as a marriage unless it was regularized, but Roman law always acknowledged the situation in which two people would live together without getting married. This state was defined as *concubinatus* or *concubinage.* Concubinage has unfavorable connotations in the English language, but it never had these in the Roman law tradition. Puerto Ricans who live consensually, or in concubinage, refer to themselves as *amancebados,* living together without marriage. The U.S. Census reports consensual unions as a recognized "civil status" and consequently asks people if they are living consensually. According to the decennial census, of all couples "living together" on the island, the following percentages were reported as "living consensually":

> 1899 34.7 percent of all unions
> 1920 26.3 percent of all unions
> 1950 24.9 percent of all unions
> 1960 13.5 percent of all unions
> 1970 6.5 percent of all unions

It is a status, therefore, that has always been culturally and officially acknowledged, and Puerto Ricans, unless they are speaking with strangers who they think may not understand, are very open about admitting that they are living consensually. They do not look on this as an immoral state, as it would be considered in many parts of the Christian world. The partners generally are not well instructed in any religious faith and consequently have no guilt feelings about living without religious marriage.** In addition, they are usually poor people with no property rights related to marriage. These simple people recognize that a man needs a woman, and a woman needs a man, and they begin to live together and bring up the children resulting from their union or from other unions that either one might have led. They judge the moral quality of the union in terms of their relationship to each other. He is a good man if he works to support the woman and children, treats them respectfully, and does not abandon them. She is a good woman if she keeps his house, cooks his meals, keeps his clothes, and raises his children properly. In fact, people in consensual unions are sometimes more

---

*The phenomenon of consensual union is widely discussed in the literature. The best insight into this cultural practice is found in Mintz (1960) A broader but less detailed description is found in Mintz's chapter. "Canamelar," in Steward (1957). A more detailed study of different rates of consensual unions in different parts of Puerto Rico is found in Dohen (1967). Some lengthy descriptions are also found in Lewis (1965) and Rogler and Hollingshead (1965).

**This does not mean they do not respect religious marriage. Many of them do not enter religious marriage because they understand its binding character and do not wish to commit themselves this way until they are sure they mean it.

concerned about the basic moral relationships than are people preoccupied with the regularization of the union. More important than the percentage of consensual unions for the whole island is the uneven distribution of consensual unions. For example, if one selected a number of representative *municipios* for low, medium, and high percentages of consensual union, it would break down as shown in Table 1. The table indicates that family patterns differ sharply from one section of the island to another. All of the low percentage *municipios* are in a small corner of the northwest tip, all of the medium-percentage *municipios* are in the central mountains, while all the high-percentage *municipios* are on the southeast corner.

The percentage of existing consensual unions has been declining sharply. It dropped from 25 percent in 1950 to 13.5 percent in 1960, and to 6.5 percent in 1970. A number of factors help to explain the decline. First, the increase in religious and spiritual care has created a wider concern for religious marriage. Second, important economic benefits have come to be associated with regularized unions; for example, widow's pensions, family benefits, social security, and admittance, particularly in New York, to public housing projects. Finally, the rapid emergence of a middle class has been important.

TABLE 1 **Percentage of All Existing Unions That Were Consensual, 1930, 1950, for Selected Municipios of Puerto Rico**

	1830	1950	1960
LOW RATES:			
Aguada	6.8	8.2	6.2
Aguadilla	11.3	14.3	6.0
Camuy	11.4	10.8	7.0
Isabela	9.6	9.4	9.0
Moca	6.3	6.9	4.0
Quebradilla	8.9	9.0	5.0
Rincon	8.5	8.6	5.0
MEDIUM RATES:			
Barceloneta	22.3	19.8	13.0
Barranquitas	15.3	15.4	7.0
Ciales	20.3	17.6	16.0
Jayuya	21.4	14.5	12.0
Orocovis	23.7	18.8	9.0
HIGH RATES:			
Arroyo	41.	35.6	14.
Cayey	42.2	34.9	20.
Coamo	41.	29.4	20.
Guayama	46.6	32.7	20.
Juana Diaz	40.5	44.5	28.
Maunabo	41.6	29.5	19.
Salinas	55.9	51.7	33.
Santa Isabel	51.6	43.8	19.

SOURCE: U.S. Bureau of the Census, U.S. Census of Population, 1930. Washington, D.C.: U.S. Government Printing Office, 1933. Vol. VI, Puerto Rico, Families, Table 18. U.S. Bureau of the Census, U.S. Census of Population, 1950. Washington, D.C.: U.S. Government Printing Office, 1953, Vol. II, Parts 51-54, Territories and Possessions, Table 39. U.S. Bureau of the Census, U.S. Census of Population, 1960. Washington, D.C.: U.S. Government Printing Office, 1963, Vol. 1, Characteristics of the Population, Vol. I, Part 53, Puerto Rico, Table 29.

Consensual union has always been a phenomenon of the poor population. As persons from the poorer classes advance to middle-class status, they become aware of regularized marriage as a middle-class value, and so they get married. Increased education and the gainful occupation and changing status of women have also contributed to the decline. In other words, the social conditions in which it was functional have disappeared.

Illegitimacy

Related to consensual unions is illegitimacy, about which at least brief mention must be made. International reports of population use the term "illegitimate" to designate the children of parents who are not married. Children of consensual unions are included in this. This is a misleading designation. In Puerto Rico, as in the Roman law tradition generally, the term "illegitimate" was never used.* A child of a marriage that was legalized, and whose rights before the law were thus protected, was called "legitimate." He was a "legal" child. "Natural" was the term used for all other children. This had a much less pejorative connotation than that associated with the term "llegitimate." A third term has come into use in Puerto Rico, the *hijo reconocido,* the recognized child.** In Puerto Rico, if the father of a child is known, whether he is living consensually with the mother, or whether the child resulted from a casual union, he is required by law to recognize the child. This gives the child a number of rights before the law, including the right to use the father's name, the right to support, and some rights of inheritance. Therefore, in examining statistics on legitimacy from areas like Puerto Rico, it is important to note that many of the children reported as illegitimate may actually be the children of stable consensual unions.

Fertility. Fertility has generally been high in Puerto Rico, although it appears to be dropping in recent years.*** This may be due largely to the migration of large numbers of young people to the mainland during their most fertile years. In any event, the rate of population increase on the island has been declining. Puerto Rico has been one of the classic examples of "population explosion," and efforts to control the population increase have been widespread, well known, and at times very controversial. The estimated natural increase of the population during the period 1887-99 was 14.3 per 1,000 population; the crude birth rate during the same period was 45.7, and the crude death rate was 31.4. The introduction of better hygiene caused the death rate to decline consistently but the birth rate to remain high, so population increase has been rapid. The average annual increase during

---

*In contrast to English common law which was concerned with illegitimacy, Roman law always acknowledged that some people would live together without getting married, in a state of concubinage. English common law, however, had the principle of common-law marriage: if a couple lived together long enough, it recognized the union as legal.

**In the late 1960s the vital-statistics reports do not use the category "recognized child" as they once did. As a result, it is difficult to determine how many there are. They had also ceased using the term *hijo natural* and began to use the standard international category "illegitimate" for children of parents not in regularized unions.

***The problem of population policy and birth control has been a troublesome issue between the government and the Catholic bishops on the island. For an analysis of the problem up to 1950, see Perloff (1950), Chapters 12 and 13. For the more modern period, Vasquez (1964) brings the data up to date. An intensive study of backgrounds of fertility was done during the 1950s in Puerto Rico. The first publication, Hatt (1952), was a survey of public attitudes toward large or small families. This was followed by Stycos (1955), which sought to determine why people said they preferred small families but continued having large ones; the final study was Hill, Stycos, and Black (1959), which reports the results of various methods to bring people to the practice of birth control.

the period 1930–35 was 18.9 per 1,000; during the period 1940-45 it was 24.9; in 1950 it was 28.6; in 1965 it had declined to 23.4; in 1970 it had declined to 15.7. Crude rates such as these are not very helpful in explaining population changes, but they give a general picture of increases and decreases. Actually, the continuing migration of Puerto Ricans to the mainland has been the safety valve of population increase. Had all the migrants remained in Puerto Rico, the population would be doubling every 20 years, a rate of growth that would have caused major problems on the island.

Family Values

Some aspects of the values of Puerto Rican family life have already been mentioned in relation to the influences that have helped to form it. In the following paragraphs, the range of values will be indicated that distinguish the Puerto Rican family from the predominant middle-class family values of the mainland.*

Personalism. The basic value of Puerto Rican culture, as of Latin cultures in general, is a form of individualism that focuses on the inner importance of the person. In contrast to the individualism of America, which values the individual in terms of his ability to compete for higher social and economic status, the culture of Puerto Rico centers attention on those inner qualities that constitute the uniqueness of the person and his goodness or worth in himself. In a two-class society in which little mobility was possible, a man was born into his social and economic position. Therefore, he defined his value in terms of the qualities and behavior that made a man good or respected in the social position in which he found himself. A poor farm laborer was a good man when he did those things that made a man good on his social and economic level. He felt an inner dignity *(dignidad)* about which the Puerto Rican is very sensitive; he expected others to have respect *(respeto)* for that *dignidad*. All men have some sense of personal dignity and are sensitive about proper respect being shown them. But this marks the Puerto Rican culture in a particular way. Puerto Ricans are much more sensitive than Americans to anything that appears to be personal insult or disdain; they do not take to practical jokes that are likely to embarrass or to party games in which people "make fools of themselves." They do not "horse around," as Americans would say in an offhand, informal manner; they are unusually responsive to manifestations of personal respect and to styles of personal leadership by men who appeal to the person rather than a program or a platform. Although the old two-class society in which these values developed has been disappearing, the values themselves are still very strong.

Personalism and Efficiency. It is this personalism that makes it difficult for the Puerto Rican to adjust easily to what Americans call efficiency. For a Puerto Rican, life is a network of personal relationships. He trusts persons; he relies on persons; he knows that at every moment he can fall back on a brother, a cousin, a *compadre*. He does not have that same trust for a system or an organization. The American, on the other hand, expects the system to work; he has confidence in the organization. When something goes wrong, his reaction is: "Somebody ought to do something about this." "Get this system going." Thus, an American becomes impatient and uneasy when systems do not work. He responds to efficiency. The Latin becomes uneasy and

---

*One or the best brief treatments of Latin values that are shared by Puerto Ricans can be found in Gillin (1960). Another good treatment is found in Wells (1969), Chapters 1 and 2.

impatient if the system works too well, if he feels himself in a situation in which he must rely on impersonal functions rather than personal relationships.

The Padrino. Related to personalism is the role of the *padrino*. The *padrino* is a person, strategically placed in a higher position of the social structure, who has a personal relationship with the poorer person for whom he provides employment, assistance at time of need, and acts as an advocate if the poor person becomes involved in trouble. The *padrino* is really the intermediary between the poor person who has neither sophistication nor innuence, and the larger society of law, government, employment, and service. He is a strategic helper in times of need, but the possibilities of exploitation in this relationship are very great. The poor person can become completely bound to the *padrino* by debt or by obligations to personal service to such an extent that his life is little better than slavery. The role of the *padrino* has decreased in Puerto Rico, but the tendency to seek a personal relationship in one's business affairs is still strong.

Machismo. Another aspect of personalism is a combination of qualities associated with masculinity. This is generally referred to as *machismo*, literally, maleness. *Machismo is* a style of personal daring (the great quality of the bullfighter) by which one faces challenge, danger, and threat with calmness and self-possession; this sometimes takes the form of bravado. It is also a quality of personal magnetism that impresses and influences others and prompts them to follow one as a leader—the quality of the *conquistador*. It is associated with sexual prowess, influence, and power over women, reflected in a vigorous romanticism and a jealous guarding of sweetheart or wife, or in premarital and extramarital relationships.

Sense of Family Obligation. Personalism is deeply rooted in the individualism that has just been described; it is also rooted in the family. As explained above, the Puerto Rican has a deep sense of that network of primary personal relationships that is his family. To express it another way, he senses the family as an extension of the person, and the network of obligations follows as described above.

Sense of the Primary of the Spiritual. The Latin generally refers to American culture as very materialistic, much to the amazement of Americans, who are conscious of human qualities, concerns, and generosity in American culture that are missing in the Latin. What the Latin means is that his fundamental concerns are not with this world or its tangible features. He has a sense of spirit and soul as much more important than the body and as being intimately related to his value as a person; he tends to think in terms of transcendent qualities, such as justice, loyalty, or love, rather than in terms of practical arrangements that spell out justice or loyalty in the conrete. On an intellectual level, he strives to clarify relationships conceptually with a confidence that if they can be made intellectually clear and precise, the relationships will become actualities. He thinks of life very much in terms of ultimate values and ultimate spiritual goals, and expresses a willingness to sacrifice material satisfactions for these. In contrast, the American preoccupation with mastering the world and subjecting it, through technological programs, to man's domination gives him the sense of reversing the system of values, of emphasizing the importance of mastering the physical universe rather than seeking the values of the spirit. It is striking to note how many important political figures are also literary men with a humanistic flair. Former Governor Muñoz Marin is a poet and is affectionately called *El Vate*, the Bard, in Puerto Rico; the former resident commissioner in Washington, Santiago Polanco Abreu, is a literary critic; some of the best known figures in public service in the Puerto Rican community in New York, such as Juan Aviles, Carmen Marrero, and Luis Quero Chiesa, are accomplished writers and artists.

Fatalism. Connected to these spiritual values is a deep sense of fatalism in Puerto Ricans. They have a sense of destiny, partly related to elemental fears of the sacred, partly related to a sense of divine providence governing the world. The popular song, "Que será, será," "Whatever will be, will be," is a simple expression of it, as is the common expression that intersperses so much of Puerto Rican speech: *Si Dios quiere*, "If God wills it." The term "destiny" recurs frequently in Puerto Rican popular songs. This quality leads to the acceptance of many events as inevitable; it also softens the sense of personal guilt for failure. If, after a vigorous effort, an enterprise does not succeed, the Puerto Rican may shrug his shoulders and remark: "It was not meant to be."

Sense of Hierarchy. The Puerto Ricans, like other Latins, have had a concept of a hierarchical world during the whole of their history. This was partly the result of the two-class system, in which members never conceived of a world in which they could move out of the position of their birth. Thus, they thought of a relationship of higher and lower classes that was fixed somewhat as the various parts of the body were fixed. This concept of hierarchy contributed to their concept of personal worth as distinct from a person's position in the social structure.

The Puerto Rican Family on the Mainland

The institution that faces the most direct shock in the migration to the mainland is the family, and the progress of Puerto Ricans can be measured to a large extent by a study of the family. First, a statistical description of Puerto Rican families can be presented, followed by an analysis of the effect of migration on the family.

It has long been recognized that the migration of Puerto Ricans is a family migration, in the sense that they either come as families or expect to stay and found their families here. This is reflected in the percentage of the population on the mainland that is married. According to the 1960 Census, of all Puerto Rican males over 14 years of age, 70 percent were married; of females, about 80 percent (Fitzpatrick, 1966). Age at marriage shows a sharp decline from first generation to second generation, indicating an adaptation to mainland patterns.

One of the most serious differences between Puerto Rican families on the mainland and on the island, revealed in the 1970 Census, is the high rate of "families with female head." On the mainland 28 per cent of Puerto Rican families were reported as having a female head, almost as high as the rate for American blacks; even more surprising is the fact that this high rate continues in the second generation: almost 26 percent of the families have a female head. This is in contrast to the 18.5 percent of families in Puerto Rico with a female head. No one has yet found a satisfactory explanation of this phenomenon. It will certainly affect Puerto Rican family life in the future.

The phenomenon of "out-of-wedlock" children is also steadily increasing in New York State. In 1957 only 11 percent of Puerto Rican births in New York State were out of wedlock; this increased to 22 percent in 1967 and 30 percent in 1969. This was considerably higher than the rate of about 20 percent in Puerto Rico in 1970.

Type of Ceremony

Another indication of change can be found in the type of religious ceremony of Puerto Rican marriages on the mainland. As indicated before, this varies considerably from one area of Puerto Rico to another. Comparison of type of religious ceremony for all marriages in Puerto Rico for 1960 with type of religious ceremony for Puerto Rican marriages in New York City for 1959 brings results as shown in Table 2.

TABLE 2 Type of Religious Ceremony for All Marriages in Puerto Rico and All Puerto Rican Marriages in New York City for Selected Years

	Civil (%)	Catholic (%)	Protestant (%)
Puerto Rico, 1949	24.3	61.4	14.3
Puerto Rico, 1960	36.2	45.8	17.6
New York City, 1949 (n. 4514)*	20.0	27.0	50.0
New York City, 1959 (n. 9370)	18.0	41.0	38.0

SOURCE: Fitzpatrick (1966).
*A small number of other types of ceremonies are included in this total.

Two things are evident from Table 2. The pattern of marriage ceremony differs considerably between Puerto Rico and New York, and the pattern in New York, as in Puerto Rico, changed greatly between 1949 and 1959. The increase in Catholic ceremonies can be explained by the widespread efforts of the Catholic archdioceses of New York and Brooklyn to develop special programs for the religious care of Puerto Rican people between 1949 and 1959. In addition, ceremonies in Pentecostal and Evangelical churches declined from 1949 to 1959, particularly between first and second generation. If the Protestant marriages performed by ministers of Pentecostal and Evangelical sects are taken separately, the decline is very evident. In 1959, 38.4 percent of first generation grooms were married by Pentecostal ministers, but only 33.3 percent of second-generation grooms; among brides, 37 percent of first generation, but only 30.1 percent of the second generation were married by Pentecostal ministers (Fitzpatrick, 1966). The consistent drop from first to second generation tends to confirm the theory that association with sects and storefront religious groups is a first-generation phenomenon. When the second generation becomes more familiar with American life, they tend to withdraw from the sects.

Intermarriage
The most significant evidence of adjustment to life on the mainland has been the increase of marriage of Puerto Ricans with non-Puerto Ricans. In his study of New York marriages for the years 1949 and 1959, Fitzpatrick (1966) established that there is a significant increase in the rate of out-group marriage among second-generation Puerto Ricans over the first. The data are presented in Table 3.

The increase in the rate of out-group marriages among Puerto Ricans in both 1949 and 1959 between the first and second generation was as great as was the increase for all immigrants in New York City in the years 1908 to 1912.* It is legitimate to conclude from this that if out–group marriage is accepted as an index of assimilation, the assimilation of Puerto Ricans in New York is moving as rapidly as the assimilation of all immigrant groups during the years 1908-12.

Changes in Values
Much more important than the statistical description of the Puerto Rican families in America or in New York City is the study of the changes in values that they face. Probably the most serious is the shift in roles of husband and wife. There is abundant evidence that this is a common experience of

---

*The data for marriages of immigrants, 1908-12 which were used in the Fitzpatrick study were taken from Drachsler (1921).

immigrants. It is provoked by a number of things. First, it is frequently easier for Puerto Rican women to get jobs in New York than Puerto Rican men. This gives the wife an economic independence that she may never have had before, and if the husband is unemployed while the wife is working, the reversal of roles is severe. Second, the impact of American culture begins to make itself felt more directly in New York than on the island. Puerto Rican women from the poorer classes are much more involved in social, community, and political activities than they are in Puerto Rico. This influences the Puerto Rican wife to adopt gradually the patterns of the mainland.

Even more direct and difficult to cope with is the shift in role of the Puerto Rican child. Puerto Rican families have frequently lamented the patterns of behavior of even good boys in America. Puerto Rican parents consider them to be disrespectful. American children are taught to be self-reliant, aggressive, and competitive, to ask, "Why," and to stand on their own two feet. A Puerto Rican child is generally much more submissive. When the children begin to behave according to the American pattern, the parents cannot understand it. A priest who had worked for many years with migrating Puerto Ricans remarked to the writer: "When these Puerto Rican families come to New York, I give the boys about forty-eight hours on the streets of New York, and the difference between his behavior and what the family expects will have begun to shake the family."

The distance that gradually separates child from family is indicated in much of the literature about Puerto Ricans in New York. In the autobiography of Piri Thomas, *Down These Mean Streets* (1967), it is clear that his family—and it was a good, strong family—had no way of controlling him once he began to associate with his peers on the streets. The sharp contrast of two life histories, *Two Blocks Apart* (Mayerson, 1965), also demonstrates the difficulties of a Puerto Rican family in trying to continue to control the life of a boy growing up in New York. His peers become his significant reference group. A considerable number of scholars and social workers attribute much of the delinquency of Puerto Ricans to the excessive confinement that the Puerto Rican families impose in an effort to protect their children. Once the children can break loose in the early teens, they break completely. When Julio Gonzalez was killed in a gang fight on the Lower East Side in reprisal for the murder of a Black girl, Theresa Gee, in 1959, he was buried from Nativity Church. Julio's father, a poor man from a mountain town in Puerto Rico, was like a pillar of strength during the wake. He was a man of extraordinary dignity and self-possession. After the funeral Mass, he went to the sacristy of the church, embraced each of the priests who had participated, and thanked them. Here was a man who sought to pass on to his son the qualities of loyalty, dignity, and strength. But when the son reached the streets, different definitions of loyalty and dignity took over. As Julio was dying, after the priest had given him the last rites of the Catholic Church, he fell into unconsciousness, mumbling: "Tell the guys they can count me; tell them I'll be there."*

Probably the most severe problem of control is the effort of families to give their unmarried girls the same kind of protection they would have given them in Puerto Rico. When the girls reach the early teens, they wish to do what American girls do: go to dances with boys without a chaperone and associate freely with girls and boys of the neighborhood or school. For a good Puerto Rican father to permit his daughter to go out unprotected is a serious moral failure. In a Puerto Rican town, when a father has brought his daughters as virgins to marriage, he can hold up his head before his community;

---

*For a lengthy discussion of this change of values and its relation to delinquency, see Fitzpatrick (1960). This is reprinted in Tyler (1962):415-21.

he enjoys the esteem and prestige of a good father. To ask the same father to allow his daughters to go free in New York is to ask him to do something that the men of his family have considered immoral. It is psychologically almost impossible for him to do this. The tension between parents and daughter(s) is one of the most difficult for Puerto Rican parents to manage. It is frequently complicated because Americans, including schoolteachers and counselors, who are not aware of the significance of this in the Puerto Rican background, advise the parents to allow the girls to go out freely.*

Finally, the classic tension between the generations takes place. The parents are living in the Puerto Rican culture in their homes. The children are being brought up in an American school where American values are being presented. The parents will never really understand their children; the children will never really understand the parents.

Weakening of Extended Kinship
Apart from the conflict between generations, the experience of migration tends to weaken the family bonds that created a supporting network on which the family could always rely. To a growing extent, the family finds itself alone. This is partly the result of moving from place to place. It is also due to the fact that the way of life in mainland cities is not a convenient environment for the perpetuation of family virtues and values. The Department of Social Services provides assistance in time of need but not with the familiar, informal sense of personal and family respect. Regulations in housing, consumer loans, schools, and courts create a requirement for professional help, and the family is less and less effective.

Replacement or Personalist Values
Closely related to all the above difficulties, and creating difficulties of its own, is the slow and steady substitution of impersonal norms, norms of the system rather than norms of personal relationships. The need to adjust to the dominant patterns of American society requires a preparation to seek employment and advancement on the basis of merit or ability. To people for whom the world is an extensive pattern of personal relationships, this is a difficult adjustment.

The process of uprooting has been described before in the extensive literature about immigrants. It leads to three kinds of adjustments. The first involves escape from the immigrant or migrant group and an effort to become as much like the established community as possible in as short a time as possible. These people seek to disassociate themselves from their past. They sometimes change their name, they change their reference groups, and seek to be accepted by the larger society. They are in great danger of becoming marginal. Having abandoned the way of life of their own people, in which they had a sense of "who they were," there is no assurance that they will be accepted by the larger community. They may find themselves in a no man's land of culture. In this stage, the danger of personal frustration is acute.

A second reaction is withdrawal into the old culture, a resistance to the new way of life. These people seek to retain the older identities by locking themselves into their old way of life.

The third reaction is the effort to build a cultural bridge between the culture of the migrants and that of the mainland. These are the people who have confidence and security in their own way of life,

---

*Protection of the girls generates its own problems in Puerto Rico, a form of "cloister rebellion" that may lead to escape from the home or elopement. It is well described in Stycos (1955), Chapter 5.

but who realize that it cannot continue. Therefore, they seek to establish themselves in the new society but continue to identify themselves with the people from whom they come. These are the ones through whom the process of assimilation moves forward.

Change and Adaptation

In view of the above discussion, it is important to discover at what level of assimilation the Puerto Rican family now stands, and how it is affected by the problem of identity. In terms of intermarriage, the data indicate that the increase in the rate of out-group marriage between first and second generation is as great as it was for all immigrants to New York, 1908-12. Replication of the study for 1969, which is now in progress at Fordham University, New York, will involve many more firsthand second-generation marriages and will give a much more reliable indication of the trend. According to the 1970 Census data, in New York State 34 percent of second-generation Puerto Rican men and 32 per cent of second-generation Puerto Rican women, married and living with their spouses, are married to non-Puerto Ricans. For Puerto Ricans outside New York the rates are much higher: 68 per cent of second-generation Puerto Rican men, 65 percent of women, married and living with their spouses were married to non-Puerto Ricans. The 1970 census reports do not discriminate between non-Puerto Rican spouses who are Hispanic and those who are not. The Fitzpatrick data include only non-Hispanic spouses among the non-Puerto Ricans. In this regard, Puerto Ricans are simply repeating the consistent pattern of immigrants who preceded them.

Second, in view of the character of the migration from Puerto Rico (i.e., the return of many Puerto Ricans from the mainland and the continuing movement of large numbers of new migrants to the mainland), there continue to be large numbers of Puerto Rican families in the early and difficult stages of adjustment to New York, struggling for a satisfactory cultural adjustment as defined by Gordon (1963) and Eisenstadt (1955).

The increase in the number of second-generation Puerto Ricans indicates that the classical problems of newcomers, the problems of the second generation, are very likely at a serious level and will continue to be so for a considerable length of time. It is not clear just how family difficulties contribute to these larger problems, but it is certain that these problems contribute immeasurably to family difficulties. In the early 1960s a group of Puerto Rican social workers founded the Puerto Rican Family Institute in an effort to assist Puerto Rican families in New York. The objective of the institute was not simply to provide family casework but to identify well-established Puerto Rican families in New York and match them as *compadres* to newly arrived families that showed signs of suffering from the strains of adjustment to the city. This was an attempt to use the traditional forms of neighborhood and family help that were characteristic of Puerto Rico. When families could be matched, the program has been very helpful. But recently the institute has found that the percentage of families with serious and immediate problems has been increasing. This may reflect the fact that as agencies around the city learn of a Puerto Rican institute, they refer their Puerto Rican problem cases to it; it may also reflect the shock of uprooting upon the newly arriving families or the disruption that occurs as the numbers in the second generation increase. The growth of militancy among the young will be another factor that will increase tension. However, in the demonstrations at City College of New York in the spring of 1969, in which militant Puerto Rican students played a major part, observers commented that the parents of the Puerto Rican students were very much on hand, supporting their sons and daughters, bringing them food, clothing, and supplies.

In the period during which the Puerto Ricans struggle for greater solidarity and identity as a community, the family remains the major psychosocial support for its members. In many cases, it is a broken family; in others, it is hampered by poverty, unemployment, illness; but it remains the source of strength for most Puerto Ricans in the process of transition. In the turbulent action of the musical *West Side Story,* when Bernardo, leader of the Puerto Rican gang, sees Tony, a youth of another ethnic group, approaching his sister Maria, Bernardo pulls Maria away from Tony to take her home; he then turns to Tony in anger and shouts: "You keep away from my sister. Don't you know we are a family people!"

During 1966 the first presentation in New York of *The Ox Cart* took place. This is a play by a Puerto Rican playwright, Rene Marques, which presents a picture of a simple farm family in the mountains of Puerto Rico, struggling to survive but reflecting the deep virtues of family loyalty and strength. Under the influence of the oldest son, the family moves to a slum section of San Juan in order to improve itself. But deterioration sets in as the slum environment begins to attack the solidarity and loyalty of the family members. The family then moves to New York; there the strain of the uprooting becomes worse, the gap between mother and children more painful, and the virtues of the old mountain family seem even more distant. After the violent death of the son, the play ends with the valiant mother setting out to go back to the mountains of Puerto Rico; there she hopes to regain the traditional values of Puerto Rican family life that were destroyed in San Juan and New York.

This is an ancient theme, and it may be as true for Puerto Ricans as it was for earlier newcomers. But if the Puerto Ricans make it on the mainland, it will be through the same source of strength that supported the immigrants of earlier times—the solidarity of the family.

References

Dohen, Dorothy M. 1967. *The Background of Consensual Union in Puerto Rico.* In *Two Puerto Rican Studies.* Cuernavaca, Mexico: Center of Intercultural Documentation.

Drachsler, Julian. 1921. *Intermarriage in New York City.* New York: Columbia University Press.

Eisenstadt, S. N. 1955. The *Absorption of Immigrants.* New York: The Free Press.

Fernandez-Marina, R. 1961. "The Puerto Rican Syndrome: Its Dynamics and Cultural Determinants." *Psychiatry* 24 (February):79-82.

——, E. D. Maldonado Sierra, and R. D. Trent. 1958. Three Basic Themes in Mexican and Puerto Rican Family Values." *Journal of Sociology* 48 (November): 167-81.

Fitzpatrick, J. P. 1960. "Crime and Our Puerto Ricans" *Catholic Mind* 58:39-50.

——. 1966. "Intermarriage of Puerto Ricans in New York City." *American Journal of Sociology* 71 (January):401.

——. 1971. *Puerto Rican Americans: The Meaning of Migration to the Mainland.* Englewood Cliffs, N.J.: Prentice-Hall.

Gillin, John. 1960. "Some Signposts for Policy." In Richard N. Adams, *et al.* (ed.): *Social Change in Latin America Today.* New York: Vintage, pp. 28-47.

Gordon, Milton. 1963. *Assimilation in American Life.* New York: Oxford University Press.

Hatt, Paul. 1952. *Background of Human Fertility in Puerto Rico.* Princeton, N.J.: Princeton University Press.

Hill, Reuben. 1955. "Courtship in Puerto Rico: An Institution in Transition." *Marriage and Family Living* 17 (February):26-34.

———, J . Mayone Stycos, and Kurt W. Back. 1959. *The Family and Population Control: A Puerto Rican Experiment in Social Change.* Chapel Hill, N.C.: University of North Carolina Press.

Landy, David. 1959. *Tropical Childhood.* Chapel Hill, N.C.: University of North Carolina Press.

Lewis, Oscar. 1965. *La Vida: A Puerto Rican Family in the Culture of Poverty—San Juan and New York.* New York: Random House.

Mayerson, Charlotte Leon (ed.). 1965. *Two Blocks Apart.* New York: Holt, Rinehart and Winston.

Mintz, Sidney. 1960. *Worker in the Cane.* New Haven: Yale University Press.

Perloff, Harvey S. 1950. *Puerto Rico's Economic Future.* Chicago: University of Chicago Press.

Roberts, Lydia, and Rose Sterani. 1940. *Patterns of Living in Puerto Rican Families.* Rio Piedras: University of Puerto Rico Press.

Rogler, Lloyd, and A. B. Hollinshead, 1965. *Trapped: Families and Schizophrenia.* New York: Wiley.

Steward, Julian. 1957. *People of Puerto Rico.* Champaign-Urbana: University of Illinois Press.

Stycos, J. Mayone. 1955. *Family and Fertility in Puerto Rico.* New York: Columbia University Press.

Thomas, Piri. 1967. *Down These Mean Streets.* New York: Knopf.

Tyler, Gus. 1962. *Organized Crime in America.* Ann Arbor: University of Michigan Press.

Vasquez, Jose L. 1964. *Fertility Trends in Puerto Rico.* Section on Bio Statistics, Department of Preventive Medicine and Public Health, School of Medicine of Puerto Rico, San Juan.

Wells, Henry. 1969. *The Modernization of Puerto Rico.* Cambridge, Mass.: Harvard University Press.

The nail that sticks up gets hammered down.
Japanese proverb

From The Italian American Family (1976)

Francis X. Femminella and Jill S. Quadagno

Historical Background

Italian Villagers

All persons who emigrated from Italy, Sicily, Corsica, and Sardinia at the end of the nineteenth century were referred to as "Italians." The name was applied by members of host societies around the world who perceived and identified them as belonging to or having a single national origin or language. This identity was not, however, a central perception of the emigrants themselves, at least not initially. The unification of Italy (1861-71) could neither easily wipe out centuries of separation, nor could it instantly supply a new mode of identification for those who knew themselves to be different.

The formation of a group cultural identity is a process necessarily continuing over generations.* Through the centuries emigrants from Italy had learned to define themselves by their association with their parents and their immediate neighbors. They belonged not to Italy but first to their families and then to their villages. For the most part, Neopolitans, Calabrians, Sicilians, Barese, etc., came to America sharing a common identification as southern Italians. When northern Italians came, they considered themselves Romans, Venetians, Piedmontese, and Genoese. From their perspective they were different peoples; they felt no closer in their relationship to one another than an American might feel to an Australian, or to a Scot (Carlyle, 1962:13ff).

Beyond merely feeling that they were different peoples, there was a pervasive prejudice held by northern Italians against southern Italians (Covello, 1967:23-33; Iorizzo and Mondello, 1971:3,4 *passim;* Lopreato, 1970:25; Rolle 1972:112). These prejudices were deeply rooted and "racial" in content. That is, northern Italians considered southern Italians to be an inferior "race" of people. The major characteristics of race prejudice and intolerance with which we are familiar in America existed in Italy also. Southern Italians were thought of as people who at best ought to be disregarded or, worse, cheated, enslaved, spat upon, and generally treated without regard for basic human dignity. In return, southern Italians despised, but, in a reflection of the psychodynamics of identification, simultaneously sought to emulate the *alt Italiani*—the high Italians of the north.

Of course, to imitate behavior requires, first of all, knowledge of the behavior, but in fact most of the inhabitants of southern Italy were financially impoverished and had little direct knowledge of northern manners and ways. What they knew of it had been learned by observing the actions of the wealthy, more educated, and more traveled local barons. These latter were landowners with extensive holdings who occupied the highest position in the stratification system of the southern Italian villages.

---

*The notion of "cultural identity" as used here is derived from a concept of "egoidentity" developed by Erik H. Erikson. See his "Identity and the Life Cycle" in George S. Klein (1959:1-171). Some of the data on which this paper is based are taken from research done by Femminella, an early portion of which was included in *Ethnicity and Ego-Identity* (1968).

Disparaged by northern Italians, *baroni* in turn looked down on their fellow villagers of lower caste. Few of these landed gentry were numbered among the immigrants to America.

This differentiation of northern and southern Italians must be neither exaggerated nor ignored if Italians in America are to be understood. Migrants have come to the Americas from all parts of the southern European boot since even before Colonial times, but the great waves of Italian migration to North America in the late nineteenth century consisted for the most part of southern Italians. On arrival, they neither expected nor received a welcoming hand from their northern Italian brothers who were small in numbers and who had arrived much earlier. If anything, they were made to feel unwanted because their presence in many cases was a source of embarrassment to the earlier immigrants who were finally extricating themselves from the prejudices they had themselves experienced upon arrival in America, and who were more securely lodged in the middle range of the work force. (Glazer and Moynihan, 1963:184).

Moreover, just as the landowners in the villages of southern Italy had imitated the northern Italians, so in this country the new *"baroni"* imitated the successful northern Italians already here. That is, northern Italian exploitation of the new immigrants in turn served as a prototype for successful southern Italian immigrant behavior. A second effect of this exploitative behavior was social psychological, reaching beyond both the individuals involved and the action and occurrences themselves. The exploitative relationships that southern Italians met reinforced those earlier sentiments of trust and distrust that have always been characteristic of Italian peasant life.* In a sense, this was socially more significant than the exploitation itself because it retarded the development of different but integrated social structures in the host society.

To explain this point, it is necessary to understand the meaning of the term *campanilismo* (Covello, 1967:135; Lopreato, 1970:103ff; Vecoli, 1964). This interesting word derives from *campanile,* meaning a steeple or belfry. Central to each of the scattered villages of the Italian countryside was the local church with its bell towers. The sound of the bell was unique and familiar to each and every person in the village, and over the centuries the attachment the villagers felt for the bell metamorphosed into a sense of loyalty to the village itself and to one's neighbors. The sound of the bell defined the boundaries of the villages (often quite literally); those who lived beyond were strangers** not to be trusted since the interests of these outsiders too often conflicted with those of the villagers themselves. The focus was not on the group and its values but on the individual and his family.

These village communities in their isolation developed manners and mores, nuances of language and dress, and human struggles and enmities that distinguished one village from another, regardless of geographical proximity. It is not surprising that when Italian villagers migrated to America, they sought out their *paisani* who had come ahead of them and as soon as possible began to re-establish many of the typical village customs and social relations, including a detachment and personal sense of being apart from the more broadly conceived polity. The centuries of defending against exploitation

---

*This notion has significance for understanding tbe *"Padroni"* relationships of earlier times and the clientele relationships of criminals in later times. Cf. L. V. Iorizzo and S. Mondello (1971:138). See also Francis A. J. Ianni (1972).

**The word "stranger" is itself pregnant with meaning and heavily laden with emotion today and through history. Cf. A. Lacoque and F. R. Vasquez, *the Newcomer and the Bible (1971).*

by northern Italians and foreign governments, and after 1860 the failure of the newly unified Kingdom of Italy to effect the Garibaldi promise of land distribution, generated mechanisms of preservation closely bound up with patterns of authority and control within the family. Clearly, these migrants from the place called Italy were not Italians; nor, for that matter, were they in the first instance "north" or "south" Italians; rather, they were persons from individual families, specific villages, and towns, which Vecoli (1964) calls "rural cities," whose life, and the meaning it held, derived from their attachment to these settings (Covello, 1967:159-168; Dore, 1968:95-122; Lopreato, 1970:101ff).

The Contadino Family in the Mezzogiorno *

Although the first Italian immigrants to arrive in America in the 1870s were from northern Italy, their numbers were small. The impact of the Italian migration, which increased rapidly after 1900, consisted largely of southern Italians from the region known as the Mezzogiorno. Between 1900 and 1930 over five million Italians came to America, and at least 80 per cent were from the southern regions of Italy (Gambino, 1974:3; Lopreato, 1970:34). In order to understand the Italian American family today, it is necessary to understand the kind of people who lived in the Mezzogiorno and the life style they brought with them to this country.

The name Mezzogiorno refers to the six provinces east and south of Rome. It has been called "the land that time forgot." Those Italians who emigrated from the Mezzogiorno were largely of the peasant class of farmers and day laborers called the *contadino* class. The *contadino* included agricultural workers who owned a tiny plot of land and leased additional land from the large landowners, the agricultural proletariat who owned no land but leased it from the *signori,* and the subproletariat consisting of day laborers, the *giornalieri,* whose daily existence depended on the whims of the weather and the nobility (Lopreato, 1970:31).

L'ORDINE DELLA FAMIGLIA. Centuries of exploitation by the landed class and the harsh exigencies of daily life led to a rejection of the social institutions of the larger society, so that the Italian *contadino* came to rely solely on the family. Within the family a complex system of rules regulating one's relations and responsibilities to the members of his family and one's posture toward the outside world was developed.

Family order, which was the only meaningful order in the lives of the *contadino,* was maintained by adhering to the norms surrounding one's responsibilities to other family members. Relationships between individuals were arranged according to a hierarchy. The first category was *la famiglia* and consisted of blood relationships, family members to whom one owed all his loyalty. *La famiglia* was supplemented by *comparaggio,* or godparents, who comprised the second category in the hierarchy. Causal acquaintances and those whose family status demanded respect made up the third category in the hierarchy. Finally, there were *stranieri,* which included all other people, such as shopkeepers and fellow workers who were objects of suspicion and as such kept at a distance (Gambino, 1974:19).

MARITAL ROLES. The *contadino* family has been described as patriarchal, yet this is somewhat misleading since it implies that all the power is held by the male members of the family. It is true that the father was the *capo di famiglia,* or head of the family, and in this role was responsible for arbitrating disputes and making decisions that affected the relations of *la famiglia* with the outside world. He was

---

*Most of the following discussion of the southern Italian family is taken from Gambino (1974).

also responsible for making a living, a feat that involved skills of wit as well as hard labor to protect his family from the threat of *la miseria,* or desperate poverty. However, the mother, as the center of the family in a society in which nonfamilial relationships were not meaningful, had a great deal of power in terms of internal matters. The southern Italian wife and mother kept the home, which was the source of all that gave meaning to life,managed all financial affairs, and arranged the marriages of her children, which were critical for survival of *la via veccchia,* the old way. In a world in which the family status was judged not by the occupation of the father but by the signs of family well-being that emanated from the household, the mother played an important role in securing that status.

In extended family relationships, the patriarchal image of the Italian family is also misleading since the major kinship ties were with the maternal relatives. The nurturing of the children was done by the mother and her female relatives who were her frequent companions, and if the mother became a widow, the responsibility for her and her children was assumed by her own family, not her husband's. "Thus, despite the pre-eminence of the husband, the wife's role in the economics of the family was considerable, comprising both management and insurance . . . Indeed, the father was formal chief executive of the family, but the actual power was shared with the mother in an intricate pattern of interactions . . ." (Gambino, 1974:26).

THE INSTITUTION OF COMPARAGGIO. The term comparaggio refers to the selection of outsiders to be admitted into the family circle in the role of godparents. This was an institution of great significance in extending the kinship ties of families in the Mezzogiorno to include individuals who were not blood relatives. It formed further protection against the intrusion of outsiders and formed links between villages that extended the influence of a single family. Because of their importance, great care was taken in the selection of godparents, who could be either one's peers or older people who were to be treated with respect. While the godparents may have participated in the baptism of the child in the church, godparents were frequently selected independent of ties to the church. It was considered an honor to be offered the role of godparent, and to refuse was considered a great insult. The privileges and obligations extended to godparents approached those of kin with blood ties, yet it was known that in a conflict one's blood relatives came first (Gambino, 974:29).

LA VIA VECCHIA. Within the family a value system was built and maintained that served chiefly to protect the individual from an essentially hostile environment. These values permeated all areas of social life not only within the family itself but in terms of the attitudes of the *contadino* toward work, education, and definitions of social status.

Of singular importance was the necessity of family ties. One's personal identity was derived from his family, and family membership was essential in terms of defining one's place in society. The most shameful condition was to be without a family (Gambino, 1974:31). A man who violated the family code and was outcast from his family was an outcast from the larger society as well. He could only become a day laborer, and even in this he was the last hired. For a female without a family the only options were to become a beggar or a prostitute. However, loyal kin were rewarded by always having a place within the family. The aged were cared for in the family, and "no one went to poorhouses, orphanages, or other institutions of charity in the Mezzogiorno except those few unfortunates without any family intimates" (Gambino, 1974:29).

The strength of familial ties also affected the attitude of the *contadino* toward work. "Work is regarded as moral training for the young. And among adults, it is regarded as a matter of pride. To work is to show evidence that one has become a man or a woman, a full member of the family" (Gambino, 1974:80). Thus work was not defined as abstract but as tangible, something that could be shown to others as a visible result of an individual's skills and efforts. The disdain for intangibles was also related to the *contadino's* attitude toward education.

While the ideal of the *contadino* was to cultivate children who were *ben educato*—well educated— the translation of this phrase is deceptive. Being educated did not refer to formal schooling but to being educated in proper behavior. "*Ben educato* meant raised with the core of one's personality woven of those values and attitudes, habits and skills that perpetuated *l'ordine della famiglia,* and thus one was attuned to the welfare of the family" (Gambino, 1974:225). In this sense, formal schooling was antithetical to proper training for manhood or womanhood, involving the influence of *stranieri* who might interfere with *la via vecchia* as well as keeping young people from the more important lessons they might learn from work.

The concept of *ben educato* was applied differently to male and female children. For a young boy, this meant first and foremost to be *pazienza,* patient. This is not to be confused with fatalism or stoicism, for it meant more than that. According to Gambino (1974:119), "the idea of *pazienza* is an ideal control of life. First and foremost, it is an ideal of inner control, of reserve." Thus, the Italian male was trained to wait and react cautiously, evaluating the events of life rather than actively pursuing a particular course. This value was expressed in a popular game played by men and boys called *morra* or throwing fingers. The game doesn't stress competition or mere chance. "It stresses cleverness in the context of chance situations, a minimodel of life" (Gambino, 1974:139). A boy was also taught to show respect to those older than himself, to acknowledge their wisdom, and to model his behavior after his male relatives. The Italian's attitudes toward the purpose of child rearing can be summarized by the old saying, "only a fool makes his children better than himself."

In the Mezzogiorno, the ideal of womanhood included not only bearing children and knowing household skills but having those supportive qualities that enable a woman to take her place as the center of the family. In raising a daughter, the family's ultimate goal was to see her settled and competent in her role as a woman (Gambino, 1974:151). From the age of 7 girls were apprenticed in learning household skills, developing the qualities of womanhood under constant supervision. Thus, an Italian girl learned manner and style as well as the crucial economic and social roles of womanhood (Gambino, 1974: 155).

The Italian Immigrant in America

Most Italian immigrants, as suggested above, came from Southern Italy. Their points of destination were the large cities of the northeastern seaboard, the central states, and, eventually for some, California. By far the largest number came in the years between 1900 and 1914—over three million, and again in 1921 when 222,260 immigrants came to these shores. Since many of the Italian immigrants planned to return home, they sought jobs with ready or immediate wages (Vecoli, 1964) rather than those which required investment of energy to be rewarded over a longer period of time.

Arriving in this country, the emigrants from the villages and cities of Italy, Sicily, Corsica and Sardinia were not respected or known for their local areas of residence but were collectively identified as Italians and Sicilians and later simply as "Italians." For many this was humiliating. In the case of the Italians who migrated to the eastern seaboard, the unkindest cut, from their point of view, was administered by fellow Catholics, the Irish (Tomasi, in Tomasi and Engel, 1970:1963-193; Vecoli, 1969:217-268) who by this time had been in the United States for two, three or more generations and had internalized nativist values, including the xenophobia toward foreigners under which they too had suffered earlier, and who still worked in construction jobs for which Italian immigrants competed.

From the viewpoint of the Irish, however, several factors militated against helping the Italian immigrants. Some had reached middle class status and saw no advantage in being identified with impoverished, illiterate, "foreign" newcomers. Others reacted strongly against the economic competition which the Italians represented. And almost all Irish were dismayed by the religious style of the Italians particularly with respect to liturgical observance, doctrinal matters, and the relationship between priest and people. These differences were sufficient to generate a resentment which often precluded cooperation between the two groups. The subjective reactions of the Italians to Irish Catholicism in the United States have been dealt with more extensively elsewhere (Russo, 1970:195-213; Femminella, 1961:233-241). What must be pointed out here is that from the viewpoint of the newly arrived *contadino* those who might have been considered closest to him outside his family and *paesani* were of little help. But while there was direct antagonism between Irish and Italian immigrants, neither group fared as well in the occupational sphere as other immigrant groups and native born persons until after World War II (Thernstrom, 1973).

In response to lack of acceptance, Italian immigrants reestablished their village life here as far as possible (Dore, 1968:95-122). This meant the creation of a new kind of *campanilismo* along with the usual distrust of strangers that goes with it. If this is confusing to non-Italo Americans who know Italians as warm and friendly people, the paradox is understandable and is explained by Friedman. He describes the peasants' way of dealing with a guest or neighbor by relating to the core of the person as long as that person is not perceived as having a competing interest (Friedman, 1960:118).

Another reaction was patient resignation, exemplified by calling upon God for help through the intercession of His saints. They also reinstituted the local *festa* (festivals on religious holidays). And they established in the early years of this century several hundreds of social and mutual benefit societies (Nelli, 1970:77-107; Vecoli, 1964; Amfitheatrof, 1973:4; Glazer and Moynihan, 1963:194). These latter were usually small groups organized around direct help to one another's families and to those from the same town in Italy but did not develop over time into larger, more complex institutions for defense of all Italians or for philanthropic purposes (Glazer and Moynihan, 1963:193-194; Vecoli, 1964).

Although the wages the immigrants received assured them survival they took equal comfort from the knowledge that there was a higher good than money—the *rispeto* or pride that comes from hard work. They were proud of their accomplishments, the more so when these resulted from toil and effort. One thanked God for talent, but one deserved praise for effort, including physical work. Honest work for the Italian was honorable and was to be performed with a sense of dignity, whatever the type of work. Digging ditches, carrying garbage, sweeping streets, shining shoes, or cleaning toilets —these were jobs that could bring a man money to feed his family here or in Italy. And if his wife and children were here already, he would manage to put some money aside to be sent back home to help his parents or other relatives who had remained in Italy. And they in turn, whenever they could, invested the money in land not only for their own use but for their sons in America in hope and preparation for their return (Vecoli, 1974:31-43).

CHAPTER 6

GENDER

Subtle and Covert Forms of Sex Discrimination (1986)

Nijole V. Benokraitis and Joe R. Feagin

How Subtle Sex Discrimination Works

Because most of us are still almost exclusively concerned with documenting and identifying the more visible and widespread types of overt sex discrimination, we are inattentive to other forms of inequality. . . . Subtle sex discrimination is considerably more harmful than most of us realize. Subtle sex discrimination has the following characteristics: (1) it can be intentional or unintentional, (2) it is visible but often goes unnoticed (because it has been built into norms, values, and ideologies), (3) it is communicated both verbally and behaviorally, (4) it is usually informal rather than formal, and (5) it is most visible on individual (rather than organizational) levels. . . .

Condescending Chivalry

Condescending chivalry refers to superficially courteous behavior that is protective and paternalistic but treats women as subordinates. This behavior ranges from simple, generally accepted rules of etiquette regarding sex (for example, opening doors for women) to more deeply entrenched beliefs that women are generally helpless and require protection and close supervision.

Chivalrous behavior implies respect and affection. That is, many men assume that referring to women as "little girl," "young lady," "little lady," and "kiddo" is a complement—especially if the woman is over thirty. Some women may be flattered by such terms of endearment. Yet, comparable references to men ("little boy," "little man") are considered insulting, demeaning, or disrespectful because they challenge men's adulthood and authority. Thus, it is acceptable to refer to women, but not men, as children.

Even when women are clearly in positions of authority, their power may be undercut through "gentlemanly" condescension. For example, one woman dean (who is responsible for, among other things, collecting, reviewing, and coordinating course schedules every semester) complained that some chairmen refuse to take her seriously. When chairs are late in submitting schedules and she calls them into her office, some emphasize her gender and ignore her administrative power: "They do things like put their arm around me, smile, and say , 'You're getting prettier every day' or 'You shouldn't worry your pretty little head about these things.'"

Chivalrous, paternalistic and "protective" behavior also limits women's employment opportunities. . . . A number of women we talked to said they were automatically excluded from some jobs because men still assume that women won't want to travel, will be unwilling to set up child-care arrangements, and "don't want to be in the public eye." Or, when women already have jobs, they will be excluded from important meetings or not considered for promotions because they should be "protected." Consider the experience of a thirty-three-year-old, unmarried store manager provided by one of our respondents:

> [Mary's] male counterparts in the company frequently were invited to out-of-town business meetings and social functions from which she was excluded. These occasions were a source for information on business trends and store promotions and were a rich source of potentially important business contacts. When [Mary] asked why she was not invited to these meetings and social gatherings, the response was that her employer thought it was "too dangerous for her to be driving out of town at night by herself...."

In most cases, it is still assumed that women need, want, or should want protection "for their own good." During a recent lunch with colleagues, for example, one of the authors was discussing prospective faculty who could fill a dean's position that was about to be vacated. The comments, from both male and female faculty, were instructive:

> Mary Ann is a very good administrator, but she plans to get married next year. I don't think she'll have time to be both a wife and a dean. Well, Susan has the respect of both faculty and administration but hasn't she been talking about having children?
>
> Tracy's been a great faculty leader and she's done an outstanding job on committees, but she's got kids. What if they get sick when important decisions have to be made in the dean's office?
>
> Sara has been one of the best chairs in the college, a good researcher and can handle faculty. [A pause] On the other hand, now that her kids are grown, she probably wants some peace and quiet and wouldn't want to take on the headaches of a dean's office. . . .

In effect, every prospective female candidate was disqualified from serious consideration because it is generally assumed that women should stay in presumably "safe" positions where their femininity, motherhood, and ability to fulfill wifely duties will remain intact.

Whether well-intentioned or malicious, chivalrous behavior is dysfunctional because it reinforces sex inequality in several ways. First, treating women as nonadults stunts their personal and professional growth. "There are problems harder to put a finger on: . . . suggestions initiated by a woman are listened to, but always a bit more reluctantly than those initiated by a man. People, sure, will listen, but we are not urged to suggest. Women, very simply, are not actively encouraged to develop."[1]

Second, chivalry justifies keeping women in low-paying jobs. Some have argued, for example, that because some women (for example, nurses and cleaning women) are encouraged to work long hours or late at night, state protective laws do not represent progressive reform but have been designed to reduce competition from female workers and to save the premium overtime and better jobs for men. Finally, chivalrous behavior can limit women's opportunities. Men's belief that women should be protected may result, for example, in men's reluctance to criticize women:

> A male boss will haul a guy aside and just kick ass if the subordinate performs badly in front of a client. But I heard about a woman here who gets nervous and tends to giggle in front of customers. She's unaware of it and her boss hasn't told her. But behind her back he downgrades her for not being smooth with customers.[2]

Thus, not receiving the type of constructive criticism that is exchanged much more freely and comfortably between men can lead to treating women like outsiders rather than colleagues.

Benevolent Exploitation

Women are often exploited. Much of the exploitation is carried off so gracefully, however, it often goes unnoticed.

Dumping. One of the most common forms of exploitation is dumping—getting someone else (i.e., a woman) to do a job you don't want to do and then taking credit for the results:

> Whenever my supervisor gets a boring, tedious job he doesn't want to do, he assigns it to me. He praises my work and promises it will pay off in his next evaluation. Then, he writes the cover letter and takes full credit for the project..... I've never been given any credit for any of the projects—and some were praised very highly by our executives. But, I suppose it's paid off because my boss has never given me negative evaluations. (Female engineer in aerospace industry)

Another form of dumping—much more elusive—is to segregate top workers by sex and depend on the women to get the work done while the men merely critique the work and implement the results in highly visible and prestigious ways. An aide in a highly placed political office said that one of the reasons her boss was extremely successful politically was because he recognized that his female aides were better, harder working, more committed, and more responsible than the male aides. Thus, he surrounds himself with such women, gives them fancy titles, and gets 60 to 70 hours of work out of them at much lower salaries than those of men. When the projects are finished, he gives a lunch for all his aides and praises the women's work. Even as the dessert is served, new projects for the women are announced. The men, however, publicize the projects and get widespread recognition.

Showcasing. "Showcasing" refers to placing women in visible and seemingly powerful positions in which their talents, abilities, and intelligence can be pulled out, whenever necessary, for the public's consumption and the institution's credibility.

One form of showcasing is to make sure that the institution's token women are present (though not participating) in the institution's meetings with the "outside." Thus, in higher education, a woman faculty member is often expected to serve on national committees (recruitment, articulation with high schools, community colleges, and colleges), grant proposals (to show the involvement of women), search committees (just in case affirmative action officers are lurking around), and a variety of external "women's-type" activities such as panels, commissions, and advisory boards. There is no compensation for these additional duties. Moreover, the women are not rewarded in later personnel reviews because this is "women's work" and because "women's work" has low status.

If an occasional committee is an important one, women chosen are typically nonfeminists who won't "embarrass" the institution/agency/organization by taking women's issues seriously. Instead, they are Queen Bees,[3] naive neophytes, women who are either not powerful or are insensitive to sex discrimination.

Another form of showcasing is giving women directorships in dead-end jobs which are considered a "natural" for women:

> There's probably less discrimination in personnel offices because the job needs a person with traditionally female skills—being nice to people, having verbal abilities, and not being a threat to anyone because a director of personnel is a dead-end job. (Director of personnel in higher education)

Technologically Based Abuses. Americans place a high value on progress, product improvements, and technological advances. ("New," "improved," or "better than ever" detergents, toothpaste, and shampoos appear on the market annually, and many people go into debt purchasing such "necessities" as home computers, microwave ovens, electronic games, and VCRs. The profits generated by such "discoveries" are not translated into higher salaries for the many women who work in "high-tech" industries. In the case of new technologies, for example, employers often convince women that their newly developed skills are inadequate and should not be rewarded:

> While office technology creates opportunities for higher pay for some of us, for many others it is used as an excuse for keeping salary levels down. An employer may ignore the new skills you have learned in order to operate your machine and argue it's the machine itself that does all the work so that you are worthless.[4]

Employers/supervisors may discourage women from pursuing personal or professional development programs that might make them more dissatisfied with or question their current subordination:

> Under the negotiated rules, secretaries were entitled to take whatever courses they wanted at a state university, tuition reimbursed. We had . . . no application form . . . although our immediate supervisors and the office supervisor knew and approved the tuition provision (after we educated them). The Queen Bee three places up on the hierarchy professed ignorance and had to be convinced anew when one of the secretaries wanted to take a history course . . . only in the last three years has anyone gone through the hassle and taken the courses. (Ex-secretary in higher education)

The implication here is that some groups of workers (especially office workers) are presumptuous in assuming that their professional development is significant enough to warrant the institution's attention or expenditures. Perhaps more importantly, college courses might lead to office workers wondering why they are performing high-tech jobs at low-tech salaries. . . .

Finally, "progress" has been a higher priority than the job hazards resulting from new technologies and automation. In most cases, the people using the new technologies are office workers—almost all of them women. The most commonly used new office equipment is the video-display terminal (VDT). There is evidence that long-term exposure to VDTs may be dangerous. Operators of VDTs experience eyestrain, neck and back pain, headaches, and blurred vision; the radiation and chemical fumes emitted by the terminals are believed to cause stress, cataracts, miscarriages, and birth defects.[5]

Yet, management has done little to improve work conditions even when many of the improvements are not costly. As one respondent put it, "Why save labor when it's cheap?"

Nudity in Advertising. One of the most widespread forms of exploitation is to use female nudity to sell everything from toothpaste to tractors. Such advertising may not be seen as exploitation because women are expected to be "decorative." The implicit message to men and women is that the primary role of women is to provide pleasure, sex, or sexual promise:

> A sexual relationship is . . . implied between the male product user and his female companion, such that the advertisement promises, in effect, that the product will increase his appeal to her. Not only will it give him a closer shave, it will also provide a sexually available woman.
>
> Often the advertisements imply that the product's main purpose is to improve the user's appeal to men, as the panty-hose advertisement which claims "gentlemen prefer Hanes." The underlying advertising message for a product advertised in this manner is that the ultimate benefit of product usage is to give men pleasure.[6]

The consistent and continuous message that advertisements send—to both men and women—is that women's roles in society are limited to two—that of housewife or sex partner. Other roles are not taken or presented seriously. Thus, women may dominate advertising space, but they are not dominant. . . .

How Covert Sex Discrimination Works

Covert sex discrimination refers to unequal and harmful treatment of women that is hidden, clandestine, and maliciously motivated. Unlike overt and subtle sex discrimination, covert sex discrimination is very difficult to document and prove because records are not kept or are inaccessible, the victim may not even be aware of being a "target," or the victim may be ignorant of how to secure, track, and record evidence of covert discrimination.

Tokenism

Despite its widespread usage since the 1970s, the term "tokenism" is rarely defined. For our purposes, tokenism refers to the unwritten and usually unspoken policy or practice of hiring, promoting, or otherwise including a minuscule of individuals from underrepresented groups—women, minorities, the handicapped, the elderly. Through tokenism, organizations maintain the semblance of equality because no group is totally excluded. Placing a few tokens in the strategically visible places precludes the necessity of practicing "real" equality—that is, hiring and promoting individuals regardless of their sex. . . .

How Tokenism Works. There are three types of commonly practiced tokenism that limit women's equal participation in the labor force. A popular form is based on *numerical exclusion,* which uses quotas to maintain a predominantly male work force:

> As soon as they come into my office, a lot of recruiters tell me exactly how many women they plan to hire and in which departments. They say things like, "This year we need two women in accounting, one in marketing, and one in data processing." Some [of the recruiters] have fairly large detailed data showing exactly how many women they should be hiring for their company.
> (What if the most qualified candidates are all women?)
>
> Most recruiters automatically assume that women are *not* the most qualified— they got high grades because they slept around, they're not serious about long-term job commitments, they don't understand the business world and so on. . . . They interview the [women] students we schedule, but rarely hire more than the one or two they're told to hire. (College job placement director)

Because male quotas are high—95 to 99 percent—it is not difficult to fill the low percentage of slots allocated to women. . . .

Sabotage

Through sabotage, employers and employees purposely and consciously undermine or undercut a woman's position. Although sabotage can be contrived and carried out by individuals, it usually involves covert agreements between two or more persons. Because sabotage is difficult to prove, it is also easy to deny. In almost all cases, it comes down to "my word against yours" because saboteurs do not leave a "paper trail."

Sabotage strategies vary by degree of sophistication, which depends on whether the woman is in a traditionally female job, a traditionally male job, or a job in which boundaries are, in principle, nonexistent because they are, in practice, not job related.

Traditionally Female Jobs. In traditionally female jobs (domestic, service, clerical), male sabotage is normative, because men at a comparable job level have higher status (owing to higher wages) or because men have supervisory positions. In terms of the latter, for example, there is a substantial literature documenting male supervisors' sexual harassment of women subordinates because, among other things, men expect women to service all their (real or imagined) needs at all levels. Thus, office workers are the most common targets of sabotage if they don't "put out."

In comparable job levels, men can use sabotage because their job functions are less vulnerable to inspection and represent higher control than those of women:

> I was hassled by the bartender and the male kitchen staff. When you're a waitress, you have to keep in the good books of the guys backing you up. If the bartender takes a dislike to you, he can slow down on your orders to the point where you get no tips at all. The kitchen staff can sabotage you in other ways. The food can be cold, it can arrive late, and orders can be all mixed up.[7]

In traditionally female jobs, male sabotage is blatant, unmasked, raw, and unsophisticated. It is used openly to control and take advantage of women's inferior job status.

Traditionally Male Jobs. In traditionally male-dominated jobs, sabotage strategies are more sophisticated. In contrast to the "good ole boys" mentality, which literally and proudly espouses a "women-are-good-for-only-one-thing" rhetoric, traditionally male job occupants react to women negatively because women are seen as potentially threatening the "old gang" cohesion, camaraderie, and esprit de corps....

In an effort to preserve long-accepted strongholds over men's jobs, men use a variety of sabotage techniques to discourage women's participation and success in traditionally male jobs:

> My co-workers would watch me talking to customers. When I went in to get the paperwork, they'd ridicule me to the customers. "She hasn't been here that long," "Women don't know much about cars." Then, they'd go over the same questions with the customers and get the sale. (Automobile salesperson)
>
> Every time there's a promotion (for corporal), I put my name in. I always get rejected even though I have seniority, have put in the same number of years on the street as the guys, and have the same firing range results as the men. When there's a temporary opening, a sergeant from another precinct is pulled into the temporary spot even when I request the assignment.... I think my supervisor is trying to mess up my work record purposely—I'm the last one to find out about special events and new cases, and I have been late for important meetings because I was told about them five or ten minutes before they start. (Female police sergeant)
>
> Ever since I became a meter reader, the guys have always teased me that I'd be attacked by dogs, raped, kidnapped, or not return.... That's scary, but I tried to ignore it.... What gets me is that sometimes I get to the customer's house and none of the

> keys I picked up fit. I have to go back to the company to get the right keys. I don't know
> who's doing it, but someone doesn't want me in this job. (Seven-year meter reader for
> a gas and electric company)

In contrast to women in female-dominated jobs, women in male-dominated jobs find that they are "set up" to fail but are not told, openly, that this is due to their gender.

Sex-neutral Jobs. The most sophisticated sabotage strategies occur in professional, technical, and administrative (and sometimes sales) jobs where sex is totally irrelevant to job performance. Because these occupations do not require physical strength but require professional or academic credentials (Ph.D., J.D., M.A., M.S.) and longer and more specialized training, there is presumably a greater objective reliance on sex-neutral qualifications. . . . One would expect, then, that sex-neutral jobs would be the least discriminatory. Such expectations have not proven to be true.

Quite to the contrary, sex-neutral jobs are often the most discriminatory because they are the most threatening to males dominating the higher echelons of the economy. The sabotage techniques are so subtle and covert that women see the sabotage long after it is too late to do anything about the discrimination:

> One mid-level manager [at a nationally known company] said she had gotten excellent
> ratings from her supervisors throughout her first year of employment. In the
> meantime, the company psychologist had called her in about once a month and
> inquired "how things were going." She was pleased by the company's interest in its
> employees. At the end of the year, one of her male peers (whose evaluations were
> known to be very mediocre) got the promotion and she didn't. When she pursued the
> reasons for her non-promotion, she was finally told, by one of the company's vice
> presidents, that "anyone who has to see the company psychologist once a month is
> clearly not management material." She had no way of proving she had been sabotaged.

In other examples, a female insurance agent is directed by the manager to nonelitist client accounts (in contrast to her male counterparts) and then not promoted because her clients take out only "policies for the poor"; and an urban renewal administrative assistant who is more qualified than her supervisors (and is frank about wanting his job) finds the information in her folders scrambled over a period of months and is told that her "administrative chaos" will lead to a demotion.

---

[1]Ethel Strainchamps, Ed., *Rooms with No View: A Woman's Guide to the Man's World of the Media* (New York: Harper & Row, 1974), p. 146.

[2]Susan Fraker, "Why Top Jobs Elude Female Executives," *Fortune,* Apr. 16, 1984, p. 46.

[3]"Queen Bees" refers to women who are convinced that they have been successful solely because of their efforts and abilities rather than recognizing that their success could not have become a reality without the sacrifices, pioneering efforts, and achievements of their female predecessors. Because of their adamant "I'm-terrific-because-I-pulled-myself-up-by-*my*-bootstraps" beliefs, Queen Bees typically either ignore or resist helping women become upwardly mobile. Thus, Queen Bees openly support men who reject sex equality and provide men (and other Queen Bees) with public rationalizations for keeping women in subordinate positions (in other words, as female drones).

[4]Ellen Cassedy and Karen Nussbaum, *9 to 5: The Working Woman's Guide to Office Survival* (New York: Penguin Books, 1983), pp. 93–94.

[5]Ibid., pp. 77–78.

[6]Alice E. Courtney and Thomas W. Whipple, *Sex Stereotyping in Advertising* (Lexington, MA: Lexington Books, 1983), pp. 103–104.

[7]Constance Backhouse and Leah Cohen, *Sexual Harassment on the Job* (Englewood Cliffs, NJ: Prentice Hall, 1981), p. 9.

Iktome and the Ignorant Girl (1984)

Brule Sioux

A pretty *winchinchala* had never been with a man yet, and Iktome was eager to sleep with her. He dressed himself up like a woman and went looking for the girl. He found her about to cross the stream. *"Hou mashke*, how are you, friend," he said. "Let's wade across together." They lifted their robes and stepped into the water.

"You have very hairy legs," said the girl to Iktome.

"That's because I am older. When women get older, some are like this."

The water got deeper and they lifted their robes higher. "You have a very hairy backside," said the *winchinchala* to Iktome. "Yes, some of us are like that," answered Iktome.

The water got still deeper and they lifted their robes up very high. "What's that strange thing dangling between your legs?" asked the girl, who had never seen a naked man.

"Ah," complained Iktome, "it's a kind of growth, like a large wart."

"It's very large for a wart."

"Yes. Oh my! An evil magician wished it on me. It's cumbersome; it's heavy; it hurts; it gets in the way. How I wish to be rid of it!"

"My elder sister," said the girl, "I pity you. We could cut this thing off."

"No, no, my younger sister. There's only one way to get rid of it, because the evil growth was put there by a sorcerer."

"What might this be, the way to get rid of it?"

"Ah, *mashke*, the only thing to do is to stick it in there, between your legs."

"Is that so? Well, I guess, women should help each other."

"Yes, *pilamaye*, thanks, you are very kind. Let's get out of this water and go over there where the grass is soft."

Spider Man made the girl lie down on the grass, got on top of her, and entered her. "Oh my," said the girl, "it sure is big, It hurts a little."

"Think how it must hurt me!" said Iktome, breathing hard.

"It hurts a little less now," said the girl. Iktome finished and got off the girl. The *winchinchala* looked and said: "Indeed, it already seems to be smaller."

"Yes, but not small enough yet," answered Spider Man. "This is hard work. Let me catch my breath, then we must try again." After a while he got on top of the girl once more.

"It really isn't so bad at all," said the ignorant *winchinchala*, "but it seems to have gotten bigger. It is indeed a powerful magic."

Iktome did not answer her. He was busy. He finished. He rolled off.

"There's little improvement," said the girl.

"We must be patient and persevere," answered Iktome. So after a while they went at it again.

"Does it hurt very much, *mashke*?" the girl asked Iktome.

"Oh my, yes, but I am strong and brave," answered Iktome, "I can bear it."

"I can bear it too," said the girl.

"It really isn't altogether unpleasant," said the girl after they did it a fourth time, "but I must tell you, elder sister, I don't believe you will ever get rid of this strange thing."

"I have my doubts too," answered Spider Man.

"Well," said the ignorant *winchinchala*, "one could get used to it."

"Yes, *mashke*," answered Iktome, "one must make the best of it, but let's try once more to be sure."

Told in Pine Ridge, South Dakota, and recorded by Richard Erdoes.

He promised me earrings, but he only pierced my ears.
Arabian saying

Son in the Afternoon (1962)

John A. Williams

It was hot and I'm a bitch when it's hot. I goosed the Ford over Sepulveda Boulevard toward Santa Monica until I got stuck in the traffic that pours from Elay into the surrounding towns. I'd had a lousy day at the studio.

I was—and still am—a writer and this studio had hired me to check scripts and films about Negroes in them to make sure the Negro movie-goer wouldn't be offended. I'm a Negro writer, you see. Anyway, the day had been tough because of a couple of verbs—slink and walk. One of those Yale guys had done a script calling for a Negro waiter to slink away from this table where a dinner party was glaring at him. I had said the waiter shouldn't slink, but walk. This Yale guy said it was essential to the plot that the waiter slink, because later on he becomes a hero. I said you don't slink one minute and be a hero the next; there has to be some consistency. The actor who played the waiter agreed with me, and so did the director. I knew this Yale guy's stuff. It was all the same, that one subtle scene packed with prejudice that usually registered subliminally. I wondered how come this guy didn't hate himself, but then, I heard he did.

Anyway . . . hear me out now. I was on my way to Santa Monica to pick up my mother, Nora. Sometimes I call her mother; sometimes I call her Nora. It was a long haul for such a hot day. I had planned a quiet evening; a nice shower, fresh clothes, and then I would have dinner at the Watkins and talk with some of the musicians making it on the scene for a quick one before they cut out to their sets to blow. After, I was going by the Pigalle down on Figueroa and catch Earl Grant. The boy really plays; he'll make it big one day. And still later, if nothing exciting happened, I'd pick up Scottie and make [134] it to the Lighthouse on the Beach or to the Strollers and listen to some sounds. I looked forward to hearing Sleepy Stein's show on the way out. So you see, this picking up Nora was a little inconvenient because we had to drive all the way into West Los Angeles. My mother was a maid for the Couchmans. Ronald Couchman was an architect, a good one I understood from Nora who has a fine sense for this sort of thing; you don't work in some hundred-odd houses during your life and not get some idea of the way a house or even a building should be laid out, if you're Nora. Couchman's wife, Kay, was a playgirl who drove a white Jaguar from one elbow-bending function to another. My mother didn't like her much; she didn't seem to care much for her son, Ronald, junior. The Couchmans lived in a real fine residential section, of course. In the neighborhood there also lived a number of actors my mother knew quite well, like the guy who used to play Dagwood.

Somehow it is very funny. I mean that the maids and butlers know everything about these people and these people, like the Yale guy, know nothing about butlers or maids. Through Nora we knew who was laying whose wife; who had money and who *really* had money; we knew about the wild parties hours before the police, and we knew who smoked marijuana, when they smoked it and where they got it. We knew all about them.

To get to the Couchmans' driveway I had to go three blocks up one side of a palm-planted center strip and back down the other. The drive bent gently, swept out of sight of the main road. The house, sheltered by slim palms, looked like a transplanted Colonial only with ugly brown shingles. I parked and walked to the kitchen door, skirting the growling Great Dane tied to a tree. I don't like kitchen doors. Entering people's houses by them, I mean. I'd done this sort of thing most of my life when I called at the places where Nora worked to pick up the patched sheets or the half-used meats and tarnished silver—the fringe benefits of a housemaid. As a teenager I'd told Nora I was through with that crap; that I was not going through anybody's kitchen door. She only laughed and said I'd learn. One day I called for her—I [135] was still a kid—and without knocking walked through the front door of this house, right through the living room. I was almost out of the room when I saw feet behind a couch. I leaned over and there was Mr. Jorgensen and his wife making out like crazy. I guess it hit them sort of sudden and they went at it like the Hell-bomb was due to drop any minute. I've been like that too, mostly in the Spring. Of course, when Mr. Jorgensen looked over his shoulder and saw me, you know what happened. I was thrown out and Nora was right behind me. In the middle of winter, the old man sick and the coal bill three months overdue. Nora was right; I learned.

My mother saw me before I could ring the bell. She opened the door. "Hello," she said. She was breathing hard like she was out of breath. "Come in and sit down. I don't know *where* that Kay is. Little Ronald is sick and she's probly out gittin' drunk again." She left me and half-walked, half-ran back through the house, I guess to be with Ronnie. I disliked the combination of her white nylon uniform, her dark brown face and the streaks of gray in her hair. Nora had married this guy from Texas a few years after the old man died. He was all right, I guess, and he made out okay. Nora didn't have to work, but she couldn't be still; she always had to be doing something. I suggested she quit work, but like her husband, I had little luck. It would have been good for her to take an extended trip around the country visiting my brothers and sisters, and once she got to Philly, she'd probably go right out to the cemetery and sit awhile with the old man.

I walked through the house. I liked Couchman's library. I thought if I knew him I'd like him. The room made me feel like that. I left it and went into the big living room. You could tell Couchman had let his wife do it. Everything in it was fast, moving, dart-like with no sense of ease. But on the walls were several of Couchman's conceptions of buildings and homes. His lines were neat, well-paced and functional.

My mother walked rapidly through the room and without looking at me said, "Just be patient, Wendell. She should be here real soon."

"Yeah," I said, "with a snootfull." I had turned back [136] to the drawings when Ronnie scampered into the room, his face twisted with rage.

"Nora!" he tried to roar, perhaps as he'd seen the parents of some of his friends roar at their maids; I'm quite sure Kay didn't shout at Nora, and I don't think Couchman would. But then, no one shouts at Nora. That is implicit in her posture, her speech and manner. "Nora you come right back here this minute!" and the little bastard stamped and pointed to a spot on the floor where my mother was supposed to come to roost.

I have a nasty temper. Sometimes it lies dormant for ages and at other times, like when the weather is hot and nothing seems to be going right, it stands poised on a springboard. It dived off. "Don't talk to *my* mother like that you little————!" I said sharply, breaking off just before I cursed. I took a step forward, wishing he'd been big enough for me to strike. "How'd you like for me to talk to *your* mother like that?"

The nine-year-old looked up at me in surprise and confusion. He hadn't expected me to say anything; I was just another piece of the furniture or something. Tears rose in his eyes and spilled out onto his pale cheeks. He put his hands behind him, twisted them. He moved backwards, away from me. He looked at my mother with a "Nora, come help me," look. And sure, there was Nora, speeding back across the room, gathering the kid in her arms, tucking his robe together.

I was almost too angry to feel hatred for myself.

Ronnie was Couchman's only kid. Nora loved him; I suppose that was the trouble, she loved him. Couchman was gone ten, twelve hours a day; the mother didn't stay around the house any longer than necessary, so Ronnie had only my mother. You know, I think kids should have someone to love, and Nora wasn't a bad sort. But somehow, when the six of us were growing up we never had her. She was gone, out scuffling to get those crumbs to put into our mouths and shoes for our feet and praying for something to happen so that all the space in between would be taken care of. Nora's affection for us took the form of rushing out into the morning's five o'clock blackness to wake some silly bitch and get her coffee; took form in her trudging five miles home every [137] night instead of taking the streetcar because we always needed tablets for school, we said. But the truth was all of us liked to draw and we went through a tablet in a couple of hours every day. Can you imagine? There's not a goddamn artist among us. We never had the physical affection, the pat on the head, the quick, smiling kiss, the "gimmee a hug" routine. All of this Ronnie was getting.

He buried his blond little head in Nora's breast and sobbed. "There, there, now," Nora said. "Don't you cry, Ronnie. Ol' Wendell is just jealous, and he hasn't got much sense either. He didn't mean nuthin'."

I left the room. Nora had hit it of course; hit it and passed on. I looked back. It didn't look so incongruous, the white and black together, I mean. Ronnie was still sobbing, his head now on Nora's shoulder. The only time I ever got that close to her was when she trapped me with a bearhug so she could whale the daylights out of me after I put an iceball through Mrs. Grant's window.

I walked outside and lighted a cigarette. When Ronnie was in the hospital the month before Nora got me to run her way the hell over in Hollywood every night to see him. I didn't like it worth a damn. All right, I'll admit it; it did upset me. All that affection I didn't get nor my brothers and sisters going to that little white boy who without a doubt, when away from her called her "our nigger maid." I spat at the Great Dane. He snarled and then I bounced a rock off his fanny. "Lay down you bastard," I muttered. He strained at his leash. It was a good thing he was tied up.

I heard the low cough of the Jaguar slapping against the road. The car was throttled down and with a muted roar swung into the driveway. The woman aimed it for me. I didn't move. At the last moment, grinning, she swung the wheel over and braked to a jolting stop. She bounded out of the car like a tennis player vaulting over a net. "Hi," she said. She tugged at her shorts.

"Hello."

"You're Nora's boy?"

"I'm Nora's son." I can't stand the word "boy."

We stood looking at each other while the dog whined. [138] Kay had a nice tan, a nice body. She was high. Looking at her, I could feel myself going into my sexy-looking bastard role; sometimes I can swing it great, and I guess this was one of the times. Maybe it all had to do with the business inside. Kay took off her sunglasses and took a good look at me.

"May I have a cigarette?"

I gave her one and lighted it.

"Nice tan," I said. Most white people I know think it's a big deal if a Negro compliments them on their tans. It's a large laugh, honest. You have all this volleyball about color and come summer you can't hold the white folks back from the beaches and the country, anyplace where they can get sun. And of course, the blacker they get, the more pleased they are. Crazy.

"You like it?" she asked. She was pleased. She placed her arm next to mine, "almost the same color," she said.

"Ronnie isn't feeling well," I said.

"Oh, the poor kid. I'm so glad we have Nora. She's such a charm. I'll run right in and look at him. Have a drink in the bar. Fix me one too."

Kay skipped inside and I went to the bar and poured out two drinks. I made hers three times stronger than mine. She was back soon. "Nora was trying to put him to sleep and she made me stay out." She giggled. I leaned over the bar and peered down her breasts as she gulped her drink. "Fix me another, would you?" For one second I was angry; I wasn't her damned servingman. I held my temper.

While I was fixing her drink she was saying how amazing it was for Nora to have a son who was a writer. What she was really saying was that it was amazing for a servant to have a son who was not also a servant. "Anything can happen in a democracy," I said. "Servant's sons drink with the madam and so on."

"Oh, Nora isn't a servant," Kay said. "She's part of the family."

Yeah, I thought. Where and how many times had I heard *that* jazz before? We were silent again and she said after it, "you like my tan, huh?"

This time I went close to her, held her arm and we [139] compared the colors.

I placed one arm around her. She pretended not to see or feel it, but she wasn't trying to get away either. In fact, while trying to appear not to, she pressed just a bit closer and the register in my brain which tells me I've got it made clicked and inwardly grinned. I looked at her. She was very high. I put both arms around her and she wrapped her arms around me, running her hands up and down the back of my neck. Then I kissed her; she responded quickly, completely.

"Mom!"

"Ronnie, come to bed," I heard Nora shout from the other room. We could hear Ronnie out there too, running over the rug. Kay tried to get away from me, push me to one side because Ronnie was coming right for the bar. "Oh, *please*," she said, "don't let him see us." I wouldn't let her push me away. "Stop!" she hissed. "He'll *see* us!" We stopped struggling, just for an instant, and we listened to the echo of the word *see*. She gritted her teeth and renewed her efforts to get away.

Me? I had the scene laid right out before me. The kid breaks in and sees his mother in this real wriggly clinch with this nigger who's just hollered at him and no matter how his mother explains it away, the kid has the image for the rest of his life.

That's the way it happened. The kid's mother hissed under her breath, *"You're crazy!"* and she looked at me as though she were seeing me for the first time. I'd released her as soon as Ronnie, romping into the bar, saw us and came to a full, open-mouthed halt. Kay went to him. He looked first at me, then at his mother. Kay turned to me, but she couldn't speak.

Outside in the main room my mother called with her clear, loud voice, "Wendell, where are you? We can go now."

I started to move past Kay and Ronnie. I wasn't angry any longer; I felt as though I might throw up. I was beginning to feel sorry for it all, but I made myself think, *"There, you little bastard, there."*

My mother thrust her face inside the door and said, [140] "Goodbye, Mrs. Couchman, see you tomorrow. 'Bye, Ronnie."

"Yes, Nora," Kay said, sort of stunned. "Tomorrow." She was reaching for Ronnie's hand as we left. I turned and saw that the kid was slapping her hand away. I hurried quickly after Nora. [141]

John A. Williams (1925–   ) was born in Jackson, Mississippi, and now lives in New York City. He has published five novels: The Angry Ones, Night Song, The Man Who Cried I Am, *and, most recently,* Sons of Darkness, Sons of Light. *He has also written three works of non-fiction and edited* The Angry Black *(revised and retitled* Beyond the Angry Black *in 1966).*

The greatest love is a mother's, then a dog's, then a sweetheat's.
Polish proverb

Why the Fear of Feminism? (1991)

Susan Jane Gilman

Ann Arbor, Mich.

I cannot tell you how many times I've heard women preface their opinions with, "Well, I'm not a feminist or anything, but we do deserve our equal rights." Or, "I don't think it's fair that women earn only 69 cents to the men's dollar, but it's not as if I'm a feminist or anything. . . ."

Although feminism is, by definition, the theory of the political, economic and social equality of the sexes, the word has become abused and distorted. Fearing that feminism means being unfeminine, anti-men and ultimately alone, many women have distanced themselves from it.

Feminism seems to present a social equivalent of Sophie's choice: Which of our children will we let die—our heart or our mind, our attractiveness or our independence? No other oppressed group experiences such a fundamental dilemma, where they feel compelled to choose between fair treatment in society and basic emotional needs. We want self-determination, but also love and intimacy. None of this is unreasonable.

For this reason it does not surprise me that women are still reluctant to see themselves as a political force. More of us are of voting age than men, but we have yet to exercise this power in a national election. We have the numbers to make employment opportunity or child care the primary issues in a campaign by threatening not to vote for the candidate who does not support them.

And yet we don't carry out this threat. Millions of women voted for Ronald Reagan and George Bush, and for countless other politicians and laws dedicated to restricting our freedoms. Only the threat to abortion has seemed to galvanize some of us—and this on both sides of the issue.

Women have argued time and again, "Why should we regard ourselves on the basis of our gender, as women first, when as human beings so many other issues concern us?"

Because, as much as we insist that we are more than wombs and homemakers, we are still regarded primarily as such by politicians and lawmakers. We can delude ourselves, but one look at recent legislation—the Louisiana abortion bill, the President's veto of the Family Leave Act—confirms our status. If we allow such policies to stand, we will have even less power to influence the things that concern us beyond "women's issues."

We would benefit by looking to the National Rifle Association. Though the N.R.A. supports unpopular ideas—that there should be absolutely no restrictions on semiautomatic weapons, for example—it gets plenty of political backing. How? It has a clear view of what is important to its members. It then singles out those issues for unwavering attention and money. If a politician believes in gun control, the N.R.A. will throw all its power behind the opponent who does not.

N.R.A. members don't get caught up in trying to prove to the world that they're not just gun nuts. And despite this, they've still managed to become one of the most powerful American interest groups.

Women have got to follow suit in three areas: equal pay and opportunity, control over our own bodies and child care. These issues cut across race and class, which often divide the women's movement. Anyone can become pregnant. Everyone wants equal pay. Most mothers are worried about securing adequate child care and parental leave.

Moreover, we need to improve the way we communicate. Today, universities are the hotbed for feminist discourse. Yet much of this discourse is irrelevant to everyday life: try telling a welfare mother or a harried secretary that they should worry about being a victim of the unconscious processes of phallocentric language.

If women are uncomfortable with the connotations of feminism, it is up to us to stop perpetuating the stereotypes. In the 1988 Olympics, Florence Griffith Joyner dressed in lace running tights. At the time, I remember thinking that this was pathetic. Why couldn't she just run?

In an ideal world, Ms. Griffith Joyner wouldn't be judged on anything but athletic ability. But until this world is created, what a woman looks like is still of major importance. And given this, it occurred to me that perhaps she decided to prove that the incongruous was not the irreconcilable, that power could be combined with femininity. At any rate, her style clearly did not compromise her running. She won.

Susan Jane Gilman is in the graduate writing program at the University of Michigan. This is adapted from an article that appeared in NY Perspectives.

The most happy marriage I can imagine to myself would be
the union of a deaf man and a blind woman.
Samuel Taylor Coleridge

The Struggle of Puerto Rican Women (1986)

Iris Zavala Martinez

When a Puerto Rican woman is asked how she is, how things are going, she often responds with *"Pues, ahi, en la Lucha"* ("Well, struggling," or "in the struggle"). Although I have not discovered the origins of this phrase, it epitomizes reality for many Puerto Rican women. We are struggling; we are in the struggle. In fact, this brief term encapsulates the broader history, as well as the daily struggles to survive—to deal with and overcome a multitude of social, economic, and personal factors—that is reflected in the lives and experiences of Puerto Rican women. It is a statement of survival, a comment on economic and social circumstances, a means of coping and perseverance; and finally, the phrase contains the seeds of a commitment to be involved, to be engaged, to be in struggle no matter what the odds.

Puerto Rican women in the United States have been portrayed in many ways. Often, there are the statistics: numbers of single heads of households, numbers on welfare, level of educational attainment, percentages using public services. The factual data, however, only draw an outline; they cannot present the complexity of the lives embodied in the numbers. Another picture is painted from the descriptions of functional style, descriptions that frequently draw upon negative stereotypes. For example, Puerto Rican women, along with Latin women in general, are often portrayed as passive, submissive, and all-suffering, or the opposite, as loud with a "hot temper." Such simplifications distort the varied lives of Puerto Rican women, taking their behavior out of context, making it seem that there is some peculiar and "cultural" reason for behaviors, which, in fact, may exist for other women too, if they are valid descriptions at all. . . .

This essay attempts to show how the interaction of social, economic, and historical pressures affects the changing lives of Puerto Rican women, thereby questioning and challenging some of the "cultural" attributes, the mental-health labels, and the myths that are used to undermine the liberating commitment to be *en la lucha*. Further this essay is directed to a vast multilevel collective of sisters, Puerto Rican and non-Puerto Rican, who seek legitimate sources of study and dialogue regarding the particular experiences of women. Ultimately, it is an effort dedicated to the sisterhood of struggle.

A Brief History

Numerous writers have analyzed the impact of colonialism and capitalism on the history, family systems, and present status of Puerto Ricans.[1] Suffice it to say here that the systematic development of capitalism in Puerto Rico not only propelled abrupt industrialization but also insured economic control of the island as an expanding market and a source of cheap labor for U.S. interests. Such complex developments meant vast changes in the fabric of life for the Puerto Rican people.

One such consequence was massive migration, especially in the 1950s and 1960s. Another was the incorporation of masses of Puerto Rican women into lower-paying and sexually segregated jobs in the labor market.[2] In the United States, immigrant Puerto Rican women increasingly did piecework in factories or unskilled work or had jobs as factory operatives, cigar makers, domestic or service workers. The resulting "proletarianization" of women in the first thirty years of this century meant involvement in labor struggles and a changing consciousness regarding sex-role relations.[3]

There has been a progressive decline, however, from the high point of 38.9 percent female involvement in the labor force set in 1950, when Puerto Rican women found employment more readily than men. By 1970 the percentage of Puerto Rican women employed was the lowest among ethnic-group women, a fact that has been attributed to "unfavorable labor-market conditions and large declines in central city industries."[4]

In fact, the sociological and mental-health literature documents the disruption to family life prompted by immigration and by the differential labor-force participation of women and men and by the increase in female-headed households. The traditional role definitions and identities of Puerto Rican men have been abruptly challenged without there being a productive way to come to grips with the changes. Women have been forced to develop themselves in the public sphere of work while maintaining subordinate roles at home or to carry on "independently" by depending on welfare.[5]

Yet, while such tensions are perhaps heightened in the United States, they also exist in Puerto Rico and elsewhere. What is perplexing, however, is the way in which traditional roles are seen as the problem for Puerto Rican women rather than the changing nature of class and gender relations resulting from changing economic and historical forces. . . . We need to be careful about embracing an overly "feminist" prescription for modern women's roles before we understand those features of "traditional" roles that help women cope with changing economic and social conditions. As Puerto Rican men have become increasingly displaced from jobs, Puerto Rican women have had to adjust to the changing situation in the home. This essay suggests that only by gaining a complex understanding of changing roles in the context of changing socioeconomic structures can we make reasonable judgments about what is "traditional" and what is "progressive" behavior for Puerto Rican women. . . .

Present-Day Reality

According to a 1978 statistical portrait of women in the United States, Puerto Rican women comprise 16 percent of all women of Spanish origin, have a median age of 22.4 years, and have the highest unemployment rate, 12.2 percent. In the 1980 census, the total Puerto Rican population was 1,823,000, of whom 985,000 were women. The median income for Puerto Ricans overall was $9,855, the lowest of all Latino groups and significantly lower that that of non-Latino families, which is $19,965. By 1983, 28.4 percent of all Latinos were living in poverty, in comparison to 12.1 percent of whites. Only 51 percent of adult Puerto Ricans were in the labor force in 1982, with Puerto Rican women's participation rate at 37 percent, in comparison to a 50 percent rate for Chicana and Cuban women.[6]

It is not surprising, therefore, that Puerto Ricans have a high rate of people on welfare. They have been increasingly forced—by high unemployment, low education, and invisible factors of institution-alization—to survive within the welfare system.

The family constellation has also changed. In 1960, 15.3 percent of Puerto Rican families were headed by women; by 1970 this figure increased to 24.1 percent. By 1982 40 percent of families were headed by women. These figures must be compared to shifts from 6 percent to 13.9 percent of white female-headed households during the same period. [7]

This brief statistical profile shows that Puerto Ricans are in a very disadvantageous situation, and Puerto Rican women even more so, particularly in comparison to both the white population and to other Latino groups. Certainly such a stark profile has implications for the overall well-being of the Puerto Rican community and for the socioemotional status of women.

The Socioemotional Profile

Before analyzing the complex interaction of various stresses on the lives of Puerto Rican women, a few examples may make the picture more concrete.[8]

Carmen is a nineteen-year-old working-class woman who came to the United States to live with an aunt, for a change of environment (*cambias de ambiente*), in hopes of learning to "do something" to earn a living and support herself. She was fleeing a very strict father, who entrusted her to his sister. Carmen was ambitious and very idealistic. She began English classes and enrolled in a vocational-training program in the community. Nine months after her arrival she had gained some ability to communicate in English and laughingly, with a heavy accent, would demonstrate her new skill.

At this time her aunt became quite ill and Carmen had to quit some of her activities to care for her. Although the aunt had teenage children who had been raised in the United States and who spoke English, they felt less obligation than Carmen to look after her. Carmen felt obliged because she felt indebted to her. She also felt that it was "expected" that she would take care of her aunt.

Two months later Carmen came into an out-patient mental-health department complaining of tension headaches, of feelings of wanting to yell and throw things, and of sudden crying spells. She made self-deprecatory remarks about how she would not amount to anything in life, how she had no skills, was not intelligent, and was selfish.

Maria is a divorced woman with three children who has been in the United States for ten years. Her husband has been gone for three years and she has been struggling to make ends meet and raise her children. She knows enough English to *defenderse,* or "get along," but she has limited vocational skills and works in a shoe factory. She works from 8:30 to 4:30, but her children get out of school at 2:30, which means that they are left alone in the afternoons, supervised by her eleven-year-old son.

The sexual overtones of comments from a fellow worker have made her feel increasingly anxious, while at home she has grown more tense about household demands. She has been growing increasingly irritated with her children, scolding them more and more often. She has not been sleeping well and has begun to calm her nerves with a *traguito,* a drink. The children have grown increasingly hard to control. When the oldest disappeared for over five hours Maria became quite agitated, lost control, and experienced an *ataque de nervios,* an anxiety attack.

Ana is a twenty-eight-year-old woman who has been raised in the United States since she was three. For two and a half years she has been married to an island-born Puerto Rican, Ernesto, who has been in the United States for the past five years. She and her spouse have been fighting increasingly over the past six months, often with the result that he storms out of the house and does not return for hours or even until the next day. Ana's family is in New York, and her husband's family is in Puerto Rico. Ernesto feels little support, is antagonistic to the "Americanos," and has difficulty holding a job.

Ana went to trade school and is a medical assistant in an area hospital. As she is bilingual, her skills are well used and she feels good about working. Ernesto constantly berates Ana and is critical of any and all of her activities, often to the point of being verbally abusive. She has been overwhelmed by his attitudes and has begun to doubt herself. Ana has become increasingly depressed and withdrawn. While suppressing intense anger at her husband she has felt helpless and upset.

While obviously not a statistical sample, Carmen, Maria, and Ana help to highlight important areas for consideration in understanding the socioemotional needs of Puerto Rican women.

All three women described here have been exposed to the general stresses on women that were mentioned earlier. In addition, they face particular problems as Puerto Rican women. First, they encounter different forms of discrimination—ethnic, class, and race—in work and community life. Second, they face the psychosocial pressures of immigration, such as the loss of homeland and dislocation. Third, they must deal with the mastery of the English language, issues of cultural identity, and other stresses associated with acculturation. Fourth, they are subject to the particular sex-role expectations of their culture. The interaction of these factors can tax the coping ability of any woman—as it has the abilities of Carmen, Maria, and Ana—and result in emotional difficulties.[9]

Of particular importance is the tension between learned "traditional" role behaviors and the woman's own developing needs, strivings that are often in conflict with the cultural and sex-role expectations. Women are to be self-sacrificing wives and mothers, subordinate to men. This is the demand of dominant elements in U.S. society, as well as of traditional Puerto Rican culture. Puerto Rican women are to accept this "reality" and not to show signs of anger, aggression, or independence. But at the same time they are to be strong and in control. Therefore, Puerto Rican women experience two forms of oppression. They are oppressed by the external, dominant Anglo system and by the socialization process and expectations of their own culture. In the words of S. Urdang, "the key to the perpetuation of such oppression is the ability of the oppressor to persuade the oppressed to cooperate in their servitude."[10]

This situation of Puerto Rican women in the United States embodies just such "double discrimination." The Puerto Rican woman is on the one hand, "entrapped within the bleak economic and political powerlessness affecting the Puerto Rican population in general. . . . On the other hand, she suffers from the socialization of sex roles that cause her to have guilt feelings about the fulfillment of her potential."[11] Along with the stress of adverse environmental and socioemotional factors, this tension and eventual conflict has various psychological symptoms. They include such problems as somatic ailings, nervousness (*los nervios alterados*), depression, fear of losing control, inability to handle children, and persistent feelings of inadequacy, powerlessness, and frustration (*no puedo hacer nada, no valgo, estoy agobiada, aborrecida*). . . .

Some . . . would focus only on the ways in which the three examples demonstrate the individual difficulties that Puerto Rican women experience in coping with their circumstances. Instead, a more liberating approach means trying to understand their emotions and behaviors in the light of the complex pressures and struggles that define reality for Puerto Rican women.

Viewed in this way, Carmen can be seen as a young woman trying to develop herself within the limits and possibilities of cultural family expectations. She has turned against herself because of her own strivings. Her frustrated attempts make her angry, but she cannot show her anger, lest she be seen as *ingrata*, or "ungrateful," by her aunt. The conflict between her striving and other people's perceived expectations of her leads to distress and to difficulty in negotiating change.

Maria presents the struggle of a woman attempting to survive without a support system. She manifests the cultural concept of *hembrismo*, which dictates that women be persevering and strong. Underlying this concept is the goal of being a *supermadre*, or great mom, a do-it-all concept probably akin to the popular idea of "superwoman" as an unrealistic goal for working women.[12] Maria struggles to provide for her children, as she has been socialized to do, and thereby enters into conflict with extreme demands of the outside world as well as those she places on herself. Although Maria has lived for some years in the United States, she has not developed supports for herself and fears failure and resorting to Aid to Families with Dependent Children, seen by her as a symbol of defeat.

Maria has experienced both sexual and class discrimination, but she ignored their psychological effects on her. She has been so intent on providing economically for her children that she has neglected their and her own emotional needs, becoming irritated and guilty; and finally, she has taken to soothing her frayed nerves with drink. Plagued by feelings of inadequacy, of not being educated enough to seek help, she has circumscribed her world to work and home, instead of seeing how forces outside her world affected her options.

In addition to concerns similar to those of Carmen and Maria, Ana reflects the conflict of "success." Her achievement of biculturality, economic status, and autonomy came at the expense of confusion and marital strife. At the same time, Ernesto is an example of the privatized reactions to economic displacement experienced by minority men. Neither Ernesto nor Ana can see the social context of their marital strife, nor how different cultural and educational experiences underlie their disagreements. They personalize a conflict that is rooted in the reality of differential experiences, of economic injustice, of colonialist history—a conflict that represents, in some ways, the struggle of a divided nation.

These examples show that life for a Puerto Rican woman can be a vulnerable one. Given this fact, the follow-up questions are: How have women coped? What have they done to overcome adversities, attitudinal limitations, and structural barriers?

Coping And Surviving

Puerto Rican women have mastered many "passive" methods of coping. For example, a common adage states that women know how to *salirse con la suya*, or "get what they want." The implication is that by using unassuming, indirect, passive, or covert methods, a Puerto Rican woman can obtain what she needs and wants. The value placed on this ability implies that a direct approach would not be successful. Thus, within existing social norms, some Puerto Rican women may learn manipulative approaches to counter oppressive familial and male attitudes and situations.[13] Such approaches respond to and emerge from a context in which assertiveness and direct expression are not allowed or valued. In fact it has often been said that Puerto Ricans have a tendency to avoid direct expressions or confrontations and to deny hostile thoughts and feelings. Given their island's history of domination by an outside force, these manifestations are not surprising. They suggest seemingly little hope for change. However, the price paid is accumulated emotions, which will seek some outlet, in somatic complaints, for example, or in an *ataque*. Coping attempts such as these, then extort a high personal price. They are private, individual efforts to deal with forces rooted elsewhere.

Puerto Rican women have also used more active, socially sanctioned strategies to seek self-esteem, survive, obtain power, and promote change. Through education, for example, individual women have tried to improve their chances of coping and surviving. Given all the forces working against her, if a Puerto Rican woman can become educated she is more employable, more economically independent, and more able to participate as a competent individual—not as the extension of some man or her children—in the community. Carmen, for example, was especially frustrated because her route to power, education, was thwarted by her aunt's illness.

Hembrismo is another overt way to cope. Through it, a woman adheres to the cultural script of motherhood, but by being exceptionally strong and powerful in linking various roles she gains power and recognition. This strategy can give a determined woman a certain adaptive strength, although it can also establish ideals that conflict with her own development and strivings. As was seen with Maria, when the objective pressures increase, the very strategy that gave strength in the past can become a barrier to flexibility.

The kinship system is most often identified as the source of support for Puerto Rican women. It can often be a first resort in times of trouble without which a woman's life is harder, as was noted for Ana. But the expectations of kin—both real and assumed—can also be a source of stress, as Carmen's distress shows.

For Puerto Rican women the reliance on extended family is culturally encouraged and often socioeconomically necessary. But extended family systems go through their own growth and conflicts and are not always the best support. In the United States kin may not be close by. While for some their absence may create a sense of isolation and loss, for others it may motivate development of networks that are not kin, such as folk healers, religious groups, and neighborhood and community groups. Such extrafamilial support systems may benefit women who are single parents or are experiencing serious emotional difficulties.[14]

Many of the increasing numbers of Puerto Rican women who are heads of their households have learned the mixed blessing of welfare as a coping strategy. While public assistance can provide women with the chance to become somewhat independent of family or men, that "freedom" may be illusive because of the ways in which it forces them to go against the dominant and respected values of the culture without really providing economic autonomy in return. The female-headed family is less a cultural phenomenon than a "functional adaptation to a specific economic situation; a situation which leaves the lower class male unable to provide long term maintenance for a family."[15] Puerto Rican women, then, have little choice but to develop their own resources and networks of support in order to survive.

---

[1]Some very good sources are Manuel Maldonado-Denis, *Puerto Rico: Una Interpretacion Historico-Social* (Mexico City: Siglo Veintiuno, 1969); Center for Puerto Rican Studies, *Labor Migration* ; and J. Inclan, "Socioeconomic Changes in Puerto Rico: The Development of the Modern Proletarian Family" (Paper circulated by the Center for Puerto Rican Studies, 1978).

[2]See Center for Puerto Rican Studies, *Labor Migration* ; and Marcia Rivera Quintero, "The Development of Capitalism in Puerto Rico and the Incorporation of Women into the Labor Force," in E. Acosta-Belen, Ed., *The Puerto Rican Woman* (New York: Praeger, 1979).

[3]Yamila Azize, *Luchas de la Mujer en Puerto Rico, 1898–1919* (San Juan: Litografia Metropolitana, 1979); and Virginia Sanchez Korrol, "Survival of Puerto Rican Women in New York Before World War II," in C. Rodriguez, V. Sanchez Korrol, and J. O. Alers, Eds. *The Puerto Rican Struggle: Essays on Survival in the United States* (New York: Puerto Rican Migration Research Consortium, 1980).

[4]See R. Santana Cooney and A. Colon, "Work and Family: The Recent Struggles of Puerto Rican Females," in *The Puerto Rican Struggle.*

[5]See E. Christensen, "The Puerto Rican Woman: A Profile," L. Miranda King, "Puertorriquenas in the United States: "The Impact of Double Discrimination," and M. Vazquez, "The Effects of Role Expectations on the Marital Status of Urban Puerto Rican Women," all in *The Puerto Rican Woman.* See also E. Mizio, "Impact of External Systems on the Puerto Rican Family," *Social Casework*, Vol. 55, No. 2 (1974): 76–89.

[6]See U.S. Department of Commerce, Bureau of the Census, "A Statistical Portrait of Women in the United States," *Current Population Reports*, Special Study, Series P–23, No. 100 (Washington DC: U.S. Government Printing Office, 1980); and "A Description of Latinos in the United States: Demographic and Sociocultural Factors of the Past and the Future," in S. Andrade, Ed., *Latino Families in the United States* (New York: Planned Parenthood Federation of America, 1983), p.17.

[7]See Santana Cooney and Colon, "Work and Family," pp. 65–66 for 1960 and 1970 data. See Council on Interracial Books for Children, *Fact Sheets on Institutional Racism,* Nov.1984, p. 7.

[8]These case examples come from my clinical work with the Puerto Rican community in Massachusetts. The names and defining characteristics have been changed.

[9]See I. Zavala-Martinez, Chap. 2, "Puerto Ricans and Mental Health: An Overview of Research and Clinical Data," in "Mental Health and the Puerto Ricans in the United States: A Critical Literature," manuscript available from the author or Hunter College, Library of Center for Puerto Rican Studies, New York; and L. Comas-Diaz, "Mental Health Needs of Puerto Rican Women in the United States," in *Work, Family, and Health.*

[10]See S. Urdang, *Fighting Two Colonialisms: Women in Guinea-Bissau* (New York: Monthly Review Press, 1979), pp. 12–17.

[11]L. Miranda, "Puertorriquenas in the United States: The Impact of Double Discrimination," in *The Puerto Rican Woman,* pp. 124–133.

[12]E. Chaney, *Supremadre: Women in Politics in Latin America* (Austin University of Texas Press, 1979).

[13]M. Lopez-Garriga, "Estrategias de Autoafirmacion en Mujeres Puertorriquenas," *Revista de Ciencias Sociales,* Vol. 20, Nos. 3, 4 (1978): 257–285.

[14]V. Garrison, "Support Systems of Schizophrenic and Non-schizophrenic Puerto Rican Migrant Women in New York City." *Schizophrenia Bulletin,* Vol. 4, No. 4 (1978): 561–595; and E. Vazquez NuHall, "The Support System and Coping Patterns of the Female Puerto Rican Single Parent," *Journal of Non-White Concerns,* Vol. 7, No. 3 (1979): 128–137.

[15]L. Morris, "Women Without Men: Domestic Organizations and the Welfare State as seen in a Coastal Community of Puerto Rico," *British Journal of Sociology,* Vol. 30, No. 3 (1979): 322–340.

There is no happiness; there are only moments of happiness.
Spanish proverb

The Struggle to Be an All-American Girl (1991)
Elizabeth Wong

It's still there, the Chinese school on Yale Street where my brother and I used to go. Despite the new coat of paint and the high wire fence, the school I knew 10 years ago remains remarkably, stoically the same.

Every day at 5 P.M., instead of playing with our fourth- and fifth-grade friends or sneaking out of the empty lot to hunt ghosts and animal bones, my brother and I had to go to Chinese school. No amount of kicking, screaming, or pleading could dissuade my mother, who was solidly determined to have us learn the language of our heritage.

Forcibly, she walked us the seven long, hilly blocks from our home to school, depositing our defiant tearful faces before the stern principal. My only memory of him is that he swayed on his heels like a palm tree, and he always clasped his impatient twitching hands behind his back. I recognized him as a repressed maniacal child killer, and knew that if we ever saw his hands we'd be in big trouble.

We all sat in little chairs in an empty auditorium. The room smelled like Chinese medicine, an imported faraway mustiness. Like ancient mothballs or dirty closets. I hated that smell. I favored crisp new scents. Like the soft French perfume that my American teacher wore in public school.

There was a stage far to the right, flanked by an American flag and the flag of the Nationalist Republic of China, which was also red, white and blue but not as pretty.

Although the emphasis at the school was mainly language—speaking, reading, writing—the lessons always began with an exercise in politeness. With the entrance of the teacher, the best student would tap a bell and everyone would get up, kowtow, and chant, "Sing san ho," the phonetic for "How are you, teacher?"

Being ten years old, I had better things to learn than ideographs copied painstakingly in lines that ran right to left from the tip of a *moc but*, a real ink pen that had to be held in an awkward way if blotches were to be avoided. After all, I could do the multiplication tables, name the satellites of Mars, and write reports on "Little Women" and "Black Beauty." Nancy Drew, my favorite book heroine, never spoke Chinese.

The language was a source of embarrassment. More times than not, I had tried to disassociate myself from the nagging loud voice that followed me wherever I wandered in the nearby American supermarket outside Chinatown. The voice belonged to my grandmother, a fragile woman in her seventies who could outshout the best of street vendors. Her humor was raunchy, her Chinese rhythmless, patternless. It was quick, it was loud, it was unbeautiful. It was not like the quiet, lilting romance of French or the gentle refinement of the American South. Chinese sounded pedestrian. Public.

In Chinatown, the comings and goings of hundreds of Chinese on their daily tasks sounded chaotic and frenzied. I did not want to be thought of as mad, as talking gibberish. When I spoke English, people nodded at me, smiled sweetly, said encouraging words. Even the people in my culture would cluck and say that I'd do well in life. "My, doesn't she move her lips fast," they would say, meaning that I'd be able to keep up with the world outside Chinatown.

My brother was even more fanatical than I about speaking English. He was especially hard on my mother, criticizing her, often cruelly, for her pidgin speech—smatterings of Chinese scattered like chop suey in her conversation. "It's not 'What it is,' Mom," he'd say in exasperation. "It's 'What *is* it, what *is* it, what *is* it!'" Sometimes Mom might leave out an occasional "the" or "a," or perhaps a verb of being. He would stop her in mid-sentence: "Say it again, Mom. Say it right." When he tripped over his own tongue, he'd blame it on her: "See, Mom, it's all your fault. You set a bad example."

What infuriated my mother the most was when my brother cornered her on her consonants, especially "r." My father played a cruel joke on Mom by assigning her an American name that her tongue wouldn't allow her to say. No matter how hard she tried, "Ruth" always ended up "Luth" or "Roof."

After two years of writing with a *moc but* and reciting words with multiples of meanings, I finally was granted a cultural divorce. I was permitted to stop Chinese school.

I thought of myself as multicultural. I preferred tacos to egg rolls; I enjoyed Cinco de Mayo more than Chinese New Year.

At last, I was one of you; I wasn't one of them.

Sadly, I still am.

Elizabeth Wong's mother insisted that she learn Chinese and be aware of her cultural background. In her essay, which first appeared in the Los Angeles Times, *Wong vividly portrays her childhood resistance to her mother's wishes and the anger and embarrassment she felt. Chinese school interfered with her being, as she puts it, "an all-American girl." Here, writing as a young adult, she recognizes in herself a sense of the loss.*

Born in 1958, Elizabeth Wong has worked as a reporter for the Hartford Courant *and the* San Diego Tribune.

A man in love mistakes a pimple for a dimple.
Japanese proverb

History of Woman Suffrage (1989)

Elizabeth Cady Stanton, Susan B. Anthony, and Matilda Joslyn Gage

The *Seneca County Courier*, a semi-weekly journal, of July 14, 1848, contained the following startling announcement:

Seneca Falls Convention.

Woman's Rights Convention.—A Convention to discuss the social, civil, and religious condition and rights of woman, will be held in the Wesleyan Chapel, at Seneca Falls, N.Y., on Wednesday and Thursday, the 19th and 20th of July, current; commencing at 10 o'clock A.M. During the first day the meeting will be exclusively for women, who are earnestly invited to attend. The public generally are invited to be present on the second day, when Lucretia Mott, of Philadelphia, and other ladies and gentlemen, will address the convention.

This call, without signature, was issued by Lucretia Mott, Martha C. Wright, Elizabeth Cady Stanton, and Mary Ann McClintock. At this time Mrs. Mott was visiting her sister Mrs. Wright, at Auburn, and attending the Yearly Meeting of Friends in Western New York. Mrs. Stanton, having recently removed from Boston to Seneca Falls, finding the most congenial associations in Quaker families, met Mrs. Mott incidentally for the first time since her residence there. They at once returned to the topic they had so often discussed, walking arm in arm in the streets of London, and Boston, "the propriety of holding a woman's convention." These four ladies, sitting round the tea-table of Richard Hunt, a prominent Friend near Waterloo, decided to put their long-talked-of resolution into action, and before the twilight deepened into night, the call was written, and sent to the *Seneca County Courier*. On Sunday morning they met in Mrs. McClintock's parlor to write their declaration, resolutions, and to consider subjects for speeches. As the convention was to assemble in three days, the time was short for such productions; but having no experience in the *modus operandi* of getting up conventions, nor in that kind of literature, they were quite innocent of the herculean labors they proposed. On the first attempt to frame a resolution; to crowd a complete thought, clearly and concisely, into three lines; they felt as helpless and hopeless as if they had been suddenly asked to construct a steam engine. And the humiliating fact may as well now be recorded that before taking the initiative step, those ladies resigned themselves to a faithful perusal of various masculine productions. The reports of Peace, Temperance, and Anti-Slavery conventions were examined, but all alike seemed too tame and pacific for the inauguration of a rebellion such as the world had never before seen. They knew women had wrongs, but how to state them was the difficulty, and this was increased from the fact that they themselves were fortunately organized and conditioned; they were neither "sour old maids," "childless women," nor "divorced wives," as the newspapers declared them to be. While they had felt the insults incident to sex, in many ways, as every proud, thinking woman must, in the laws, religion, and literature of the world, and in the invidious and degrading sentiments and customs of all nations, yet they had not in their own experience endured the coarser forms of tyranny resulting from unjust laws, or association with immoral and unscrupulous men, but they had souls large enough to feel the wrongs of others, without being scarified in their own flesh.

After much delay, one of the circle took up the Declaration of 1776, and read it aloud with much spirit and emphasis, and it was at once decided to adopt the historic document, with some slight changes such as substituting "all men" for "King George." Knowing that women must have more to complain of than men under any circumstances possibly could, and seeing the Fathers had eighteen grievances, a protracted search was made through statute books, church usages, and the customs of society to find that exact number. Several well-disposed men assisted in collecting the grievances, until, with the announcement of the eighteenth, the women felt they had enough to go before the world with a good case. One youthful lord remarked, "Your grievances must be grievous indeed, when you are obliged to go to books in order to find them out."

The eventual day dawned at last, and crowds in carriages and on foot, wended their way to the Wesleyan church. When those having charge of the Declaration, the resolutions, and several volumes of the Statutes of New York arrived on the scene, lo! the door was locked. However, an embryo Professor of Yale College was lifted through an open window to unbar the door; that done, the church was quickly filled. It had been decided to have no men present, but as they were already on the spot, and as the women who must take responsibility of organizing the meeting, and leading the discussions, shrank from doing either, it was decided, in a hasty council round the altar, that this was an occasion when men might make themselves pre-eminently useful. It was agreed they should remain, and take the laboring oar through the Convention.

James Mott, tall and dignified, in Quaker costume, was called to the chair; Mary McClintock appointed Secretary, Frederick Douglass, Samuel Tillman, Ansel Bascom, E. W. Capron, and Thomas McClintock took part throughout the discussions. Lucretia Mott, accustomed to public speaking in the Society of Friends, stated the objects of the Convention, and in taking a survey of the degraded condition of woman the world over, showed the importance of inaugurating some movement for her education and elevation. Elizabeth and Mary McClintock, and Mrs. Stanton, each read a well-written speech; Martha Wright read some satirical articles she had published in the daily papers answering the diatribes on woman's sphere. Ansel Bascom, who had been a member of the Constitutional Convention recently held in Albany, spoke at length on the property bill for married women, just passed the Legislature, and the discussion on woman's rights in that Convention. Samuel Tillman, a young student of law, read a series of the most exasperating statutes for women, from English and American jurists, all reflecting the *tender mercies* of men toward their wives, in taking care of their property and protecting them in their civil rights.

The Declaration having been freely discussed by many present, was re-read by Mrs. Stanton, and with some slight amendments adopted.

Declaration of Sentiments

When, in the course of human events, it becomes necessary for one portion of the family of man to assume among the people of the earth a position different from that which they have hitherto occupied, but one to which the laws of nature and of nature's God entitle them, a decent respect to the opinions of mankind requires that they should declare the causes that impel them to such a course.

We hold these truths to be self-evident: that all men and women are created equal; that they are endowed by their Creator with certain inalienable rights; that among these are life, liberty, and the pursuit of happiness; that to secure these rights governments are instituted, deriving their just powers from the consent of the governed. Whenever any form of government becomes destructive of these ends, it is the right of those who suffer from it to refuse allegiance to it, and to insist upon the institution of a new government, laying its foundation on such principles, and organizing its powers in such form, as to them shall seem most likely to effect their safety and happiness. Prudence, indeed, will dictate that governments long established should not be changed for light and transient causes; and accordingly all experience hath shown that mankind are more disposed to suffer, while evils are sufferable, than to right themselves by abolishing the forms to which they were accustomed. But when a long train of abuses and usurpations, pursuing invariably the same object evinces a design to reduce them under absolute despotism, it is their duty to throw off such government, and to provide new guards for their future security. Such has been the patient sufferance of the women under this government, and such is now the necessity which constrains them to demand the equal station to which they are entitled.

The history of mankind is a history of repeated injuries and usurpations on the part of man toward woman, having in direct object the establishment of an absolute tyranny over her. To prove this, let facts be submitted to a candid world.

He has never permitted her to exercise her inalienable right to the elective franchise.

He has compelled her to submit to laws, in the formation of which she had no voice.

He has withheld from her rights which are given to the most ignorant and degraded men—both natives and foreigners.

Having deprived her of this first right of a citizen, the elective franchise, thereby leaving her without representation in the halls of legislation, he has oppressed her on all sides.

He has made her, if married, in the eye of the law, civilly dead.

He has taken from her all right in property, even to the wages she earns.

He has made her, morally, an irresponsible being, as she can commit many crimes with impunity, provided they be done in the presence of her husband. In the covenant of marriage, she is compelled to promise obedience to her husband, he becoming, to all intents and purposes her master—the law giving him power to deprive her of liberty, and to administer chastisement.

He has so framed the laws of divorce, as to what shall be the proper causes, and in case of separation, to whom the guardianship of the children shall be given, as to be wholly regardless of the happiness of women—the law, in all cases, going upon a false supposition of the supremacy of man, and giving all power into his hands.

After depriving her of all rights as a married woman, if single, and the owner of property, he has taxed her to support a government which recognizes her only when her property can be made profitable to it.

He has monopolized nearly all the profitable employments, and from those she is permitted to follow, she receives but a scanty remuneration. He closes against her all the avenues to wealth and distinction which he considers most honorable to himself. As a teacher of theology, medicine or law, she is not known.

He has denied her the facilities for obtaining education, all colleges being closed against her.

He allows her in Church, as well as State, but a subordinate position, claiming Apostolic authority for her exclusion from the ministry, and, with some exceptions, from any public participation in the affairs of the Church.

He has created a false public sentiment by giving to the world a different code of morals for men and women, by which moral delinquencies which exclude women from society, are not only tolerated, but deemed of little account in man.

He has usurped the prerogative of Jehovah himself, claiming it as his right to assign for her a sphere of action, when that belongs to her conscience and to her God.

He has endeavored, in every way that he could, to destroy her confidence in her own powers, to lessen her self-respect, and to make her willing to lead a dependent and abject life.

Now, in view of this entire disenfranchisement of one-half the people of this country, their social and religious degradation—in view of the unjust laws above mentioned, and because women do feel themselves aggrieved, oppressed, and fraudulently deprived of their most sacred rights, we insist that they have immediate admission to all the rights and privileges which belong to them as citizens of the United States.

In entering upon the great work before us, we anticipate no small amount of misconception, misrepresentation, and ridicule; but we shall use every instrumentality within our power to effect our object. We shall employ agents, circulate tracts, petition the State and National legislatures, and endeavor to enlist the pulpit and the press in our behalf. We hope this Convention will be followed by a series of Conventions embracing every part of the country.

The following resolutions were discussed by Lucretia Mott, Thomas and Mary Ann McClintock, Amy Post, Catherine A. F. Stebbins, and others, and were adopted:

WHEREAS, The great precept of nature is conceded to be, that "man shall pursue his own true and substantial happiness." Blackstone in his Commentaries remarks, that this law of Nature being coeval with mankind, and dictated by God himself, is of course superior in obligation to any other. It is binding over all the globe, in all countries and at all times; no human laws are of any validity if contrary to this, and such of them as are valid, derive all their force, and all their validity, and all their authority, mediately and immediately, from this original; therefore,

Resolved, That such laws as conflict, in any way, with the true and substantial happiness of woman, are contrary to the great precept of nature and of no validity, for this is "superior in obligation to any other."

Resolved, That all such laws which prevent woman from occupying such a station in society as her conscience shall dictate, or which place her in a position inferior to that of man, are contrary to the great precept of nature, and therefore of no force or authority.

Resolved, That woman is man's equal—was intended to be so by the Creator, and the highest good of the race demands that she should be recognized as such.

Resolved, That the women of this country ought to be enlightened in regard to the laws under which they live, that they may no longer publish their degradation by declaring themselves satisfied with their present position, nor their ignorance, by asserting that they have all the rights they want.

Resolved, That inasmuch as man, while claiming for himself intellectual superiority, does accord to woman moral superiority, it is pre-eminently his duty to encourage her to speak and teach, as she has an opportunity, in all religious assemblies.

Resolved, That the same amount of virtue, delicacy, and refinement of behavior that is required of woman in the social state, should also be required of man, and the same transgressions should be visited with equal severity on both man and woman.

Resolved, That the objection of indelicacy and impropriety, which is so often brought against woman when she addresses a public audience, comes with a very ill-grace from those who encourage, by their attendance, her appearance on the stage, in the concert, or in feats of the circus.

> *Resolved,* That woman has too long rested satisfied in the circumscribed, limits which corrupt customs and a perverted application of the Scriptures have marked out for her, and that it is time she should move in the enlarged sphere which the great Creator has assigned her.
>
> *Resolved,* That it is the duty of the women of this country to secure to themselves their sacred right to the elective franchise.
>
> *Resolved,* That the equality of human rights results necessarily from the fact of the identity of the race in capabilities and responsibilities.
>
> *Resoloved, therefore,* That, being invested by the Creator with the same capabilities, and the same consciousness of responsibility for their exercise, it is demonstrably the right and duty of woman, equally with man, to promote every righteous cause by every righteous means; and especially in regard to the great subjects of morals and religion, it is self-evidently her right to participate with her brother in teaching them, both in private and in public, by writing and by speaking, by any instrumentalities proper to be used, and in any assemblies proper to be held; and this being a self-evident truth growing out of the divinely implanted principles of human nature, any custom or authority adverse to it, whether modern or wearing the hoary sanction of antiquity, is to be regarded as a self-evident falsehood, and at war with mankind.

At the last session Lucretia Mott offered and spoke to the following resolution:

> *Resolved,* That the speedy success of our cause depends upon the zealous and untiring efforts of both men and women, for the overthrow of the monopoly of the pulpit, and for the securing to woman as equal participation with men in the various trades, professions, and commerce.

The only resolution that was not unanimously adopted was the ninth, urging the women of the country to secure to themselves the elective franchise. Those who took part in the debate feared a demand for the right to vote would defeat others they deemed more rational, and make the whole movement ridiculous.

But Mrs. Stanton and Frederick Douglass seeing that the power to choose rulers and make laws, was the right by which all others could be secured, persistently advocated the resolution, and at last carried it by a small majority.

Thus it will be seen that the Declaration and resolutions in the very first Convention, demanded all the most radical friends of the movement have since claimed—such as equal rights in the universities, in the trades and professions; the right to vote; to share in all political offices, honors, and emoluments; to complete equality in marriage, to personal freedom, property, wages, children; to make contracts; to sue, and be sued; and to testify in courts of justice. At this time the condition of married women under the Common Law, was nearly as degraded as that of the slave on the Southern plantation. The Convention continued through two entire days, and late into the evenings. The deepest interest was manifested to its close.

The proceedings were extensively published, unsparingly ridiculed by the press, and denounced by the pulpit, much to the surprise and chagrin of the leaders. Being deeply in earnest, and believing their demands pre-eminently wise and just, they were wholly unprepared to find themselves the target for the jibes and jeers of the nation. The Declaration was signed by one hundred men, and women, many of whom withdrew their names as soon as the storm of ridicule began to break. The comments of the press were carefully preserved, and it is curious to see that the same old arguments, and objections rife at the start, are reproduced by the press of to-day. But the brave protests sent out from this Convention touched a responsive chord in the hearts of women all over the country.

PUERTO RICANS

POPULATION: *137 million and still counting*	**PHYSICAL CHARACTERISTICS:** *Bantam Weights, Featherweights, Lightweights*
RELIGION: *Welfare* **PRACTICING:** *Minus holiday death toll, 108 million*	**RACIAL TRAITS (GOOD):** *Hot-blooded, colorful wardrobes, starting to go back where they came from* **RACIAL TRAITS (BAD):** *Tropical disease carriers* *Spanish accents* *Birth rate increasing*
LOCATION: *En route from Puerto Rico*	**DIET STAPLE:** *Bananas*

CHAPTER 7

HERITAGE

What Makes Something Funny? (1989)
John J. Macionis

The Sociological Approach to Humor

The most fascinating thing about using the sociological perspective, especially for people just beginning to study the discipline, is how familiar social patterns suddenly take on strange new meanings. Humor is a case in point: Virtually everyone laughs in response to particular events or information, but few people ever think much about why *we* laugh. What is it, in other words, that makes something funny in the first place? And, to put the matter in broader terms, why is humor such an essential part of social life?

Humor is, indeed, vital to our everyday lives. To see this clearly, simply imagine going through a day's activities without sharing a joke with a friend, responding with a good laugh to an unexpected event, or using a grin to lighten a tense moment. Truly, "a place where people never laugh" is tantamount to hell itself, just as the label "devoid of humor" is equivalent to denying a person a basic dimension of humanity.

The first step in a sociological understanding of humor is to recognize that it is a distinctly human activity. Other forms of life are social (ants, for instance); some animals even have the rudimentary ability to utilize symbols (such as chimps); but only humans are sufficiently at home in the world of symbols to make use of humor. What are the links among humans, symbols, and humor? Simply put, humans do not exist directly within the natural world; rather, we mediate the experience of the world with *meanings*. In other words, our senses do not in themselves constitute reality but provide input that is fashioned into a reality for ourselves, human beings live within a world made symbolic. Humor involves a special case of socially constructed meanings.

Essentially, humor is a human response to two inconsistent meanings or realities. Since social life is largely patterned in more or less predictable ways, one of these realities is usually "conventional."

This means just that it is consistent with cultural expectations linked to the situation at hand. Because the other reality differs from this one, it can be termed "unconventional," implying that it violates cultural expectations in some significant way. Any joke, therefore, has two symbolic parts joined together as "double meanings." Consider for example, a conventional question posed to Groucho Marx by a woman sitting at a table in a restaurant: "Would you join me?" "Why?" snapped Groucho in response, "Are you coming apart?" In this case, of course, the double meanings involve the word "join" in its social or physical senses.

Another extremely basic example of humor is one of the trademark jokes of standup comic Henny Youngman, who (while talking about anything) says, "Take my wife . . . *please!*" In this case, the conventional meaning lies in the fact that Youngman, in the midst of talking about some issue, appears to be alluding to his wife for purposes of illustration: "Take my wife. . . ." After just enough time to let this reality become established in the minds of the audience, however, he completes the joke by adding the single word "*please!*" which emphatically introduces the contrasting and unconventional reality: This man is trying to get rid of his wife! The value of such simple jokes is that they reveal the basic structure—two contrasting realities—of all humor.

The conventional reality with which the "punch line" collides need not always be stated explicitly. This is not surprising since the conventional understandings of situations can remain implicit and still be recognized. Thus, humor can be found in single statements such as the earnest assertion of Mark Twain that "Reports of my death have been greatly exaggerated." In this case, of course, the conventional reality left implicit is that people are either living or they are dead. Contrasting with this implicit definition of the situation is the explicit and deliberately ambiguous statement that death is a matter of degree. Note, too, a second level of contrasting reality: For someone who is speaking to suggest that he is even slightly "dead" is patently absurd.

"Getting" a Joke

In any instance of humor, anyone who does not clearly understand both the conventional and the unconventional realities embedded in a joke or situation may complain of not "getting it." This simply means that the person does not understand both realities well enough to perceive their incongruity.

Sometimes, however, the process of "getting" a joke is a bit more complex. In many jokes or other situations with a potential for humor, a crucial piece of information may not be stated explicitly. The audience must then piece together the stated elements and inferentially complete the joke in their own minds. For this reason, some humor is more demanding than other humor, and may be lost on young children, for instance. An example requiring some inferential gymnastics is the following joke, which might have been heard on the streets of any Polish city during the recent clash between Solidarity supporters and government troops:

1: What's the difference between a dead dog lying in the road and a dead government soldier lying in the road?
2: I dunno. What's the difference?
1: There are skid marks in front of the dog.

The three bits of information we are asked to imagine are (1) a dog lying dead on the road, (2) a government soldier lying dead on the road, and (3) skid marks in front of the dog. But finding the humor here depends on drawing out two additional pieces of information. First, the inference can be made that there are no skid marks in front of the government soldier; this leads, second, to the conclusion that a passing Solidarity supporter struck the government soldier *deliberately*. At this point, two opposing meanings emerge: a conventional notion ("killing is wrong") in contrast to an unconventional idea ("except for bumping off government soldiers").

Why would anyone want to make humor difficult in this way? Simply because the humor response is *accentuated* by pleasure at having completed the puzzle necessary to "get" the joke. In part, this pleasure is satisfaction at one's mental abilities. In addition, inferentially completing a joke confers "insider" status on a member of an audience. Turned around, we can understand the frustration of not "getting" a joke: evidence of mental inadequacy coupled to being socially excluded. Not surprisingly, then, at one time or another we have all faked "getting" a joke we did not actually understand, and tactfully explained a joke to an unenlightened companion.

Forms of Comedy

The fact that humor is generated in patterned ways is evident in comedy performances, which typically take one of several forms.

(1) Straight Man/Funny Man. Unquestionably, this is one of the most popular of all comedy formats. Well-known examples include the great comedy teams of Stan Laurel and Oliver Hardy, Dean Martin and Jerry Lewis, Lucille Ball and Desi Arnaz, George Burns and Gracie Allen, and Dan Rowan and Dick Martin. In each case, one individual promotes conventional understandings of situations (thus the term "straight man") while the other tends toward the unconventional (the "funny man"), so that humor flows readily from their interaction.

Also understandable in these terms is the propensity of lone comedians (such as Johnny Carson or David Letterman) to work with rather flat sidekicks (such as Ed McMahon or Paul Schafer). At the same time, the essentially binary character of humor tends to discourage three-member comedy teams. There have been exceptions, of course. One noteworthy case is the Three Stooges, although elements of the straight-man/funny-man format are found in Moe's tendency to be more conventional than the other two. Even more interesting is the case of the Marx Brothers—originally five in number. Early films include four of the brothers (Groucho, Harpo, and Chico each played a version of the funny man, while Zeppo countered as the straight man). Not surprisingly, this was a somewhat awkward format for their humor. By the time of the best Marx Brothers films in the mid-1930s (such as *A Night at the Opera* and *A Day at the Races*), Zeppo had departed. Although Zeppo's withdrawal was often attributed to being "colorless" in the face of his zany brothers, he was simply unnecessary. Groucho (as "funny man") played extremely effectively against such "straight-man" characters as Margaret Dumont, while at times himself becoming straight man to brother Chico (as in the famous Tuttsi-Fruttsi scene in *Races*). Against this backdrop, the third main Marx Brother, Harpo found his success in silence, often contributing humor by engaging various minor (and unsuspecting) characters.

(2) Assuming a Character. This is a common format for comedians who tend to work alone. Well-known examples of created "characters" include many by Lily Tomlin and Don Mondello's Father Guido Sarducci.

Working alone, a comedian using this performance is virtually compelled to be a "funny man," playing against the "straight man" implicit in cultural convention. A humorous character, then, is likely to be outlandish in some respect. At the same time, however, rather than being unique, the character should represent a "type" of person. By representing a familiar, if unconventional, segment of society, the audience has greater ability to grasp the contrasting meanings. "Jim" on "Taxi," for instance, is popular among middle-aged people familiar with the unconventional reality represented by the "burned-out druggie" of the 1960s.

(3) Impersonations. Another staple of performance comedy, impersonations generate humor by contrasting the expected behavior of some person being portrayed (a conventional reality) with what is actually observed (usually unconventional). For this reason, most comedians favor impersonations of well-known members of the establishment. Not only will the audience know the character being presented, but they will also be familiar with this character in decidedly conventional terms. Chevy Chase, for example, has long been known for his portrayals of Gerald Ford, exaggerating to great effect this President's propensity for physical awkwardness.

Topics of Humor

Comedians pride themselves in the ability to make a joke about anything. But what is funny depends on what is conventional within any culture, explaining why people around the world do not laugh at the same things.

For example, a friend who recently returned from Moscow claimed she had heard several people jokingly indicate that for Christmas they were hoping to receive "an onion wrapped in toilet paper." To the Moscovite, this is a reference to two items recently in short supply; the humor lies in treating as special that which ought to be utterly routine. To most Americans unaware of these shortages, however, onions and toilet paper *are* utterly routine, so that the line falls flat. For the same reason, of course, what is funny varies within a society, according to geographical region, by age cohort, and especially by ethnicity.

In all cases, however, humor tends to flourish around issues or topics that lend themselves to double meanings—in short, what is controversial. As children, the first jokes most of us learned were probably concerned with the American taboo of the past—sex. The mere mention of what is "unmentionable" can bring paralyzing laughter to young faces.

Since it involves playing with reality, humor is a powerful force within any society. Thinking in terms of the structural-functionalist paradigm, humor is a universal means of releasing potentially disruptive sentiments, or a cultural "safety valve." To men anxious about changing conceptions of gender, for example, feminist jokes provide needed release of what might build toward full-blown misogyny. In the same way, Gentiles may joke about Jews, blacks about whites, and so on. On an international level, we can imagine how "Soviet jokes" have probably become popular in Afghanistan in recent years, just as "Yankee jokes" are no doubt making the rounds in Managua. On a more situational level, of course, humor serves as a vital form of tact. A smile, grin, or laugh can simply and easily convey the idea that someone's personal embarrassment is not to be taken seriously.

From a social-conflict point of view, humor can be understood as a form of political action. This may appear odd at first glance since humor is, by definition, what is not to be taken seriously. Indeed, the safety valve in humor lies precisely in the fact that if called to account for a joke at the expense of some category of people, the comedian will immediately offer the defense that "I didn't mean anything by it—it's only a joke." But humor also contains an element of hostility when it plays to stereotypes with which everyone is familiar but which are no longer part of polite conversation.

Moreover, a thin line separates what is funny from what is offensive. In the Middle Ages, the word "humor" referred to the balance of bodily fluids that determined a person's state of health or sickness. To be "out of humor" was, in this sense, to be "sick." This explains why the most pious and conventional people—or the most zealous revolutionaries—are sometimes charged with having no sense of humor. The sting lies in the assertion that one is stuck in a single frame of meaning, lacking the basically human ability to shape and reshape reality.

But while humor is built on challenging what is conventional or taken for granted, every culture is likely to shield some sentiments or events from humor. Perhaps they are simply too powerful to be taken lightly: A case in point was the 1986 space shuttle disaster. Few "space shuttle" jokes emerged, and those that did were widely condemned as "sick." In short, humor is embedded in society: What is—and what is not—to be taken lightly can hardly be separated from the larger social system.

Humor and Social Marginality

Finally, based on the argument so far, one suspects that the greatest contribution to humor comes not from the most "established" people but from those at society's margins. White Anglo-Saxon Protestants (WASPS), historically the most socially prominent of Americans, have certainly not dominated the world of comedy. Indeed, there are even jokes about how dour WASPs are:

> How does a male WASP propose to a female WASP?
> He says, "How would you like to be buried with my people?"

On the other hand, the margins of society are logically the place from which conventional social patterns can be taken lightly. The wit of an Oscar Wilde, for instance, can hardly be separated from living the marginal life of an intellectual and homosexual in Victorian England. Similarly, although supporting research results are lacking at present, racial and ethnic minorities (and especially Jews, who, like Wilde, have historically emphasized intellectualism and have been forced to the margins of society) seem to be disproportionately represented among America's comedians.

In sum, the sociological perspective provides intriguing insights about humor. Indeed, the sociological enterprise (about which there are very few jokes) itself has much in common with humor in its ability to discern unconventional meanings in everyday life.

An Indian Father's Plea (1990)

Robert Lake (Medicine Grizzlybear)

Dear teacher, I would like to introduce you to my son, Wind-Wolf. He is probably what you consider a typical Indian kid. He was born and raised on the reservation. He has black hair, dark brown eyes, and an olive complexion. And like so many Indian children his age, he is shy and quiet in the classroom. He is 5 years old, in kindergarten, and I can't understand why you have already labeled him a "slow learner."

At the age of 5, he has already been through quite an education compared with his peers in Western society. As his introduction into this world, he was bonded to his mother and to the Mother Earth in a traditional native childbirth ceremony. And he has been continuously cared for by his mother, father, sisters, cousins, aunts, uncles, grandparents, and extended tribal family since this ceremony.

From his mother's warm and loving arms, Wind-Wolf was placed in a secure and specially designed Indian baby basket. His father and the medicine elders conducted another ceremony with him that served to bond him with the essence of his genetic father, the Great Spirit, the Grandfather Sun, and the Grandmother Moon. This was all done in order to introduce him properly into the new and natural world, not the world of artificiality, and to protect his sensitive and delicate soul. It is our people's way of showing the newborn respect, ensuring that he starts his life on the path of spirituality.

The traditional Indian baby basket became his "turtle's shell" and served as the first seat for his classroom. He was strapped in for safety, protected from injury by the willow roots and hazel wood construction. The basket was made by a tribal elder who had gathered her materials with prayer and in a ceremonial way. It is the same kind of basket that our people have used for thousands of years. It is specially designed to provide the child with the kind of knowledge and experience he will need in order to survive in his culture and environment.

Wind-Wolf was strapped in snugly with a deliberate restriction upon his arms and legs. Although you in Western society may argue that such a method serves to hinder motor-skill development and abstract reasoning, we believe it forces the child to first develop his intuitive faculties, rational intellect, symbolic thinking, and five senses. Wind-Wolf was with his mother constantly, closely bonded physically, as she carried him on her back or held him in front while breast-feeding. She carried him everywhere she went, and every night he slept with both parents. Because of this, Wind-Wolf's educational setting was not only a "secure" environment, but it was also very colorful, complicated, sensitive, and diverse. He has been with his mother at the ocean at daybreak when she made her prayers and gathered fresh seaweed from the rocks, he has sat with his uncles in a rowboat on the river while they fished with gillnets, and he has watched and listened to elders as they told creation stories and animal legends and sang songs around campfires.

He has attended the sacred and ancient White Deerskin Dance of his people and is well-acquainted with the cultures and languages of other tribes. He has been with his mother when she gathered herbs for healing and watched his tribal aunts and grandmothers gather and prepare traditional foods such as acorn, smoked salmon, eel, and deer meat. He has played with abalone shells, pine nuts, iris grass string, and leather while watching the women make beaded jewelry and traditional native regalia. He has had many opportunities to watch his father, uncles, and ceremonial leaders use different kinds of songs while preparing for the sacred dances and rituals.

As he grew older, Wind-Wolf began to crawl out of the baby basket, develop his motor skills, and explore the world around him. When frightened or sleepy, he could always return to the basket, as a turtle withdraws into its shell. Such an inward journey allows one to reflect in privacy on what he has learned and to carry the new knowledge deeply into the unconscious and the soul. Shapes, sizes, colors, texture, sound, smell, feeling, taste, and the learning process are therefore, integrated—the physical and spiritual, matter and energy, conscious and unconscious, individual and social.

This kind of learning goes beyond the basics of distinguishing the difference between rough and smooth, square and round, hard and soft, black and white, similarities and extremes.

For example, Wind-Wolf was with his mother in South Dakota while she danced for seven days straight in the hot sun, fasting, and piercing herself in the sacred Sun Dance Ceremony of a distant tribe. He has been doctored in a number of different healing ceremonies by medicine men and women from diverse places ranging from Alaska and Arizona to New York and California. He has been in more than 20 different sacred sweat-lodge rituals—used by native tribes to purify mind, body, and soul—since he was 3 years old, and he has already been exposed to many different religions of his racial brothers: Protestant, Catholic, Asian Buddhist, and Tibetan Lamaist.

It takes a long time to absorb and reflect on these kinds of experiences, so maybe that is why you think my Indian child is a slow learner. His aunts and grandmothers taught him to count and know his numbers while they sorted out the complex materials used to make the abstract designs in the native baskets. He listened to his mother count each and every bead and sort out numerically according to color while painstakingly making complex beaded belts and necklaces. He learned his basic numbers by helping his father count and sort the rocks to be used in the sweat lodge—seven rocks for a medicine sweat, say, or 13 for the summer solstice ceremony. (The rocks are later heated and doused with water to create purifying steam.) And he was taught to learn mathematics by counting the sticks we use in our traditional native hand game. So I realize he may be slow in grasping the methods and tools that you are now using in your classroom, ones quite familiar to his white peers, but I hope you will be patient with him. It takes time to adjust to a new cultural system and learn new things.

He is not culturally "disadvantaged," but he is culturally "different." If you ask him how many months there are in a year, he will probably tell you 13. He will respond this way not because he doesn't know how to count properly, but because he has been taught by our people that there are 13 full moons in a year according to the native tribal calendar and that there are really 13 planets in our solar system and 13 tail feathers on a perfectly balanced eagle, the most powerful kind of bird to use in ceremony and healing.

But he also knows that some eagles may only have 12 tail feathers, or seven, that they do not all have the exact same number. He knows that the flicker has exactly 10 tail feathers; that they are red and black, representing the directions of east and west, life and death; and that this bird is considered a "fire" bird, a power used in native doctoring and healing. He can probably count more than 40 different kinds of birds, tell you and his peers what kind of bird each is and where it lives, the seasons in which it appears, and how it is used in a sacred ceremony. He may have trouble writing his name on a piece of paper, but he knows how to say it and many other things in several different Indian languages. He is not fluent yet because he is only 5 years old and required by law to attend your educational system, learn your language, your values, your ways of thinking, and your methods of teaching and learning.

So you see, all of these influences together make him somewhat shy and quiet—perhaps "slow" according to your standards. But if Wind-Wolf was not prepared for his first tentative foray into your world, neither were you appreciative of his culture. On the first day of class, you had difficulty with his name. You wanted to call him Wind, insisting that Wolf somehow must be his middle name. The students in the class laughed at him, causing further embarrassment.

While you are trying to teach him your new methods, helping him learn new tools for self-discovery and adapt to his new learning environment, he may be looking out the window as if daydreaming. Why? Because he has been taught to watch and study the changes in nature. It is hard for him to make the appropriate psychic switch from the right to the left hemisphere of the brain when he sees the leaves turning bright colors, the geese heading south, and the squirrels scurrying around for nuts to get ready for a harsh winter. In his heart, in his young mind, and almost by instinct, he knows that this is the time of year he is supposed to be with his people gathering and preparing fish, deer meat, and native plants and herbs, and learning his assigned tasks in this role. He is caught between two worlds, torn by two distinct cultural systems.

Yesterday, for the third time in two weeks he came home crying and said he wanted to have his hair cut. He said he doesn't have any friends at school because they make fun of his long hair. I tried to explain to him that in our culture, long hair is a sign of masculinity and balance and is a source of power. But he remained adamant in his position.

To make matters worse, he recently encountered his first harsh case of racism. Wind-Wolf had managed to adopt at least one good school friend. On the way home from school one day, he asked his new pal if he wanted to come home to play with him until supper. That was OK with Wind-Wolf's mother, who was walking with them. When they all got to the little friend's house, the two boys ran inside to ask permission while Wind-Wolf's mother waited. But the other boy's mother lashed out: "It is OK if you have to play with him at school, but we don't allow those kind of people in our house!" When my wife asked why not, the other boy's mother answered, "Because you are Indians and we are white, and I don't want my kids growing up with your kind of people."

So now my young Indian child does not want to go to school anymore (even though we cut his hair). He feels that he does not belong. He is the only Indian child in your class, and he is well-aware of this fact. Instead of being proud of his race, heritage, and culture, he feels ashamed. When he watches television, he asks why the white people hate us so much and always kill our people in the movies and why they take everything away from us. He asks why the other kids in school are not taught about power, beauty, and essence of nature or provided with an opportunity to experience the world around them firsthand. He says he hates living in the city and that he misses his Indian cousins and friends. He asks why one young white girl at school who is his friend always tells him, "I like you, Wind-Wolf, because you are a good Indian."

Now he refuses to sing his native songs, play with his Indian artifacts, learn his language, or participate in his sacred ceremonies. When I ask him to go to an urban powwow or help me with a sacred sweat-lodge ritual, he says no because "that's weird" and he doesn't want his friends at school to think he doesn't believe in God.

So, dear teacher, I want to introduce you to my son, Wind-Wolf, who is not really a "typical" little Indian kid after all. He stems from a long line of hereditary chiefs, medicine men and women, and ceremonial leaders whose accomplishments and unique forms of knowledge are still being studied and recorded in contemporary books. He has seven different tribal systems flowing through his blood; he is even part white. I want my child to succeed in school and life. I don't want him to be a dropout or juvenile delinquent or to end up on drugs and alcohol because he is made to feel inferior or because of discrimination. I want him to be proud of his rich heritage and culture, and I would like him to develop the necessary capabilities to adapt to, and succeed in, both cultures. But I need your help.

What you say and what you do in the classroom, what you teach and how you teach it, and what you don't say and don't teach will have a significant effect on the potential success or failure of my child. Please remember that this is the primary year of his education and development. All I ask is that you work with me, not against me, to help educate my child in the best way. If you don't have the knowledge, preparation, experience, or training to effectively deal with culturally different children, I am willing to help you with the few resources I have available or direct you to such resources.

Millions of dollars have been appropriated by Congress and are being spent each year for "Indian Education." All you have to do is take advantage of it and encourage your school to make an effort to use it in the name of "equal education." My Indian child has a constitutional right to learn, retain, and maintain his heritage and culture. By the same token, I strongly believe that non-Indian children also have a constitutional right to learn about our Native American heritage and culture, because Indians play a significant part in the history of Western society. Until this reality is equally understood and applied in education as a whole, there will be a lot more schoolchildren in grades K-2 identified as "slow learners."

My son, Wind-Wolf, is not an empty glass coming into your class to be filled. He is a full basket coming into a different environment and society with something special to share. Please let him share his knowledge, heritage, and culture with you and his peers.

Lake reports that Wind-Wolf, now 8, is doing better in school, but the boy's struggle for cultural identity continues.

Robert Lake (Medicine Grizzlybear), is a member of the Seneca and Cherokee Indian tribes, is an associate professor at Gonzaga University's School of Education in Spokane, Wash.

The Appalachian Voice (1987)
Eli Flam

Shoals of immigrants continue to settle in the United States, well into its third century as a nation, and many who are long here still seek to home in on their heritage. How do people from elsewhere become Americans while dealing with the voices and values they bring with them? Until the middle of the twentieth century, the melting-pot theory held sway. It postulated that individuals and groups from all over the globe should largely give up their languages and ways to become assimilated in a homogeneous mass. But in recent decades, the notion of an American "stew" has gained favor, by which constituent tongues and cultures keep their identities and so add to the flavor and substance of the nation.

Appalachia was settled by the nation's earliest immigrants, and its residents are one of its most misunderstood groups. Mostly of Scots-Irish stock, they first settled the extensive mountainous region from Pennsylvania to Alabama well before the Revolutionary War. They represent a rock-ribbed past, a rugged heritage.

"My people have always been teachers on my mother's side," said Laura Milton Hodges. "The first ones came to Appalachia way before the Revolutionary War. . . .The books on our shelves were by philosophers, and on history, and even Greek plays, and English literature.

"We're also farmers, and that's real important. The main thing is, though, you have to value your own culture. Then you can go anywhere, fit in anywhere."

Hodges teaches remedial English and reading at Watauga High School in the northwest corner of North Carolina. She lives in Vilas, four miles from where she grew up in southern Appalachia. Her husband runs a bulldozer business; their 19-year-old son, Roy Lee, Jr., works with him. Two daughters, 26-year-old Joy Pritchett and 24-year-old Gay Isaacs, also live in Watauga County and continue the family patterns of studying and teaching.

More than twenty million people live in Appalachia, a thickly wooded area, roughly the size of Great Britain, that covers largely mountainous, often isolated areas from Alabama and Mississippi on the south to Pennsylvania and New York on the north. In between lie large chunks of Georgia, South Carolina, North Carolina, Tennessee, Kentucky, West Virginia, Maryland, and Ohio.

Early settlers found land for the taking and either negotiated treaties (often broken) or fought with the Cherokees, Appalaches, and other Indian tribes. Theodore Roosevelt wrote in his *Winning of the West* that

> the Watauga folk were the first Americans who, as a separate body, moved into the wilderness to hew out dwellings for themselves and their children, trusting only to their own shrewd heads, stout hearts, and strong arms, unhelped and unhampered by the power nominally their sovereign.

In other words, they were independent-minded. Their language, crafts, and culture have reflected this through the centuries. But living apart, often in remote hollers and valleys without decent roads or means to earn a fair income, also brought widespread substandard living conditions. "The very name of the region," wrote native son Harry Caudill in 1973, "has become synonymous with poverty and backwardness."

Concerted political action in Washington led in 1965 to the Appalachian Regional Development Act and an initial $1.2 billion for a five-year program to build roads, schools, hospitals, and sewage treatment plants and to reclaim eroded land. Local development districts (LCDs) carried programs forward. At the same time, the bluegrass and country music rooted in the area spread to other parts of the United States and the world. Stars of the Grand Ol' Opry in Nashville, Dolly Parton, Johnny Cash, and a slew of other performers became public and television standouts. Writers from Appalachia found new audiences.

But on the other side of the coin, new and old stereotypes—quaint talk, moonshinin', and a lot of down-home orneriness—were stirred up via comic strips, musicals, and television sitcoms like *L'il Abner, Hee Haw, and The Beverly Hillbillies*. It all had a whiff of George Washington Harris' roughhouse hero of more than a century ago, Sut Lovingood.

In one yarn, Lovingood drew a farrago of raillery about the appearance of horse and self from the "crowd of mountaineers full of fun, foolery, and mean whiskey" in front of Pat Nash's grocery. Responded Sut:

> I say, you durn'd ash cats, jis' keep yer shuts on, will ye? You never sees a rale hoss till
> I rid up; you's p'raps stole ur owned shod rabbits ur sheep wif borrerd saddils on, but
> when you tuck the fus' begrudgin look jis' now at this critter, name Tarpoke, yu were
> injoyin a sight ove nex' tu the bes' hoss what ever shell'd nubbins ur toted jugs, an he's
> es ded as a still wum, poor ole Tickytail!

Journalist-author Harris, a committed secessionist from Tennessee, used Lovingood as a stick to beat the Yankees from 1854 until he died in 1869. The satirical character appeared in the local press and a New York newspaper, *Spirit of the Times*. Harris had a "Rabelaisian touch," said J. Franklin Meine in his *Tall Tales of the Southwest*, portraying Sut as "simply the genuine naive roughneck mountaineer, riotously bent on raising hell." Writing in the *New Yorker* in 1955, Edmund Wilson, however, saw "extravagant language and monstrously distorted descriptions. Unlike Rabelais, he is always malevolent and always extremely sordid."

Education and the regional language

"About 95 percent of my kids at school are mountain-born, native children," Laura Milton Hodges observes. "Like us, they also have that extended family, and a lot of their grandparents use some of what we may call antiquated forms of English. We use double and triple negatives when we want to emphasize something like. 'It don't make no nevermind,' and we sometimes don't say isn't, we say ain't.

"A lot of times, teachers either from the inside or the outside will try to shake it out of the kids, to shame them. If you put them down and make them ashamed, you're making them ashamed of their family and of the home they live in.

"And so we have to find ways to make them realize what a wonderful tradition, a long history they have and the reasons they speak that way. Then they're more interested in 'popular,' current grammar, and they can better themselves. A lot of those who get ashamed, they drop out of school, and they end up cleaning motel rooms, or cooking in restaurants, now that we have tourism."

Appalachian high school dropout rates still run higher than the overall U.S. average. The tendency persists despite programs like those at Watauga or the Support Center in Cobbleskill, N.Y., where in six years the rate dropped from 12 to 7 percent, or efforts by well-known figures like country singer Tom T. Hall, himself a dropout. One Kentucky school superintendent says teachers' attitudes have to change. They have a tendency to downgrade a newcomer whose older siblings didn't do well, for example, or whose parents "never did amount to a hill of beans." Added a parent: "Whatever a child has got on his back and no matter how ticky his hair is, no matter what hole he comes out of, he deserves the same chance as Sally sitting over here in a ruffled dress."

Since the 1960s and 1970s, most grade schools have retention programs. Many have enriched, upgraded, and adapted their curricula. Newly built community colleges and special technical schools coordinate classes geared to new industries and manufacturers coming into a county. Some area universities, like Appalachian State in North Carolina and Radford in Virginia, have created Appalachian studies programs. Berea College in Kentucky focused on mountain people and issues.

The so-called regional language was widely believed to be closely related to Elizabethan English. But like the exuberant growth in valley, forest, and upland, speech in Appalachia has embraced and intertwined with elements from the original Indians, early French trappers, German settlers, and blacks with whom the Scots–Irish pioneers worked in lumber camps, coal mines, cotton mills, and textile plants.

A nineteenth-century observer, Anne Newport Royall, said, "Like Shakespear[e], they make a word when at a loss: *scawm'd* is one of them, which means spotted." The widely acknowledged abilities of Appalachians as storytellers often are credited to a rich Scots–Irish oral heritage. Legendary frontiersman Davy Crockett once described himself as

> fresh from the backwoods, half-horse, half-alligator, a little touched with snapping turtle, can wade the Mississippi, leap the Ohio, ride a streak of lightening, slide down a honey locust and not get scratched.

This way with words was put to partisan use during the fierce union organizing battles in the 1920s and 1930s in coal fields on the western side of the mountains. The song "Which Side Are You On?" still galvanizes the faithful, far and wide. Miner's wife Florence Reece of Ellistown, Tennessee, wrote at the outset: "We're starting our good battle,/ We know we're sure to win,/ Because we've got the gun thugs/ A-lookin' very thin."

Prefixing a verb with an *a*, as in "A-lookin' very thin," is a common construction. In fact, to be common is a virtue in Appalachia, as in the sentence, "He's a mighty common man"—said of business mogul or preacher, bank president or shopkeeper, nabob or neighbor.

Hard times caused some inhabitants to leave Appalachia in the 1960s before the pendulum swung more favorably with development efforts in the 1970s. Another miner's wife, Sarah Ogan Gunning of Harlan, Kentucky, caught the keening lament of these place-minded people with her version of "A Girl of Constant Sorrow." The singer bids farewell to her home state, then mourns: "My mother, how I hated to leave her,/ Mother dear who now is dead,/ But I had to go and leave her/ So my children could have bread."

Neighbors and kin

"In defining our culture," Laura Milton Hodges continued, "I'll have to talk about the values that people maybe don't realize. First of all I'd say family is the highest priority. Stories about our being clannish and protective of each other—well, that's pretty true. I'm a neighbor to a lot of my kin, for example."

A brother lives four miles away, as did their parents when alive, and aunts, uncles, and others who left for military service or to work away have come back to retire. "We have our family right close," the North Carolina teacher said.

"Now we have television and movies, and all sorts of influences from the outside that teach a popular English and bring in different values. If you go out into the world, maybe you put on a little different accent, you change your grammar, and you try to polish it up—but when you go home, you're gonna have to communicate so you can speak that old language again. It comes easy, and for my kids, they have some kind of a pride—sometimes they'll use *ain't* in defiance, especially if it's somebody puttin' them down.

"We're so proud of people who've made it in the world, the Carter family, June Carter Cash and Johnny. We're proud that Dolly Parton grew up in the mountains of Tennessee and knows all the homecookin' things she does on national TV, and that colleges just love bluegrass and country music, and that our native singers go to, why, Carnegie Hall, and are well-accepted.

"But a lot of kids I know don't realize all this. They think it's just something you do in the kitchen, or square dancing. A little later in their lives, some of them do find out, and it is a matter of pride."

A literature coming of age

Appalachian writers have come of age. Some four hundred have been "mapped" by two English professors at Radford University. In addition to such figures of the past as Thomas Wolfe, Sherwood Anderson, Jesse Stuart, and James Agee, a number of newer authors have been saluted—for example, the late Breece D'J Pancake, Pinckney Benedict, Jayne Anne Phillips, Lee Smith.

Lee Smith grew up in a large extended family in the western Virginia town of Grundy, tucked between steep, rugged, mountains. Politics, community affairs, and just plain "yarning"—embroidering stories anew with each telling—were the stuff of front porch conversation, and now form the core of her novels. Smith usually focuses on ordinary people in southern Appalachian towns who get tangled in toils of love, lust, marriage, and family concerns.

Oral History covers a hundred years in the history of a mountain family branded with bad luck. *Black Mountain Breakdown,* about a young woman struggling in tightly meshed, down-home surroundings, has been compared to "reading *Madame Bovary* while listening to Loretta Lynn and watching *The Guiding Light*." In her sixth and latest work, *Family Linen,* the heroine is a small-town beautician named Candy.

And still the lilt and tilt of a certain kind of Southern patois loops and larrups through all the tangled tales. One strand evokes the kind of recondite romanticism espoused by Sidney Lanier, a contemporary of George Washington Harris, creator of Sut Lovingood. Another tracks up through as strong a writer as Anne W. Armstrong, who wrote *This Day and Time* in 1930. Ivy Ingoldsby, deserted by her husband and left with a young son in the East Tennessee mountains, frets in the following paragraph about neighbor Doke's cow to an aristocratic summer visitor:

> "I tell ye," she would complain angrily to Old Mag or Mrs. Philips, "I tell ye, ef I had me a gun, I 'ud as leave to shoot the sorry critter as no, me a-workin' hard the endurin' day, an' a sight to do atter I gits home of a night, me a-needin' my sleep, an' then a-havin' to git up from the bed an' run her off! Of course, Doke hain't got no chancet to keep his critters up. He's done burnt all his fence-rails for firewood. . . . But Doke,

> he's got to do somethin' about that old cow o' hisn. I 'ud put the law on him. I 'ud take a writ, on'y I'm afeared he 'ud witch Enoch or burn me down. I do know Duke Odum is the aggravatin'est man on earth—I won't except none!"

The central, abiding role of women in Appalachia recurs in literature and life. In *Esquire*, Phillip Moffitt called his late grandmother, Etta Lee, "one of a special breed of women who . . . as [she] used to tell me, 'took their strength from the mountains and from living day to day.'" As a five-year-old, Moffitt lay

> for hours on end underneath a tall pine tree on an old homemade quilt . . . listening to her . . . real stories, without rose coloring, adult stories of human weakness, of betrayal, of domination—stories without heroes and happy endings, but also without self-pity or defeat. Life as it is.

He realized later, like one of Laura Milton Hodges' students,

> that despite my outward drive for success and worldly accomplishment [he became editor-in-chief and president of *Esquire*], I too was of those hills and valleys, and my days, like [those of Etta Lee], could be filled with the sweet sadness of observing life from the isolation of the dark mountains.

Tourism, coal mining, and hardship

"On our side of the mountains," Milton Hodges—as many friends call her—said, "we don't have coal or minerals except for the mica and feldspar, but we've got tourism and a new influx of people who are buying up second homes and trying to pass laws to keep the mountains beautiful. They don't want to see filling stations, but that may be our boys' talent, or a second job so we don't have to sell the land to develop it.

"It's real hard because all of us, all the mountain folks, hate to see the development, and there's not one man who didn't cry when he had to sell an acre of a farm his great-granddaddy got a grant for, fighting in the Revolutionary War. We also realize we have to eat, and we may not put up a little log cabin replica of a moonshine still, we may just have to do something real, like fixing cars.

"We're a little on their side too, but we have to eat, and we want to stay where we are."

To do so, farmers raise tobacco, trees, and "the best cabbage in the South," the Watauga County native declared, on nearby Beech Mountain, where cool weather helps the crop. Ginseng, the much sought-after root locally called *sang*, is found in the woods. Originally shipped almost exclusively to China, it now is prized in urban American markets as well.

Federal and state projects have helped the area, "but most of it was a temporary shot in the arm. We have centers for our older citizens now, but you can't help a people unless it comes from them. They had classes, for example, on how to make strawberry preserves. Now you tell me that's not ludicrous, because our mountain women have always known how to do that. With my job, I still can and freeze things, cure hams and work up pig meat."

Some help has come to the Beech Mountain area from three brothers—Harry, Grover, and Spencer Robbins. After prospering in the lumber business, the brothers built a golf course and clubhouse, and laid out a mammoth project keyed to the highest ski runs in the East—clustered resort homes, a modern airport, and a snazzy monorail to hook all the planned activities together. These projects provided jobs for many residents of Beech Mountain.

All three brothers also rescued *Tweetsie,* a little train that earned its nickname from the sound of its whistle. In the 1930s, the brothers often rode *Tweetsie* from Boone, North Carolina, to visit a grandmother in Fosco. First to cross the Blue Ridge Mountains when track was laid into Tennessee in 1881, *Tweetsie*—as it is lettered on the side of the coal car—went out of business in the 1940s after the Watauga River overflowed and tore up a lot of track. In the late 1950s, the Robbins brothers located the train in Hollywood, where it had been used in the movies. With some help from Gene Autry, they brought it back home and reopened the old line.

Over in Kentucky and Tennessee, most families still tend gardens and keep a few animals, but coal mining still is the main outside employment. Traditional craftsmanship centers on hand-carved wooden dolls, hand-sewn quilts, gun cabinets, furniture, needlework, and musical instruments. Death and accidents still are stark facts of life in the tight, dangerous adyta far below the ground, although strip mining, a highly mechanized process that scars the land unsparingly unless landscaped afterward, has come to the region.

Billy Gaylor, from Fonde, Kentucky, followed father, brother, and grandfather as a coal miner. After a bad accident in a tunnel, he said, "Not one man out of the whole crowd thought about themselves, they wondered about the others. There's a closeness, a bond between us underground." An informal survey in Letcher County showed that all miners had either been injured themselves, quit because of coal dust afflictions, or had friends hurt and killed in rock slides, afterdamp explosions, or other disasters.

Hardship has been a way of life in Appalachia from the first settlement, but it has taken very hard times to force people to seek work and new horizons elsewhere. Fred Dotson, from Lee County, Virginia, found a good job as layout and quality control inspector at a Plymouth factory in Detroit in the mid-1950s.

"But I was homesick," he told *Appalachia* magazine. "I don't care much for inside work." His father was there also, "and homesick real bad, too," Fred's wife, Audrey, said. "We were there almost four years—three of our six kids were born there. And I'll tell you this, it's a hard place for children. You just can't keep kids fastened up in an apartment all the time, but we couldn't let them out the door either."

Coming home

"Seems like people always come back," Laura Milton Hodges said. "We don't have as much migration at this time as we did into the fifties. People were going to Detroit and Cleveland and Flint and anywhere they could get jobs. It was just like they'd died and gone to heaven when they got their paychecks, but really they hadn't, because of the places they had to live.

"It took their freedom and some of their spirit. I've heard them talk. . . . You couldn't believe people were so close together living, and you could hear what your neighbors were doin'. . . .They kind of stayed together, though, among themselves, the kind of people they understood."

Hodges, who took part in the Festival of American Folklife in Washington D.C., last summer, was fooling with a piano in her hotel one evening when an older man with a banjo asked if she knew how to play "I'll Fly Away."

"We started," she said, "and he hit the same licks I did, just exactly like I was back home. He didn't talk like me, but when I looked at him and he looked at me, I knew where he was from. He had changed his way of talking, but he was from twenty miles away, and still remembered the old mountain style of music, certain beats, little embellishments. It was just like I found a friend, right there. This was homefolks.

They got together with a Caribbean group with lute and bongos, Mexican musicians, and some Chinese participants whose daughter Margaret loved to dance and learned to do the mountain flatfoot.

"We'd take turns," Laura Hodges exclaimed, "for each culture. I felt as accepted there as I've ever felt in my life. You don't see that all over these United States, but there I made a lot of friends. And our dances, we weren't that far apart.

"I was raised not to have prejudice, as much as possible, and I'm proud my mother and daddy put that to me."

Misnomers and stereotypes

In eastern Tennessee, a group of dark-skinned people called Melungeons remains something of a mystery, as with other apparently triracial mixtures. They are believed to be part black, part Indian, and part French, Portuguese, or Jewish. Several books and a number of articles have been written about them. Bonnie Ball, in *The Melungeons: Their Origin and Kin* (1969), traces the name to a slight transformation of the French word, *melangeon*, for mixed breed. While acknowledging the presence of French trappers and traders in the area centuries ago, she also speculates that the reputed lost colony of North Carolina may also have provided a source for the Melungeons.

Long ill-treated by many whites in the area, they were encouraged to attend community meetings by a local organizer, Ellen Rector. "They don't talk exactly like we do," Rector told Kathy Kahn in *Hillbilly Women*, "but they're real good to talk up at our meetings. I don't hardly know who is a Melungeon around here. They've called us all Melungeons. What ain't called Melungeons is called *hillbillies*."

The word *hillbilly* itself may derive from a combination of *hill* and *Billy*, a name popular among the Scots-Irish settlers. Sweet William, a flower from the British Isles, is prevalent in Appalachia (along with more than half the species of plants found throughout the Eastern United States). Many old ballads featured a young man named William, as in "Barbara Allen," where the namesake dies for Sweet William, and a boyfriend in a latter-day song is *Common Bill.*

Cratis Williams, the "father of Appalachian studies," adds to the discussion of this misnomer. During the period of industrialization following the Civil War, Williams argues, people began calling Appalachians *mountaineers* (a term that residents consider a misnomer). The term *hillbilly* was in use at that time, but it was only applied to the poor white residents of Alabama and Mississippi sandhills and piney woods. Williams points out that only recently has *hillbilly* become synonymous with *mountaineer.*

Sensitivities ran higher when outsiders used the name a decade or so ago, Eric Olson, librarian at Appalachia State University, commented, especially in the burlesque television shows of *Hee Haw* and *The Beverly Hillbillies.* Some of that has passed (along with the shows) because of a stronger, more positive sense of identity within the area. Nevertheless, Olson noted, Appalachians remain one of the few groups of "minorities" that still are or can be made fun of publicly without much outcry.

"Somebody asked me the other night," Hodges said, "what the *hillbi*—he caught himself and said, in a northern accent, what the hill people do for entertainment. I didn't take offence, but it's an example of what we always hear, and I told him we go to lectures and symphony concerts, we love those. Then we make music in the kitchen with the kids, too.

"And he was really shocked. He was wanting me to tell him, I guess, that we make a little moonshine, that we sit back and drink it, and have a free-for-all, because somewhere in the back of people's minds, I think they want there to be a race of people, an ethnic group that's still a little on the romantic wild side."

A region of *growingness*

Some two hundred years ago, William Bartram, son of a Quaker farmer from Philadelphia and America's leading botanist, crisscrossed Appalachia as settlement was first taking hold. In his book, *Travels*, he writes about coming upon a rich sylvan scene replete with a "meandering river gliding through," strolling turkeys, prancing deer, and "companies of young, innocent Cherokee virgins" gathering the lushest fruit imaginable, reclining under the shade "of floriferous and fragrant native bowers . . . disclosing their beauties to the fluttering breeze, and bathing their limbs in the cool, fleeting streams" while yet other groups "more gay and libertine," played yet more lascivious games.

By the 1960s, Harry Caudhill, in his landmark volume, *Night Comes to the Cumberlands*, wrote:

> Though fabulous wealth has been generated in Appalachia, the mountaineers' share
> in it has been held to a minimum. . . . To the industrialists who opened the coal mines,
> set up the great saw mills, operated the quarries, built the railroads and hauled away
> the resources, the population was a made-to-order source of cheap labor. . . . The
> debasement of the mountaineer is a tragedy of epic proportions.

Progress has been made in the twenty-five years since those words helped jog official Washington and many others to take remedial steps, and since Charles Kuralt touched a nerve for millions of viewers with his program, *Christmas in Appalachia*. Measures have been taken to improve health, education, transportation, and unemployment. But the old ways remain on many sides.

Post offices still serve as general store, church, and school. Place names remind one of violence and hard times: Squabble, Gouge-eye, Shooting Creek, Vengeance, Hell Mountain, and Long Hungry, Bone Valley, Poor Fork, Needmore, Weary Hut, and Broken Leg. Humor comes in with Shake a Rag, Squeeze Betsey (a tight place between two cliffs), and Chunky Gal. And mountains, showing that gift for a turn of phrase, go by Hogback, Hound Ears, Standing Indian, The Devil's Courthouse, Sharp Top, and Naked Place.

Yet that bedrock question of whence derives the region's flavorful speech draws this flat-out statement by eminent philologist James Robert Reese:

> Although the language of the area has been referred to as Elizabethan English, Early
> English, and American Anglo-Saxon, very little scientific investigation of it has been
> completed and published.

In an article carried in the bountiful anthology, *Voices from the Hills*, Reese continues:

> Too many items of the supposed mountain dialect, such as the pronunciations
> indicated by the occasional spellings of *gin* (again I get home), *sich, ye, borry, jest, hain,
> jit, gin'rally, kem* (came), *fer* (far) *larnt, denamite* (dynamite), *rench*, (rinse), *cheer*
> (chair) and hundreds of others, as well as morphological variants such as *housen,
> beastes, postes, nestes, waspers* and even such phonological generalizations as the
> appearance of /t/ in final position in such words as *behind, end, and shed* not only had
> been recorded as common in other areas of the country, but were spoken by persons
> who were neither socially nor culturally related to the mountaineer.

Reese concludes that the *way* Appalachians speak and write, what he calls "rhetorical sources" and not any dialect as such, are fit subjects for study for those who want to understand the area's culture. He finds that the dialects are not dying, only changing, but he fears for the deeply rooted "art of oral rhetoric." Its three main ingredients: "the conscious belief that it is important, a closeness to the mountain land, and time to sit and talk."

In the meantime, a no less distinguished linguist, Earl F. Schrock, Jr., delved into Anne Armstrong's novel *This Day and Time* several decades after it was published, in connection with his own detailed two-year survey of southern Appalachian speech. He credited Armstrong with a sensitive ear for phonetic spelling. Schrock sees peculiar verb and adjective usages falling away, chiefly due to radio and television, and exposure to people from other areas, and even notes a continuing attachment to double or even triple negative exclamations (Hain't no use lightin' no lamp"), a love of God ("Laws a mercy"), and heavy use of comparative and superlative suffixes ("He was the most moaningest-fullest hound I ever did see").

Also enlightening are the comments of three artists. Lester Pross, who grew up in New York's Appalachian region and became head of the art department at Berea College in Berea, Kentucky, told *Appalachia* magazine:

> Although I've traveled and lived in other countries and been strongly influenced intellectually by what I've seen, my paintings continue to reflect the *growingness* of this part of the world, the beauty and variety of the landscape.

Frank Fleming, one of seven children of poor farmers in Bear Creek, Alabama, whose ceramic sculptures invariably have animals in them, said, "I guess when I was growing up living so close to the land like we did, we got so we kind of trusted animals more than we did people."

David Lucas, who returned to hometown Haymond, Kentucky, after working as a welder for U.S. Steel in Gary, Indiana, was inspired to work full-time as an artist by a visit to the Chicago Art Institute. In talking about his painting, *Hoeing Potatoes*, he said, "People around here are always digging in the ground. They plant, they strip for coal, they bury people."

Harry Caudill, noting that Appalachia was "the nation's first frontier," added that "it may be foretelling America's final form." Appalachian-Americans represent not only a complex, rugged past but also an evolving present in the ever-shifting mosaic of life in the United States.

Additional Reading

James Agee, *A Death in the Family*, McDowell, Oblensky, New York, 1957. Reprinted by Grossett & Dunlap, 1972.

Anne W. Armstrong, *This Day and Time*, Alfred Knopf, New York. Reprinted by the Research Advisory Council, East Tennessee State University, 1970.

W. J. Cash, *The Mind of the South*, Alfred Knopf, New York, 1941.

Harry Caudill, *Night Comes to the Cumberlands*, Little, Brown, Boston, 1962.

Rebecca Caudill, *My Appalachia*, Holt, Rinehart and Winston, New York.

Thomas D. Clark, *Travels in the Old South, A Bibliography*, University of Oklahoma Press, Norman, Oklahoma, 1956.

David Crockett, *A Narrative of the Life of David Crockett of the State of Tennessee*, Tennesseanna edition, University of Tennessee Press, 1973.

George Washington Harris, *Sut Lovingood's Yarns,* 1867. Reprinted by College and University Press, New York, 1963.

Robert J. Higgs and Ambrose N. Manning, eds., *Voices from the Hills,* Frederick Ungar, New York, and Appalachian Consortium Press, 1975.

Bessie, James, *Anne Royall's U.S.A.,* Rutgers University Press, New Brunswick, New Jersey, 1972.

Robert L. Kincaid, *The Wilderness Road,* Bobbs-Merrill, New York, 1966.

John Parris, *Roaming the Mountains,* Citizen-Times Publishing Company, Asheville, N.C.

Bruce and Nancy Roberts, *Where Time Stood Still,* Crowell-Collier Press, New York.

Theodore Roosevelt, *The Winning of the West,* Review of Reviews Co., 1889.

Jesse Stuart, *Kentucky Is My Land,* Dutton, 1952.

Jack E. Weller, *Yesterday's People,* University of Kentucky Press, 1971.

Billy Edd Wheeler, *Song of a Woods Colt,* Drake House Publishers, distributed by Grossett & Dunlap, New York, 1969.

Eliot Wigginton, ed., *The Foxfire Book,* Anchor Press/ Doubleday, New York, 1972.

Cratis D. Williams, "The Southern Mountaineer in Fact and Fiction," (Ph.D. diss., New York University, 1961).

Eli Flam is a free-lance writer who has traveled widely in Appalachia and is a son of immigrants.

A man can't get rich if he takes proper care of his family.
Navajo saying

Power, Powerlessness and the Jews (1990)
David Vital

One of the inescapable facts of modern Jewish life is that the destruction of European Jewry by the Germans in World War II led to no sea change in the ethos and mores of Jewish people as whole.

Here and there, small and scattered groups, and some isolated individuals, did try to take the measure of some events. Some reordered their lives. Some, although very few, sought to reconcile their previously established private views and beliefs with what they had now learned and were now obliged to conclude. Certain issues and questions, hitherto ignored, or raised and discussed only in defined and somewhat limited sectors, took on enhanced importance. But by and large, the huge defeat the Jewish people had suffered in the course of the war waged against them led to no deep reappraisal. Not one of the great public institutions resolved on radical restructure, let alone dissolution. No individual personality of real note, no leader of real prominence, resolved on retirement from public life. And even beyond the "establishment," no really new diagnosis of the condition of Jewry emerged, no fresh ideas were offered to the public for consideration and reflection. Certainly none was taken up.

Such was the case even so far as the Zionists were concerned. It is perfectly true that they were able to argue—quite correctly—that their analyses of the Jewish situation had been tragically, but persuasively, validated by events. But even they—faced as they were in those days with the other great crisis of Jewry in this century, the fight for political independence in the Middle East—made no more than a simple and limited and, so to speak, pragmatic attempt to reorder their view of the Jewish condition as a whole and of the Diaspora in particular. As for the Diaspora, which is here my principal concern, there too little or nothing of real consequence changed, or indeed has changed to this day, although Jewish life in the Diaspora continues to flourish and, if anything, is more attractive than ever (to judge by the number and flow of migrants). In all this, the profoundly conservative character of the Jews is fully manifest—and not for the first time.

II.

Still, fifty years have now elapsed since the outbreak of World War II, and rather longer than that since the profundity of Nazi Germany's hostility to the Jewish people became clear, along with some true estimate of the support the Jews might expect to receive from other states and societies in the hour of their darkest peril. It is now only a little less than forty-five years since what actually occurred during the war passed into common knowledge. Time enough, in other words, to begin taking stock of the consequences for Jewry of the all-but-total elimination of what was unquestionably its heartland, its veritable core: the great Eastern European mass.

It cannot be stressed too often or too strongly that in Poland and the Baltic countries, in Russia and Rumania, in Czechoslovakia and Hungary were to be found those communities that together constituted the Jewish people in its essential European form: the most homogeneous, the most coherent, the least assimilated, least self-conscious, most compact, and far and away the most lively and remarkable of Jewish conglomerations in modern times. It is not too much to say that to all intents and purposes these communities *were* the Jewish nation—all others, no matter how distinguished or ancient or prosperous, being peripheral to them. It was out of the human resources gathered in this great reservoir of people, talent, and energy that the two chief Jewish communities in our times, in the United States and in Israel, were very largely constructed. It was within this society that the terms of virtually all the major internal issues in modern Jewry, both cultural and political, were set and once seemed likely to be decided, and it was upon the movement of ideas and people in and out of that great network that the future of the Jews seemed most likely to depend.

The injury done to the Jewish people as such by the annihilation of that pulsating society is therefore beyond measure and imagination. After the war, the Jewish people could not be even remotely what it once had been. Worse, it could not be what many of its members had very reasonably hoped that it might become. For instance, it was always understood that from this pool the Jewish community in Palestine (the *yishuv*), and the Jewish state-to-be, would draw its future population. The problems and the afflictions of East European Jewry had precipitated, motivated, and nourished the Zionist movement in the first place, and it was Jews from Eastern Europe who had brought the *yishuv* to the point of economic and social take-off several years before the onset of World War II. The loss to contemporary Israel of that community from which the Zionists had always drawn strength, and for which they had always believed they were laboring, remains incalculably vast.

In brief, the European catastrophe did more than leave a void in Jewry. It left it with an injury that will not be repaired. What, then, has contemporary Jewry learned, what might it learn, from its loss? I propose to approach this question indirectly, by asking a somewhat different and (it might seem) retrospectively useless question, namely, what could have saved the Jews in Europe?

We know what did *not* save them. The Jews of Europe were not saved by the mitigating effect of their persecutors' and murderers' cold self-interest. That is to say, the old, well-worn argument offered up by one generation of Jews after another to the ruling power of the day and place—to the effect that they would prove *useful* to state, economy, and society—and clutched at again by the desperate people of one ghetto after another in occupied Europe, this time by and large fell on deaf ears. Even the status of slaves was largely refused them—on principle, and as a matter of high state and social policy.

Nor were the Jews saved in any appreciable numbers by the civilized societies, polities, institutions, and churches of the day, even those which were declared enemies of Germany and all its works, or which at one time or another had had the opportunity to act in charity on the Jews' behalf. Some turned a blind eye; some shrugged; some prevaricated; some appealed to weighty political and social argument for doing this or refraining from doing that. Need one rehearse the hardly unthinking cruelties committed by the West European and North American democracies, from explicit requests to the Germans to imprint the passports of Jews with an identifying mark, the better to keep them out; through blanket refusals to alter by one jot or tittle the relevant immigration laws; to an essential ambivalence on the issue of the physical elimination of Jewry from the European scene?

Nor were the Jews saved or given material assistance by those indigenous forces who were indeed fighting the common enemy in the territories of the new German empire, and who had every military reason to enlarge their ranks and increase the scope and intensity of their otherwise admirable resistance. What could be more miserable than the response of the Polish Home Army to the pleas of the fighters in the Warsaw Ghetto for arms: not an outright refusal, to be sure, but a pathetic handful of weapons tossed to the Jews in barely disguised contempt and disbelief? What could be more horrifying than the fate that awaited the Jews who managed to evade ghettoization, or who escaped from death camps into the surrounding forests, and wishing no more than to pursue the fight, were unlucky enough to fall into the hands of the wrong group of partisans?

It is true that to every one of these generalizations there were exceptions: instances of the most remarkable decency and generosity, of commitment to the basic moral dictates of humanity—to say nothing of immense courage in circumstances of extreme danger. Many Jews owed their lives to individuals or small groups scattered throughout Europe, not excluding Germany itself, or Poland for that matter, who offered shelter and lifesaving assistance in a dozen forms. But they were just that: exceptions. The rule was otherwise. And the rule was plainly a function of the fundamentals of the Jewish condition. Not their wartime condition; rather, their condition from time immemorial. Indeed, one great singularity of the Holocaust (there are others) is that it tells us in stronger, clearer, less deniable terms than any other event in the history of the Jews what lies at the basis of the Jewish condition.

In a famous essay, *Galut* ("Exile"), the late historian Yitzhak Baer remarks on the great change that overcame the Jews in late antiquity:

> In the 7th century, the Jews still took an active military part in the struggle for control of Palestine between Rome and Persia, between Rome and Islam, which they interpreted in eschatological terms. But from then on, the nation definitely submitted to the admonitions of its teachers. God had made His will manifest; it was His will that the Jews should bear the yoke of foreign nations.

And Baer goes on:

> The Jews left the ranks of warring nations and put their fate altogether in the hands of God—a unique historical fact to which no historian has yet given its proper importance.

These lines, originally written in German and published in Berlin in 1936, could stand as the epitaph for European Jewry. The war against the Jews was nothing if not supreme testimony to their powerlessness—to the direct and horrific consequences of their having "left the ranks of the warring nations and put their fate altogether in the hands of God." Except, of course, that God, or let us say Providence, was inscrutable; in practice, it was into the hands of their rulers that the Jews consigned their fate. Therein the tragedy and, at the same time, the paradox.

The ancient view, deeply ingrained in the Jewish psyche, was to regard what the redactors of the Mishnah called "the ruling power" (*ha-ra-shut*) with grave suspicion. The advice the ancient rabbis offered the people was to exercise all possible care in their dealings with that power, in fact to steer clear of it altogether if that were possible. But much of the force of this injunction came to be lost in modern times, notably in the West but in parts of Central Europe as well, as the twin processes of formal emancipation and cultural switch altered the terms of life for Jews out of all recognition.

The old, proud prudence and the underlying distrust that informed it gave way to a curious and historically unprecedented combination of dependence and humility. This can be seen at work in the singularly trustful and at the same time quite humble, not to say servile, spirit in which, in December 1942, the most prominent figure of the day in American Jewry, Rabbi Stephen S. Wise, approached his head of state. By that time, the essentials of what was happening to the European Jews were already quite well known, not only to Wise and his senior colleagues among American Jewish leaders but to the State Department and President Roosevelt himself. Wise wrote to Roosevelt apologizing for proposing to add to the President's wartime burdens and restating the basic facts of what he there and then defined as "the most overwhelming disaster of Jewish history." He went on to remind the President that, "together with the heads of other Jewish organizations," he had succeeded in keeping the reports of the "unspeakable horrors" taking place in Europe out of the press. Finally, he asked the President to receive a delegation. To what specific purpose? "We hope above all that you will speak a word which may bring solace and hope to millions of Jews who mourn, and be an expression of the conscience of the American people."

Solace and hope. . . . It is easy enough, especially in retrospect, to see the pathetic inadequacy of Wise's petition. But Wise's wartime conduct, along with that of others who failed to make an ultimate, consistent effort to muster their admittedly small and fearfully insufficient forces in the struggle on behalf of the Jews of Europe, can be understood only in terms of a profound and pervasive sense of weakness—an overwhelming, paralyzing conviction of the utter vulnerability and helplessness of the Jews wherever they might be, and thus of the extreme unwisdom of opposing or crossing or even merely irritating the "ruling power."

The deeper implications of the refusal of the American government to allow the war effort to be in any way compromised in the public mind by association with a Jewish cause or interest, even that of mere physical rescue, constitute a separate topic; in any case, it is now water under the bridge. What is surely not water under the bridge, however, is the continuing, contemporary difficulty of the Jews themselves in dealing with problems related to power—especially and crucially insofar as these bear on the collective affairs of Jewry itself.

III.

A quick reading of the map of modern Jewry shows the most notable divisions of opinion and behavior corresponding to the fundamental contemporary division between the Jews of the state of Israel and the Jews who are citizens of other states. Israel is evidently, and by design, a power-political structure. To use Baer's terminology, it is one of the world's "warring nations." In contrast, Diaspora Jewry is in no significant, operative sense a coherent political entity of any description. Plainly, it neither provides nor permits a structure of power, much less a structure of power capable of sustaining conflict with hostile peoples and societies.

But this is only half the story. The deeper and much more telling distinction in contemporary Jewry is not geographical political but philosophical.

In the contemporary West, generally speaking, the respect for the rights of man and the citizen, the rule of law, certain well-tried methods of patient, peaceful resolution of conflict be negotiation—all these and more have come to be seen not only as immensely desirable in themselves and infinitely preferable to other, darker principles, techniques, and instruments, but as actually in evidence. They operate, they are available, and, all things considered, they are maintained in fairly good repair. Moreover, the Jews of Western Europe and North America have been among the notable beneficiaries of these principles and of the workings of their accompanying institutions. What could be more natural, then, than their attachment to a view of society which is intrinsically optimistic, altruistic, moralistic, legalistic, and above all *principled?*

But there is another outlook. To the east and to the south of the fortunate lands of Western Europe and North America things were, and have long remained, otherwise—and not for the Jews alone, but for all. There is no need to recite even in abbreviated form the catalogue of afflictions which have overcome virtually all the peoples of Central and Eastern Europe, of the Middle East and Central Asia, of both Northern and sub-Saharan Africa, and of Southern Asia and the Far East in our own times and before our eyes. The world outside the West is a hard world. In lands in which violence, cruelty, tyranny, and hatred are endemic, there is every reason for the ordinary person to conclude that safety does not lie in any reliance on the rules of law and common morality, perhaps not even on the native decency and good will of individual men and women. There, one tends easily and naturally to a much greater measure of skepticism and distrust of the "other" than is usual—or perhaps even necessary—in the West. In a hard world one relies, if one can, on oneself. In a hard world, it is no more than prudent to learn hard lessons.

But are these the lessons that the Jews as a people have learned from their very particular and very hard experience in the recent past? Or is it the case that those Jews who have found a place for themselves in one or another of the fortunate lands have learned—or taught themselves—a lesson very different from the one learned by those less fortunately situated?

As time elapsed after the destruction of European Jewry, as the initial shock wore off, different communities could be seen—and today can be seen still more clearly—not only to be very differently placed, but indeed to inhabit different mental and philosophical universes. The consequences of this split are visible everywhere, most ominously in disagreements over the aims and methods, and even the propriety, of collective action by Jews where such action must rely on the autonomous employment of instruments of influence and power. They also make themselves felt in an almost emblematic way in contemporary discussions of the meaning, for Jews, of the Holocaust.

It is not that there is anything in those discussions analogous to the political ferocity of the *Historikerstreit* (historians' conflict) in West Germany. Nor, so far as I can make out, is there any great public debate going on between explicit and identifiable schools of thought. Nevertheless, there are questions that do manifestly gnaw at thinking Jews, and to which very different answers are given.

Was the Holocaust one of a class of more or less comparable events? Or was it, on the contrary, unique? How to situate the Holocaust in the Jews' *own* history? Was it specific to its time and place? Or was it, on the contrary, characteristic of, perhaps a function of, the exilic condition itself—as Baer implicitly and later many others explicitly would contend? If so, was it then in some crucial sense not only an event in, but an event peculiar to, Jewish history, and comprehensible ultimately only in its terms—that is to say, in terms of the longstanding and immensely bitter conflict in which Jews have been embroiled with their European neighbors and rulers for 1,500 years and more?

One can see why, in the West, the last view is likely to be unpopular. For one thing, it suggests that in one crucial respect Nazi Germany was less eccentric, more representative, than contemporary Westerners generally like to think. And many Jews in the Diaspora would similarly reject such a view. Their reasons for doing so were well illustrated a few years ago in the mixed response to Claude Lanzmann's extraordinary documentary film about the Holocaust, *Shoah*.

Reviewing that film for the BBC's *Listener*, a critic who described herself as "a British child of Jewish origin" began by citing an earlier review of the film by Pauline Kael in the *New Yorker*. Miss Kael had raised the following demurral:

> [Lanzmann] succeeds in making the past and the present seem one, and this appears to be an aesthetic victory. . . . It has another aspect, though; implicitly the film says that the past and the present are one—that this horror could happen again. See, the Polish peasants are still talking about how the Jews killed Christ and hoarded gold.

The British critic then drove this objection home:

> Kael has a point. Lanzmann's unwillingness to put the events into historical context leaves him open to the accusation of pessimism. . . . Analysis which might have made the Holocaust understandable and specific to its era is missing.

All this is exceedingly telling. Take the terminology itself: Lanzmann is open to an "accusation" of pessimism, the inevitable corollary being that had he rendered the Holocaust "understandable," that is, by showing it to be "specific to its era," he would, in effect, have removed, an obstacle to optimism. But is optimism the proper position to hold? And *was* the Holocaust an isolated event or was it an event whose causal roots ran so deep and were so pervasive that they may run beneath and through contemporary society as well? Plainly, neither of these two critics, nor very many other members of the contemporary Western intelligentsia, would be prepared to tolerate such a view of the Jewish condition. Few, regardless of origins, loyalties, and political convictions, are even prepared to examine it.

Can one blame them? It is exceedingly painful to acknowledge that in a hundred different ways the Jews as a people are still beset by a seemingly ineradicable refusal to accord them such standards or status, or to ascribe to them such significance or qualities, as are normally and unquestioningly accorded and ascribed to other peoples and denominations. It is painful partly because it entails a profound disappointment. So many things have changed for the better in the postwar world, at least on the surface; surely we are entitled to believe that they have changed for good? It is painful, too, because the greater part of Jewry suffers today, perfectly understandably, from a kind of war-weariness: an intense desire for peace, for a relaxation of tension, for a condition in which all stress and conflict, to say nothing of the constraints and dictates of an exceptional status, might finally be consigned to the past.

But suppose one does venture to look beneath the surface; what does one find, and what is one to make of it? What are we to make of the endemic anti-Semitism in contemporary, *judenrein* Poland? Or of ostensibly anti-Israel but in fact manifestly old-style, Protocols-of-the-Elders-of-Zion-type propaganda mounted for decades now by the Soviet bloc and the majority of Arab states—both for domestic and for foreign consumption—and lately making its way into mainstream newspapers and magazines in Western Europe? Or of the particular edge that has been lent in recent years to the tension between American blacks and American Jews? Or of the never-ending reiteration of the belief that in some deep sense Jews are themselves responsible for all attacks upon them—as when in October 1980 the Prime Minister of France lamented the death of non-Jews in the assault on the synagogue in the Rue Copernic in Paris on the grounds that they, presumably unlike the Jewish victims, were "innocent"? Or when the Greek Minister of Justice determined recently that the killing of a little Jewish boy in a synagogue in Rome was an action that fell quite properly "within the domain of the struggle to regain the independence of the [killer's] homeland"?

It is not my purpose to offer a catalogue of charges, let alone a catalogue of woes, but rather to suggest that while the forms have changed and in some places the content as well, and while the intensity of hostility has diminished, there is still reason to doubt that the world has made its peace with the Jews in its midst, or that Jews are entitled to feel peace with the world around them. It seems more likely that there has been a truce of sorts since the end of World War II, and that though the truce holds, more or less, signs of erosion are now beginning to be visible.

If these signs are not always apparent, it is only because the immediate object in view has changed. The villain is no longer so much the alien Jewish intruder into European and American society, cast as an incorrigibly vulgar and hateful agent of economic, political, or cultural corruption, burrowing under the old order, opening the gates of the city to carriers of moral plague. Instead, it is Israel and its people who play the role of whipping boy. The image is no longer T.S. Eliot's notorious

> The rats are underneath the piles,
> The Jew is underneath the lot. . . . .

It is more likely to be the British poet Peter Reading's image of "a fat juicy jeep of Israelis" in Lebanon being shot at by a little Arab boy and shooting back because,

> . . . Well,
> nobody looks for a motive from these Old
>   Testament shitters—
> thick hate is still in the genes.

How profound, though, is the difference? To what other national state or society is so much obsessive, venomous attention paid, so much evil ascribed, so little forgiven? About what other geographically remote people do serious Western literary lights write hostile *poetry?*

IV.

The notion that the killing-off of the Jews of Europe ended the ancient conflict between the Jewish people and their neighbors appears to have less substance than many thought. But if, on the non-Jewish side, the conflict has been renewed, on the Jewish side the capacity to resist may be weaker today than ever before. And this is so precisely because of the great slaughter. Firstly, the amputation of European Jewry from the body of the Jewish people drastically reduced it in numbers, in talent, and in where I can only describe as the *will* to collective life. Secondly, it accelerated the (already occurring) breakup of Jewry into ever less cohering communities, each imbued with a distinct culture and language, each subject to specific influences and needs and so, inevitably, each intent on social purposes of its own definition.

To all this has been added, finally, the paradoxical tendency on the part of many Jews in the Diaspora, and even to some extent in Israel as well, to think of the Holocaust itself as that event in the history of the Jews which necessarily overshadows all others—as, in short, an archetype. The tendency is so to magnify and particularize the Holocaust in Jewish terms, so to associate the Jewish people with it, so to fix the image of the Jews in terms of this vast and hugely injurious calamity as to drown out virtually all other voices and to smother virtually all other developments, facets, and qualities of Jewish life, history, and culture.

But if the Holocaust is the archetypical event in the history of the Jews, Jews themselves become archetypical victims. And this thesis is as damaging in its way as is the seemingly opposite idea that the Holocaust can only be understood as a specific instance of the all-too-numerous horrors which humankind has inflicted on itself. Actually, the two ideas, which appear to run counter to each other, in a crucial respect are mutually reinforcing; and both sap the foundations of Jewish collective life.

It is simply untrue that the long war conducted both against Judaism and the Jews in Europe (and the Middle East too), of which the events in Europe were the culminating and most horrible chapter, is of a class with other crusades, massacres, decimations, and slaughters. So to hold is to misconstrue not only Jewish but European history and the history of the Muslim world as well. There is nothing to be gained and much to be lost by such a gigantic exercise in the sweeping of unpleasantness into the capacious memory holes which societies retain for such purposes.

But for Jews, perhaps an even greater danger lurks in the opposite tendency. It is one thing to retain the memory of the Holocaust as a catastrophe whose causes need to be studied not only for their own sake but in the interests of finally reordering the life of the Jews as individuals and as a people. It is quite another to establish that memory as the primary reference point in the internal communal life of the Jews and in relations between Jews and other peoples. To do so is to make of the Jews a people of invalids, of victims, of death. Thus, in the minds of others; thus, bit by bit, in their own minds as well. Little can be so destructive of the inner life and stability of Jewry, of its sense of itself as an old and, despite everything, honored member of the family of nations, or of its capacity to sustain the manifold pressures which the present and the future surely hold in store.

David Vital, who teaches international politics at Tel Aviv University and Jewish history at Northwestern, is the author of a three-volume series on the formative years of the Zionist movement. The present essay, in somewhat different form, was delivered at an international conference,, "Lessons and Legacies: The Meaning of the Holocaust in a Changing World," held at Northwestern in November.

If God lived on earth, people would break his windows.
Jewish proverb

The Brutal Bargain (1991)

Norman Podhoretz

One of the longest journeys in the world is the journey from Brooklyn to Manhattan—or at least from certain neighborhoods in Brooklyn to certain parts of Manhattan. I have made that journey, but it is not from the experience of having made it that I know how very great the distance is, for I started on the road many years before I realized what I was doing, and by the time I did realize it I was for all practical purposes already there. At so imperceptible a pace did I travel, and with so little awareness, that I never felt footsore or out of breath or wary at the thought of how far I still had to go. Yet whenever anyone who has remained back there where I started—remained not physically but socially and culturally, for the neighborhood is now a Negro ghetto and the Jews who have "remained" in it most likely reside in the less affluent areas on Long Island—whenever anyone like that happens into the world in which I now live with such perfect ease. I can see that in his eyes I have become a fully acculturated citizen of a country as foreign to him as China and infinitely more frightening.

That country is sometimes called the upper middle class; and indeed I am a member of that class, less by virtue of my income than by virtue of the way my speech is accented, the way I dress, the way I furnish my home, the way I entertain and am entertained, the way I educate my children—the way, quite simply, I look and I live. It appalls me to think what an immense transformation I had to work on myself in order to become what I have become: if I had known what I was doing I would surely not have been able to do it, I would surely not have wanted to. No wonder the choice had to be blind; there was a kind of treason in it: treason toward my family, treason toward my friends. In choosing the road I chose, I was pronouncing a judgment upon them, and the fact that they themselves concurred in the judgment makes the whole thing sadder but no less cruel.

When I say that the choice was blind, I mean that I was never aware—obviously not as a small child, certainly not as an adolescent, and not even as a young man already writing for publication and working on the staff of an important intellectual magazine in New York—how inextricably my "noblest" ambitions were tied to the vulgar desire to rise above the class into which I was born; nor did I understand to what an astonishing extent these ambitions were shaped and defined by the standards and values and tastes of the class into which I did not know I wanted to move. It is not that I was or am a social climber as that term is commonly used. High society interests me, if at all, only as a curiosity; I do not wish to be a member of it; and in any case, it is not, as I have learned from a small experience of contact with the very rich and fashionable, my "scene." Yet precisely because social climbing is not one of my vices (unless what might be called celebrity climbing, which very definitely *is* one of my vices, can be considered the contemporary of social climbing), I think there may be more than a merely personal significance in the fact that class has played so large a part both in my life and in my career.

But whether or not the significance is there, I feel certain that my longtime blindness to the part class was playing in my life was not altogether idiosyncratic. "Privilege," Robert L. Heilbroner, has shrewdly observed in *The Limits of American Capitalism*, "is not an attribute we are accustomed to stress when we consider the construction of our social order." For a variety of reasons, says Heilbroner, "privilege under capitalism is much less 'visible,' especially to the favored groups, than privilege under other systems" like feudalism. This "invisibility" extends in America to class as well.

No one, of course, is so naïve as to believe that America is a classless society or that the force of egalitarianism, powerful as it has been in some respects, has ever been powerful enough to wipe out class distinctions altogether. There was a moment during the 1950's, to be sure, when social thought hovered on the brink of saying that the country had to all intents and purposes become a wholly middle-class society. But the emergence of the civil-rights movements in the 1960's and the concomitant discovery of the poor—to whom, in helping to discover them, Michael Harrington interestingly enough applied, in *The Other America,* the very word ("invisible") that Heilbroner later used with reference to the rich—has put at least a temporary end to that kind of talk. And yet if class has become visible again, it is only in its grossest outlines—mainly, that is, in terms of income levels—and to the degree that manners and style of life are perceived as relevant at all, it is generally in the crudest of terms. There is something in us, it would seem, which resists the idea of class. Even our novelists, working in a genre for which class has traditionally been a supreme reality, are largely indifferent to it—which is to say, blind to its importance as a factor in the life of the individual.

In my own case, the blindness to class always expressed itself in an outright and very often belligerent refusal to believe that it had anything to do with me at all. I no longer remember when or in what form I first discovered that there was such a thing as class, but whenever it was and whatever form the discovery took, it could only have coincided with the recognition that criteria existed by which I and everyone I knew were stamped as inferior: we were in the *lower* class. This was not a proposition I was willing to accept, and my way of not accepting it was to dismiss the whole idea of class as a prissy triviality.

Given the fact that I had literary ambitions even as a small boy, it was inevitable that the issue of class would sooner or later arise for me with a sharpness it would never acquire for most of my friends. But given the fact also that I was fiercely patriotic about Brownsville (the spawning-ground of so many famous athletes and gangsters), and that I felt genuinely patronizing toward other neighbor-hoods, especially the "better" ones like Crown Heights and East Flatbush which seemed by comparison colorless and unexciting—given the fact, in other words, that I was not, for all that I wrote poetry and read books, an "alienated" boy dreaming of escape—my confrontation with the issue of class would probably have come later rather than sooner if not for an English teacher in high school who decided that I was a gem in the rough and who took upon herself to polish me to as high a sheen as she could manage and I would permit.

I resisted—far less effectively, I can see now, than I then thought, though even then I knew that she was wearing me down far more than I would ever give her the satisfaction of admitting. Famous throughout the school for her altogether outspoken snobbery, which stopped short by only a hair, and sometimes did not stop short at all, of an old-fashioned kind of patrician anti-Semitism, Mrs. K. was also famous for being an extremely good teacher; indeed, I am sure that she saw no distinction between the hopeless task of teaching the proper use of English to the young Jewish barbarians whom fate had so unkindly deposited into her charge and the equally hopeless task of teaching them the proper "manners." (There were as many young Negro barbarians in her charge as Jewish ones, but I doubt that she could ever bring herself to pay very much attention to them. As she never hesitated to make clear, it was punishment enough for a woman of her background—her family was old-Brooklyn and, she would have us understand, extremely distinguished—to have fallen among the sons of East European immigrant Jews.)

For three years, from the age of thirteen to the age of sixteen, I was her special pet, though that word is scarcely adequate to suggest the intensity of the relationship which developed between us. It was a relationship right out of *The Corn is Green*, which may, for all I know, have served as her model; at any rate, her objective was much the same as the Welsh teacher's in that play: she was determined that I should win a scholarship to Harvard. But whereas (an irony much to the point here) the problem the teacher had in *The Corn Is Green* with her coal-miner pupil in the traditional class society of Edwardian England was strictly academic, Mrs. K.'s problem with me in the putatively egalitarian society of New Deal America was strictly social. My grades were very high and would obviously remain so, but what would they avail me if I continued to go about looking and sounding like a "filthy little slum child" (the epithet she would invariably hurl at me whenever we had an argument about "manners")?

Childless herself, she worked on me like a dementedly ambitious mother with a somewhat recalcitrant son; married to a solemn and elderly man (she was then in her early forties or there-abouts), she treated me like a callous, ungrateful adolescent lover on whom, she had humiliatingly bestowed her favors. She flirted with me and flattered me, she scolded me and insulted me. Slum child, filthy little slum child, so beautiful a mind and so vulgar a personality, so exquisite in sensibility and so coarse in manner. What would she do with me, what would become of me if I persisted out of stubbornness and perversity in the disgusting ways they had taught me at home and on the streets?

To her the most offensive of these ways was the style in which I dressed: a tee shirt, tightly pegged pants, and a red satin jacket with the legend "Cherokees, S.A.C." (social-athletic club) stitched in large white letters across the back. This was bad enough, but when on certain days I would appear in school wearing, as a particular ceremonial occasion required, a suit and tie, the sight of those immense padded shoulders and my white-on-white shirt would drive her to even greater heights of contempt and even lower depths of loving despair than usual. *Slum child, filthy little slum child.* I was beyond saving; I deserved no better than to wind up with all the other horrible little Jewboys in the gutter (by which she meant Brooklyn College). If only I would listen to her, the whole world could be mine: I could win a scholarship to Harvard, I could get to know the best people, I could grow up into a life of elegance and refinement and taste. Why was I so stupid as not to understand?

In those days it was very unusual, and possibly even against the rules, for teachers in public high schools to associate with their students after hours. Nevertheless, Mrs. K. sometime invited me to her home, a beautiful old Brownstone located in what was perhaps the only section in the whole of Brooklyn fashionable enough to be intimidating. I would read her my poems and she would tell me about her family, about the schools she had gone to, about Vassar, about writers she had met, while her husband, of whom I was frightened to death and who to my utter astonishment turned out to be Jewish (but not, as Mrs. K. quite unnecessarily hastened to inform me, *my* kind of Jewish), sat stiffly and silently in an armchair across the room, squinting at his newspaper through the first *pince-nez* I had ever seen outside the movies. He spoke to me but once, and that was after I had read Mrs. K. my tearful editorial for the school newspaper on the death of Roosevelt—an effusion which provoked him into a full five-minute harangue whose blasphemous contents would certainly have shocked me into insensibility if I had not been even more shocked to discover that he actually had a voice.

But Mrs. K. not only had me to her house; she also—what was even more unusual—took me out a few times, to the Frick Gallery and the Metropolitan Museum, and once to the theater, where we saw a dramatization of *The Late George Apley,* a play I imagine she deliberately chose with the not wholly mistaken idea that it would impress upon me the glories of aristocratic Boston.

One of our excursions into Manhattan I remember with particular vividness because she used it to bring the struggle between us to rather a dramatic head. The familiar argument began this time on the subway. Why, knowing that we would be spending the afternoon together "in public," had I come to school that morning improperly dressed? (I was, as usual, wearing my red satin club jacket over a white tee shirt.) She realized, of course, that I owned only one suit (this said not in compassion but in derision) and that my poor parents had, God only knew where, picked up the ideas that it was too precious to be worn except at one of those bar mitzvahs I was always going to. Though why, if my parents were so worried about clothes, they had permitted me to buy a suit which made me look like a young hoodlum she found it very difficult to imagine. Still, much as she would have been embarrassed to be seen in public with a boy whose parents allowed him to wear a zoot suit, she would have been somewhat less embarrassed than she was now by the ridiculous costume I had on. Had I no consideration for her? Had I no consideration for myself? Did I want everyone who laid eyes on me to think that I was nothing but an ill-bred little slum child?

My standard ploy in these arguments was to take the position that such things were of no concern to me: I was a poet and I had more important matters to think about than clothes. Besides, I would feel silly coming to school on an ordinary day dressed in a suit. Did Mrs. K. want me to look like one of those "creeps" from Crown Heights who were all going to become doctors? This was usually an effective encounter, since Mrs. K. despised her middle-class Jewish students even more than she did the "slum children," but probably because she was growing desperate at the thought of how I would strike a Harvard interviewer (it was my senior year), she did not respond according to form on that particular occasion. "At least," she snapped, "they reflect well on their parents."

I was accustomed to her bantering gibes at my parents, and sensing, probably, that they arose out of jealousy, I was rarely troubled by them. But this one bothered me; it went beyond banter and I did not know how to deal with it. I remember flushing, but I cannot remember what if anything I said in protest. It was the beginning of a very bad afternoon for both of us.

We had been heading for the Museum of Modern Art, but as we got off the subway, Mrs. K. announced that she had changed her mind about the museum. She was going to show me something else instead, just down the street on Fifth Avenue. This mysterious "something else" to which we proceeded in silence turned out to be the college department of an expensive clothing store, de Pinna. I do not exaggerate when I say that an actual physical dread seized me as I followed her into the store. I had never been inside such a store; it was not a store, it was enemy territory, every inch of it mined with humiliations. "I am," Mrs. K. declared in the coldest human voice I hope I shall ever hear, "going to buy you a suit that you will be able to wear at your Harvard interview." I had guessed, of course, that this was what she had in mind, and even at fifteen I understood what a fantastic act of aggression she was planning to commit against my parents and asking me to participate in. Oh no, I said in a panic (suddenly realizing that I *wanted* her to buy me that suit), I can't, my mother wouldn't like it. "You can tell her it's a birthday present. Or else I will tell her. If I tell her, I'm sure she won't object." The idea of Mrs. K. meeting my mother was more than I could bear: my mother, who spoke with a Yiddish accent and of whom, until that sickening moment, I had never known I was ashamed and so ready to betray.

To my immense relief and my equally immense disappointment, we left the store, finally, without buying a suit, but it was not to be the end of clothing or "manners" for me that day— not yet. There was still the ordeal of a restaurant to go through. Where I came from, people rarely ate in restaurants, not so much because most of them were too poor to afford such a luxury—

although most of them certainly were—as because eating in restaurants was not regarded as a luxury at all; it was, rather, a necessity to which bachelors were pitiably condemned. A home-cooked meal was assumed to be better than anything one could possibly get in a restaurant, and considering the class of restaurants in question (they were really diners or luncheonettes), the assumption was probably correct. In the case of my own family, myself included until my late teens, the business of going to restaurants was complicated by the fact that we observed the Jewish-dietary laws, and except in certain neighborhoods, few places could be found which served kosher food; in midtown Manhattan in the 1940s, I believe there were only two and both were relatively expensive. All this is by way of explaining why I had had so little experience of restaurants up to the age of fifteen and why I grew apprehensive once more when Mrs. K. decided after we left de Pinna that we should have something to eat.

The restaurant she chose was not at all an elegant one—I have, like a criminal, revisited it since—but it seemed very elegant indeed to me: enemy territory again, and this time a mine exploded in my face the minute I set foot through the door. The hostess was very sorry, but she could not seat the young gentleman without a coat and tie. If the lady wished, however, something could be arranged. The lady (visibly pleased by this unexpected—or was it expected?—object lesson) did wish, and the so recently defiant but by now utterly docile young gentleman was forthwith divested of his so recently beloved but by now thoroughly loathsome red satin jacket and provided with a much oversized white waiter's coat and tie—which, there being no collar to a tee shirt, had to be worn around his bare neck. Thus attired, and with his face supplying the touch of red which had moments earlier been supplied by his jacket, he was led into the dining room, there to be taught the importance of proper table manners through the same pedagogic instrumentality that had worked so well in impressing him with the importance of proper dress.

Like any other pedagogic technique, however, humiliation has its limits, and Mrs. K. was to make no further progress with it that day. For I had had enough, and I was not about to risk stepping on another mine. Knowing she would subject me to still more ridicule if I made a point of my revulsion at the prospect of eating nonkosher food, I resolved to let her order for me and then to feign lack of appetite or possibly even illness when the meal was served. She did order—duck for both of us, undoubtedly because it would be a hard dish for me to manage without using my fingers.

The two portions came in deep oval-shaped dishes, swimming in a brown sauce and each with a sprig of parsley sitting on top. I had not the faintest idea of what to do—should the food be eaten directly from the oval dish or not?—nor which of the many implements on the table to do it with. But remembering that Mrs. K. herself had once advised me to watch my hostess in such a situation and then to do exactly as she did, I sat perfectly still and waited for her to make the first move. Unfortunately, Mrs. K. also remembered having taught me that trick, and determined as she was that I should be given a lesson that would force me to mend my ways, she waited too. And so we both waited, chatting amiably, pretending not to notice the food while it sat there getting colder and colder by the minute. Thanks partly to the fact that I would probably have gagged on the duck if I had tried to eat it—dietary taboos are very powerful if one has been conditioned to them—I was prepared to wait forever. And in fact it was Mrs. K. who broke first.

"Why aren't you eating?" she suddenly said after something like fifteen minutes had passed. "Aren't you hungry?" Not very, I answered. "Well," she said, "I think we'd better eat. The food is getting cold." Whereupon, as I watched with great fascination, she deftly captured the sprig of parsley between the prongs of her serving fork, set it aside, took up her serving spoon and delicately used those two esoteric implements to transfer a piece of duck from the oval dish to her plate. I imitated the whole operation as best I could, but not well enough to avoid splattering some partly congealed sauce onto my borrowed coat in the process. Still, things could have been worse, and having more or less successfully negotiated my way around that particular mine, I now had to cope with the problem of how to get out of eating the duck. But I need not have worried. Mrs. K. took one bite, pronounced it inedible (it must have been frozen by then), and called in quiet fury for the check.

Several months later, wearing an altered but respectably conservative suit which had been handed down to me in good condition by a bachelor uncle, I presented myself on two different occasions before interviewers from Harvard and from the Pulitzer Scholarship Committee. Some months after that, Mrs. K. had her triumph: I won the Harvard scholarship on which her heart had been so passionately set. It was not, however, large enough to cover all the expenses, and since my parents could not afford to make up the difference, I was unable to accept it. My parents felt wretched but not, I think, quite as wretched as Mrs. K. For a while it looked as though I would wind up in the "gutter" of Brooklyn College after all, but then the news arrived that I had also won a Pulitzer Scholarship which paid full tuition if used at Columbia and a small stipend besides. Everyone was consoled, even Mrs. K.: Columbia was at least in the Ivy League.

The last time I saw her was shortly before my graduation from Columbia and just after a story had appeared in the *Times* announcing that I had been awarded a fellowship which was to send me to Cambridge University. Mrs. K. had passionately wanted to see me in Cambridge, Massachusetts, but Cambridge, England was even better. We met somewhere near Columbia for a drink, and her happiness over my fellowship, it seemed to me, was if anything exceeded by her delight at discovering that I now knew enough to know that the right thing to order in a cocktail lounge was a very dry martini with lemon peel, please.

As editor-in-chief of Commentary, *Norman Podhoretz today is a member of the New York literary establishment. He received a B.A. degree from Columbia University in 1950 at the age of twenty, and a further B.A. from Cambridge University in England two years later. He has written a number of books, including* Breaking Ranks *(1979),* The Present Danger *(1980),* Why We Were in Viet Nam *(1982),* The Bloody Crossroads *(1986), and* Making It *(1964), from which the following selection is taken.*

Like Alfred Kazin (see "The Kitchen"), Podhoretz is a child of Jewish immigrants from Eastern Europe. He grew up in Brooklyn where, as he tells it, he wanted as a teenager to conform to the ways of his peers, children of poor immigrant origin whose sights were definitely not set on an intellectual career. Podhoretz describes his early, fierce resistance to one of his high school teachers who was determined to turn the "dirty slum child" into a Harvard swan. He wins some of his battles with her, but in the end he loses the war. Looking back he sees the "brutal bargain" he struck. Getting his new identity was a wrenching process of gain and loss.

A Sense of Community (1973)

Cora Sarjeant Wilder

A recent edition of *The New York Teacher* told of more than 5,000 parents, students and teachers from all corners of Rockland County who gathered at the 2nd Annual Language Fair held at Nanuet Mall on April 1. This festive event originated with the idea of "recognizing the diverse cultures that enrich America." The countries represented were France, Greece, Israel, Italy, Germany, Spain, Scotland, and Wales. To my distress, there was no indication that Africans and their descendants, who formed the largest non-British group in the thirteen colonies during the formative years of American language and culture, had in any way provided any amount of enrichment.

About two years ago, a *New York Times* editorial entitled "Jazz, Jitter, and Jam" aptly recalled that the myth of white supremacy had for too long prevented America from acknowledging its African heritage but that the time had come for American schoolchildren, both white and black, to study the African, as well as the European, contributions to the language and culture of their nation.

The focus of this editorial reiterates the influence of our dance and the fact that films made in some remote African villages contain perfect examples of the Charleston. No need to recall the influence of our art and the fact that in 1907, Picasso altered the faces on his huge canvas, Les Demoiselles d'Avignon, to resemble African masks, marking the beginning of Cubism—a turning point in Western art. No need to repeat, either, the influence of our "blues" which has become the inspiration of popular music throughout society. Perhaps some mention of our food would have been in order though; "soul food"—a form of cookery that developed from the need for economy, simplicity and creativity—is a form which the average housewife might now be well-advised to note. However, at that time, we were not in the throes of this period of inflationary food prices.

Rather, the editorial noted that in the western half of Africa, from whence over 10 percent of Americans trace their ancestry, the language of Mandingo was (and is presently) spoken either as a first or second language by a substantial number of African "immigrants" to the U.S. and not surprisingly, the influence of Mandingo can be traced in the development of the American language.

The fact is, moreover, that many well-known Americanisms are in actuality Africanisms—O.K. being a notable example. Reportedly, attempts have been made to trace its origin in English, French, German, Finnish, Greek, and Choctaw, but O.K. can be shown to derive from similar expressions in a number of West African languages and to have been used in Black Jamaican English more than 20 years before its use by whites in New England.

In addition, over 80 Americanisms appear to have an African or probable African origin, including such items as: jazz, jitter and jitter-bug, hep (as in a jam session), to jive, to tote, to goose, to bug someone, to lam (meaning to go), to dig (meaning to understand, appreciate), uh-huh and uh-uh (for yes and no), ofay and honkie(as names for the white man), cocktail, guy, yam, goober (peanut), gumbo (okra), and bogus. Many such words are said to be direct loan words from Africa.

Black American expressions like "be with it," "do your thing," and "bad mouth" (to talk badly about someone) are word-for-word translations from phrases widely used in West African languages, including Mandingo.

Any recognition of America's diverse heritage demands recognition, too, of West Africa and for informed educators to avoid or overlook this fact is erroneous and naive—perhaps, devious. Is it any wonder the concern for Negro History Week, community control, and the like? Rollo May, in his recent book *Power and Innocence,* notes that affirming one another is the basis of social organization; that is, acknowledging the significance and importance of one another is basic to community. This can be interpreted to mean that "community power" becomes insignificant when the "power of community"—the integrative capacity of community—is asserted and affirmed rather than ignored.

Let it be known, too, that no program can be developed in the earnest hope of promoting "a better understanding among all" when it fails to provide a balanced view of the community and of American heritage and when it fails to give young Americans especially an understanding of human societies beyond the confines of the Western world.

Cora Sargeant Wilder, Chair Social Sciences Department, Rockland Community College

---

A lawyer and a wagon-wheel must be well greased.
German proverb

ITALIANS

POPULATION: *16,384,336*	**PHYSICAL CHARACTERISTICS:** *Garlic breath, greasy, pinky rings*
RELIGION: *Dashboard idolatry* **PRACTICING:** *16,384,336*	**RACIAL TRAITS (GOOD):** *Will not kill members of the immediate family.* **RACIAL TRAITS (BAD):** *Gangsters*
LOCATION: *Mulberry Street, N.Y.C.*	**DIET STAPLE:** *Garlic*

CHAPTER 8

RACE AND ETHNICITY

Significant Supreme Court Decisions
American Heritage Magazine

24. **Plessy v. Ferguson (1896).** Homer Adolph Plessy, a light-skinned Louisiana black man, was arrested for sitting in a railroad car reserved by Louisiana law for whites. In a New Orleans court his lawyers argued that the law was unconstitutional, but Judge John H. Ferguson ruled against them, on the ground that the railroad had provided separate but equally good cars for blacks, as the law required. This line of reasoning was upheld by the Supreme Court. The case is remembered today mainly for the dissent of Justice John Marshall Harlan. "Our Constitution is color-blind," Harlan wrote. "The arbitrary separation of citizens, on the basis of race . . . is a badge of servitude wholly inconsistent with civil freedom."

25. **Brown v. Board of Education of Topeka (1954).** This is the famous school-desegregation case in which the Court unanimously overturned *Plessy v. Ferguson.* "In the field of public education," Chief Justice Earl Warren stated, "the doctrine of 'separate but equal' has no place."

26. **Roe v. Wade (1973).** Norma McCorvey (or Jane Roe), a woman prevented from having an abortion by a Texas law, sued to have the law overturned. Henry Wade, a Dallas district attorney, pushed the case up to the Supreme Court. Texas claimed that the case should have been dismissed as moot, since the plaintiff had already had her baby. In a controversial decision the Court ruled in McCorvey's favor, establishing the right of women to have abortions during the early months of pregnancy.

The Worst Supreme Court Decision

27. **Dred Scott v. Sandford** (1857). A slave, Dred Scott sued for his freedom on the ground that his master, an Army surgeon, had taken him into Illinois and then the Wisconsin Territory, where slavery had been barred by Congress in the Missouri Compromise. The Court whose majority decision was read by Chief Justice Roger B. Taney, ruled that the Missouri Compromise was unconstitutional because it violated the property rights protected by the Fifth Amendment, since it denied slave owners the right to take their property wherever they wanted to. In effect, this decision opened all the West to slavery, infuriated the North, and pushed the nation more precipitously toward civil war.

When the cat and mouse agree, the grocer is ruined.
Persian proverb

Five Black Troublemakers (1991)

American Heritage Magazine

173. Denmark Vesey (ca. 1767-1822) was a slave who purchased his freedom after winning a lottery and organized an elaborate uprising among South Carolina slaves. However, the authorities got wind of the scheme, and Vesey and thirty-five other blacks were hanged, despite the fact that no actual uprising had taken place.

174. Sojourner Truth (ca. 1797-1883) was a leading black abolitionist in the decades before the Civil War, unusual in that she campaigned for women's rights as well as for the ending of slavery. At a women's rights convention in 1851 she said: "The man over there says women need to be helped into carriages and lifted over ditches, and to have the best place everywhere. Nobody ever helps me into carriages or over puddles, or gives me the best place—and ain't I a woman?…I have ploughed and planted and gathered into barns, and no man could head me—and ain't I a woman?"

175. Frederick Douglas (ca. 1817-1895), a Baltimore slave, escaped to New York in 1838. He became an abolitionist, developed an extraordinary ability as a speaker, and published an abolitionist paper, the *North Star*. During the Civil War he helped raise black regiments and in later life continued to campaign for full equality for blacks and for women.

176. Marcus Garvey (1887-1940), an ardent black nationalist, founded the Universal Negro Improvement Association. By the mid-1920s the association had nearly a million members and Garvey had created the Black Star steamship line and other all-black businesses. He hoped to establish an independent black nation in Africa the success of which would compel whites to accept blacks as equals. Eventually, however, his companies failed and he was convicted of fraud and deported to his native Jamaica.

177. Malcolm X (1925-1965), born Malcolm Little, was a "hustler" who was converted to the Black Muslim faith while in prison. Having become one of the most radical Muslim critics of white America, a black nationalist who opposed integration of any sort on the ground that white people were devils, he began to moderate his position after extensive travels in the Middle East and Africa. His career was cut short when he was assassinated after he had begun to criticize other Muslim leaders.

Promoting Pluralism (1988)

Joseph Giordano and Irving M. Levine

The depiction of ethnic characters in the media has been the subject of hot debate for decades. The feeling still exists among leaders of many ethnic groups that very little has changed in the negative and stereotyped way they are portrayed. On the other hand, media managers believe that they have become more culturally sensitive and often view the demand of ethnic groups as out of touch with the realities of the industry. The truth lies somewhere in the middle.

Unquestionably, more minority and ethnic characters and scenes can be seen than in the days of *Father Knows Best* and *Ozzie and Harriet.* But TV programs and films are still marred by the low visibility of certain groups and the stereotyping of others. While the news media played an important role in the 1960s by vividly documenting in pictures the struggle for civil rights, today too many radio and TV stations deliberately try to hype ratings by showcasing extremists and bigots. Their appearance often works to increase tensions between ethnic groups. Today's media are rarely as crude in depicting ethnic groups as greeting cards and "truly tasteless" joke books, and the stereotypes that occur are presented in a more sophisticated form. Nevertheless, they do reinforce bigotry.

Is change hopeless? We think not. In spite of this long and somewhat negative history we do think that the time is ripe for positive changes.

Creative cooperation between media professionals and ethnic groups may now be more propitious than ever. The following combination of factors lead us to that conclusion:

- A number of ugly racial confrontations in the past few years—e.g., in Howard Beach, New York, and Forsyth County, Georgia—may have served the same function as the urban riots of the 1960s: to remind Americans of how deep the racial divisions are in this country, how explosive they can be, and the important role the media can play in reducing or enlarging those tensions.
- Historical, sociological and psychological research continues to show that ethnic ties are far more than an immigrant phenomenon; rather, they help shape an individual's character and personal story line for generations beyond immigration. Conversely, individuals who deny or are cut off from their ethnic identities often suffer lowered self esteem.
- Whether we're talking about new technology like 100-plus-channel TV and VCRs or growing ethnic outlets like minority television outlets and ethnic magazines, the growth of the media provides more forms for media expression.
- Mass media programming, particularly TV, is becoming more authentic, both in terms of the variety of characters shown (as in the colorful ethnic, as well as gender and class, interactions of *Cagney and Lacey, St. Elsewhere, thirtysomething* and *Hill Street Blues)* and in the presentation of such once-taboo topics as spouse abuse and teenage suicide. As the networks learned in such mini-series as *Roots* and *Holocaust*, delving into an ethnic group's story can make for programming that is educationally enriching, dramatically compelling and commercially profitable.
- In the area of news coverage, radio and TV stations are becoming more self-critical than in the past, as evidenced by the presence of such articulate inside critics as Bill Moyers, and the number of stations that have initiated and maintained regular contact with ethnic group leaders.
- The emergence of a new generation of writers, such as Maxine Hong Kingston, Richard Rodriguez, and Paul Cowan (respectively, Chinese-, Mexican-, and Jewish-American) are providing the mass media with

a greatly expanded pool of story ideas. Each ethnic group has a rich history and folk tradition which the mass media barely have begun to plumb.

Both media professionals and ethnic group leaders will benefit if they take advantage of this new climate by reaching out to each other.

For their part, media leaders should recognized that there is a real audience for programs and films that portray a fully pluralist America. Such TV series as *The Cosby Show, L. A. Law, Frank's Place, A Year in the Life,* and films including *La Bamba* and *The Color Purple* already show that there is a substantial audience for "real"—stereotype-breaking and ethnically diverse—characters.

Authenticity becomes even more important in light of Lichter and Lichter's Study (1988) of how adolescents react to ethnic characters on prime time TV shows (see story on p. 5). They view the characters as typical of the groups they represent. Therefore, TV programs must involve not only a certain variety of non-stereotyped ethnic characters but, more positively, characters who reflect the values and styles of their traditions

Segments on *thirtysomething, A Year in the Life* and *L. A. Law* deal with meaningful feelings about intermarriage. For example, when the Christian mother on *A Year in the Life* first refuses to participate in the Jewish naming ritual but then talks alone to her infant daughter about her Hebrew name, we experience her conflict.

New Dimensions

Media leaders generally have viewed ethnic America as consisting of pressure groups. A new, more sympathetic perspective on American pluralism means perceiving its groups as resources, both in terms of creative personnel and story ideas.

It would involve reaching out to attract and help train directors, producers, writers, actors, camera people and other personnel from many ethnic backgrounds. For example, the major TV networks and PBS might sponsor contests, with significant cash awards, or the best original plays on ethnic America. Schools of communication and film, as well as TV and radio stations and film companies, also should consider including curricula on "The Ethnic Dimension of News and Entertainment" in their base training and continuing-education programs.

The most concrete contribution the mass media can make is to develop, and adhere to, guidelines for good ethnic programming and news coverage. Some examples are to present characters who speak in correct accents, to avoid negative stereotypes (the "dumb Pole," "drunk Irishman," "inscrutable Chinese" or "Italian gangster"), to cover racial or other intergroup tensions in a way that fairly and knowledgeably covers each side's interests and avoids stoking intergroup tensions. News coverage in particular should avoid giving the most coverage to the most extreme, hate-mongering views.

Reaching Out

For their part, ethnic group leaders also need to adopt a less adversarial stance toward the media. Before complaining about coverage of their group or otherwise engaging in advocacy, they must come to understand how the media work, and the complex structural, commercial, creative and social dynamics to which they are subjected. When it comes to TV, for example, they need to understand how many individuals are involved in covering a news story or shaping a series, and how the intense ratings wars affect programming. For better or worse, the media are comprised of businesses (whose primary focus is what will enhance the bottom line).

Appreciating the corporate dimension of the mass media does not mean that ethnic advocates should not, or cannot, influence them. But it does imply that they must develop the interpersonal, public relations and other skills to ensure their being heard.

Part of this process is to know not only when to challenge, but also when to support. Rather than simply complain, ethnic leaders should applaud quality programming involving ethnic content. They should do so particularly when a station or film company has taken a risk with material that previously was considered parochial or "too controversial."

Ethnic America also has an obligation to promote such risk-taking, to broaden horizons and confront stereotypes, by educating media corporations.

At the same time, if ethnic leaders want media executives to tap their creative resources, they have the obligation to develop their resources to the fullest. Ethnic groups in America must more adequately support their own writers, artists or filmmakers. They need to undertake comprehensive, well-organized oral history projects and have at least one museum documenting that group's story in both the "old country" and in America. Many groups do all of these things, but don't adequately connect with media representatives who might be convinced to take seriously the material that is available for good authentic programming.

Finally, ethnic groups would comprise a more potent force in influencing the media if they entered into coalitions rather than going at it alone. The more extensive experience of some groups (for example, Jews and blacks) in what has been called "the art and science of influence" could benefit other groups, while the strength of *all* groups would be enhanced by a sharing of expertise.

Ultimately, the goal of such coalition-building within ethnic America is not to confront the media but to build bridges to it. For ethnic America and the mass media need each other. Each group in this country needs to be seen and to be portrayed fairly, by the major channels of communication in order to get its message across to the general American public. Conversely, the mass media, which are ever in danger of being stale in their entertainment programming and superficial or inaccurate in their news coverage, need to utilize ethnic diversity as an inexhaustible source of creative renewal.

Joseph Giordano, a family therapist, is director of the American Jewish Committee's Center on Ethnicity, Behavior and Communications and is co-chairman of the Italian American Foundation's Media Institute. Irving M. Levine, a major leader of the "new ethnicity" movement, is the American Jewish Committee's Director of National Affairs and the founder/director of AJC's Institute of American Pluralism.

Tell the truth and run.
Japanese proverb

He Won't Forget the 'Forgotten Holocaust'
Marcia Froelke Coburn (1988)

"Ukrainians have been trying to tell their story for years. Nobody's been interested. This is a story of a forgotten holocaust. The death of 7 million people, deliberately planned by Joseph Stalin."

To Myron Kuropas, the story is simple and horrifying. Nuances, circumstances, interpretations—all cease to be relevant. What matters, he says, is the truth, even when it's cold, hard, not very pretty.

And the fact that it has been ignored—or even deliberately covered up—is, to him, just as shocking, just as much an indictment of man's inhumanity as the original, terrible tale.

"Ukrainians have been trying to tell their story for years," Kuropas says. "Nobody's been interested. Nobody wants to hear about Ukrainians." So, when faced with someone who's willing to listen, Kuropas—Ph.D. from the University of Chicago, author, public school teacher, supreme vice president of the Ukrainian National Association—begins slowly, from the beginning.

"This is a story of a forgotten holocaust," he says. "The death of 7 million people, deliberately planned by Joseph Stalin.Ukraine—not *the* Ukraine, which I'll explain later—has been part of the U.S.S.R. since about 1920." Before that, the country was independent; then it experienced two Bolshevik invasions and, eventually, lost the battle.

Even so, Kuropas says, the first five to seven years after being annexed, Ukraine retained some level of independence. "It had its own institutions, its own ethnonational culture, literary societies, publishing houses, schools. It was a renaissance time.

"But in 1929, Stalin introduced the collectivization policy, by which all the individually owned or worked farms would be joined together to make collective ones."

The idea was to move the soviet Union from an antiquated, rural nation to an industrialized one. "To do that the government needed money, which meant they had to sell things on the open market. And what better than wheat, since they had Ukrainian farms, located in the breadbasket of the world?"

There was, naturally, resistance to the idea of collective farms. "Incredible resistance," Kuropas says. "People were shot, liquidated, sent to Siberia. Still, they resisted. But every year, more and more farms were collectivized. By 1931, about 85 percent of the total Ukrainian farms had been brought under this system; a year later, it was almost 90 percent. And every year, the government raised the percentage of wheat that went to the state."

By all historical accounts, the harvests of 1932 were particularly meager. "It is estimated that it was at least 17 percent less than normal," Kuropas says, "yet the Soviet authorities demanded more wheat. If people didn't give it, [government agents] expropriated it and stored it in bins. When the people began to starve and attack the storage bins, they were shot. Stalin put the army in, and they took out pigs, cows, anything that moved. To make sure the people weren't stealing anything—and this is documented—agents went through feces of people to see if they could find corn kernels. It was a horrendous experience; 7 million people perished."

Those statistics, he explains, are based on the comparison of the 1926 census with the one in 1936. "That shows a drop of 3 million in the population, plus adding in the Soviet projected statistics on births, and the figure come out to 7 million," Kuropas says. "Yet there are Soviet dissidents who have written books that suggest approximately 12 million died."

Whatever the staggering number of victims, 18,000 Ukrainian-Americans—including Kuropas, his wife, the former Alexandra Waskiw, and their two sons—gathered in Washington, D.C., last month to commemorate what the Washington Post recently called "a monstrous but almost forgotten act of genocide a half-century ago."

How could such an act be swept away? To Kuropas, the answer is a conspiracy motivated by leftist sympathies. "No reporters were allowed into the Ukraine, but somehow one from the British papers got in and took photographs. But when the Soviets denied that any famine took place, the U.S.S.R. correspondents for the *New York Times* and the *Nation* backed them up. The only American paper that printed the story was a Hearst paper, the Chicago American, but that was in 1935 and they put the date of the famine as 1934. Naturally, everyone could deny that there had been a famine in 1934—rightfully so—and the story became known as 'more of Hearst's fiction.'"

The reasons Kuropas talks of a conspiracy can be found in a 1982 issue of the Ukrainian Weekly, printed on the same page as a photograph of the infamous edition of the Chicago American. There Kuropas writes of "the radical left [which] reveled. . . . The Soviet Union had something for everyone. Liberals found social equality, wise and caring leaders, reconstructed institutions and intellectual stimulation. Rebels found support for their causes: birth control, sexual equality, progressive education, futuristic dancing, Esperanto."

"I think these kinds of statements should really be slugged out in academic journals, not newspapers," says an East Coast-based Soviet Studies professor, who asked not to be identified. "Undoubtedly, there was a famine, and, undoubtedly, some Americans at one time tended to romanticize the Soviet experiment. But I think bandying these kinds of charges and accusations about comes dangerously close to red-baiting."

Not surprisingly, Kuropas sees it differently. "In the U.S., Ukrainians are viewed as people who have quaint customs, sing nice songs, wear cute costumes. We are, supposedly, people who are a little bit confused when it comes to world history. We don't understand what has really taken place. Yet Americans are the ones who don't really understand what has taken place, as evidenced by the use of the term *the* Ukraine. I'm always asked where *the* Ukraine is, and I always answer 'between *the* Russia and *the* Poland.' Using 'the' suggests something is part of a greater whole, when actually that's not the case here."

Kuropas says he has been fighting such misunderstandings and semantics all his life. Born in Chicago to Ukrainian-born parents. he grew up on the city's North Side, with close ties to the local Ukrainian community. He attended public schools, then Loyola University, where he earned a B.S. in psychology. After obtaining an M.A. at Roosevelt, also in psychology, he went to the University of Chicago, where he got a Ph.D. in education. His thesis was on Ukrainian-American immigration.

He started his career as a public school teacher, then assistant principal, then principal. Along the way, he married the Ukrainian-born Alexandra, and they had two children, Stephen and Michael. For several years he was the regional director of ACTION, where he developed the Project Senior Ethnic Find, "an outreach Vista program for the ethnic elderly in Illinois, Indiana, Michigan and Ohio." He wrote a textbook called *Ukrainians in America* (Lerner, $6.95). He contributed a section to an anthology, *Ethnic Chicago* (W.B. Eerdmans). In 1976 he became President Gerald Ford's special assistant on ethnic affairs for one year. Then he worked for several months with Sen. Robert Dole (R-Kan.), organizing an ethnic advisory council concerning human rights in Eastern Europe.

"Then I had to re-evaluate what I was doing," he says. "I hardly had any time to spend with my wife or family." Together, they decided to leave Washington, settle down in the DeKalb area, and spend their time on what mattered most; first, each other, then promoting understanding of Ukranian causes. "I returned to the public school system, first as a principal," Kuropas says. "Now I'm teaching third grade."

Wait a minute. Third grade? A university of Chicago Ph.D., a former special assistant to the president, a previous legislative assistant to a U.S. senator? "Yes, yes," Kuropas says, laughing a little. "I find it even more unbelievable than you do. Well, about three years ago I had a misunderstanding with the superintendent of schools, and I was demoted. It was, I guess, a conflict of style. We differed on our approaches to education and teaching. I'm more concerned with basics than other things and, well, it was just a different approach and emphasis than the superintendent wanted."

Still, the inevitable issue has to be raised: Maybe Kuropas is a guy who just can't help taking things too far. "Sure, perhaps some people would say that," he says. "Probably. But then I could bring in lots of people who really support me. I fought it [the demotion] the full route, with a closed and an open hearing—and I lost. One guy who voted against me is a carpet layer. This is the kind of person who decided my future."

Yet Kuropas says that, overall, he's happy teaching third grade. "This has given me more time to do other things." Harvard University Press will be publishing his partly rewritten dissertation soon; and then there is the issue of the Ukrainian famine. Kuropas says his two main goals are to have the famine taught as a regular part of a school's curriculum and eventually to have a TV docudrama produced so the tragedy will reach a mass audience.

"We Ukrainians—and there are 60,000 of us in the Chicago area—think our story should be remembered and told and taught the same way the Nazi holocaust is, mainly because it is an international crime, just like the Holocaust in Germany."

At the moment, all Kuropas can do is tell the story to whoever will listen—and finding listeners is not always easy, he admits. "People don't care," he says. And then, perhaps, people are startled by his references to the "mostly liberal" American press as exemplified by Time and Newsweek—a statement that could give both Democrats and Republicans pause. But Kuropas doesn't care; he's on a crusade and he won't be swayed. "This is a forgotten holocaust," he says, "and that's not right. This story should be told."

From Heredity, Race and Society (1946)

L.C. Dunn and Theodosius Dobzhansky

It is an old human habit to believe that one's own family or race is better then the neighbors, but it is a relatively new idea to ascribe this superiority to inherited biological qualities. The Greeks of more than 2,000 years ago felt quite sure that they were better than barbarians, barbarians being generously defined as all non-Greeks; but they regarded the barbarian as inferior not because there was anything wrong with his body, but because his table manners, so to speak, were so bad. The Greeks could also detect the same superior attitude in other peoples of antiquity. As far back as the fifth century B.C. Herodotus, the great historian, wrote with subtle irony that Persians "look upon themselves as very greatly superior in all respects to the rest of mankind, regarding others as approaching to excellence in proportion as they dwell nearer to them; whence it comes to pass that those who are the farthest off must be the most degraded of mankind."

Later, it was not a Roman "race" that ruled so much of the civilized world but Roman ideas of government, Roman law, Roman discipline and military achievement; and many a "barbarian" acquired this belief in Roman superiority by becoming a Roman citizen.

Mohammedans are often, though quite wrongly, regarded as intolerant, yet they always accepted without discrimination anyone who embraced their religion. The early Christians in general adopted the same attitude, paying little attention to biological or racial differences, since they regarded as fundamental those differences in behavior which, like those of the Pharisees, arose from differences in beliefs.

In medieval lore one of the three wise men who came [107]* to Christ in Bethlehem was pictured as a Negro. As recently as 250 years ago Peter the Great of Russia imported, among other marvels, a Negro boy. This lad had a hard time convincing a prospective Russian father-in-law that in spite of the blackness of his skin he was not related to the devil, but eventually he married into the Russian aristocracy, and his great-grandson, Alexander Pushkin, became the greatest of Russian poets and one of the great poets of the world.

The idea of biological superiority based on race appears in the Old Testament. Here it is quite clear that Jehovah made his covenant with Abraham and "with his seed," that is, with those descended biologically from Abraham. In the New Testament there are vivid descriptions of the conflict between this view and the radical, even revolutionary, doctrine of the universal brotherhood of man.

The issue is still joined. Many people declare it to be the "white man's burden" to rule men of all other colors. And so anxious have some white men been to lay this burden upon themselves that they used their superior weapons to fight and kill colored people, and incidentally other whites, for their privilege. Again it became useful to the German Nazis to think that their neighbors were biologically degraded. The world could only be benefited by the killing of Slavs and Jews and other "inferior races." Truly, race superiority is very useful when armies are on the march.

---

*In the texts of the selections, bracketed numbers indicate the pagination of the original sources. When a page in the original ends with a hyphenated word, we have indicated the original pagination after the entire word.

But if ideas about war and conquest are as old as history, at least one factor has come into the world in recent times. This is the knowledge of human races and of human biology which is emerging from the studies of may scientists specializing in this subject. Military leaders and politicians have been learning how to use real or assumed scientific discoveries to add an appearance of respectability to their propaganda. Such propaganda, even when directed to evil ends, can not accomplish its purpose if we know the facts of human biology. What then is the truth about race? What has science to say about it? [108]

Race Classification

About one fact of cardinal importance practically all scientists are agreed: All men belong to a single species, and there are no divisions between any varieties of men like those barriers which separate the species of animals. All kinds of human beings can mate and have offspring, regardless of geographic origin, color, or other biological difference. All have the same general characteristics, which caused the first great classifier of animals and plants, the Swedish naturalist Linnaeus, in 1738 to assign all men to the species *Homo sapiens* (Homo for *man*, sapiens for *wise*, an opinion which we should probably only dare express in Latin!). Linnaeus placed this species at the pinnacle of the animal kingdom.

Linnaeus knew, of course, that the men who inhabit the different parts of the world are not all alike, and so he divided the human species into four varieties, as follows:

> *americanus* (American Indian)—Tenacious, contented, free; ruled by custom
> *europaeus*—Light, lively, inventive; ruled by rites
> *asiaticus*—Stern, haughty, stingy; ruled by opinion
> *afer* (African)—Cunning, slow, negligent; ruled by caprice

The first classification was, as we see, based on characters of the mind and not of the body. The fault of this classification was that it didn't classify: contented, lively and negligent people can be found everywhere.

A little later (1775) the German scholar Blumenbach, founder of anthropology, the scientific study of man, proposed to divide men according to skin color into five varieties and to each of these varieties was given the name "race," a term which had been employed earlier by the French scientist Buffon. The five "races" of Blumenbach were:

> Caucasian or white
> Mongolian or yellow [109]
> Ethiopian or black
> American or red
> Malayan or brown

This was a biological classification which obviously described existing differences between large populations inhabiting different parts of the world.

Other anthropologists thought that skin color was too superficial a trait and they resorted to measurements of parts and proportions of the body, particularly of the head. Races were recognized by head shape in conjunction with particular combinations of other traits, nearly all of which were present to some degree in all "races" and which were not constant with any race. Head shape as we know may differ sharply within the same family, even among brothers and sisters.

The use of such methods led to a great multiplication of races. Deniker in 1889 recognized 29 of them distinguished by hair form, with skin color and nose shape as subsidiary traits. In 1933 von

Eickstedt set up three basic races, "Europid," "Negrid" and "Mongolid," with 18 "subraces," 3 "collateral races," 11 "collateral subraces" and 3 "intermediate forms." In 1950, the American anthropologists Coon, Garn, and Birdsell recognized 6 "putative stocks"—Negroid, Mongoloid, White, Australoid, American Indian, and Polynesian—and 30 different races.

No agreement has emerged from such efforts as to what constitutes a race. The confusion is made worse by those who fail to distinguish groups resembling each other biologically from those united in a national or language community. "American" as applied to citizens of the United States can certainly designate no biological unit. There is no "American race" (unless it be the red men displaced by the immigrants from Europe); nor is there a Swiss race or a French race. A nation may consist of more than one race, and several nations, like those of the British Commonwealth, may be biologically alike. The inhabitants of northern Germany resemble physically the inhabitants of Denmark and Sweden more than they do the south Germans, who in turn are physically similar to [110] some Frenchmen, Czechs and Yugoslavs. You will not be able to distinguish by sight some Swedes, Finns and Russians, yet they speak very different languages.

It is very easy to be deceived by differences amongst peoples even more superficial and easily acquired than language or ideas or religion. Dress and decoration, even hair-do, may make some people seem dissimilar as a group from the very population from which they are descended. If one were to arrange a guessing contest as to what "race" certain particular Europeans belong to, it would have to be conducted either without any clothing or decoration at all or with the neutral uniform of dress and hair style which the clothiers and permanent wavers of the city are spreading throughout all populations. "Racial" differences have often been inferred from characters almost as transitory as these.

The misuse of "race" for political and military purposes has brought the term "race" into such disrepute that many people, including some scientists, propose to abandon the term altogether as applied to human groups. It is true that it is used in many ways. By "the human race" we certainly do not mean the same thing as "the races of man"; nor does the latter convey the same meaning of race as is intended in a discussion of the "races of Europe"; and yet there are human entities for which the term race, if properly used, could stand.

If change of name could cure some of the ills which the race notion, or rather the misuses of the notion, have brought about, then it might be better to convey the idea of race in other words. Some have used "ethnic group" in place of race; but unfortunately "ethnic group prejudice" is easily exchangeable for "race prejudice"; and one can hate "ethnic groups" just as venomously as real or imaginary races.

Anyone can see that the inhabitants of Chinatown differ in appearance from those living on Park Avenue, and that Pullman porters as a group differ from train conductors as a group. These are facts which require expression and understanding, and they will not disappear behind a changed name. There is no doubt that the popular [111] idea of race as well as that held by the older anthropology are both invalid, but it takes some effort to see where the fallacy lies.

How Races are Distinguished

How does a layman and how does a scientist arrive at the idea of race? Suppose that we consider the inhabitants of an American city, such as New York. We know the different kinds of people who live in different sections of the city, in Harlem, in Little Italy, in the Norwegian colony in Brooklyn, and so on. As laymen we recognize the facial and bodily traits which are usual in the different groups. In Harlem the majority of people have dark skins, tightly curled hair, broad noses and thick lips, and we know that these have come from African ancestors. In the Norwegian colony we find many tall people, many blonds, and many with blue eyes; whereas those of Italian descent tend to be shorter, brunette and dark-eyed. Amongst those of South German or Swiss descent we are more likely to find medium stature, brown hair, fair skin, and round heads.

We might conclude that among these neighbors in the city we can identify four groups or races: African, north European, central European and south European. Some anthropologists have called these Negro, Nordic, Alpine, and Mediterranean. If asked to describe what Negroes of Nordics are like we may make a sort of composite picture of all the Negroes or all the Nordics that we know; or we may pick out one or a few individuals who have struck us as "typical" and describe their qualities as those of Negroes and Nordics in general.

The Anthropologist has generally used refinements of these methods. He has combined the measurements and descriptive notes taken on a number of persons of a certain group and has calculated the *average* stature, average head shape, and the averages of other bodily characters. He gives this set of averages as the characteristic of the group. [112]

At this point, whether we have reached it by "scientific" or by lay men's methods, the trouble begins. In the first place, we may make the mistake which has been so common in the past, of assuming some necessary connection between the physical characters which we have observed or measured and mental and cultural characters of the group. The skin color, hair shape and lip thickness of Negroes is known to be inherited and to develop as well in northern Harlem as in equatorial Africa. It is known also that most northern Negroes live in slums, enjoy jazz and engage in manual or menial labor. One is likely to jump to the conclusion that the economic and social and cultural position of the Negro is also inherited and will continue regardless of education and opportunity. But it is obvious this does not follow from the facts at all.

Difficulties of Race Classification

If we avoid succumbing to the above error, we must then learn to resist the temptation, which is even stronger, to identify individuals with races. Negroes and Nordics and Alpines differ *as groups,* but mistakes are bound to be made if one tries to place every person that one meets in one of these groups. Perhaps not many mistakes will be made in assigning persons to the Negro group on the one hand or to the Nordic on the other; but a veritable avalanche of mistakes will be made in trying to separate Nordics, Alpines and Mediterranean. Anthropologists armed with all their measurements are in little better position than the layman when it comes to deciding to which of these European "races" a given person belongs. The averages may describe very well the ideal Nordic or Alpine, but ideals and averages are abstractions, and it is just a lucky accident if the person whose race we wish to determine happens to have all his traits coincide exactly with the averages for any one race. If we make many measurements and calculate averages for all of them we may find ourselves in the predicament that no actually existing man or woman of any race anywhere conforms to the race [113] ideal. Since every individual differs from any other individual, everyone belongs to his own special race; but to say that makes the race concept absurd.

Not only individuals but also whole groups of people are frequently difficult to place in any one race. Our ideas about Nordics come from our acquaintance with Norwegians and Swedes, and our ideas about the Alpines from observations on southern Germans. Now, inhabitants of northern and central Germany are on the whole intermediate between Nordics and Alpines; yet, among them individuals may be found who are just as "typical" Nordics and "typical" Alpines as can be found anywhere. What race do these people belong to? We may try to escape the difficulty by saying that both Nordic and Alpine "bloods flow in their veins," or simply that there are racial mixtures or hybrids. But a moment's reflection will show that this leads into another difficulty no less serious than the first.

Pure Races?

If you say that something is a mixture, you imply that pure ingredients which have been mixed together exist somewhere, or have existed in the past. But where are the pure Nordics, pure Alpines, pure Mediterraneans, etc.? Wherever you go, you find that only very few, if any, inhabitants of a country conform to any possible notion of racial purity and uniformity. For example, you will meet a lot of tall, blond and blue-eyed persons in the city of Oslo, Norway, but you will find there also many individuals with brown eyes and dark hair. There is nothing to indicate that the possessors of these un-Nordic colorations are any less native to the city than are the blue-eyed blonds. Similarly, blue-eyed blonds are met with occasionally among Spaniards, most of whom are brunets.

As a last resort, one may suppose that, although no countries inhabited by "pure" Nordics and "pure" Alpines (or by any other "pure" race for that matter) exist at present, such countries did exist in the past. This [114] supposition is actually implied in most popular discussions of the "race problem." Back in some distant Golden Age people zealously kept their race "pure," and this made them strong and wise. Recently they allowed themselves to become mixed or "mongrelized," and the twilight of humanity is about to swallow us as a consequence. Such notions are, however, definitely refuted by scientific data. Race mixture has been going on during the whole of recorded history. Incontrovertible evidence from studies on fossil human remains shows that even in prehistory, at the very dawn of humanity, mixing of different stocks (at least occasionally) took place. Mankind has always been, and still is, a mongrel lot.

To be sure, the growth of the world's population in the last two hundred years, coupled with the development of the means of travel and communication, has enormously speeded up the process of mixing of the human races. Mixing of at least closely related races (such as those living in different European countries) appears, however, to be biologically desirable rather than the reverse. A gradual increase of the average stature has been going on in most civilized countries of the world during at least the last hundred years. This becoming taller is due in part to improvement of hygienic conditions and to better nutrition, but in part also to the lifting of barriers which in the past separated different peoples so that "tall" genes could spread more widely. However that may be, nothing can be more certain than that pure races in man never existed and can not exist.

But suppose that the population of a country, a city, or an island were isolated from any immigrants from the outside and allowed to breed for many generations within itself, would not this population eventually become a "pure" race? Here we come to a matter of crucial importance for the understanding of the whole problem of race. "Pure" races could exist only if heredity were like a fluid transmitted through "blood," and if the hereditary "bloods" of the parents mixed and fused in their offspring. We know that this does not happen. The experiments of Mendel and the calculations of [115] Hardy and Weinberg showed that heredity is transmitted not as fluids which can be mixed and diluted, but in discrete packages called genes, so that a child inherits just 1/2 of the genes each of its parents possesses, and that brothers and sisters receive different sets of genes. The old race notion is based on the "blood" theory of heredity; and the old idea of race is just as fallacious as the blood theory.

Suppose that individuals with blue eyes and blond hair, and with dark eyes and black hair, exist in a certain population. If the hereditary "bloods" were to mix, all individuals in this population would eventually show a uniform mixture of light and dark complexion; they would all have light brown eyes and hair. Actually the genes for the different eye and hair colors do not mix. Populations descended from Europeans will always have individuals with dark and light brown and blue eyes, and with black, brown, and blond hair. They will always stay mixed, and will never become uniform or "pure."

When a trait, such as the skin color in Negroes and whites, is determined by cooperation of several genes, it may seem that the hybrids, the mulattoes, are all uniformly coffee-colored. But we know that this is in reality not so, because Mendelian segregation takes place. Although the average skin hue in mulattoes is intermediate between black and white, individuals with very light and with very dark skins are also born. Anyone who has observed the Negroes in the United States knows how tremendously they vary in their physical traits. Now, most of them are of course hybrids, descendants of persons of African and of European origin. Supposing that no more Negro-white crosses occur from now on, the American Negroes may eventually become a little more homogeneous than they are at present, but certainly nothing resembling complete uniformity will ever be reached. Some anthropologists consider this variable group a race in the making, designated as American Colored.

We can see where the old race notion went astray. It assumed, tacitly or explicitly, that a race is a "community of blood." If that were so, the racial "ideal" obtained by [116] averaging the characteristics of a group of peoples who have intermarried for generations would have some meaning: this "ideal" would approximately correspond to the type which would eventually be reached if this group were to continue intermarrying without any immigration from the outside. The heredity of any individual would be determined by the race from which he sprang. Every one of us would be, in a very real biological sense, blood of our race's blood and bone of our race's bone. The fact is, however, that every group of people consists of individuals who have certain genes in common but differ in other genes. Parents always differ in several, and probably in many genes. Their children differ in some genes both from their parents and from each other. The hereditary diversity of a group, be it a family, a clan, or a race, persists indefinitely. The heredity of an individual is only partly determined by the race from which he sprang. The diversity, the variation, found within a race is more important than the racial averages.

Definition of Race

People differ in the color of skin, eyes, hair, in stature, bodily proportions, and in many other traits. Each trait is determined by several, often by many, genes. How many variable genes there are in man is unknown; certainly hundreds, possibly thousands. Because of this, some of us have blue and others brown eyes, some have prominent and others flat noses, some are tall and others short. Such differences are, of course, common among people of the some country, state, town, members of a family, and even brothers and sisters. We do not suppose that every person with blue eyes belongs to a different race from everybody with brown eyes. It would be absurd to do so because blue and brown-eyed children are frequently born to the same parents. It happens, however, that certain genes are more frequent among the inhabitants of some countries than of others. Thus, blue eyes are very common in most parts of the United States but rather [117] rare in most parts of Mexico. It is this and similar differences which make it possible to say that the inhabitants of the United States are in general racially distinct from the inhabitants of Mexico. Races can be defined as populations which differ in the frequencies of some gene or genes. [118]

Do Human Races Differ in Mental Capacity?

Breeds of dogs differ markedly in temperament, in responsiveness to particular kinds of training, and hence in the uses to which they may best be put by man. Although almost any dog can be trained when young to be of some use, one would not, for choice, try to train a dachshund to be a sheepherder, or a shepherd dog to hunt rabbits. Similarly, the differences in temperament between polo ponies and draft horses, which are certainly conditioned in part by their heredity, fit them for different functions. These breed differences have been accentuated by selective breeding by men who had these different functions in view. It has often been argued by analogy that differences in biological heredity lie at the bottom of intellectual, emotional, and temperamental differences between races and between cultural and social groups.

Another argument runs as follows: Races arise as a part of the evolutionary process, by which populations within a species become adapted to a particular environment. Racial variation in skin color has, for example, been viewed in this way. If biological evolution has caused races of man to diverge in physical characters, should it not have done the same for the mental capacities and aptitudes of these people?

Both of these arguments by analogy are unconvincing, because they are based on a misunderstanding of the nature of biological heredity. It has been pointed out repeatedly in this book that what is inherited is not this or that trait, but the manner in which the developing organism responds to its environment. Now, the amount as well as the kind of variation which a trait shows in different environments is decided by the hereditary make-up of the organism. For example, individuals who carry [131] the genes for the O, A, or B blood groups have the respective blood groups regardless of their state of health, the climate they live in, or the nutrition which they receive. The blood group is rigidly fixed by heredity. But the skin color is not so rigidly fixed, since it can change rather rapidly depending upon the exposure of the skin to sunlight. Finally, whether or not an individual gets into conflicts with the law depends upon the person's upbringing and circumstances, and also upon the kind of laws which the society sees fit to establish. Human behavior is, then, quite plastic and can be changed by the living conditions.

The important problem is why some traits are more and others less fixed or plastic. The fixity or plasticity of a trait is a matter of evolutionary adaptation. By and large, the traits which are important for the survival in all the environments which a species or a race normally encounters are fixed; the development of the organism is so "buffered" against external disturbances that the trait almost invariably appears. Thus, man is almost always born with and grows up having the same set of internal organs, of physiological functions, and with a capacity to reason and to learn from experience.

But it is also advantageous for the safety of the organism to have some traits change rather easily when the environment changes. For example, dark skin pigmentation is advantageous during summer vacation on the seashore. But little skin pigment is supposedly advantageous to secure a supply of vitamin D (the "sunlight" vitamin) when sunlight is scarce. The genetic constitution which is most favorable in a changeable climate is, then, one which permits the development of darker or lighter skin colors at different seasons and in different climates.

The relative fixity of the temperamental make-up of horse or dog breeds is, then, understandable. These breeds have been fashioned by man and intended for different uses. A great Dane with the temper of a fox terrier might be dangerous, and a fox terrier with the temperament of a great Dane would be boring. The [132] genetic component is important by selection and breeding. But has there been a similar selection in the evolution of man?

It is obvious that different social positions and different trades call for somewhat different behavior patterns. The qualities most useful in a military leader are not the same which are most favored in a writer or a scientist, and vice versa. The mentality of a nomadic hunter is usually different from that of a farmer. But the pre-eminent requirement of living in any human society is very nearly always the same: it is the ability to learn from experience and to adjust one's behavior to the needs and circumstances. This requirement is fundamental for living in any culture or civilization, for the most primitive to the most complex. Accordingly, the process of selection which has been, and still is, most powerful and persistent in human evolution is that for the ability to learn new ways of behavior, new techniques of doing things, and new skills.

In short, the human species as a whole has developed away from genetic specialization and fixity of behavior, and toward educability. This is true for all races of man and for all climates. Therein lies the most important biological feature of the evolutionary pattern of mankind. Breed of dogs or of horses have been deliberately fashioned for performance of different services by making their genes different. Man is certainly capable of pursuing a great variety of ways of life. But he is enabled to do so by different training and education, not by acquiring different genes. This does not mean that the genetic differences among men do not affect their mentality. But from the vantage point of evolutionary biology we can see that such differences are not fundamental. Far more important is the fact that human capacities are developed by training from childhood on. Pathological cases aside, human personality is shaped mainly by the patterns of interpersonal relations which prevail in a given culture, and by the individual experiences of each member of a community. This genetically conditioned [133] educability has guaranteed the success for mankind a biological species; and has, in turn, permitted progressively more advances cultural developments.

Concluding Remarks

Although universal uniformity of men appeals to some people, there is no reason why monotonous sameness should be our goal. On the contrary, such a prospect appears bleak in the extreme. Psychological and cultural differences among individuals and groups furnish the leaven of creative effort which carries mankind toward ever greater achievements. The question of whether or not human races differ in hereditary psychological traits for the time being must be regarded as open. We know that a variety of different civilizations have existed and exist in the world. The differences between them certainly can not be accounted for by the biological differences between the groups of people who created, developed, and maintained these civilizations. The differences between the so-called "race psychologies" are determined by the cultural differences to an extent assuredly greater than they may be influenced by biological heredity. Furthermore, psychic differences between individuals are certainly much greater than the average differences between nations or races.

We have seen that the psychic trait which has been, and still is, most favored in human evolution is the ability to profit from experience, the educability. Now, educability does not make all men alike. The exact opposite is true. The survival advantage of the ability to learn and to be trained consists precisely in that the development for a person can be turned in any one of many possible directions, as necessity may demand. Educability permits, then, a vastly greater diversity of human personalities than could possibly arise if human mentality were genetically fixed, as it is, for example, in the inhabitants of the anthill. Far from fostering mental uniformity, human evolution has led to increasing diversity. [134]

Regardless of how the problem of the relations between biological heredity, individual and group psychology, and culture may eventually be settled, the variety of human cultures will appear to us an inspiration rather than a curse if we learn to respect, to understand, and to admire them. In the realm of culture there is enough room to accommodate the diversified contributions not only of different individuals but also of every nation and race. It is a waste of time to discuss which particular contributions are superior and which inferior. There is no common measure applicable to the works of a poet, an artist, a philosopher, a scientist, and the simple kindness of heart of a plain man. Humanity needs them all. [135]

L. C. Dunn (1893-   ), a geneticist who has worked extensively on the biology of race, is Professor of Zoology at Columbia University, the author of Heredity *and* Variation *and the co-author of the standard textbook,* Principles of Genetics.

Theodosius Dobzhansky (1900-   ) was born in Russia and is an internationally recognized authority on genetics and evolution. His books include Genetics and the Origin of Species; Evolution, Genetics and Man; The Biological Basis of Human Freedom; *and* Mankind Evolving: the Evolution of the Human Species.

Contention is better than loneliness.
Irish proverb

The Woman Who Beat the Klan (1987)

Jesse Kornbluth

In her dream, there was a steel-gray casket in her living room. Who was the dead man laid out in a gray suit? She couldn't tell. And every time she moved closer to the coffin, someone she didn't know said, "You don't need to see this." But Beulah Mae Donald knew that she did, and so she woke from her dream at two in the morning in <u>Mobile, Ala., on March 21, 1981</u>. The first thing she did, she later said, was to look in the other bedroom, where her youngest child slept. Michael, 19, wasn't there. She telephoned one of her six other children. Though Michael had watched television with his cousins earlier in the evening, he had left before midnight.

Mrs. Donald drank two cups of coffee and moved to her couch, where she waited for the new day. At dawn, Michael still wasn't home. To keep busy, she went outside to rake her small yard. As she worked, a woman delivering insurance policies came by. "They found a body," she said, and walked on. Shortly before 7 A.M., Mrs. Donald's phone rang. A woman had found Michael's wallet in a trash bin. Mrs. Donald brightened—Michael was alive, she thought. "No, baby, they had a party here, and they killed your son," the caller reported. "You'd better send somebody over."

A few blocks away, in a racially mixed neighborhood about a mile from the Mobile police station, Michael Donald's body was still hanging from a tree. Around his neck was a perfectly tied noose with 13 loops. On a front porch across the street, watching police gather evidence, there were members of the well known United Klans of America, one the largest and, according to civil rights lawyers, the most violent of the Ku Klux Klans. Less than two hours after finding Michael Donald's body, Mobile police would interview these Klansmen. Lawmen learned only much later, however, what Bernie Jack Hays, the 64-year-old Titan of the United Klans, was saying as he stood on the porch that morning. "A pretty sight," commented Hays, according to a fellow Klansman. "That's gonna look good on the news. Gonna look good for the Klan."

For Bennie Hays, the 25 policemen gathering around Michael Donald's body represented the happy conclusion to an extremely unhappy development. That week, a jury had been struggling to reach a verdict in the case of a black man accused of murdering a white policeman. The killing had occurred in Birmingham, but the trial had been moved to Mobile. To Hays—the second-highest Klan official in Alabama—and his fellow members of Unit 900 of the United Klans, the presence of blacks on the jury meant that a guilty man would go free. According to Klansmen who attended the unit's weekly meeting, Hays had said that Wednesday, "If a black man can get away with killing a white man, we ought to be able to get away with killing a black man."

On Friday night, after the jurors announced they couldn't reach a verdict, the Klansmen got together in a house Bennie Hays owned on Herndon Avenue. According to later testimony from James (Tiger) Knowles, then 17 years old, Tiger produced a borrowed pistol. Henry Francis Hays, Bennie's 26-year-old son, took out a rope. Then the two got in Henry's car and went hunting for a black man.

Michael Donald was alone, walking home, when Knowles and Hays spotted him. They pulled over, asked him for directions to a night club, then pointed the gun at him and ordered him to get in. They drove to the next county. When they stopped, Michael begged them not to kill him, then tried to escape. Henry Hays and Knowles chased him, caught him, hit him with a tree limb more than a hundred times, and, when he was no longer moving, wrapped the rope around his neck. Henry Hays shoved his boot in Michael's face and pulled on the rope. For good measure, they cut his throat.

Around the time Mrs. Donald was having her prescient nightmare, Henry Hays and Knowles returned to the party at Bennie Hays's house, where they showed off their handiwork, and, looping the rope over a camphor tree, raised Michael's body just high enough so it would swing.

The Mobile Police Chief was certain from the very beginning that the Klansmen were involved. Despite that, the police soon arrested three young men they described as "junkie types." When it became clear these men had no involvement in the killing, they were released—and, at the District Attorney's invitation, the Federal Bureau of Investigation entered the case. That investigation produced no useful evidence, however, and it seemed that the killers would go unpunished. It took two years, a second F.B.I. investigation and a skillfully elicited confession to convict Tiger Knowles of violating Michael Donald's civil rights and Henry Hays of murder. Hays, who received the death sentence, is that rarest of Southern killers: a white man slated to die for the murder of a black.

At that point, a grieving mother might have been expected to issue a brief statement of gratitude and regret, and then return to her mourning. Beulah Mae Donald would not settle for that. From the moment she insisted on an open casket for her battered son—"so the world could know"—she challenged the silence of the Klan and the recalcitrance of the criminal justice system. Two convictions weren't enough for her. She didn't want revenge. She didn't want money. All she ever wanted, she says, was to prove that "Michael did no wrong."

Mrs. Donald's determination inspired a handful of lawyers and civil rights advocates, black and white. Early in 1984, Morris Dees, co-founder of the Southern Poverty Law Center, suggested that Mrs. Donald file a civil suit against the members of Unit 900 and the United Klans of America. The killers were, he believed, carrying out an organizational policy set by the group's Imperial Wizard, Robert Shelton. If Dees could prove in court that this "theory of agency" applied, Shelton's Klan would be as liable for the murder as a corporation is for the actions its employees take in the service of business.

Mrs. Donald and her attorney, State Senator Michael A. Figures, agreed to participate in the civil suit. Last February, an all-white jury in Mobile needed to deliberate only four hours before awarding her $7 million. In May, the Klan turned over the deed to its only significant asset, the $225,000 national headquarters building in Tuscaloosa. Meanwhile, Mrs. Donald's attorney moved to seize the property and garnish the wages of individual defendants. "The Klan, at this point, is washed up," says Henry Hays, from his cell on death row.

On the strength of evidence presented at the civil trial, the Mobile District Attorney was able to indict Benny Hays and his son-in-law, Frank Cox, for murder; their trial, scheduled to begin in February, will complete Beulah Mae Donald's long and painful campaign to insure that her son's lynching will be the last Alabama will ever see.

When six veterans of the Confederate Army founded the Ku Klux Klan in 1865, their intent was to relieve the boredom of life in a small Tennessee town. After giving themselves titles intended to sound preposterous, the members of this secret society decided to add costumes—and their hooded robes encouraged them to commit acts of violence they would never have dared to undertake without disguise. By 1867, they were beginning to terrorize blacks; Jews and Catholics were to follow.

In the 1920's, at the height of its popularity, the Klan had about 5 million members, more in the North than in the South; in that decade alone, Klansmen lynched as many as 900 blacks. The modern

Klan has, by contrast, only about 5,000 to 7,000 members—and they are split into four groups, with no national leader. Michael Donald's murder, the first Klan killing in Alabama in years, was more an expression of impotent rage than it was testimony to a resurgence of the white-sheeted Klan.

In the 1970's, if the Mobile Klansmen were known for anything, it was for the business cards they printed up and handed out to the elderly ladies they helped across downtown streets. But there were still reasons they might believe they could kill a black in Mobile and go free.

Although about one-third of Mobile's population is black, not a single one was elected to Mobile's top governing body from 1911 to 1985. In the mid-1970's, when a police squad was formed to prevent robberies, minority leaders charged that its real purpose was to harass blacks. In 1977, their belief gained credibility when members of this squad took an innocent black man into custody and encouraged him to confess to a burglary by putting a rope around his neck, tossing it over a tree and pulling him onto his tiptoes. The squad was disbanded, but race relations didn't improve significantly.

Beulah Mae Donald, who was born in 1919, grew up isolated from most of this. She left school in the 10th grade to have a child; by 1962, when Michael was born, she says she was so exhausted that she had to spend a year in the hospital. She'd always worked—"I had a sorry husband," she says—and when her marriage ended soon after Michael's birth, she moved her brood into a Mobile housing project and began to raise them alone. "I wasn't able to get everything for them," she recalls, "but I let them know the value of things." Her method was love and religion. On Sunday, she would take her family to church in the morning and remain there all day. "I'm a strong believer," she explains. "I don't know about man, but I know what God can do."

As Mrs. Donald recounted her story on a sweltering summer afternoon, one grandchild rested on her couch. Another came in from the dusty yard to ask for a cold drink. "You have water, now, you hear," Mrs. Donald told him. "You can't go on drinking all my juice like you do." She loved this boy, she explained to her visitor, but she was having trouble teaching him that the family's resources are limited—she has not yet received any money form the Klan, and supports herself on $400 a month from Social Security and what little she makes working with retarded children. "He complained that he's going back to school without any new clothes," she said. "I told him, 'Well, you may not *get* any.'"

Michael never looked to his mother to provide for him, Mrs. Donald said. From early childhood, "If he came home and I was lying down, he'd know something was wrong, and he'd do little things to help—that's the kind of boy he was." Michael worked hard at trade school, gave his mother most of the money he made and played basketball on a community team. Smoking, she said, was his only vice. "I told him not to smoke," she recalled. "He'd say, 'I'm going to college. Can't I have a cigarette?'"

Considering the kind of boy he was, Mrs. Donald knew that Michael had done nothing to provoke his murder; from the beginning, she suspected that the Klan was involved. So did Winston J. Orr, the veteran Mobile policeman who was, from 1981 to 1984, Chief of Police. But Orr was working against a number of factors that made a thorough investigation unlikely. In the early 1980's, Mobile had one of the highest per capita murder rates in America—and no homicide squad. To make matters worse, Orr's detectives ignored the fact that on the night of the murder, Klansmen had burned a cross on the Mobile County Courthouse lawn. Instead, they speculated that Michael Donald might have been having an affair with a white co-worker at The Mobile Press Register, where he'd had a part-time job. Or, they thought, he might have been involved in a drug deal that went sour.

Mrs. Donald was so eager to help the police that she allowed them to search Michael's room for drugs. They tore the room apart—and found none. In June 1981, when their investigation fizzled and the three initial suspects were released, one of Beulah Mae Donald's daughters and some friends picketed the courthouse. In August, Michael Figures, her attorney, organized a protest march. The Rev. Jesse Jackson came to Mobile to lead it. "Don't let them break your spirit," he told the 8,000 marchers. But that summer, as Mrs. Donald prayed for the Lord to take her away, she had only one consolation. At least, she told herself, Michael hadn't suffered the fate of so many murdered black men—his body hadn't been thrown in the river.

What Mrs. Donald needed was an advocate within the system. Fortunately, Thomas H. Figures—her attorney's brother—had in 1978 become the Assistant United States Attorney in Mobile, and he is, by any measure, a formidable advocate. After earning an M.B.A. at Indiana University and a law degree at the University of Illinois, he had moved to New York in 1971 to become a corporate counsel at Exxon. In 1973, "before the money got so good I couldn't leave," he resigned, returned to Mobile, and joined the District Attorney's office. As Assistant United States Attorney, he had watched the first F.B.I. investigation of the Michael Donald murder with growing dismay. His highest priority became getting the Justice Department to authorize a second F.B.I. investigation.

Figures's request arrived in Washington just as the Justice Department was thinking of closing the case. "As an act of appeasement to me—or to convince me that a second investigation would come to the same conclusion—I was allowed to work with a second F.B.I. agent, James Bodman," Figures recalls. "I'll never forget the first thing Bodman said. He asked me, 'Why the hell do you want to reopen this can of worms?' But then he got interested in it, and we worked on it every day. We had lunch together, we talked at night—people started calling us 'the odd couple.'" In a sense, they were; both are from the deep South, but Figures is black, and Bodman is white.

After hearing a lot of lies and following many unproductive leads, Figures and Bodman uncovered one key fact: On the night of the murder, Tiger Knowles had returned to Bennie Hays's house with blood on his shirt. With this new evidence, the Justice Department convened an investigative grand jury in Mobile. Incredibly, the Klansmen called to testify did not bring lawyers with them. In short order, one witness told the grand jury that young Henry Hays had admitted everything to him. This got back to Tiger Knowles, who began to worry that Henry Hays would confess—and, by trading testimony against Knowles for a reduced sentence, leave him bearing the greater burden of guilt.

In June of 1983, Knowles confessed to F.B.I. agent Bodman. After pleading guilty to violating Michael Donald's civil rights, he was placed in the Federal witness protection program—a fairly standard accommodation for Klan informers—and sentenced to life in prison. In December, when Henry Hays was tried for capital murder, Knowles appeared as a prosecution witness. Largely on the strength of his testimony, a jury of 11 whites and one black found Hays guilty and sentenced him, too, to life in prison.

That didn't seem sufficient punishment to Judge Braxton Kittrell Jr., who rejected the sentence in February 1984 and directed that Henry Hays be electrocuted. In 1986, the Alabama Court of Criminal Appeals set aside the death sentence. Later that year, however, the Alabama Supreme Court upheld Judge Kittrell's decision. "We cannot imagine," the justices wrote, "a case in which the death penalty is more justified."

Henry Hays has a surprising ally in his struggle not to die in the electric chair. "You can't give life, so why take it?" asks Beulah Mae Donald. "You kill an innocent person, that person stays with you day and night."

Morris Dees, who engineered the civil suit for Mrs. Donald, understands her reliance on the Lord. Born in Alabama in 1936, he was raised in the Baptist heartland. Like his schoolmates, he wanted to be a farmer; unlike them, he was also a born salesman, who used his blond hair, blue eyes and effervescent personality to make a fortune.

Dees's business career began at the University of Alabama when his mother sent him a birthday cake. That inspired Dees to send postcards to his schoolmates' parents. asking if they'd like his 'Bama Cake Service to deliver birthday cakes to their sons and daughters. "We got 25 percent response," Dees says. "You couldn't do that in the real world." After graduation from the University of Alabama law school, Dees formed a direct-mail publishing company that eventually shipped 5 million cookbooks a year. He sold his company in 1970, then turned his attention to politics.

"I got interested in George McGovern strictly because of his views on Vietnam," Dees says. He and a colleague wrote a seven-page letter for the candidate. "Everybody laughed at it, said it was too long. McGovern said he couldn't send it out. I said O.K., but I mailed 350,000 copies anyway. In direct mail, a good response is a 1 to 2 percent return; our letter pulled 17 percent, with an average contribution of $25."

In the 1972 Presidential campaign, Dees's letters garnered an unheard-of $24 million. Dees asked only for permission to use McGovern's mailing list to approach potential contributors to his Southern Poverty Law Center. The Center became active in death row cases and defended the rights of poor workers, white and black, who were felt to be victims of discrimination.

In 1979, Dees and Bill Stanton, the center's research director, took on their first case involving the Klan. They became interested in the possibility of finishing off the Klan through civil litigation, and, to help law enforcement officials, they founded Klanwatch, an investigative unit that tracks Klan activities and publishes a newsletter. Klansmen noticed; the S.P.L.C. became the Klan's favorite opponent.

In 1983, Klansmen torched S.P.L.C. headquarters in Montgomery; in 1984, when Denver talk-show host Alan Berg was murdered by a far-right fanatic, Dees was No. 2 on the killer's hit list. In that same year, Louis Beam, a leader of a paramilitary Klan, challenged Dees by registered mail to a duel. "Your mother," he wrote, in part, "why I can just see her now, her heart just bursting with pride as you, for the first time in your life, exhibit the qualities of a man." Then Beam "visited" the S.P.L.C. in an apparent effort to intimidate Dees.

From its new headquarters, dubbed the Southern Affluence Law Center because of its stylish glass-and-steel architecture, the S.P.L.C. undertook its most massive anti-Klan project in 1984— using Mrs. Donald's civil suit to dismantle Robert Shelton's branch of the Klan.

Shelton's men had been involved in the beating of Freedom Riders at the Birmingham bus station in 1961, in the 16th Street Baptist Church bombing in Birmingham in 1963 and in the shooting of Viola Liuzzo near Selma in 1965. The challenge for Dees, Stanton and S.P.L.C. investigator Joe Roy was to locate former Klansmen who would testify that they were acting under orders when they participated in those beatings and killings—and, if possible, convince Klansmen involved in more recent racial incidents to come forward.

In the 18 months it took to prepare the case, Beulah Mae Donald says, Morris Dees didn't neglect her. "We didn't meet until the trial, but Morris and I would talk on the phone. He'd say, 'You still ready to go through with this?' And he did everything possible—he sent $35, $50 every few weeks. He helped when we needed it."

Although Mrs. Donald hadn't attended the 1983 trial, she decided to push herself and go to the civil trial. "If they could stand to kill Michael," she reasoned, "I can stand to see their faces." But she couldn't look at Tiger Knowles, the first witness, as he gave the jurors an unemotional account of the events leading up to the murder. And she cried silently when Knowles stepped off the witness stand to demonstrate how he helped kill her son.

Mrs. Donald was more composed when former Klansmen testified what they had been directed by Klan leaders to harass, intimidate and kill blacks. She had no difficulty enduring defense witnesses—the six Mobile Klansmen and the lawyer for the United Klans of America cross examined Dees's witnesses, but called none of their own. Just four days after the trial had started, it was time for the closing arguments.

At the lunch break on that day, Tiger Knowles called Morris Dees to his cell. He wanted, he said, to speak in court. "Whatever you do, don't play lawyer," Dees advised him. "Just get up and say what you feel."

When court resumed, the judge nodded to Knowles. "I've got just a few things to say," Knowles began, as he stood in front of the jury box. "I know that people's tried to discredit my testimony. . . . I've lost my family. I've got people after me now. Everything I said is true. . . . I was acting as a Klansman when I done this. And I hope that people learn from my mistake. . . . I do hope you decide a judgment against me and everyone else involved."

Then Knowles turned to Beulah Mae Donald, and, as they locked eyes for the first time, begged for her forgiveness. "I can't bring your son back," he said, sobbing and shaking. "God knows if I could trade places with him, I would. I can't. Whatever it takes—I have nothing. But I will have to do it. And if it takes me the rest of my life to pay it, any comfort it may bring, I hope it will." By this time, jurors were openly weeping. The judge wiped away a tear.

"I do forgive you," Mrs. Donald said. "From the day I found out who you all was, I asked God to take care of y'all, and He has."

Four hours later, the jury announced its $7 million award.

A few months after the verdict, Mrs. Donald was still recovering form the courtroom drama. She had been inundated by so many congratulatory letters—"The mail lady was mad"—that she had Morris Dees take them away. When visitors she didn't know came to see her, she told them they were at the wrong house. The medication she was taking for her tired legs wasn't helping—until she absolutely had to be up and about, she was determined to rest.

Soon, she said, the Klan building will be sold. The Klan's money will make her too prosperous to remain in this housing project. Then she will have to leave her $94-a-month apartment, with its cinderblock walls, steep steps and sad memories. Even now, she says, her daughters are looking for a new apartment, convenient to her church and most of her 32 grandchildren.

In her new home, her family hopes, she'll find some peace. Mrs. Donald, now 68, doesn't have much expectation of that. "When the trial was over, the jurors came down and told me, as people do, that they felt for me," she says. "But the verdict didn't make me feel better. What happened to Michael—I live it day and night. I was just surprised that a white jury could do this."

For all her sorrow, Beulah Mae Donald emphasized that she won't succumb to bitterness. "What is a dream to me is that money comes out of this," she says, contemplating the irony of human loss and monetary gain. "I don't need it. I live day to day, like always. But there's some sad people in the world who don't have food to eat or a decent place to stay. I've been there. I know what it means to have nothing. If the Klan don't give me a penny, that's O.K. But if they do, I'm going to help a lot of people who don't have none."

Jesse Kornbluth is a contributing editor of Vanity Fair and a screenwriter.

It is better to be a coward for a minute than dead for the rest of your life.
Irish proverb

Rediscovering Malcolm X (1990)

Vern E. Smith, Regina Elam, Andrew Murr and Lynda Wright

He strode across the stage, tall and strong, with the bearing, as a friend would say later, of a shining black prince. It was a Sunday in Harlem and the faithful had gathered. He wore his conservative dark suit, the sort favored by accountants and be-bop men, and saluted the crowd with a greeting born of hope. *"As-salaam alei-kum,"* "Peace be unto you." And the crowd answered *"Wa-alei-kum salaam,"* "And unto you be peace." It was not to be. There was a disturbance in the rear of the Audubon Ballroom. His guards started toward it. A smoke bomb went off. Three gunmen came forward and, with a sawed-off shotgun and pistols, they killed Malcolm X.

It will be 25 years this week since the assassination. But in black America his message is enjoying a prominence he never knew as a preaching prophet. His life is the subject of rap songs, films and a stream of books and dissertations. Set against a backdrop of inner cities ravaged by crack, crime and AIDS, and a larger society that has grown impatient or indifferent to the cause of African-Americans, Malcolm's maxims on self-respect, self-reliance and economic empowerment seem acutely prescient.

He has also become the public icon of the street brother trying to "get over." And a quiet hero to those in the black bourgeoisie who every so often allow themselves to wonder why they have to keep fighting the power. "There's something in Malcolm which touches the core of younger people," says Howard Dodson of the Schomburg Center for Research in Black Culture. "He was willing to stand up, to talk straight. Malcolm was a man—a real man."

Actually, he was many men. A son of a preacher turned teenage burglar. A prisoner, then a member of the Nation of Islam, popularly known as Black Muslims. A black separatist in Manhattan, ultimately a mainstream Muslim embraced by Arabs in Mecca. "Malcolm lived five or six lifetimes all in one," says his brother Wilfred Little, now 70. "Each one was as if another person had been born and lived another life." For white America, or at least that segment not assigned his autobiography in college, his image froze in the early '60s as the threatening, street-corner speaker so different from the wholesome civil-rights workers. "We're nonviolent with people who are nonviolent with us," he declared in 1964. "But we are not nonviolent with anyone who is violent with us."

Integration was not part of his agenda. He argued that black Americans needed human rights, not civil rights. "By this he meant a new social contract between people and the state that presumed that full employment was a human right, that no one should go hungry," says Manning Marable, a University of Colorado professor who is writing a study of Malcolm's political life.

Malcolm never stopped evolving. He departed from the Chicago-based Black Muslim movement after their leader, the autocratic Elijah Muhammad, suspended him for callously remarking after John F. Kennedy's assassination that "the chickens coming home to roost never did make me sad." But Muhammad also feared Malcolm's independence and his increasingly public criticism. On his own, Malcolm continued to preach. "The black man should control the politics of his own community, and the politicians who are in his own community," he argued, as well as the economic resources that meant jobs within that community.

A pilgrimage: In 1964 Malcolm made a pilgrimage to Mecca and became an orthodox Muslim. When he returned, says researcher Paul Lee, "he removed a blanket indictment against white folks.

His basic line was, 'To judge a man because he's white gives him no out. He can't stop being white. That's just like judging us because we're black.' When he said that, one of the brothers jumped up and tried to grab him." Sara Mitchell-Brown, now a Macon, Ga., schoolteacher, served as the coordinating secretary of Malcolm's Organization of Afro-American Unity. She recalls his efforts to assimilate all his conflicting experiences as a difficult process. "His attempt to establish a sincerely aggressive image minus the menacing quality promoted in the media was a burdensome task for him," she says. It was cut short by three gunmen acting on the Black Muslims' desire to be rid of a meddlesome priest.

It is, of course, just an accident of Muslim practice, but having abandoned his "slave" surname, Malcolm could be popularly referred to only by his given name. This became, as memory blurred into history, an assumption of familiarity, and an invitation to intimacy that is now being accepted. In the black community, he is a growing presence. Mainstream record and bookstores have begun to cash in, cutting into the street market in Malcolm memorabilia that has long flourished in urban neighborhoods. "When it gets warm the most important artifact you can sell is a T shirt or something with Malcolm's picture on it," says Cornell University professor James Turner, the national chairman of the Malcolm X Commemoration Commission.

On the radio, Malcolm can be heard in a sound bite from a speech that opens "Self-Destruction," a rap single recorded by The Stop the Violence Movement, a consortium of black rap artists. On television he can be seen in music videos produced by other rappers, some of whom have dedicated albums to him. The most famous artistic use of Malcolm's words came in "Do The Right Thing," Spike Lee's searing film about life in the black ghetto. Lee's coda consists of two quotes. One from Martin Luther King Jr. preaches the doctrine of nonviolence. The other, from Malcolm X, uses his slogan, "by any means necessary." That juxtaposition embodies one of the debates in black America. What is the continuing relevance of King's message? It may be morally impeccable, but is that sufficient any longer? The times and conditions have obviously changed, even as the themes of both have been converted into needlepoint samplers. That doesn't make for good contemporary debate, but it does allow Malcolm's voice to be clearly heard.

No walls: "Our generation said, 'Just topple the walls of segregation'," says Turner of Cornell. "The walls are down but the barriers to social justice are still there. Young people are asking, 'Who are we, in this time?' Malcolm speaks to that." He does, but as Turner and the others remind us, his message was complex. "He's getting attention, but I still think he's misunderstood," Malcolm's eldest daughter, Attallah Shabazz, recently told the Los Angeles Times. "[Young people are] inspired by pieces of him instead of the entire man… They think 'by any means necessary' means with a gun, as opposed to with a book or getting an 'A' in school."

In some respects, his life is more telling than his words. "One of the attractions to many young black people is that Malcolm began as a social deviant," says Marable of Colorado. "Yet he radically transformed himself—through his own initiative. His life is the process of the worst becoming the best." Consider, too, his image as a strong black man, which is so compelling to youngsters. Powerful and manly, he stayed married to one woman and was devoted to her and his daughters.

Malcolm understood that African Americans had white enemies, and black ones also. He had no tolerance for self-hatred, however petty, including his own; his autobiography includes a wrenching description of straightening his hair with lye. A gifted minister, he wasn't trying to save souls; he wanted to free minds. As the writer Peter Goldman argued in his book, "*The Death and Life of Malcolm X*," "What interested Malcolm first was the decolonization of the black mind—the wakening of a proud, bold impolite new consciousness of color and everything color means in white America." Near the end of his life he also encouraged black Americans to think globally. "He really felt that we didn't have a chance just struggling internally," says Paul Lee. "He didn't want to emphasize our minority status because black people already hated themselves enough."

Malcolm X is dead. On anniversaries like these, it is tempting to play the old parlor game: what if he had lived? How might he have confronted the crack epidemic or street crime that mainly takes its toll on blacks? We can't know for sure, but presumably he would have done more than ponder the passage of time.

Trust in Allah, but tie your camel.
Arabian proverb

The Negro Question (1950)

Albert Einstein

I am writing as one who has lived among you in America only a little more than ten years. And I am writing seriously and warningly. Many readers may ask: "What right has he to speak out about things which concern us alone, and which no newcomer should touch? I do not think such a standpoint is justified. One who has grown up in an environment takes much for granted. On the other hand, one who has come to this country as a mature person may have a keen eye for everything peculiar and characteristic. I believe he should speak out freely on what he sees and feels, for by so doing he may perhaps prove himself useful.

What soon makes the new arrival devoted to this country is the democratic trait among the people. I am not thinking here so much of the democratic political constitution of this country, however highly it must be praised. I am thinking of the relationship between individual people and of the attitude they maintain toward one another.

In the United states everyone feels assured of his worth as an individual. No one humbles himself before another person or class. Even the great difference in wealth, the superior power of a few, cannot undermine this healthy self-confidence and natural respect for the dignity of one's fellow-man.

There is, however, a somber point in the social outlook of Americans. Their sense of equality and human dignity is mainly limited to men of white skins. Even among these there are prejudices of which I as a Jew am clearly conscious; but [132] they are unimportant in comparison with the attitude of the "Whites" toward their fellow-citizens of darker complexion, particularly toward Negroes. The more I feel an American, the more this situation pains me. I can escape the feeling of complicity in it only by speaking out.

Many a sincere person will answer me: "Our attitude towards Negroes is the result of unfavorable experiences which we have had by living side by side with Negroes in this country. They are not our equals in intelligence, sense of responsibility, reliability."

I am firmly convinced that whoever believes this suffers from a fatal misconception. Your ancestors dragged these black people from their homes by force; and in the white man's quest for wealth and an easy life they have been ruthlessly suppressed and exploited, degraded into slavery. The modern prejudice against Negroes is the result of the desire to maintain this unworthy condition.

The ancient Greeks also had slaves. They were not Negroes but white men who had been taken captive in war. There could be no talk of racial differences. And yet Aristotle, one of the great Greek philosophers, declared slaves inferior beings who were justly subdued and deprived of their liberty. It is clear that he was enmeshed in a traditional prejudice from which, despite his extraordinary intellect, he could not free himself.

A large part of our attitude toward things is conditioned by opinions and emotions which we unconsciously absorb as children from our environment. In other words, it is tradition—besides inherited aptitudes and qualities—which makes us what we are. We but rarely reflect how relatively small as compared with the powerful influence of tradition is the influence of our conscious thought upon our conduct and convictions.

It would be foolish to despise tradition. But with our growing self-consciousness and increasing intelligence we must [133] begin to control tradition and assume a critical attitude toward it, if human relations are ever to change for the better. We must try to recognize what in our accepted tradition is damaging to our fate and dignity—and shape our lives accordingly.

I believe that whoever tries to think things through honestly will soon recognize how unworthy and even fatal is the traditional bias against Negroes.

What, however, can the man of good will do to combat this deeply rooted prejudice? He must have the courage to set an example by word and deed, and must watch lest his children become influenced by this racial bias.

I do not believe there is a way in which this deeply entrenched evil can be quickly healed. But until this goal is reached there is no greater satisfaction for a just and well-meaning person than the knowledge that he has devoted his best energies to the service of the good cause. [134]

Albert Einstein (1879-1955), the world-famous theoretical physicist, is best known as the formulator of the theory of relativity. He was born in Germany but lived in the United states from 1933 until his death. Among his books ar The Meaning of Relativity *and* The World As I See It.

One man's folly is another man's wife.
Helen Rowland

Complexion (1991)

Richard Rodriguez

Complexion. My first conscious experience of sexual excitement concerns my complexion. One summer weekend, when I was around seven years old, I was at a public swimming pool with the whole family. I remember sitting on the damp pavement next to the pool and seeing my mother, in the spectators' bleachers, holding my younger sister on her lap. My mother, I noticed, was watching my father as he stood on a diving board, waving to her. I watched her wave back. Then saw her radiant, bashful, astonishing smile. In that second I sensed that my mother and father had a relationship I knew nothing about. A nervous excitement encircled my stomach as I saw my mother's eyes follow my father's figure curving into the water. A second or two later, he emerged. I heard him call out. Smiling, his voice sounded, buoyant, calling me to swim to him. But turning to see him, I caught my mother's eye. I heard her shout over to me. In Spanish she called through the crowd: 'Put a towel on over your shoulders.' In public, she didn't want to say why. I knew.

That incident anticipates the shame and sexual inferiority I was to feel in later years because of my dark complexion. I was to grow up an ugly child. Or one who thought himself ugly. (*Feo.*) One night when I was eleven or twelve years old, I locked myself in the bathroom and carefully regarded my reflection in the mirror over the sink. Without any pleasure I studied my skin. I turned on the faucet. (In my mind I heard the swirling voices of aunts, and even my mother's voice, whispering, whispering incessantly about lemon juice solutions and dark, *feo* children.) With a bar of soap, I fashioned a thick ball of lather. I began soaping my arms. I took my father's straight razor out of the medicine cabinet. Slowly, with steady deliberateness, I put the blade against my flesh, pressed it as close as I could without cutting, and moved it up and down across my skin to see if I could get out, somehow lessen, the dark. All I succeeded in doing, however, was in shaving my arms bare of their hair. For as I noted with disappointment, the dark would not come out. It remained. Trapped. Deep in the cells of my skin.

Throughout adolescence, I felt myself mysteriously marked. Nothing else about my appearance would concern me so much as the fact that my complexion was dark. My mother would say how sorry she was that there was not money enough to get braces to straighten my teeth. But I never bothered about my teeth. In three-way mirrors at department stores, I'd see my profile dramatically defined by a long nose, but it was really only the color of my skin that caught my attention.

I wasn't afraid that I would become a menial laborer because of my skin. Nor did my complexion make me feel especially vulnerable to racial abuse. (I didn't really consider my dark skin to be a racial characteristic. I would have been only too happy to look as Mexican as my light-skinned older brother.) Simply, I judged myself ugly. And, since the women in my family had been the ones who discussed it in such worried tones, I felt my dark skin made me unattractive to women.

Thirteen years old. Fourteen. In a grammar school art class, when the assignment was to draw a self-portrait, I tried and tried but could not bring myself to shade in the face on the paper to anything like my actual tone. With disgust then I would come face to face with myself in mirrors. With disappointment I located myself in class photographs—my dark face undefined by the camera which had clearly described the white faces of classmates. Or I'd see my dark wrist against my long-sleeved white shirt.

I grew divorced from my body. Insecure, overweight, listless. On hot summer days when my rubber-soled shoes soaked up the heat from the sidewalk, I kept my head down. Or walked in the shade. My mother didn't need anymore to tell me to watch out for the sun. I denied myself a sensational life. The normal, extraordinary, animal excitement of feeling my body alive—riding shirtless on a bicycle in the warm wind created by furious self-propelled motion—the sensations that first had excited in me a sense of my maleness, I denied. I was too ashamed of my body. I wanted to forget that I had a body because I had a brown body. I was grateful that none of my classmates ever mentioned the fact.

I continued to see the *braceros,* those men I resembled in one way and in another way, didn't resemble at all. On the watery horizon of a Valley afternoon, I'd see them. And though I feared looking like them, it was with silent envy that I regarded them still. I envied them their physical lives, their freedom to violate the taboo of the sun. Closer to home I would notice the shirtless construction workers, the roofers, the sweating men tarring the street in front of the house. And I'd see the Mexican gardeners. I was unwilling to admit the attraction of their lives. I tried to deny it by looking away. But what was denied became strongly desired.

In high school physical education classes, I withdrew, in the regular company of five or six classmates, to a distant corner of a football field where we smoked and talked. Our company was composed of bodies too short or too tall, all graceless and all—except mine—pale. Our conversation was usually witty. (In fact we were intelligent.) If we referred to the athletic contests around us, it was with sarcasm. With savage scorn I'd refer to the 'animals' playing football or baseball. It would have been important for me to have joined them. Or for me to have taken off my shirt, to have let the sun burn dark on my skin, and to have run barefoot on the warm wet grass. It would have been very important. Too important. It would have been too telling a gesture—to admit the desire for sensation, the body, my body.

Fifteen, sixteen. I was a teenager shy in the presence of girls. Never dated. Barely could talk to a girl without stammering. In high school I went to several dances, but I never managed to ask a girl to dance. So I stopped going. I cannot remember high school years now with the parade of typical images: bright drive-ins or gliding blue shadows of a Junior Prom. At home most weekend nights, I would pass evenings reading. Like those hidden, precocious adolescents who have no real-life sexual experiences, I read a great deal of romantic fiction. 'You won't find it in your books,' my brother would playfully taunt me as he prepared to go to a party by freezing the crest of the wave in his hair with sticky pomade. Through my reading, however, I developed a fabulous and sophisticated sexual imagination. At seventeen, I may not have known how to engage a girl in small talk, but I had read *Lady Chatterley's Lover.*

It annoyed me to hear my father's teasing: that I would never know what 'real work' is; that my hands were so soft. I think I knew it was his way of admitting pleasure and pride in my academic success. But I didn't smile. My mother said she was glad her children were getting their educations and would not be pushed around like *los pobres.* I heard the remark ironically as a reminder of my separation form *los braceros.* At such times I suspected that education was making me effeminate. The odd thing, however, was that I did not judge my classmates so harshly. Nor did I consider my male teachers in high school effeminate. It was only myself I judged against some shadowy, mythical Mexican laborer—dark like me, yet very different.

Language was crucial. I knew that I had violated the ideal of the macho by becoming such a dedicated student of language and literature. *Machismo* was a word never exactly defined by the persons who used it. (It was best described in the 'proper' behavior of men.) Women at home, nevertheless, would repeat the old Mexican dictum that a man should be *feo, fuerte, y formal.* The three *F's,*' my mother called them, smiling slyly. *Feo* I took to mean not literally ugly so much as ruggedly handsome. (When my mother and her sisters spent a loud, laughing afternoon determining ideal male good looks, they finally settled on the actor Gilbert Roland, who was neither too pretty nor ugly but had looks 'like a man.') *Fuerte,* 'strong,' seemed to mean not physical strength as much as inner strength, character. A dependable man is *fuerte. Fuerte* for that reason was a characteristic subsumed by the last of the three qualities, and the one I most often considered—*formal.* To be *formal* is to be steady. A man of responsibility, a good provider. Someone *formal* is also constant, a person to be relied upon in adversity. A sober man, a man of high seriousness.

I learned a great deal about being *formal* just by listening to the way my father and other male relatives of his generation spoke. A man was not silent necessarily. Nor was he limited in the tones he could sound. For example, he could tell a long, involved, humorous story and laugh at his own humor with high-pitched giggling. But a man was not talkative the way a woman could be. It was permitted a woman to be gossipy and chatty. (When one heard many voices in a room, it was usually women who were talking.) Men spoke much less rapidly. And often men spoke in monologues. (When one voice sounded in a crowded room, it was most often a man's voice one heard.) More important than any of this was the fact that a man never verbally revealed his emotions. Men did not speak about their unease in moments of crisis or danger. It was the woman who worried aloud when her husband got laid off from work. At times of illness or death in the family, a man was usually quiet, even silent. Women spoke up to voice prayers. In distress, women always sounded quick ejaculations to God or the Virgin; women prayed in clearly audible voices at a wake held in a funeral parlor. And on the subject of love, a woman was verbally expansive. She spoke of her yearning and delight. A married man, if he spoke publicly about love, usually did so with playful, mischievous irony. Younger, unmarried men more often were quiet. (The *macho* is a silent suitor. *Formal.*)

At home I was quiet, so perhaps I seemed *formal* to my relations and other Spanish-speaking visitors to the house. But outside the house—my God!—I talked. Particularly in class or alone with my teachers, I chattered. (Talking seemed to make teachers think I was bright.) I often was proud of my way with words. Though, on other occasions, for example, when I would hear my mother busily speaking to women, it would occur to me that my attachment to words made me like her. Her son. Not *formal* like my father. At such times I even suspected that my nostalgia for sound—the noisy, intimate Spanish sounds of my past—was nothing more that effeminate yearning.

High school English teachers encouraged me to describe very personal feelings in words. Poems and short stories I wrote, expressing sorrow and loneliness, were awarded high grades. In my bedroom were books by poets and novelists—books that I loved—in which male writers published feelings the men in my family never revealed or acknowledged in words. And it seemed to me that there was something unmanly about my attachment to literature. Even today, when so much about the myth of the *macho* no longer concerns me, I cannot altogether evade such notions. Writing these pages, admitting my embarrassment or my guilt, admitting my sexual anxieties and my physical insecurity, I have not been able to forget that I am not being *formal.*

So be it.

1982

POLISH

POPULATION: *Too many already*	**PHYSICAL CHARACTERISTICS:** *Unpronounceable names* *Play polkas and mazurkas*
RELIGION: *Bowling*	**RACIAL TRAITS (GOOD):**
PRACTICING: *All the leagues*	**RACIAL TRAITS (BAD):** *Become football brutes*
LOCATION: *Buffalo, New York*	**DIET STAPLE:** *Anything*

CHAPTER 9

STEREOTYPES

Teaching the Mudheads How to Copulate (1984)
Pueblo

The Mudheads are not very bright. Long ago they didn't know many things, even very simple, everyday actions. So a man tried to instruct them.

He tried to teach them how to go up a ladder. He showed them how to do it, and they tried to copy him, but they couldn't. One tried to go up the ladder with his feet upmost, standing on his head. Another tried to climb the back of the ladder. A third kept falling through the rungs, while a fourth got all tangled in the rungs. They just couldn't do it.

Then the man tried to teach them how to build a house. He showed them the right way to do it, and they tried to imitate his actions. But one started with the roof and made the others hold up the ceiling while he tried to build downward from it. Another put together a house with no doors and windows. He built it from the inside, and when he wanted to go out, he found he had walled himself in. The others had to break down the walls to let him out. Still another made the mud bricks out of sand. When it rained, his house collapsed into a sandpile. Try as they would, the Mudheads just couldn't do it right.

Then the man tried to show them a really simple thing—how to sit on a chair. They watched and tried to do as he did. One sat on top of the chair back and tumbled over. Another sat underneath the chair. Another sat on the chair with his back to the front. A fourth tried to sit upside down with his head where his rump ought to have been. They just couldn't get the point.

"Well," said their instructor, "I'll try one thing more. I'm going to show you how to copulate." There was a fat old woman who hadn't had a man in her for a long time. "They can all practice on me," she said, "I don't mind." So she lifted up her manta and bent over, and the instructor copulated with her in the simplest way—from the back as dogs do. The Mudheads watched closely, and then they all wanted to try. But none of them could find the right opening. One did it in the anus, another in the knee bend, another in the arm bend, another in the armpit, another in the navel, another in the ear. They tried and tried. They really wanted to do it right, but they couldn't. "I give up on you," said the instructor. The fat old woman just laughed.

Told in several versions during a sacred clown dance and pantomime at Zuni Pueblo, 1964, and recorded by Richard Erdoes.

Love teaches even asses to dance.
French proverb

The Things They Say behind Your Back
William Helmreich

All about stereotypes

"Everyone knows that most Italians either belong to the Mafia or have a relative who does. And of course they're great shoemakers and tailors, though they tend to gamble too much."

"Do you know that the first present the new Pope got was a pair of slippers with gold initials inside them that said T.G.I.F. Now you know what that stands for. Right?"

"Sure. It stands for Thank God It's Friday. We say it every week at the office."

"Wrong. It means Toes Go In First. You know how those Polacks are."

"The problem with this country is that the Jews control everything. They run the TV stations, movies, newspapers, and whatever else they can get their grubby hands on. Worst of all, they're cheap and sneaky."

"The Blacks think they got everything coming to them. They can't think ahead more than one day. They never come on time when you make an appointment with them. All they wanna do is drink, shoot up, and play the numbers."

"Now you take the Japanese. There's a people that are hardworking, smart, and ambitious. But remember—you can never turn your back on them, even for a minute. They're really sly and treacherous. And don't ever talk politics with them. They're so chauvinistic it's ridiculous, even though, you know, they just imitate everything we do."

The well-known journalist and writer Walter Lippmann called "these pictures in our heads" stereotypes. Basically, a stereotype is an exaggerated belief, oversimplification, or uncritical judgement about a category. The category may be a neighborhood, a city, a newspaper, members of a profession, believers in a religion, or even a highway (e.g., "The Long Island Expressway is *always* packed.") Although stereotypes are most often exaggerations or distortions of reality, they are often accepted by people as fact. When they concern a highway, they do little damage, but when they are used to indict an entire group of people, great harm can be done.

Naturally, not all stereotypes about different nationalities are negative. Some, in fact, are quite complimentary. "The Italians are very family oriented," "the French are great lovers," and "the Chinese are so courteous," are examples of stereotypes that reflect well on various peoples. Nevertheless, they are equally exaggerated generalizations and a person who accepts such statements as factual can easily believe less positive views.

Groups are sometimes responsible for creating, or at least abetting, their own stereotypes. This is especially true when the stereotype is a positive one. Thus, an after-dinner speaker at an Irish affair may begin his speech by saying something like, "As we know, the Irish have always been regarded as good politicians." The Jewish American Princess (JAP) is another case in point. While not a very positive statement about the Jewish people, it has been given a tremendous boost in popularity by the Jews themselves, particularly Jewish comedians, who have found it makes great copy.

When people employ stereotypes they are usually making judgements about a given individual's potential to fit into a certain category based upon that person's racial or ethnic origins. In other words, they say that a Pole is more likely to be stupid because he is Polish, an Italian more apt to talk with his hands because he is Italian, and so forth. Some people even believe such traits to be true of all members of a given group. What needs to be determined is when a statement about a member of a certain group has little basis in fact and when it has a good deal of basis in fact. In short, to what extent is a stereotype based on reality?

Why do we often stereotype people, even when deep down we "know better than that"? A great deal has been written about this question, with almost as many answers given as there are types of people. Among the most common explanations is that it is simply a very efficient way of coping with our environment, an environment so complex that we have to break it down into categories before we can understand it. It would clearly be impossible for us to function if everything that happened were dealt with on an individual basis. Without stereotypes everything would be treated as if it were taking place for the first time. Thus, stereotypes are convenient though often inaccurate. Frequently they eliminate the need to learn about people for those who simply do not, either because of fear or sheer laziness, wish to make the effort.

Another cause of stereotypes may be the cultural background of the individual. Most cultures encourage prejudiced attitudes toward other groups. These attitudes are ingrained in people beginning with early childhood, and are therefore very difficult to overcome. In general, the longer one has such attitudes, the harder it is to change them. In one study done on this question, a group of whites were shown a photograph of a white person holding a razor blade while arguing with a Black person in a New York City subway. They were shown the photo for a split second and then asked to write down what they saw on a slip of paper. More than half of the respondents said that they saw a *Black* man holding a razor blade against the throat of a *white* man. Culture is such a strong factor that persons who do not themselves agree with particular stereotypes will remain silent simply because they "want to be like everybody else."

Quite often people are unable to accept the blame for their own shortcomings, and when this happens they search for convenient targets upon whom they can vent their frustrations. Some of the more typical victims are friends, parents, and others who are "safe" because they won't reject you for such outbursts, providing that it doesn't happen too often. In many cases, however, people select minority group members as scapegoats because they are powerless, relatively speaking, and/or easily identifiable. Thus General Brown talked about "the Jewish lobby," as did Billy Carter, and former Governor George Wallace talked about "Nigras and pointyheads."

Professors Bruno Bettelheim and Morris Janowitz have argued that stereotypes are often caused by a complex process known as projection. When people accuse others of motives or characteristics they sense in themselves but can't admit to openly, it is called projection. Noted psychologist Gordon Allport, in his famous work *The Nature of Prejudice,* notes that in Europe, where there is no large Black population, the Jew is the one accused of unbridled sexual lust, violence, and filth. Americans, having peoples such as Blacks, Puerto Ricans, and Chicanos to personify these traits, find it unnecessary to use Jews for this purpose. As a result, Americans can attribute other, more specialized, traits to Jews, such as defensiveness, aggressiveness, and shrewdness.

Stereotypes also allow us to justify our behavior toward a group that we already dislike or are mistreating. In other words, they enable us to rationalize our actions. An example would be General Westmoreland's comment during the Vietnam War. When asked to justify the napalming of innocent villagers, he replied, "These Asians don't value life the way we do." Further evidence for the use of stereotypes to rationalize behavior comes from the fact that people often assign contradictory stereotypes to members of a group. The writer Harry Golden once said, "The Jew is probably the only person who can be called a communist and a capitalist—by the same person—and at the same time."

The media also play a role in stereotypes, though it is more a case of reinforcing rather than creating stereotypes. Certain TV shows portray the Irish, Jews, Blacks, and other groups in a stereotyped manner. The same is true of films, plays, and magazines. Still, the media mainly reflect our pre-existing attitudes as opposed to inventing them.

Do stereotypes actually cause prejudice? Not necessarily. More often they justify prejudice, but in doing so they reinforce prejudice. It is difficult to separate one from the other. If one has a stereotyped view of a nationality, it can result in prejudice toward that group, and if one is prejudiced one can either create or find stereotypes justifying one's attitudes. Whatever the case, since stereotypes often guide our behavior, an understanding of them is extremely important.

Knowing the causes of stereotypes is indeed helpful—and there are many books on the subject—but it does not tell us *how particular stereotypes developed*. Growing up in a certain culture may result in a person having negative views toward, say, Italians, but it does not tell us how that culture *acquired* these views in the first place. Understanding that people pick on certain groups when they need a scapegoat does not tell us why *particular* groups are chosen as scapegoats and not others. Why the Jews and not the Danes? Why the Poles and not the Bulgarians? To answer this question, we need to know much more.

Many stereotypes change over time because they are often a function of political, economic, and social developments. For example, American views of the Chinese and Japanese have been linked by researchers to U.S. relations with China and Japan at different times in history. When such relations were good, the stereotypes in this country tended to be positive; when they deteriorated, the stereotypes focused on the negative characteristics.

How have particular groups come to be identified with particular characteristics? Puerto Ricans are not thought of as grasping in a business sense, but Jews are. Blacks are sometimes categorized as lazy and shiftless, but the Chinese are not. We have the fighting Irish, the stupid Poles, the clannish Italians, the cold and insensitive WASPs. Where did these ideas originate?

A major thesis of this book is that, contrary to what many people may think, a large number of stereotypes possess more than a kernel of truth. There is, as we shall demonstrate, some basis for saying that Jews are aggressive, Blacks musically gifted, the Irish heavy drinkers, and Orientals inscrutable. True, the *majority* of stereotypes do not fall into this category, but it is important to know which do, which do not, and why.

Another important thesis advanced here is that all racial and ethnic stereotypes stem, in some measure, either from the historical experiences and culture of the group or from the historical experiences and culture of the nations that had contact with the group. In cases where the stereotypes are negative but contain some truth, we will try to understand them and not deny their existence. Though certain unpleasant truths may emerge from such an analysis, the long-range effect will be to increase our understanding of why people do the things they do and how the group to which they belong helps shape their attitudes and values.

Stereotypes are often vicious and can be exceedingly dangerous. We have only to recall what happened to Jews in Europe because of the blood libels leveled against them by Christians, as well as the fate of Black men accused of lusting after white women. If this is so, then why bother to write about stereotypes, especially when many have some validity? Does such information simply become ammunition for the Archie Bunkers of America?

The answer to this last question is yes—if it is done in a flip, insensitive, and unscientific manner. Programs such as "All in the Family" can legitimate prejudice largely because they are only seen as family entertainment. Thus the message that is transmitted becomes, "It's okay to put down Poles, Hispanics, and Blacks, and anyone who objects is either oversensitive or a spoilsport." That is neither the intent nor approach of this book. While readers will hopefully find the material entertaining, the main goal is to inform and enlighten. By examining the various stereotypes logically, point by point, a clearer picture should emerge about the different groups that make up American society and why they are viewed in certain ways by others. A careful examination of this problem will, in this writer's view, reduce rather than increase prejudice.

There are some jokes in this book. They are there not to ridicule the members of the groups under discussion but to show how popular the stereotypes themselves are. It should in no way be assumed that telling such jokes will either increase or decrease prejudice. The evidence on this question is, as of now, inconclusive. Some groups have far more negative stereotypes than others. The reader glancing through the Contents will find, for example, that almost all of the stereotypes attributed to Blacks, namely, lazy and shiftless, violent, stupid, and so forth, are negative. This does not mean that any of them are true or that Blacks possess no positive traits. Black people have made enormous contributions throughout history and have innumerable positive characteristics. But it is not the purpose of this book to detail them. Rather, the focus is on how *others* perceive (read: Stereotype) Blacks. That Afro-Americans are seen so negatively by white America is , more than anything else, a reflection of the depths of racism in this country, and it is this reality that a book like the present one attempts to evaluate.

The groups selected for discussion in this book were chosen either because of their size or because they are among the most maligned in American society. The stereotypes themselves are based both on general impressions and scientific studies that show how different groups are perceived by Americans. Some of the stereotypes exist in the country from which the people came, while others do not. The focus here is on how Americans see them.

It should be understood that what is being presented here is really a *overview* of some of the most commonly held stereotypes. Hundreds of pages could probably be devoted to each of the stereotypes, but that is not our goal here. The first group to be considered is one of the oldest and most often stereotyped peoples in the world—the Jews.

They talk of my drinking, but never my thirst.
Scottish proverb

The Myth of the Matriarch (1990)
Gloria Naylor

The strong black woman. All my life I've seen her. In books she is Faulkner's impervious Dilsey, using her huge dark arms to hold together the crumbling spirits and household of the Compsons. In the movies she is the quintessential Mammy, chasing after Scarlett O'Hara with forgotten sunbonnets and shrill tongue-lashings about etiquette. On television she is Sapphire of *Amos 'n' Andy* or a dozen variations of her—henpecking black men, herding white children, protecting her brood from the onslaughts of the world. She is the supreme matriarch—alone, self-sufficient and liking it that way. I've seen how this female image has permeated the American consciousness to the point of influencing everything from the selling of pancakes to the structuring of welfare benefits. But the strangest thing is that when I walked around my neighborhood or went into the homes of family and friends, this matriarch was nowhere to be found.

I know the statistics: They say that when my grandmother was born at the turn of the century as few as 10 percent of black households were headed by females; when I was born at mid-century it had crept to 17 percent; and now it is almost 60 percent. No longer a widow or a divorcée as in times past, the single woman with children today probably has never married—and increasingly she is getting younger. By the time she is 18, one out of every four black unmarried women has become a mother.

But it is a long leap from a matrifocal home, where the father is absent, to a matriarchal one, in which the females take total charge from the males. Though I have known black women heading households in different parts of the country and in different social circumstances—poor, working class or professional—none of them has gloried in the conditions that left them with the emotional and financial responsibility for their families. Often they had to take domestic work because of the flexible hours or stay in menial factory or office jobs because of the steady pay. And leaving the job was only to go home to the other job of raising children alone. These women understood the importance of input from black men in sustaining their families. Their advice and, sometimes, financial assistance were sought and accepted. But if such were not forthcoming, she would continue to deal with her situation alone.

This is a far cry form the heartwarming image of the two-fisted black woman I watched striding across the public imagination. A myth always arises to serve a need. And so it must be asked, what is it in the relationship of black women to American society that has called for them to be seen as independent Amazons?

The black woman was brought to America for the same reason as the black man—to provide slave labor. But she had what seemed to be contradictory roles: She did the woman's work of bearing children and keeping house while doing a man's work at the side of the black male in the fields. She worked regardless of the advanced stages of pregnancy. In the 19th century the ideal of the true woman was one of piety, purity, domesticity and submissiveness; the female lived as a wife sheltered at home or went abroad as a virgin doing good works. But if the prevailing belief was that the natural state of women was one of frailty, how could the black female be explained? Out in the fields laboring with their muscled bodies and during rest periods suckling infants at their breasts, the slave women had to be seen as different from white women. They were stronger creatures: they didn't feel pain in childbirth; they didn't have tear ducts. Ironically, one of the arguments for enslaving blacks in the first place was that as a race they were inferior to whites—but black women, well, they were all a little *more* than women.

The need to view slavery as benign accounted for the larger-than-life mammy of the plantation legends. As a house servant, she was always pictured in close proximity to her white masters because there was nothing about her what was threatening to white ideas about black women. Her unstinting devotion assuaged any worries that slaves were discontented or harbored any potential for revolt. Her very dark skin belied any suspicions of past interracial liaisons, while her obesity and advanced age removed any sexual threat. Earth mother, nursemaid and cook, the mammy existed without a history or a future.

In reality, slave women in the house or the field were part of a kinship network and with their men tried to hold together their own precarious families. Marriages between slaves were not legally recognized, but this did not stop them from entering into living arrangements and acting as husbands and wives. After emancipation a deluge of black couples registered their unions under the law, and ex-slaves were known to travel hundred of miles in search of lost partners and children.

No longer bound, but hardly equal citizens, black men and women had access to only the most menial jobs in society, the largest number being reserved solely for female domestics. Richard Wright wrote a terribly funny and satirical short story about the situation, "Man of all Work." His protagonist is unable to find a job to support his family and save his house from foreclosure, so he puts on his wife's clothes and secures a position as a housekeeper. "Don't stop me. I've found a solution to our problem. I'm an army-trained cook. I can clean a house as good as anybody. Get my point? I put on your dress. I looked in the mirror. I can pass. I want that job."

Pushed to the economic forefront of her home, the 19th century mammy became 20th century Sapphire. Fiery, younger, more aggressive, she just couldn't wait to take the lead away from the man of the house. Whatever he did was never enough. Not that he wanted to do anything, of course, except hang out on street corners, gamble and run around with women. From vaudeville of the 1880s to the advent of *Amos 'n' Andy,* it was easier to make black men the brunt of jokes than to address the inequities that kept decent employment from those who wanted to work. Society had not failed black women—their men had.

The truth is that throughout our history black women could depend upon their men even when they were unemployed or underemployed. But in the impoverished inner cities today we are seeing the rise of the *unemployable.* These young men are not equipped to take responsibility for themselves, much less the children they are creating. And with the increasing youth of unwed mothers, we have grandmothers and grandfathers in their early thirties. How can a grandmother give her daughter's family the traditional wisdom and support when she herself has barely lived? And on the other side of town, where the professional black woman is heading a household, usually because she is divorced, the lack of a traditional kinship network—the core community of parents, uncles, aunts—makes her especially alone.

What is surprising to me is that the myth of the matriarch lives on—even among black women. I've talked to so many who believe that they are supposed to be superhuman and bear up under all things. When they don't, they all too readily look for the fault within themselves. Somehow they failed their history. But it is a grave mistake for black women to believe that they have a natural ability to be stronger than other women. Fifty-percent of black homes being headed by females is not natural. A 40 percent pregnancy rate among our young girls is not natural. It is heartbreaking. The myth of the matriarch robs a woman caught in such circumstances of her individuality and her humanity. She should feel that she has the *right* at least to break down—once the kids are put to bed—and do something so simple as cry.

Gloria Naylor won the American Book Award in 1983 for her first novel, The Women of Brewster Place. *Her new novel is* Mama Day.

Bed is the poor man's opera.
Italian proverb

... And the Maligning of the Male (1990)

Ishmael Reed

Being a black man in America is like being a spectator at your own lynching. Everybody gets to make a speech about you but you: white supremacists, feminists, conservatives, liberals, sociologists, psychologists, demographers—all manner of experts, editorial writers and columnists, many of whom seem to live in cozy places like Georgetown or Palo Alto.

Every time you try to tell your story, you're interrupted or called paranoid. As a black male writer, sometimes you have to be strident to get your point across, to get somebody to pay attention. You feel like the man yelling fire in a crowded theater. You just can't seem to get the gag off, so you engage in what to society is muffled incoherency.

If people only knew the truth, they wouldn't prejudge you, you think. If they only know the statistics that puncture the lies that are circulating about black men, they wouldn't get you mixed up with the one percent with whom the media are so thrilled—the bums and deadbeats. Every time you see footage of a drug bust on TV you see black males. Yet the Drug Enforcement Administration has said that a number of ethnic groups, including Orientals and Israelis, are involved in drug trafficking. The news shows don't show the Chinese gangs that now supply 40 percent of the heroin in New York.

As with the persecuted Jews in Germany, somebody is always trying to pin the Star of David on your clothes, but in this country it's very convenient. You wear the Star of David on your skin. Your style disturbs people—Bernard Goetz says he shot the black teenagers on the subway because he was threatened by their body language. Even the white avant-garde shares this view. Norman Mailer's "white negro" in his infamous essay of that title is an irresponsible psychopath who lives constantly on the edge.

When Susan Brownmiller, in her money-making book on rape, *Against Our Will,* wrote that to foster his manhood the black man contributes to the "specter of the black man as a rapist," she was indulging in group libel. You know that the majority of convicted rapists in the U.S. are white males. At the university where you work, the student newspaper for several years carried stories about black rapists, but then, thanks to the feminist movement, it was revealed that the most frequent type of rape occurring on campus was date rape—white fraternity guys who were refusing to take no for an answer.

You don't live in a true pogrom, but if you are caught in a neighborhood where you don't belong, you might be placed under surveillance or you might be killed. You've read a number of accounts of professional black men who've been taken for muggers. The Reverend Floyd Flake, a black congressman whose district includes Howard Beach in New York City, went into a store there and had a hard time convincing some whites that not only wasn't he a threat to them, he was actually their federal representative.

In *The Washington Post* columnist Richard Cohen said that shopkeepers were perfectly justified in denying all young black men entrance to their stores on the basis of the actions of a few. So, when a local merchant complained about the behavior of a particular black customer, you told him that the next time all the black people in the world had a meeting, that black man's conduct would be the first item on the agenda.

Despite this daily slander, most black men hold down jobs, however menial, and many have proved their loyalty to their country. During the first years of the Vietnam war black men were 13 percent of the grunts but took a quarter of the casualties. In today's Vietnam movies you don't see these men or, if you do, they're dope-smoking buffoons.

On a television talk show in San Francisco you spoke of some of the emotional land mines that a black man has to traverse each day. You cannot really communicate what it feels like to look into your rearview mirror and see a cop pull in behind you. It's the little hurts that build up. After the show, black men came up on the street and shook your hand. They stopped their cars on the freeway and yelled over to you. You had hit a nerve.

These are the cartoon images presented of black men: the criminal, the athlete, the clown, the entertainer, the good nigger, the brute. (Harold Ross, the first editor of *The New Yorker*, seemed to sum it up for the media when he said, "Coons are either funny or dangerous.") These images create tension, literally. Black men suffer from high blood pressure, they get strokes and cancer more often than whites. If you don't have a sense of humor, you become a scowling time bomb, striking out at people who are dear to you. James Baldwin told of how his father punished his family for the humiliations he received each day at work in the white world. A lot of black men, hating themselves, turn their aggression on one another in the streets.

As a novelist and essayist, you believe that black kids should be exposed, not only to you and your writing, but to black scientists, inventors, engineers, architects generals. How many children know that 5,000 black men fought in the Revolutionary War, those immortalized in Robert Lowell's beautiful poem "For the Union Dead"?

How can the United States become a truly great society if it continues to cling, like Linus to his blanket, to the racist idea that black men somehow are at the root of all social problems? You proposed on a magazine article that white men and black men should meet in a national conference to discuss their differences and common interests, but nobody took you up on the suggestion. It's almost as if they don't want the situation to change. You think that Jimmy the Greek shouldn't have been fired by CBS for what he said about the breeding of black athletes. He should have been made to take a year's course in ethnic studies at some university instead. Better still, there could be a College for Racists, maybe along the lines of the "reeducation" camps North Vietnam set up for the defeated generals of the South.

For all of the wounds, for all of your humiliation, it could be worse. You could be a white man. You feel sorry for the good, decent and fair white men in this society. While you might be associated with creepy crack merchants, small-time hustlers and gold-chain thieves, nobody is associating you with perpetrators of genocide, or with the people who created slavery and invented the Bomb. Crowds in world capitals aren't shaking their fists at you and calling you the great Satan, nor are they hanging you in effigy. When you suffer a setback in life, you can always claim that it's because of racism, and most of the time you will probably be right. What's a white man's excuse for failure? You used to joke that, with all of the opportunities that white men have in this society, any one of them who ended up less than President of the United States should be considered a flop.

You don't have that kind of pressure. You hear every day on the news that the public will never elect a black President. Nobody expects you to be a white savior, a James Bond, an Indiana Jones or

Superman. Imagine how that kind of pressure feels. Women and all the minorities in this country, not just the blacks, seem to have the same grievances about white males, lumping the good ones in with the bad with such epithets as "power structure." You wonder how white men are able to withstand it. Maybe that's why they're the group with the highest suicide rate. And so as a black man you are beleaguered, but at least you're not Atlas, carrying the world on your shoulders.

Ishmael Reed's last novel was Reckless Eyeballing *(1986). A collection of his essays,* Writin' Is Fightin', *will be published in July by Atheneum.*

A License Plate Debate:
Italian Slurs or Pride? (1990)

San Francisco Journal

Like many of the proud sons and daughters of Palermo, Naples and Genoa, Dominic Troncale is not shy about advertising his ethnic heritage. He wears a shirt that says "Full-Blooded Italian."

He also tools around in a brown Oldsmobile with a license plate that reads "A DAGO 2." And therein lies the heart of a bitter debate that has pitted Italian-American against Italian-American and that has led to scores of hearings around the state to determine which individual license plates are acceptable and which are offensive.

The 68-year-old Mr. Troncale, of Covina, says it is his right to call himself anything he wants on his license plate, adding that "it will be a cold day" before he voluntarily gives up his plate, a gift form his wife a dozen years ago.

His license plate, however, offends the Sons of Italy, a 85-year-old group with 14,000 members in California and 85,000 nationwide. The Sons of Italy Grand Lodge of California, based in San Francisco, has prodded the California Department of Motor Vehicles to recall all personalized license plates with some combination of the words "dago" or "wop," terms that sting most Italian-Americans.

In 1989 the Virginia Department of Motor Vehicles revoked one plate because of a complaint from the Sons of Italy. But in California, which registers twice as many cars and trucks as any other state, the current recall is California's first of an entire series of license plates and involves hundreds of drivers.

Last month the department gave 33 drivers three options: A refund, a free change of the license plate lettering or a hearing before an administrative law judge. The refunds for the "vanity" plates come to about $35 if it is a first-year plate, or $20 if it is a renewal plate.

Many of the owners turned in their plates or changed them, but 162 others, including Mr. Troncale, opted for the hearing, in the hope that the decision might go their way and they could keep their plates. Since mid-September, hearings have been held all over the state, and a first ruling is expected soon.

"I have not seen any of these people who are the least bit reluctant to share their views," said Judge Stephen Smith, with the Office of Administrative Hearings in Sacramento, who has conducted most of the hearings so far.

The plate owners say the emblems are, at the least, harmless and, at best, a badge of ethnic pride.

"We're living in the 90s now, not the 20s," said Ted Muscolo, a 43-year-old mortgage banker from Glendora. The license plate on his white 1990 Corvette reads "4TOP-WOP."

"Not just friends and family but clients know me by it," said Mr. Muscolo. "It's worked in my favor."

Richard Armento, president of the social justice committee of the Sons of Italy Grand Lodge of California, has another view. It would be fine with him, Mr. Armento said, if people wanted to put such words anywhere, even spray paint their house with them. But allowing them on license plates, he said, is wrong because "it looks like the state of California condones that."

Mr. Troncale, waiting anxiously for a November hearing in Los Angeles, said the issue is not his license plate. Instead, he said, it is his right to call himself whatever he wants.

"My dad used to belong to the Sons of Italy a long, long time ago," he continued. "In those days they WERE the sons of Italy and they banded together for security in a strange country. When the immigrants came here all had dirty names. That's just the way life was and beer was a nickel."

But for Philip Piccigallo, national executive director of the Sons of Italy, the consensus of the experts who compile dictionaries and define the words at issue as terms of contempt is enough reason to try to remove the license plates.

"While we recognize people's rights to freely express themselves," Mr. Piccigallo said, "it does not mean they have the right to harm the cumulative reputation of an entire group of people."

I didn't know he was dead; I thought he was British.
Unknown

The Burden of History (1989)

Jewell Handy Gresham and Margaret B. Wilkerson

Our children are being destroyed, and we are in grave danger. And everybody knows it.
Everybody.   Toni Morrison

Three times in the history of this Republic, a momentous event occurred which provided an opportunity for a national course of action to redress the injustices suffered by the descendants of African peoples in this land.

The first was the Revolutionary War, which resulted in the making of the Constitution; the second, the Civil War, was followed by the shaping of Reconstruction; and the third was the mid-twentieth-century civil rights movement, which made possible a second reconstruction to redress the failures of the first.

Each time the challenge was not met.

On the failure of the first, historian Leon Litwack observed in his 1987 presidential address to the Organization of American Historians on "The Bicentennial and the Afro-American Experience":

> It had been the genius of the Founding Fathers to sanction, protect, and reinforce the enslavement of black men and women in the same document that promised to "establish justice, insure domestic tranquillity...promote the general welfare, and secure the blessings of liberty" to Americans. It had been the genius of the founders to build safeguards for slavery in the Constitution without even mentioning slavery by name. The legitimization of slavery was the price of the new federal union.

Sixty-five years after the Civil War, writing on Reconstruction in the 1930s, W.E.B. Du Bois conducted a massive examination of the historical literature on slavery and the post-Civil War era. He came away "literally aghast" at what white scholars had done, not only to an entire people but to the integrity of the subject matter and disciplines of study. It was, he wrote, "one of the most stupendous efforts the world ever saw to discredit human beings, an effort involving universities, history, science, social life and religion."

Were Du Bois alive today, only two decades after the black revolution of the 1950s and 1960s, he would be equally aghast. To his list of those seeking to discredit African-Americans he would add politicians at all levels of government, academic and journalistic opinions molders, heavily corporate-endowed think tanks and an assortment of others. Litwack observes:

> The significance of race in the American past can scarcely be exaggerated. Those who seek to diminish its critical role invariably dismiss too much of history—the depth, the persistence, the pervasiveness, the centrality of race in American society, the countless ways in which racism has embedded itself in the culture, how it adapts to changes in laws and public attitudes, assuming different guises as the occasion demands.

The distinguished women who are contributors to this issue were asked to write from their own individual experiences on a particular topic related to the latest era of relentless trashing of black men, women and children as scapegoats for the national ills, amounting to a psychic assault no people should be asked to endure.

This issue makes no attempt to be comprehensive relative to all of the myths concocted about the black experience or of the present wretched conditions of masses of black Americans. On the latter, much is annually addressed by such organizations as the Urban League on the state of Black America, the Children's Defense Fund and the National Black Child Development Institute on the plight of children (and comprehensive remedial programs) and numerous others. The areas of deep concern to African-Americans, in any case, are far too many and too complicated for any small group of writers to venture to address the whole without the accompanying voices of men and women from across the spectrum of the black community.

Among the topics being addressed, two of critical importance relating to black health and crime (apart from drugs) are not being discussed independently. Regarding black health, the grim statistics extending from birth to an often too-early grave are readily available elsewhere. Their implications are genocidal. The 1988 release of a report by the National Center for Health Statistics showing a decline of the life span of American blacks for the second year in a row is a case in point. No other industrial nation in the world shows a decline in the life expectancy of a segment of its population for two consecutive years!

Crime in America involves economic, political, social, mystical and simultaneously fearful and titillating phenomena, and African-Americans are most often victims before they are perpetrators. It is therefore impossible for many black Americans to look upon the crisis of crime in America as it affects black people and the society at large without exploring the basic question: Who are the real criminals?

We believe that the desperate plight of the masses of black infants, children and youth in America represents a crime against humanity, and it is this intolerable set of circumstances in all its dimensions that we ask the nation to address NOW.

This issue therefore ends with a "Challenge to the Nation for the Year 2000." To pose it, we chose artist/activist Ossie Davis, known and beloved by many across the country for his dedicated artistry as a stage and screen actor, writer and television host, and for his commitment to positive social change that has long led him to play a central role in the affairs of black people and the nation.

In a special issue to which black women are the contributors, what could be more fitting than the choice of an African-American father beloved by innumerable numbers of people to deliver a challenge to society on behalf of our children. Happily, the value system of the man and the people made it unnecessary to request that he make his appeal as well on behalf of all members of the human race.

Does TV Shape Ethnic Images?

S. Robert Lichter and Linda S. Lichter

The landscape from *Amos 'n' Andy* to *The Cosby Show* is littered with ethnic shows and characters who have entertained audiences and troubled anti-defamation groups. A long line of Italian mafiosi, black servants and Hispanic banditos, to name a few stereotypes, have attracted condemnation from community organizations. Yet surprisingly little is known about how audiences react to such characters. Much of the concern is directed at young people. Do they see ethnic characters as either positive or negative role models, as real people or mere figments of fantasy?

To find out, we asked over 1,200 students at a public high school in the Howard Beach area of Queens in New York City about their attitudes towards race and ethnicity in real life and on television. The school was chosen because it contained a multi-ethnic population, with large numbers

---

Television Teachings:
Strange New World Lurks Behind the Tube

Is television a learning tool and an accurate reflection of the real world?
Here are some examples of the major findings in the Lichters' study:

1. **Many students see television entertainment as realistic.**
   - 40 percent of those surveyed say they learn a lot from TV.
   - 25 percent say TV shows what life is really like.
   - 24 percent say people on TV are like real life.

2. **Blacks, more than any other group, use TV to learn about life.**
   - 51 percent say they learn a lot from TV.
   - 30 percent say the same things happen in TV and real life.
   - 23 percent identify often with ethnic TV characters.

3. **Television influences the positive images of ethnic groups in real life.**
   - 26 percent say TV influences their racial and ethnic attitudes.
   - The more students like TV characters, the more they regard them as typical of their ethnic group.

4. **Ratings of television characters cut across racial lines.**
   - Television's black characters received the most favorable ratings, even among non-black students.
   - Italian characters are rated as most typical of their real-life ethnic group by both Italian and non-Italian students.
   - All ethnic characters received favorable ratings.
   - Jewish students respond most positively to ethnic characters across the board.

Source: *Television and Ethnic Images Among Howard Beach Youth*

of black, Hispanic, and Italian-American students, and smaller groups of Irish and Asian descent. Two months after the survey was completed during the fall of 1986, this obscure Queens school suddenly became the focus of unwanted national attention when several of its students were charged with murder following a racial attack. Suddenly, the study was also about race relations in Howard Beach.

The results provide some reassurance that the attack did not necessarily reflect widespread racial antagonism. Most members of the racial and ethnic groups surveyed say they are willing to invite those from their ethnic groups into their homes. Negative stereotypes are the exception rather than the rule, although about one in three students holds negative images of blacks and Italian Americans. But negative images of other groups as "lazy," "stupid," "violent," etc., are often balanced by those who held positive images of the same groups as "friendly," "kind," "honest," and the like.

Any expression of negative stereotyping or ethnic prejudice is grounds for concern and condemnation, but it was a relief to find that such attitudes were not pervasive.

Creating Reality

Even so, there was enough mutual suspicion and intolerance to lend urgency to the question of television's role in forming or reinforcing ethnic attitudes. Television is a major part of these students' lives, accounting for a substantial portion of their leisure time. Two out of five watch television over four hours a day, and one in six watches at least six hours daily.

More importantly, many regard television as a learning tool and an accurate reflection of the real world. Forty percent say they learn a lot from TV, and one in four agrees that "TV shows what life is really like," and "people on TV are like real life."

Interestingly, the different ethnic groups tended to watch television for somewhat different reasons. Black students were the heaviest TV watchers and were also the group most likely to use television as a learning tool. Of these students, over half said they learn a lot from TV and one-third said it teaches them things they don't learn in school. In light of these findings, it is perhaps not surprising that blacks were also the group most likely to see television as a reflection of real life.

At the other end of the spectrum, Jewish students were least likely to see this correspondence between TV and the real world. The findings suggest that young people in different ethnic groups vary in their susceptibility to the various appeals of TV entertainment and the use to which they put information they gain from watching television. Yet, these ethnic variations do not change the fact that, overall, a surprising number of teenagers see the fantasy factory as a mirror of reality.

Role Models

For many, this linkage between real life and TV's version of life is relevant to their perceptions of race and ethnicity. About one-third of those with an opinion say that the ethnic characters they see on television affect their attitudes toward ethnic groups in real life. If many young people admit that their ethnic perspectives flow partly from television, then their opinions of TV characters take on a special importance. We asked them to rate a list of twenty ethnic characters ranging from *Cosby*'s Cliff Huxtable to George Jefferson, from *Hill Street*'s heroic Frank Farillo to *Taxi*'s tiny tyrant Louis DePalma, and from the Jewish Lieutenant Samuels of *Cagney and Lacey* to the Asian Detective Yemana of *Barney Miller*. The ratings were based on two scales: how favorably the students regarded the various characters and how "typical" they considered them to be of their respective ethnic groups.

The result? The students view virtually all these characters not only in positive terms but as typical members of their ethnic group. This was true whether or not the students themselves were members of the character's ethnic group. There was a general tendency to rate characters from one's own group favorably, but responses to the characters themselves often seemed to override any loyalties to ethnic groups.

Again, however, ethnic variations did exist within these general trends. Black students not only responded very favorably to ethnic characters in general, they were also most likely to regard these characters as typical of real-life groups. By contrast, Jewish students were least likely to see these characters as reflecting reality, even though they responded to them most positively. Generally, each group of students rated as most typical characters of their own ethnic background, suggesting that television may affect ethnic self-perception more than images of other groups. So the good news is that young people have positive feelings about TV's ethnic characters, and these associations may carry over into their images of real life groups. The bad news is that their positive identifications extend to less than exemplary characters. Black and Italian-American parents might be startled at the thought of George Jefferson or Louis DePalma as role models for their children. Even more startling is the notion that these characters are widely accepted as "typical" of blacks and Italians respectively.

Yet the study suggests that the continuing appearance of an ethnic character, whether positive or negative, may legitimize him or her as an individual worthy of admiration, if not emulation. The results also show, however, that the more positive or favorable the response to a TV character, the more likely that the student sees the character as typical of his or her ethnic group. Thus, TV may influence ethnic stereotyping mainly *by encouraging viewers to identify the positive traits of television characters with the ethnic groups they represent.*

Portrayal Power

Television's power to legitimize character and behavior may exceed the intentions of its creators. This is reminiscent of some troubling findings that emerged from studies of *All in the Family*. When Norman Lear made Archie Bunker a lovable bigot, he took care to portray Archie's biases as reprehensible. The idea was to get viewers to laugh at his bigotry, to attack intolerance with ridicule. But surveys showed that intolerant viewers *identified* with Archie and allowed his sentiments to reinforce their own.

TV's tendency to create its own consensus seems to justify the often-expressed concern of America's racial and ethnic groups about the way they are portrayed in television entertainment. There is ample cause for concern. While research show that television holds no magical power to change firmly held beliefs, it can add powerful reenforcement to attitudes already held. For example, one study demonstrated that prejudiced viewers see Archie Bunker as an admirable character. It is only those with more tolerant attitudes who realize that Archie is actually the focus of humorous disapproval. This role of television as a reinforcer and crystallizer of existing attitudes is significant even if few people actually form their opinions of cultures or races based on what they see on TV. If the audience views certain ethnic and racial groups in a negative manner and television portrayals confirm those images, then TV entertainment may be reassuring those people that their images of certain ethnic and racial groups as foolish, lower class, inarticulate, or criminal are correct.

Many have also expressed concern that negative stereotypes may particularly affect the members of those groups portrayed by giving them a negative self-image. The absence or low status of their television counterparts may encourage them to limit their own aspirations. Surveys also show that many people actually admit to using TV to guide them in their own social and personal situations. This dependence on television as an educational tool for living is particularly strong for those with little education.

Television exercises its greatest power over those who do not hold strong opinions or who have no opinion or information about a particular topic or group of people. Here television may be playing a vital informational role. In dealing with a variety of socially relevant topics such as racial and ethnic relations, TV not only entertains, it conveys values and messages that people may absorb unintentionally. This is particularly the case with young people.

S. Robert and Linda S. Lichter are co-directors of the Center for Media and Public Affairs in Washington, D.C. Dr. Robert Lichter is DeWitt Wallace fellow at the American Enterprise Institute.

Why Students Watch Television

Most students spend a large portion of their free time in front of the set. But their reasons for finding the time worth spending vary widely.

	Asian	Black	Latino	Jewish	Italian	Irish	All
It brings my family together	18%	23%	20%	10%	14%	13%	18%
I learn a lot from it	35	51	36	24	28	31	40
It shows how others solve problems I have	41	38	36	31	34	27	37
I get to know different people	35	42	33	24	26	27	34
Teaches things I don't learn in school	26	32	26	16	17	11	27
Shows what life is really like	29	28	27	14	19	13	25
I learn how to act	9	12	11	2	7	2	10
It keeps me from being bored	94	86	78	86	88	89	85

Source: From *Television and Ethnic Images Among Howard Beach Youth*

Man's Most Dangerous Myth: The Fallacy of Race

Ashley Montagu

The purpose of this book has been to clarify the reader's thinking upon the much-vexed and usually tendentiously discussed problem of "race," to induce the reader to rethink his basic convictions regarding human relations, and to present the whole problem in such a way as to encourage him to draw his own conclusions concerning the kind of solution or solutions that would be most effective in solving the "race" problem.

In the preceding chapters we have discussed and considered some of the "causes" of the "race" problem. It would seem evident that the removal of the conditions which give rise to these causes would suggest itself as the most obvious approach to the solution of the problem. If we eliminate these conditions, we shall eliminate the effects which they produce.

We saw that the term "race" itself, as it is generally applied to man, is scientifically without justification, and that as commonly used the term corresponds to nothing in reality. We saw that the word is predominantly an emotionally loaded one, and we were able to trace something of its rise and development in what has invariably been a background or matrix of strong feeling and prejudiced thought. Men may pretend that they are masters of reason when they are in fact creatures of emotion. It was Oliver Goldsmith who wrote:

> Logicians have but ill defin'd
> As rational the human kind;
> Reason, they say, belongs to man,
> But let them prove it if they can.

Reason and intellect play a minor role in the lives of men, and what part they do play is often confused and fragmented. Symonds, in a study on the methods by which teachers solve personal problems[1] found that "very few of the larger problems of life are adjusted to through reason. The intellect is used rarely by persons in meeting the larger problems and issues of life and few individuals are able to use their reasoning powers except in limited situations. The large part of adjustment is carried on through the impulses, emotions," and similar mechanisms.[2]

As Oscar Wilde so wryly remarked: "I wonder who it was defined man as a rational animal. It was the most premature definition ever given. Man is many things but he is not rational." Or as another poet, Walter de la Mare, put it, "*raw homo* that is, with little admixture of *sapiens*."

Sapience here lies in frankly facing the fact that most people are emotional creatures who use their minds mostly in order to support their prejudices. Prejudice is a passion with a logic all its own. It is of little use attempting to correct this logic by demonstrating its falsity, for it is not the logic which is the cause of the prejudice, but the prejudice which is the cause of the false logic. Hence, we would be more effectively employed in trying to understand the sources of this prejudice than in hectoring the insecure logicians. All of us have prejudices of some sort. The important thing is to recognize that we do, and do something about freeing ourselves from them, or if that is not possible, controlling them.

It is said that "The truth shall make ye free." But most men wish neither to know the truth nor to be free.[3] Most men wish to know the kind of things that will support them in the culture of which they are a part. Whatever contributes to that end is "true." That is their pragmatic test of truth. It is all too readily understandable. Men live by the values they learn from their culture. What teachers in the classroom and instructors in the lecture hall may tell them has its importance, but what matters most is what actually goes on in the world. We may preach equality, but if we practice discrimination the hypocritical lesson will not fail to be learned. What is done, *not* what is said, is the reality in which most men believe. A culture lives what it believes; that is, it acts out what it really believes in, it does not live by what it aspires to be. Men will fight to the death for what they believe, but not for the ideals in which they have no faith. These they will combat if they conflict with their own conception of reality. For the support of such conceptions men do not generally require the sanction of scientifically established facts. Emotions, prejudices, and metaphysics are usually quite sufficient. As Stephen Spender has remarked: "Very few people in the world's history have died for the sake of 'being definite,' thinking clearly, and behaving morally without the background of a belief in any metaphysical system. As we hare already seen, "race" is the metaphysical which for most men constitutes such a conception of reality. The child picks up attitudes long before he becomes familiar with the facts. It is difficult to convince a child that there is no such thing as "race," nor can one successfully explain the facts to him, however simply and clearly one may present them, when outside the classroom, on the street, at home, everywhere about him, he sees that "race" is a "real" thing. To make him see that this "real" thing has been arbitrarily created would be a reasonably simple matter in the hands of a good teacher, but whatever he did would be largely undone by the world outside the classroom unless conditions outside the classroom were favorable, which, as we know, they generally are not.

I would not for this reason lightly regard the teaching of the facts about "race" in the schools; on the other hand, I recommend such teaching unequivocally and unreservedly.[4] It should, however, be made clear here that we must not expect too much from such attempts at education in the schools, for the so-called "education" received at school is only a small part of that larger education which men receive from direct contact with the world. It is the world men live in, not the school, and what the world teaches that are to them real. What the school teaches is largely unreal and theoretical. The three *r*'s are in many instances the only concrete things with which it leaves them. The fourth, and most important of the *r*'s is omitted, *relations*, human relations.

This is the sad and tragic state to which we have come. The dissociation between what is taught in the schools and what is taught by real life has become so glaring that the schools and all who are associated with them have fallen into something like contempt, since as measured by the standard of successful achievement in the "real world" they do not measure up at all. "That's all right for a school child" is a common saying, or "That's academic."

Children learn early that "race" prejudice, unlike other antisocial behavior, is socially sanctioned and has the approval of "respectable" people.[5]

It is, or should be, clear, then, that education in the schools is not enough, since what is taught in the schools is not what men believe, and men will not act upon what they do not believe. As the seventeenth-century Portuguese philosopher Francisco Sanchez put it, "ideas taught do not have greater power than they receive from those who are taught." What, then, must we do to persuade men to implement the right ideas with the power of their convictions? To present to them the right ideas is only half the task; we must also provide them with the proper supports for such ideas and eliminate the conditions which render the support of such ideas difficult. If we can remove those conditions and substitute others for them, we shall have made possible a substantial change in the beliefs of men and in many of the notions upon which they customarily act.

Do we know what those conditions are? I think we do, at least a goodly number of them. We have seen that frustration and aggression are linked factors which play an important role in preparing the individual personality for "racial" hostility unless the conditions are such as to favor such a development. These conditions are always artificially constructed in economic, political, and social frameworks wherein "racial" hostility can be used to advantage by the individual or by the group within that framework.

Clearly, any culture or part of a culture which finds it necessary to create and maintain hostilities between different groups of men, instead of encouraging their social development by mutual exchange and cooperation of interests to the advantage of all, is sick. For the great principle of biological as well as of social development is cooperation, not antagonism.

We have already seen that modern science has demonstrated that there is strong reason to believe that cooperation and altruism have played more important roles in the evolution of animal species, but especially of man, than have the egoistic forces in nature. A healthy competition is desirable in any society; but it must be a competition "with" not a competition "against," it must be a competition to cooperate, to cooperate in the interest not alone of the individual or his particular group but in the interest of all society, and not only of society as a whole but of all men everywhere. No man can be free until all his fellow men are free. Race prejudice arises from man's failure to make use of his own potentialities, particularly his powers to relate himself to other beings, to establish human ties. Those who exploit their society for their own interest, whether they are aware of it or not, are working against the interest of their society. They produce imbalances, top-heaviness, disoperative rather than cooperative conditions. Obviously, where self-interest is the dominant motive of the individuals in a society, the society will be characterized by a fundamental spirit of disorganization. In such a society the individual thinks of himself first, of society last. He will so order his conduct as to attain his ends as quickly as possible without any concern for the consequences to society. If Negroes or members of any other ethnic or so-called "minority" group can be utilized, to their disadvantage, in the attainment of those ends, there are pitifully few individuals in our culture who would hesitate not to use them so—the Declaration of Independence, the Bill of Rights, the teaching of the churches, of the schools, and common human decency notwithstanding.

Who is to blame for this sorry condition? Surely not the common man! When he leaves school and enters the workaday world and attempts to behave in a humane manner he soon discovers that he is not likely to prosper. In order to survive he finds it necessary to adapt himself to the conditions of life as he finds them—which he usually does. In doing so he fails both himself and his society, for, let us ask ourselves, to what is it that we adapt ourselves? Without enumerating the unhappy catalogue, we may answer at once: to conditions as we find them. We accept and adapt ourselves to evil as if it were a good, to the principle of expediency rather than that of integrity; to the principle of competition rather than cooperation. Are these responses to the challenges of being human a reflection of a failure of nerve, of courage? I do not think so. On the other hand, I believe that most men accept the world for what it is, believing that it is so ordered by some immutable power and that things are as they are because that is the way they are, and little, if anything, can be done to change them. "You can't change human nature" is the common expression of this viewpoint.

If what I have said is true, them our only hope lies in education of the right sort. If we can succeed in reorganizing our system of education from top to bottom, making our principal purpose the cultivation of human beings, we shall have gone a long way toward achieving a new society.

Our educational systems have not, in fact, been educational systems at all; they are really systems of instruction. We instruct, we do not educate; and otherwise we leave the individual to shift as well he may for himself. We leave our children with information, *not* with knowledge; we teach them to act before we teach them to reflect. Instruction in reading, writing, and arithmetic does not constitute a sufficient preparation for living with complex human beings in a rather complex world. In order to live happily and efficiently in such a world it is necessary to understand not only the nature of human beings but also how they came to be as we now find them, both culturally and physically. Surely our first and last task in education should be to inspire our growing citizens with a full understanding and appreciation of humanity; in what it means to be human.[6] The facts, the spiritual teachings, and the examples are all ready to our hand. What is to prevent us from weaving them into the pattern of the lives which we have in our making? School boards, vested interests, and corrupt politicians are strong forces in our society; but stronger forces than they have been moved in the past and will be moved again. There are no irresistible forces.

It is fatuous to assert that human beings live in the type of society they deserve. The fact is that most human beings have little to do with the making of the society in which they live. They are brought up in it and generally accept it more or less unquestioningly. They may suffer to some extent themselves and be the cause of suffering in others; but they accept this kind of suffering as inevitable—in the nature of things. Their social consciousnesses are structured in terms of their culture.

How, then, under such conditions, can we ever hope to solve the "race" problem? Obviously, by altering those conditions to such an extent as to produce a profound awareness in every person of his proper place in society, to make him aware of the fact that he must become an active, not a passive, instrument in the government of his society and that government can be, and must be, for the benefit of all the people without discrimination of color, class, or creed.

One cannot teach human beings these things merely by uttering them. They can only be made part of an attitude of mind if they are understood at an early age as part of a whole integrated system of education in humanity, in human relations.

The facts of life assume a meaning only when they are related to action in living. The meaning of a word lies in the action it produces. We can teach children to believe in humanity, and we can teach them to act upon what they believe. We can teach them the truth about the present character of our society, and equip them to play their part in improving it, instead of subtly priming them to support the status quo.

To teach children the facts about the meaning of the many varieties of mankind is alone insufficient; as I have said, such teaching can achieve little unless it becomes part of a planned, integrated, complete experience in the meaning and significance of humanity.

There have been few attempts to teach children to become human beings, and yet that is what our schools should principally be doing Our schools must be converted into institutes for the teaching of the art and science of human relations, learning the art of being a human being, and the reasons why it is necessary to be one. "Race" problems are essentially problems in human relations, and "race" problems are but one of the many indications of our failure in human relations. The necessary change can be brought about by the educators of this and other lands. It is the educators of the young who are the true, unacknowledged legislators of the world. The opportunity beckons to them to bring into existence, by their example and by their teaching, a new world of humanity. Surely it is unnecessary for our educators to wait until they are forced into action by the pressure of public opinion. It is educators who produce the trained incapacity for humane living for which the parents have usually well and truly laid the foundations. It is the educators, and the parents, who are capable of changing all this, of making truly humane beings of the wards in their charge. The enterprise must be a joint one, between parents and teachers. But where the parents have failed the teacher should not also fail. Parents of the coming generations must be taught to love their children, to endow them with that sense of inner security which will fortify them against all exterior assaults upon their integrity, and by loving them thus teach them to love all others. But this is where teachers must take the lead. It is this which they must teach those who are to become parents and those who are already parents. We shall have neither peace nor harmony in the world until we have made human beings with peace nor harmony in themselves. It has been estimated that it costs about $150, 000 to a kill a man in modern warfare; we could make an almost perfect human being for considerably less. Would it not be worth trying?

How shall we try? What are the specifications for the blueprint for action? What the educators must do is, I think, obvious: they must become aware of their strategic advantage, and they must, alone or in cooperation, take it upon themselves to reorganize the education of the young along the line I have indicated; to teach humanity first and to regard all other education as subordinate to this. "The best place to think through and practice intelligent human relations is in the classroom. The best laboratory for human engineering is in the school room where democracy has its best opportunity and its greatest challenge."[7]

As for a blueprint for action, each teacher must work that out for himself in adjustment to the local situation which he knows best. Approaches to the solution of the "race" problem must be made at all levels, but ultimately it is the individual teacher upon whom our reliance must be placed. Good teachers are more important than anything they teach. An integrated program in human relations throughout the school system is indispensably necessary, a program to include teachers as well as pupils, but it does not have to start that way. It can commence with a small group of teachers, and failing such a group, with but a single one. Let such a one say to himself: "I am only one; but I am one. I cannot do everything; but I can do something. What I can do I ought to do; and, by the grace of god, *I will.*"

---

[1]Symonds, "How Teachers Solve Personal Problems," *Journal of Educational Research*, Il (1941), 80-93.
[2]Symonds, *The Dynamics of Human Adjustment*, pp. xii-xiii.
[3]Fromm, *Escape from Freedom*; Montagu, "Escape from Freedom," Psychiatry, V (1942), 122-29; Montagu, *Man in Process*; Montagu, *The Humanization of Man*.
[4]It has been shown, for example, that college graduates are, on the whole, better informed about the facts of "race" and more understanding in the matter of ethnic relations than high school graduates; the latter, in turn, rank higher in these respects than grammar school graduates. Here, then, is good evidence of the value of *general* education in producing better intergroup understanding. see Allport, "Is Intergroup Education Possible?" *Harvard Educational Review*, XV (1945), 83-86.
[5]Allen et al., "Social Awareness in a City High School," *Intercultural Educational News*, VIII 1(1946), 1-7; Radke and Trager, "Children's Perceptions of the Social Roles of Negroes and Whites," *Journal of Psychology*, XXIX (1950), 1-33; Trager and Yarrow, *They Learn What They Live*.
[6]See Montagu, *On Being Human*; Montagu, *The Direction of Human Development*; Montagu, *Man in Process*; Montagu, *The Humanization of Men*.
[7]Bishop, "Democracy Demands Co-operative Living," *Education*, LXVIII (1946), 12-18.

What Makes White Right? (1968)

Chuck Stone

Is it the color white sui generis which makes it right?

Or is it the military and political power of the white race that defines rectitude for all peoples—regardless of race, creed, or color?

We live in a society which is structured on a most fundamental and universal premise: if it's white, it's right.

In this conceptual framework, "white" is more than just a color.

It's a civilization, a frame of mind.

When we were kids, we used to chant a sassy ditty:

> If you're white, you're all right.
> If you're yellow, you're mellow.
> If you're brown, you can stick around.
> If you're black, step way back.

We thought this was cute.

But what a bunch of subconscious bigots we were, so full of self-hatred, so full of self-shame.

Without realizing it, we had incorporated into our thinking the two conceptual antipodes which place the color white at one end of the scale of social acceptability and black at the other end, representing rejected untouchableness.

Rather than dare question the political doctrine and intellectual rational of white supremacy, we simply adopted it.

We joined the majority group which had already colored us a "contrast conception."

Few people have expressed this sad truth more ably than Lewis C. Copeland, who wrote a marvelous article back in 1939 called "The Negro as Contrast Conception."

Read these truths:

> Relations between white and black people in the South have given rise to a distinctive conception of the Negro. As a natural outcome of the juxtaposition of two divergent ethnic groups, white people have sharply distinguished themselves from black people. It is not surprising then to find that there has been a marked tendency to conceive of the Negro in terms of contrast. In fact, one may speak of the Negro as a "contrast conception". . . .
>
> The popular conception of Negro character is dramatically portrayed in folk beliefs, fables, anecdotes, jokes, songs, and literature. To sound natural the anecdote must be told in the dialect which whites attribute to Negroes and which is believed to be peculiar to them. In striking contrast to the colored characters, the white characters speak in the most polished and stilted phrases. The things white people laugh at in Negro life are significant, for these are the traits that are considered distinctive.

It always disturbed me that ten per cent of America's population could grow up in a culture insulted and ridiculed nightly by two white men who were regarded as great comedians.

The stigma of "Amos 'n' Andy" gave American culture a blood transfusion of racism it will never completely throw off.

But if you place "Amos 'n' Andy" in the catalogues of history, it is almost of contemporary racist vintage.

America was a johnny-come-lately when it came to polarizing black and white.

For centuries, Europeans had been doing it with notorious success.

A white slave could escape his bondage and be absorbed into society's mainstream. A black slave was always the "heathen."

In order to justify enslaving the colored heathens, however, an ethical rationale had to be discovered.

Gaines De Sepulveda, a brilliant theologian, helped pave the way in 1550 when he debated Las Cases at Valladolid on the right of Spaniards to wage wars of conquest against the Indians.

Argued Sepulveda, it's all right to enslave the Indians "(1) because of the gravity of their sins. . . .; (2) because of the rudeness of their heathen and barbarous natures, which oblige them to serve those of more elevated natures, such as the Spaniards possess; (3) for the spread of the faith."

The Portuguese in Mozambique and Angola readily accept this logic today in their tenacious perpetuation of these two countries as colonies.

However, white supremacy has even deeper historical roots than a debate in 1550. This all-embracing doctrine is timeless, extending back into mores, customs, and almost petty nuances of habit.

So much so that a mere thirty-five per cent of the world's population of 3.1 billion has been able to con the other sixty-five per cent or 2.0 billion colored people that the thirty-five per cent were, in fact, their superiors—and still are.

I've read few things which have spelled out so eloquently the doctrine of "white makes right" than the passage from Herman Melville's classic, *Moby Dick.*

In discussing the neurotic fascination Captain Ahab had for Moby Dick, Melville does a delightful delineation on the white-right syndrome in Chapter Forty-Two, titled "The Whiteness of the Whale."

The historical greatness of what it is to be white is reflected in this passage:

> Aside from these more obvious considerations touching Moby Dick, which could not but occasionally awaken in any man's soul some alarm, there was another thought, or rather vague, nameless horror concerning him, which at times by its intensity completely overpowered all the rest. . . .
>
> It was the whiteness of the whale that above all things appalled me. . . .
>
> Though in many natural objects, whiteness refiningly enhances beauty, as if imparting some special virtue of its own, as in marbles, japonicas, and pearls; and though various nations have in some way recognized a certain royal pre-eminence in this hue given the barbaric, grand old Kings of Pegu placing the title 'Lord of the White Elephants' above the modern kings of Siam unfurling the same snow-white quadruped in the royal standard; and the Hanoverian flag bearing the one figure of a snow-white charger! and the great Austrian Empire, Caesarian, heir to overlording Rome, having for the imperial color the same imperial hue; and though this pre-eminence in it applies to the human race itself, giving the white man ideal mastership over every dusky tribe; and though besides, all this, whiteness has been even made significant of gladness, for among the Romans a white stone marked a joyful day; and though in other mortal sympathies and symbolizings, this same hue is made the emblem of many touching, noble things—the innocence of brides, the benignity of age; though among the Red Men of America the giving of the white belt of wampum was the deepest pledge of honor; though in many climes, whiteness typifies the majesty of Justice in the ermine of the Judge, and contributes to the daily state of kings and queens drawn by milk-white steeds; though even in the higher mysteries of the most august religions it has been made the symbol of the divine spotlessness and power; by the Persian fire worshippers, the white forked flame being held the holiest on the altar; and in the Greek mythologies, Great Jove himself being made incarnate in a snow-white bull; and though to the noble Iroquois, the mid-winter sacrifice of the sacred White Dog was by far the holiest festival of their theology, that spotless, faithful creature being held the purest envoy they could send to the Great Spirit with the annual tidings of their own fidelity; and though directly form the Latin word for white, all Christian priests derive the name of one part of their sacred vesture, the alb or tunic, worn beneath the cassock; and though among the holy pomps of the Romish faith, white is specially employed in the celebration of the Passion of our Lord; though in the Vision of St. John, white robes are given to the redeemed, and the four-and-twenty elders stand clothed in white before the great white throne and the Holy One that sitteth there white like wool; yet for all these accumulated associations, with whatever is sweet, and honorable, and sublime, there yet lurks an elusive something in the innermost idea of this hue, which strikes more of panic to the soul than that redness which affrights in blood.

Indeed, not only the country, but western civilization, is still quite safe. White folks are still on top.

And white is still right because history says so. But y'all just never did know why before, did you?

B.C.   Johnny Hart

Hi and Lois   Mort Walker and Dik Brown

Hagar the Horrible   Dik Brown

The Unbearable Being of Whiteness (1988)

Barbara Ehrenreich

This column is addressed to my fellow white people and contains material that we would prefer to keep among ourselves. God knows we have suffered enough already from the unique problems that have confronted white people over the centuries: the burden of bringing Christianity to heathens so benighted that they usually preferred death. The agony of sunburn. But now we face what may be the biggest problem of all. You know what I mean, brothers and sisters, *low self-esteem.*

It started with the Asian menace. Many years ago "Made in Japan" applied chiefly of windup toys and samurai movies. No one thought twice about sending their children off to school with the sons and daughters of laundrymen and chop suey chefs. But now, alas, the average white person cannot comprehend the inner workings of the simplest product from the Orient, much less read the owner's manual.

In the realm of business, our most brilliant blue-eyed MBAs admit they are as children compared to the shoguns of Mitsubishi and Toshiba. As for education, well, the local high school is offering a full scholarship to the first Caucasian to make valedictorian. And what white parents have not—when pressed to the limit by their brutish, ignorant, dope fiend children—screamed, "Goddamn it, Tracey [or Sean], why can't you act more like an Asian-American?"

Yes, I know the conventional explanation: white people lack convincing role models. Consider the president, whose own son grew up believing—hoping?—that his true parents were the black help. Or consider the vice president, a man so bedeviled by bladder problems that he managed, for the last eight years, to be in the men's room whenever an important illegal decision was made. Or consider how long it took, following the defeat of Robert Bork, for the conservatives to find a white man who was clean-shaven, drug-free, and had also passed his bar exam.

Then there were the nonblack Democratic candidates, who might be considered the very flower of white manhood. For months, none of them could think of anything to say. Political discourse fell to the level of white street talk, as in "Have a nice day."

Then, stealthily, one by one, they began to model themselves after Jesse Jackson. Even the patrician Al Gore, surely one of the whitest men ever to seek public office, donned a windbreaker and declared himself the champion of working people. Richard Gephardt borrowed Jackson's rhyme about how corporations "merge" with each other and "purge" workers. Soon he was telling moving stories about his youth as a poor black boy in the South, and how he had inexplicably turned white, clear up to and including his eyebrows.

Confronted with the obvious superiority of the black candidate, many white voters became perplexed and withdrawn. We had liked to think of blacks as simple folk with large thighs and small brains—a race of Head Start dropouts, suitable for sweeping floors and assisting blond cops on TV. In fact, there is clear evidence of black intellectual superiority: in 1984, 92 percent of blacks voted to retire Ronald Reagan, compared to only 36 percent of whites.

Or compare the two most prominent men of television, Bill Cosby and Morton Downey, Jr. Millions of white Americans have grown up with no other father figure than "Cos." Market researchers have determined that we would buy any product he endorses, even if it were a skinlightener. No one, on the other hand, would buy anything form Downey, unless it was something advertised anonymously in the classified section of *Soldier of Fortune*.

Perhaps it is true, as many white people have secretly and shamefully concluded, that these facts can only be explained by resorting to genetic theories of IQ. But I still like to think there are environmental explanations. A generation ago, for example, hordes of white people fled the challenging, interracial atmosphere of the cities and settled in the whites-only suburbs. Little did we know that a life-style devoted to lawn maintenance and shrub pruning would, in no time at all, engender the thick-witted peasant mentality now so common among our people.

At the same time, the white elite walled themselves up in places like Harvard to preserve white culture in its purest form. Still others, the brightest of our race, retired to Los Alamos to figure out how to bring the culture to a prompt conclusion. Unfortunately, our extreme isolation from people of alternative races meant there was never anyone around to point out the self-destructive tendencies inherent in white behavior, which is still known collectively as "Western Civilization."

Let's face it, we became ingrown, clannish, and retarded. Cut off from the mainstream of humanity, we came to believes that pink is "flesh-color," that mayonnaise is a nutrient, and that Barry Manilow is a musician. Little did we know that all over the world, people were amusing each other with tales beginning, "Did you hear the one about the Caucasian who…"

I know. It hurts. Low self-esteem is a terrible thing. Some white men, driven mad by the feeling that people are laughing at them, have taken to running around the streets and beating on random persons of color or threatening to vote Republican.

Believe me, that kind of acting out won't help. If white people are ever to stand tall, we're going to have to leave our cramped little ghetto and stride out into the world again. Of course, there'll be the inevitable embarrassments at first: the fear of saying the wrong thing, of making mathematical errors, of forgetting the geography of the southern hemisphere. But gather up little Sean and Tracey and tell them, "We can do it! If we study and try very hard, even we can *be somebody!*"

Too clever is dumb.
German proverb

The Arab Image (1988)

Jack G. Shaheen

America's bogeyman is the Arab. Until the nightly news brought us TV pictures of Palestinian boys being punched and beaten, almost all portraits of Arabs seen in America were dangerously threatening. Arabs were either billionaire, bombers, bedouin bandits, belly dancers or bundles in black—rarely victims. They were hardly ever seen as ordinary people practicing law, driving taxis, singing lullabies or healing the sick. Though TV newscasts may portray them more sympathetically now, the absence of positive media images nurtures suspicion and stereotype.

Historically, the Arab lacks a human face. Media images are almost invariably hostile and one-sided. They articulate to, perhaps are even responsible for, the negative stereotype Americans have of Arabs. As an Arab-American, I have found that ugly caricatures have had an enduring impact on Americans of Arab heritage. For the prejudiced, during the Gulf War, all Arabs, including some of the three million Americans with Arab roots, became to many, "camel jockeys," "ragheads" and "sandsuckers." Whenever there is a crisis in the Middle East Arab-Americans are subjected to vicious stereotyping and incidents of violence and discrimination.

I was sheltered from prejudicial portraits at first. My parents came from Lebanon in the 1920s; they met and married in America. Our home in the steel city of Clairton, Pennsylvania, was a center for ethnic sharing—black, white, Jew and gentile. There was only one major source of media images then, at the State movie theater where I was lucky enough to get a part-time job as an usher. But in the late 1940s, Westerns and war movies were popular, not Middle Eastern dramas. Memories of World War II were fresh, and the screen heavies were the Japanese and the Germans. True to the cliché of the times, the only good Indian was a dead Indian. But when I mimicked or mocked the bad guys, my mother cautioned me. She explained that stereotypes hurt; that they blur our vision and corrupt the imagination. "Have compassion for all people, Jackie," she said. Experience the joy of accepting people as they are, and not as they appear in films, she advised.

Mother was right. I can remember the Saturday afternoon when my son, Michael, who was seven, and my daughter, Michele, six, suddenly called out: "Daddy, Daddy, they've got some bad Arabs on TV." They were watching that great American morality play, TV wrestling. Akbar the Great, who liked to hear the cracking of bones, and Abdullah the Butcher, a dirty fighter who liked to inflict pain, were pinning their foes with "camel clutches." From that day on, I knew I had to try to neutralize the media caricatures.

I believe most researchers begin their investigations because they have strong feelings in their gut about the topic. To me, the stereotyping issue was so important I had to study it. For years I watched hordes of Arabs prowl across TV and movie screens. Yet, a vacuum existed in the literature: research on TV and movie Arabs did not exist. My research began with television because visual impressions from the tube indoctrinate the young. Once a stereotypical image becomes ingrained in a child's mind, it may never wither away.

Investigating television's Arabs began as a solo effort. But members of my family, friends, and colleagues assisted by calling attention to dramas I might otherwise have missed. For several years, I examined *TV Guide* and cable and satellite magazines. Daily, I searched for Arab plots and characters, then taped, studied, and categorized them. To go beyond personal observations, I interviewed more than thirty industry leaders, writers, and producers in New York and Los Angeles. In the spirit of fairmindedness, I invited image makers, those influential purveyors of thought and imagination, to offer sparks of decency that illuminate, rather than distort, our perception of others.

It hasn't been easy. Images teach youngsters whom to love, whom to hate. With my children, I have watched animated heroes Heckle and Jeckle pull the rug from under "Ali Boo-Boo, the Desert Rat," and Laverne and Shirley stop "Sheik Ha-Mean-ie" from conquering "the U.S. and the world." I have read more than 250 comic books like the "Fantastic Four" and "G.I. Combat" whose characters have sketched Arabs as "lowlifes" and "human hyenas." Negative stereotypes were everywhere. A dictionary informed my youngsters that an Arab is a "vagabond, drifter, hobo and vagrant." Whatever happened, my wife wondered, to Aladdin's good genie?

To a child, the world is simple: good versus evil. But my children and others with Arab roots grew up without ever having seen a humane Arab on the silver screen, someone to pattern their lives after. It seems easier for a camel to go through the eye of a needle than for a screen Arab to appear as a genuine human being.

Hollywood producers must have an instant Ali Baba kit that contains scimitars, veils, sunglasses and such Arab clothing a *chadors* and *kufiyahs*. In the mythical "Ay-rabland," oil wells, tents, mosques, goats and shepherds prevail. Between the sand dunes, the camera focuses on a mock-up of a palace from "Arabian Nights"—or a military air base. Recent movies suggest that Americans are at war with Arabs, forgetting the fact that out of 21 Arab nations, America is friendly with 19 of them.

Audiences are bombarded with rigid, repetitive and repulsive depictions that demonize and delegitimize the Arab. One reason is because since the early 1900s more than 500 feature films and scores of television programs have shaped Arab portraits.

I recently asked 293 secondary school teachers from five states—Massachusetts, North Carolina, Arkansas, West Virginia, and Wisconsin—to write down the names of any humane or heroic screen Arab they had seen. Five cited past portraits of Ali Baba and Sinbad; one mentioned Omar Sharif and "those Arabs" in *Lion of the Desert* and *The Wind and the Lion*. The remaining 287 teachers wrote "none."

Nicholas Kadi, an actor with Iraqi roots, makes his living playing terrorists in such films as the 1990 release "Navy Seals." Kadi laments that he does "little talking and a lot of threatening—threatening looks, threatening gestures." On screen, he and others who play Arab villains say "America," then spit. "There are other kinds of Arabs in the world," says Kadi. "I'd like to think that some day there will be an Arab role out there for me that would be an honest portrayal."

The Arab remains American culture's favorite whipping boy. In his memoirs, Terrel Bell, Ronald Reagan's first secretary of education, writes about an "apparent bias among mid-level, right-wing staffers at the White House" who dismissed Arabs as "sand niggers."

Sadly, the racial slurs continue. Posters and bumper stickers display an Arab's skull and an atomic explosion. The tag: "Nuke their ass and take their gas."

At a recent teacher's conference, I met a woman from Sioux Falls, South Dakota, who told me about the persistence of discrimination. She was in the process of adopting a baby when an agency staffer warned her that the infant had a problem. When she asked whether the child was mentally ill, or physically handicapped, there was silence. Finally, the worker said: "The baby is Jordanian."

To me, the Arab demon of today is much like the Jewish demon of yesterday. We deplore the false portrait of Jews as a swarthy menace. Yet a similar portrait has been accepted and transferred to another group of Semites—the Arabs. Print and broadcast journalists have started to challenge this stereotype. They are now revealing more humane images of Arabs, a people who traditionally suffered from the ugly myths. Others could follow that lead and retire the stereotypical Arab to a media Valhalla.

The civil rights movement of the 1960s not only helped bring about more realistic depictions of various groups; it curbed negative images of the lazy black, the wealthy Jew, the greasy Hispanic and the corrupt Italian. These images are mercifully rare on today's screens. Conscientious imagemakers and citizens worked together to eliminate the racial mockery that had been a shameful part of the American cultural scene.

It would be a step in the right direction if movie and TV producers developed characters modeled after real-life Arab-Americans. We could then see a White House correspondent like Helen Thomas, whose father came from Lebanon, in "The Golden Girls," a lawyer patterned after Ralph Nader on "L.A. Law," or a Syrian-American playing tournament chess like Yasser Seirawan, the Seattle grandmaster.

Politicians, too, should speak out against the cardboard caricatures. They should refer to Arabs as friends, not just as moderates. And religious leaders could state that Islam, like Christianity and Judaism, maintains that all mankind is one family in the care of God. When all imagemakers rightfully begin to treat Arabs and all other minorities with respect and dignity, we may begin to unlearn our prejudices. The ultimate result would be an image of the Arab as neither saint nor devil, but as a fellow human being, with all the potentials and frailties that condition implies.

Jack G. Shaheen, born in 1935, teaches mass communications at Southern Illinois University in Edwardsville. He has also taught at the American University in Beirut and the University of Jordan in Amman. He is the author of The TV Arab *(1984).*

The Israelis are the Doberman pinschers of the Middle East.
They treat the Arabs like postmen.
                                        Franklyn Ajaye

GERMANS

POPULATION: *Figures unreliable*	PHYSICAL CHARACTERISTICS: *Thick!*
RELIGION: *Deutschland Uber Alles* PRACTICING: *Whenever nobody is looking*	RACIAL TRAITS (GOOD): *Start wars, Drink beer* *Like to march and wear uniforms* RACIAL TRAITS (BAD): *Lose wars, Beer belly* *Still cla·ming the Kaiser* *was a gentleman and* *Hitler was misunderstood*
LOCATION: *Milwaukee and Buenos Aires*	DIET STAPLE: *Jews*

Study Guide

Chapter 1

Acculturation

Acculturation may be defined as the modification of the culture of a group or an individual as a result of contact with a different culture. The more prolonged the interaction and the greater the amount of borrowing that occurs the more profound the acculturation. Obviously, when there is constant interaction between peoples of different cultural backgrounds, as in the United States, acculturation is an important aspect of life.

At this point, however, it will be useful to define *culture*. Culture includes all those learned and shared beliefs, customs, skills, habits, traditions and knowledge common to the members of a given society. Culture may be seen as the distinctive way of life of a particular group of people. Some describe it as a given group's design for living.

Culture usually refers to something made by human beings, rather than something that occurs in nature. For instance, the ocean, the beach, and the fish are not part of one's culture. But, how one *thinks about*, and what one *does with* the natural environment (the ocean, the beach and the fish), is very dependent upon one's culture. For at least the past 500 years the general attitude of western civilization has been the belief that human beings are, in some sense, apart from nature, that nature is something to be "conquered," to be controlled, to be used. The American Indian cultures, on the other hand, viewed nature in a very different manner. Rather than seeing themselves as being opposed to nature, they believed (and most still do), that the human being is a vital part of nature. Since we are a part of nature it is not wise to interfere with nature or try to control or use it. Clearly, different cultural groups perceive the world in very different ways. When these groups interact, interchange ideas, beliefs, even argue and fight, acculturation takes place. The beliefs and attitudes of any group can, and do, change. Thus, the modern American of Western European heritage and tradition is now beginning to view the environment and nature in a fashion much closer to that of the Native American.

Thus acculturation in many instances leads to human advancement. It is the locked-up views of the ethnocentric that prevents cultural interaction and thwarts the kind of exchange that leads to human growth and development. Certainly groups or individuals who intentionally refuse to interact, exchange ideas, and engage in borrowing tend to hold back human advancement. No social group or culture can assume that it has the best responses to human issues at all times and under all circumstances. Unfortunately, to refuse to expose oneself to other groups and ideas and values, while stifling personal growth, does give the individual a sense of comfort and security.

EXERCISES:

1. Name some values, attitudes and beliefs that you hold that are significantly different from your parents. Your grandparents. Can you identify any way in which acculturation played a part in changing any of the above?

2. How many of the values and beliefs which you still accept and live up to can you directly attribute to your cultural background?

    Example: Bill and Gretta Hansa want their children to celebrate Christmas on Christmas eve (exchange presents, etc.) because Bill's grandparents always celebrated the eve before and he has warm and affectionate memories of Christmas eve which he wants to share with his kids. Gretta grew up in a tradition which always celebrated the holiday on Christmas morning. However, her relationship with Bill has led to acculturation and she now thoroughly enjoys the idea of exchanging gifts on the evening before the holiday.

3. Consider a belief or value that you accept without question. See if you can attribute it to your cultural background.

CHAPTER 2

CLASS

Most Americans believe they live in a classless society. At least the American ideology promotes the idea that through diligence and a bit of luck anyone can "rise above" his or her social class. Certainly up until the present time the reality of upward mobility has often been labeled an "American religion." Nevertheless, as we all know, there are significant variations in standards of living, status of occupation, and the possibility of upward mobility among American citizens.

Social class has been defined in many ways. However, all refer to a hierarchical stratification, or "layering," of people in social groups, communities and societies. Membership in a given social class category is one of the ways used to distinguish one individual or group from another in such a way as to assign "worth." The urge to organize people into layers almost appears to be a trait found in most, if not all, cultures. While many Americans define class membership in terms of income, (Gilbert and Kahl, 1982) it is important to understand that money alone does not determine one's social class. Rather, one's social class standing depends on a combination of prestige, power, influence and income (Webb and Sherman, 1982).

Traditional measures of class in the United States therefore, include family income, father's occupation, prestige of one's neighborhood, the power one has and the level of education achieved by the family head. Ethnicity and race, unfortunately, often reduce one's level of social class even when the above criteria have been met. In other cultures, markers of social class may include such things as bloodline and family name, caste into which one was born and whether or not one does physical labor.

For purposes of this book, we will divide American society into five classes (Webb and Sherman, 1982). At the top of the hierarchy is a very small upper class consisting mostly of those who have inherited social privilege from others. This group is often referred to as having "old money." Second there is a large upper middle class, whose members are usually professionals, corporate executives, leading scientists, and the like. This group usually has had an extensive amount of higher education, and while family background is not especially important, manners, tastes and patterns of behavior are.

The third (or middle) social class is often referred to as the lower middle class. Persons in this group are mostly employed in white-collar jobs and earning middle level incomes. They are typically small business persons, teachers, social workers, nurses, salespersons, bank tellers and so forth. This is the largest American social class and encompasses a wide range of occupations and income. Americans in this class tend to value being respectable and having a sense of belonging. Friendliness and keeping up appearances are also considered important. Fourth in the hierarchy of social class is the working class, whose members are chiefly blue-collar workers, or employees in low-paid service occupations. Working class families typically have to struggle with poor job security, limited fringe benefits, and often work that is either more dangerous or "dirtier" than that of the classes above them.

Finally at the bottom of the hierarchy is the lower class. These individuals are often referred to as the "working poor" or even the "underclass." The latter term refers to people who have been in poverty so long that they seem to be unable to take advantage of any available options for moving up the social ladder. Clearly, poverty is both the chief problem and the major characteristic of this group of Americans.

Complicating the issues of social class is the fact that there is a large overlap between lower-middle-class, working class, and lower class membership and membership in minority groups. Black-Americans, Hispanic-Americans, and Native-Americans are the most economically deprived people in the United States. In addition, often their minority status limits their opportunity to attain better occupations, education and income and thus move up on the hierarchy.

EXERCISES:

1. Make a list of the proverbs you heard as a child growing up. Identify the underlying value(s) learned from each and try to get in touch with how such values have influenced your thinking and perhaps your life.

2. The following proverbs are scattered throughout your text. Identify an underlying value expressed in each and give a similar proverb from your own cultural background.

   African: Speak softly and carry a big stick, you will go far.
   Arabian: Trust in Allah, but tie your camel.
   French: Love teaches even asses to dance. *love lends grace to even the most lowly individual.*
   German: Too clever is dumb.
   Haitian: Do not insult the mother alligator until you have crossed the river.
   Irish: It is better to be a coward for a minute than dead for the rest of your life.
   Italian: Bed is the poor man's opera.
   Japanese: A man in love mistakes a pimple for a dimple.
   Jewish: If God lived on earth, people would break His windows.
   Spanish: There is no happiness; there are only moments of happiness.
   Yugoslavian: Tell the truth and run.

3. Think of the town in which you live, can you identify neighborhoods by social class?

4. In your high school did students tend to group together by social class? If not, how did their groupings seem to be determined?

5. List ten occupations not included in the above introduction. Make sure that you include two from each of the five social classes.

6. Decide which social class you are a member of. What do you believe you would have to do to rise to the next higher group?

Gilbert, D. and Kahl, J., *The American Class Structure*, Homewood, Il: Dorsey, 1982.

Webb and Sherman, *Schooling and Society*, 2nd Ed. New York: Macmillan, 1989.

CHAPTER 3

COMMUNICATING

Communication is an interaction in which two or more persons both send and receive messages. In this process they both present themselves and interpret each other. Expressions of friendship, affection and love depend upon a person's ability to communicate his or her feelings. So, of course, do expressions of anger, mistrust and hatred. It is certainly true that one can't *not* communicate. One's silence communicates, as does body motions and sounds such as sighs and grunts. Any two persons in communication with each other bring to the situation a set of understandings and expectations that shape the nature of their communication. It must also be remembered that both verbal and nonverbal communications are part of the same system. A person who is speaking, for example, is also displaying some facial expression, is standing or sitting in a particular way, and may be using a particular set of gestures. Sometimes the verbal and nonverbal channels of communication may be in sync, thus conveying the same message, while at other times they may contradict each other thus making communication difficult to interpret.

Human communication uses both *illocution* and *locution.* For example, a person might say, "It's cold in this room." This is illocution, a set of words placed in sequence that conveys a particular content. The literal meaning of the above sentence is clear, however, what is the intended message? Hearing someone say "It's cold," you may need to consider whether the intended message is (a) "Shut the door behind you;" (b) "Turn up the heat;" or (c) "This is a crummy, drafty apartment;" or any of numerous other possibilities. Human beings also use *paralanauage* which can also confuse the meaning of a statement, especially for one not familiar with the culture of the speaker. "*Man he's great!*," carries a very different message than "Yeah, he's a great one Examples of paralanguage include speech modifiers such as pitch, rhythm, intensity and pauses. In addition, such things as laughing, winking, yawning and groaning are other examples.

Culture and social status also have a role to play in communicating. Typically Americans place great value on "looking one in the eye." Eye contact is seen as an indication of one's ability to relate to others; it is also an indicator of the honesty of the message. However, in some cultures women are taught to lower their eyes and avoid eye contact. Under these circumstances, the message communicated may become quite confused. High status persons tend to gaze at a person more fixedly when they are speaking than when they are listening. On the other hand, the lower status person is more likely to gaze when listening and less when speaking to a person considered to be of higher status. The effectiveness of such behavior in communicating power is clear. Social psychologists speak of *display rules* or socially accepted circumstances in which one can express certain emotions and feelings in a given society. Cultures vary greatly in what emotions can be expressed; how they can be expressed; and under what circumstances.

EXERCISES:

1. Sit in a room with another person and see how long you can *not* communicate. Try this for about five minutes and then ask your partner to tell what he or she feels you have communicated during this time. How accurately did your partner pick up your obviously nonverbal communication?

2. With which person in your life do you have the greatest amount of eye contact? What do you think this indicates about your relationship with that person?

CHAPTER 4

CUSTOMS

A *custom* is a practice followed as a matter of course among a people. In some cases, it can become a common practice or usage so long established that it takes on the force or validity of law. Basically, however, a custom is usually a practice or habitual behavior based on tradition rather than written law or contract. People speak of an "unwritten law," meaning a common practice which members of a group adhere to even though it is not a written law. It is not a law in America to celebrate Mother's Day, however, most Americans would feel guilty if they did not.

A significant example of the power of custom is the fact that no matter how liberated we claim we are, we are still more or less prisoners of the history of American sexual customs. From the day we were born, long before we began to appreciate our sexual nature, we were subjected to conditioning from others in our family and society who had grown up in an earlier time when values, attitudes, and lifestyles were more or less different from what we have grown accustomed to. We often think that we start with a clean slate, however we tend to forget that we are born into the ever-developing fabric of American sexual customs.

EXERCISES:

Customs affect our behavior in many areas of living, however, for purposes of simplicity the following exercises will focus on sexual customs.

1. What are some of the more important factors that influence our developing sexual customs?

2. What historical events may have had the most influence on your parents' sexuality?

3. What positive and negative attitudes about sex did you learn from your parents, that you can trace back to specific events in your childhood and adolescence?

Chapter 5

Family

The family is a basic social unit. It may consist of a single parent with one or more children; be a nuclear family with mom, dad and kids; or it may be an extended family with many individuals of different generations all making up the family unit. Like all human responses to the realities of life one finds great diversity in the characteristics, structure, roles, child rearing practices and values as one studies the family.

What follows is a very brief and generalized overview of some of the family groups that make up modern America. Of course, intermarriage and time have changed many of the traditional family structures, however, many of these traditional structures and values still find expression in many ways.

American Indians. Since they were here first it is proper to begin with them. In each culture, patterns of values are passed on by the family, and the Indian is no exception. However, there are important differences between the Indian family and the modern "American" family. In modern America the basic unit is expected to be the family of procreation; the nuclear family. The traditional pattern of Indian family organization was quite different, with three generations involved and multiple parental functions delegated among aunts and uncles as well grandparents. Grandparents were often more available for infant and toddler care and thus continued a relationship of great importance between child and grandparent throughout the life span. The parent generation was occupied with basic life issues such as hunting, food cultivation and food preservation. Parenting roles, when not given to grandparents, were shared by several adults. All this tended to free the biological parents for a much looser, more pleasure-oriented association with their children. For children the extended family meant ties from birth allowing bonding to several parental figures. This provided a security of affection and of standards of behavior, as well as a variety of role models. In traditional Indian society sex roles were quite specific. The responsibility for teaching self-discipline and for establishing the proper limits and the development of skills were the province of the same-sex parental figures. Modern Indian families are quite interested in keeping alive the language, folkways, crafts and values associated with their tribal identities.

Black Families. Although influenced by the oppressive forces of slavery and today's society, the strong kinship bonds among Black families today can be traced to historical origins in Africa. Each aspect of life was permeated by the African belief in strong kinship bonds. Although all Africans were not engaged in agriculture, the land was extremely important to the entire community. It was owned not by individuals but by the tribal or familial group. Mbiti (1970) stresses that the "survival of the tribe" was primary and that kinship controlled tribal life and provided a sense of bonding between individuals. Unlike the European premise of "I think, therefore, I am," the African philosophy is, "We are, therefore, I am."

Slavery was a major disruption to the close kinship and family ties. People were torn from their home and tribe and thrust into servitude. Men and women were not allowed to legalize their marriages, either in the African tribal way nor the European manner. Black men were used as breeders to increase the labor supply and children and parents often separated. Despite extremely difficult conditions, family life remained important. Slaves sought to maintain the high value placed on the family and tribal relation of their African heritage. It is from this heritage of shared loyalty and strong kinship bonds that Black Americans descend. Reliance upon a strong kinship network, not necessarily drawn along "blood" lines, remains a major mode for coping with the pressures of an oppressive society. White (1972) has pointed to the number of "uncles, aunts, big mamas, boyfriends, older brothers and sisters, deacons, preachers and others who operate in and out of the Black home."

Mexican Families. In Mexican society, the nuclear family is embedded in an extended family network. The boundaries of the nuclear family are flexible with respect to the inclusion of relatives such as grandparents, aunts, uncles and cousins. Children who are orphaned or whose parents are separated may be included in the household. Single, divorced or widowed relatives may also live with the nuclear family. Interdependence, between generations and among others of the same generation characterize this kind of support network. Many family functions such as care taking and disciplining of children, financial responsibility, companionship, emotional support and problem solving are shared. The family protects the individual, and it demands loyalty. The values of family proximity, cohesiveness, and respect for parental authority are present throughout a person's lifetime. Autonomy and individual achievement are not especially emphasized. Honesty and preservation of one's *dignidad* (dignity) are basic values. Mexicans often pride themselves as being *pobre pero honesto* (poor but honest). Birth rates among Mexicans are considerably higher than among Anglo-American families. This large size is a major structural influence on many aspects of family life.

Irish Families. Although the Irish never expressed a strong interest in romantic love, they did have a surprising number of female rulers and heroines. Irish women have traditionally dominated family life. As one writer stated it: "The Irish woman had a hardy spirit, an undaunted courage and, in asserting herself, an uninhibited brass." (Potter, 1960) Irish women have a greater degree of independence than women of other ethnic groups. Irish families often paid as much attention to the education of their daughters as to their sons, and there are more Irish women in white collar and professional jobs than in most other cultures (Blessing, 1980). Usually the Irish woman found her social life mostly through the Church. Here the veneration of the Virgin Mary reinforced the view of women as independent and dominant (Kennedy, 1978). Irish women have traditionally been considered as morally superior to men. While they seem to defer to the husband's authority, they hold the family reins tightly in their own hands.

The Irish place less emphasis upon marriage than most other cultures, and romance in marriage is not the most important concept. The Irish tend to view people moralistically. One is either good or bad, strong or weak, bad guy or victim. Thus the family often designates a good child and a bad or weak one. It was common to hear a mother say: "my Sean, poor Dennis, and that Maureen." Discipline in Irish families is maintained by belittling, shaming or ridicule (Spiegel, 1971). Children are typically raised to be polite, respectable, obedient and well behaved. They are not usually made the center of attention or especially fussed over for fear of spoiling them or giving them a "swelled head."

Italian Families. In Italian there are two words meaning wall. One is for inside walls as in a building and the other is for the walls bordering on the outside. This distinction, not found in English, probably reflects the importance Italians place on boundaries. Inside the family, all emotions are seen as understandable. The Italian does not have problems with the denial of feelings found in many other cultures. There are clear values of right and wrong behavior, however, they are primarily based upon the effect they have on the family. Disgrace to the family is a major crime in the Italian home. Taking advantage of a family member is considered a grievous kind of betrayal. At all costs the family honor must be preserved. The major difficulty in an Italian family arises when family values conflict with the values of an individual.

There is little place for the separate nuclear family in Italian culture. The network of significant others includes aunts, uncles, cousins, *gumbares* (old friends), along with godparents, all of whom assume a major role in child-rearing. Unlike WASPs, who raise their children to be independent and self sufficient. (WASP parents think themselves to be failures if their children do not leave home on schedule). Italian parents raise children to be mutually supportive and to contribute to the family. Separation from the family is not desired, nor easily accepted. In the traditional Italian family the father was the head and the mother its heart. She was expected to derive her primary pleasure from nurturing her family. Her personal needs came second to those of her husband. In exchange, however, she received protection and security from all outside pressures and threats.

Jewish Families. It is difficult to describe an ethnic group that has thousands of years of history and yet no single language or country of origin. In addition, their ethnic identity and religious life are often so interwoven as to be indistinguishable. Increasing our difficulty is the fact that there are three main branches of religious Judaism in the United States: Orthodox, Conservative and Reform; each with its own set of principles, beliefs and ritual practices. Therefore, for this undertaking we will examine family life among the largest group of American Jewry (around 75%) which has its roots in Eastern Europe (Russia, Poland, etc.).

Eastern European Jewish families place primary emphasis on the following: centrality of the family; suffering as a shared value; intellectual achievement and financial success; and verbal expression of feelings.

In the Jewish culture the family is seen as a sacred institution; it is a violation of God's law not to marry. Marriage and raising children have been at the center of Jewish tradition. The Jewish father is traditionally seen as a good parent, husband and provider, and the Jewish woman as a devoted wife and the mother of intelligent children. After marriage, the obligations to the extended family continue to be important. Living far away is not accepted as an excuse for not staying connected or for failing to fulfill family obligations. Their long history of persecution has led to the assumption that suffering is a basic part of life. This suffering is expressed in a popular Yiddish saying, *Shver zu zein a yid* ("It's tough to be a Jew"). It is interesting that in both the Irish and the Jewish cultures suffering occupies a central position in the family ethos. However, in Irish families it is assumed that one suffers because one deserves punishment for one's sins while in the Jewish family the predominant view is that one suffers because "of what the world has done to you." This sense of persecution is part of a cultural heritage and is usually assumed with pride. It binds Jews with their heritage; with the suffering of Jews throughout history. Jewish Americans value verbal ability, the capacity to articulate their thoughts. In many families, children's opinions are highly valued, and it is not unusual for parents to take pride in the contributions their children make to the solution of problems. There is a less clear-cut boundary between parents and children than in many other ethnic groups. Child-rearing in the Jewish family is achieved typically through reasoning, explanation and rationality. Jewish parents tended to be permissive, over protective, and concerned about their children's happiness. Children, in turn, were expected to provide their parents with *naches*. This can be delivered in the form of achievement, financial success, marriage and grandchildren. Failure to provide some *naches* is considered unacceptable and therefore the cause of much guilt.

Blessing, P.J. Irish. In S. Thernstron (Ed.), *The Harvard Encyclopedia of American Ethnic Groups*. Cambridge: Harvard University Press, 1980.

Kennedy, R.E. *The Irish: Marriage, Immigration and Fertility*. Berkeley: University of California Press, 1978.

Mbiti, J.S. *African Religions and Philosophies*. Garden City, N.Y. Anchor Books, Doubleday, 1970.

Potter, G. *To The Golden Door*. Boston: Little Brown, 1960.

Spiegel, J. *Interplay between Individual, Family and Society*.

(J. Papajohn, Ed.). New York: Science House, 1971.

White, J. Towards a Black Psychology. In R. Jones (Ed.). *Black Psychology*. New York: Harper and Row, 1972.

CHAPTER 6

GENDER

One is either a man or a woman for reasons beyond the obvious external sexual anatomy of male and female. Recent research would indicate that the hormones that mold our external sexual anatomy before birth also create some definite male-female differences in specific areas of our brains. Before we are born many things happen to us that will eventually make us "masculine" or "feminine," male or female. The term *gender* encompasses all those elements that make us either male or female. Some of these elements effect us prior to birth; others exert their influence after we are born.

From birth on we teach children the meaning of gender. Because of the social values we attach to maleness or femaleness we condition children to respond in certain ways we consider appropriate to males or females. Baby boys are dressed in blue, given trucks or footballs, and bounced roughly by moms and dads alike. Girls are seen as "sugar and spice and everything nice," treated more delicately, given dolls to play with in an attempt to teach them mothering and nurturing. In a sense we are all brain washed (literally conditioned) to fit the gender roles or stereotypes accepted as correct and desirable for members of our society. Boys in our culture are rewarded for being assertive and aggressive. The same behavior in girls is typically seen as pushy and domineering. Every known culture has a tendency to stereotype gender roles for males and females. In some cultures the stereotyping is very evident and pervasive, while in other cultures the gender-role stereotyping is more lay-back and less obvious.

This raises some key questions that an educated person should begin to consider. For example, are boys more aggressive because of genetic differences or because of sexual stereotyping and conditioning? Are girls naturally superior verbally or is it also the result of the reward system to which girls are subject? Why are boys on average better in mathematics than girls? It is not our purpose to answer these questions at this point, however, it is important that they be discussed and their significance understood and appreciated.

The terms *sex* and *gender* are commonly used interchangeably, although they actually are very different things. Let us consider a few terms. *Gender Identity* is the self-awareness we have of ourselves as being male or female. Our sexual anatomy, the makeup of our brain and the hormones coursing through our body and the social conditioning that takes place after birth are all different but inseparable aspects of our gender identity. This identity we privately experience within ourselves. *Gender role*, on the other hand, involves everything we do or say to indicate to others and ourselves that we are male and female. This includes our sexual behavior, our being "turned on," and the way in which we express our sexual arousal. Gender role is very much involved with the many expectations, rewards and punishments, we receive from our parents, family, peers and society. To convey our gender identity to others, we tend to behave in those masculine or feminine ways our culture assigns to men and women.

Gender roles and sexual anatomy are very obvious and important factors in our sexuality, but they are not the entire picture, our sexuality is a distinct part of our personality. We are sexual persons, and our sexuality includes our sex, our gender, our gender identity, our gender role, and everything else, no matter how intangible, that makes us the sexual beings we are. We cannot separate our sexual anatomy and hormonal make-up from our up-bringing or our behavior. Our awareness of our sex and gender grows out of our constantly changing views of ourselves and the way we respond to the expectations and messages we receive from others.

EXERCISES:

1. Describe an *androgynous* person. Why do many thinking persons feel that this is the ideal state for both male and female individuals?

2. Name the five behaviors that you personally believe are most identifiable in a healthy person of your sex.

3. Describe a mature adult person in terms of personality traits.

4. Describe a typical female person in terms of personality traits.

5. Describe a typical male person in terms of personality traits.

6. Did you experience a latency period (a time when you did not want to be with kids of the opposite sex) when you were growing up? If you did, what were your feelings (fears, expectations, etc.) when your feelings for the opposite sex changed at puberty? Try to describe them in detail and at length.

7. When you were growing up, what were the typical terms you heard used to describe male and female persons? i.e. "dumb blond," "fragile female," "just like a man."

CHAPTER 7

HERITAGE

Heritage comes from the French "to inherit" and in our context means all those things that make up our ethnicity and culture that have been passed on to us as the result of one's birth and upbringing. It includes the components of one's *cultural, ethnic* and *religious* background as well as the process of *socialization* which caused one to internalize these components.

Socialization is the process through which a society teaches its members the "rules" for living in that society. It also teaches its young the values, the beliefs, customs — in short, all those things that make up a given culture. Most of these "rules" are internalized and accepted as "givens;" things one does not even think about or question. Things such as male/female roles, what is and is not funny, when one can cry, etc. are internalized in the individual through the process of socialization. For example, in some American ethnic groups becoming educated is much more important than in others. Children in these groups grow up with the internalized view of "me as a college student." Socialization therefore includes one's name, the place where one was brought up, and the parents and other relatives and significant adults who helped one internalize the value system of the group.

The *cultural component* includes one's entire family, one's language, and one's participation in the rituals and value system of the group. Culture is the sum of the beliefs, practices, habits, likes, dislikes, norms, customs, rituals and so forth that one learns as the result of being born into a given group. It is important to note that language makes culture and culture makes language. The words a cultural group uses to describe an event affects one's thoughts and feelings about that event, and the feelings and thoughts a group has about an event can cause the development of the language used to deal with and describe that event. For example, in Spanish one says: "The pencil fell from my hand," while in English the same event is described as: "I dropped the pencil." In the English version the individual takes full responsibility for the falling of the pencil, while in Spanish, nature or even the pencil itself, play a more important role.

Religion can be defined as the belief in the divine or super human power or powers to be obeyed and worshipped as the creator(s) of the universe. It includes a system of beliefs, practices and ethical values. Religions usually include moral rules (commandments) and universal principles. For instance, "Thou shalt not commit adultery," is a rule for living in a monogamous society. "Do unto others as you would have others do unto you," is a universal principle that can be applied in all human situations. The more fundamentalistic the religion is the greater the emphasis upon rules as opposed to universal principles. The religion component includes the extended family, organized group membership and participation and historic beliefs.

Ethnic background or *ethnicity*. The word, ethnic stems from the Greek word *ethnikos* meaning national or gentile and *ethnos* meaning nation or people. In modern America it usually means a member of a minority group who retains the customs, values, language or social views of his or her original group. Clearly, one's identification with his or her ethnic group is an important factor. As new generations are born and raised in contact with other ethnic groups and receive the "majority" view of life in school and the through the media, the identification with the ethnic group of birth often declines. Intermarriage is also a factor in the "watering-down" of one's ethnic identity. However, ethnicity remains a vital force in America, a major form of group identification, and a major determinant of family patterns and belief systems. The premise of equality, on which the United States was founded, required one to give primary allegiance to our national identity, fostering the myth of the "melting pot," the notion that group distinctions between people were unimportant. However, we have not "melted." There is clear evidence that ethnic values and identification are retained for many generations after immigration (Greely, 1981) and they play a significant role in determining one's life style. Second, third and even fourth generation Americans, in addition to new immigrants, differ from the dominant culture in lifestyles, values, and behavior. Ethnicity is a powerful influence in determining identity. A sense of belonging and of historical continuity is a basic human need. We may ignore it or cut it off by changing our names, rejecting our families and social backgrounds, but we do so to the detriment of our well being. (McGoldrick, 1982).

Culture, religion and ethnicity are united within each person and cannot be isolated from each other. One cannot understand and appreciate the meaning of heritage without recognition of this fact.

CHAPTER 8

RACE AND ETHNICITY

Race has been described as Man's most dangerous myth (Montagu, 1965). It is, of course, neither a myth nor dangerous when it refers to local geographic or global human population distinguished as a more or less distinct group by genetically transmitted physical characteristics. It does, however, become a dangerous myth when it implies the belief that physical and mental traits are linked, that the physical differences are associated with pronounced differences in mental capacities, and that these differences can be measured with "IQ" tests and cultural achievement. Even when using the scientists definition one must constantly remember the fact that all human beings are so much mixed with regard to origin that between different groups of individuals intergradation and "overlapping" of physical characteristics is the rule. To believe that one group constitutes a "master race" as Hitler attempted before and during World War II can lead to unbelievably horrible consequences. It is easy to see that an African Negro and a white Englishman must have had a somewhat different biological history, and that their obvious physical differences would justify the biologist in classifying them as belonging to two different races. In this sense a number of human races have been arbitrarily recognized. However, this is not the sense in which most of the older anthropologists, and most race classifiers, slave traders and racists use the term. It is this unscientific attempt to separate groups of human beings into "superior" and "inferior" classifications that constitutes the myth of "race."

Ethnicity is a term used to describe a human group whose members share a common historical heritage. When asked to complete the statement, "I am _____" with as many descriptors as can be thought of, those statements that reflect identification with a collective or reference group are often indicative of one's ethnic identity. When one responds that she or he is Jewish, Polish or Italian, one is identifying with a group of people who share a common heritage, history, celebrations and traditions, who may enjoy similar foods, or speak a common language other than English. A sense of peoplehood, or the feeling that one's own destiny is somehow linked with that of others who share this knowledge, reflects identification with an ethnic group.

One cannot discuss ethnicity without considering ethnic assimilation and acculturation. A typology has been suggested by Banks, (1990), which identifies six stages of ethnic assimilation.

In Stage 1, which he calls *ethnic psychological captivity*, the individual believes the negative myths concerning his/her group that the larger or dominant cultural group has developed. Stuck at this level, the person is usually ashamed of his or her group, and therefore develops low self-esteem and even self-rejection.

In Stage 2, *ethnic encapsulation*, the individual spends the major portion of his or her time within one's own group. This results in a high degree of ethnocentrism which alienates the individual from others. Strong negative feelings toward those who are different usually emerge, especially if the individual feels that his or her group is in someway threatened.

In Stage 3, *ethnic identity clarification,* the person at this stage has accepted him or her self and has a rather clear sense of their own group. The individual in this stage is now able to respond positively to others.

In Stage 4, *Biethnicity,* the individual at this stage has developed the skills necessary to participate fully and effectively in two ethnic cultures. Many African-Americans or Jewish-Americans have learned to function effectively in the daily work setting while returning to private lives that are more reflective of their own ethnic group. Persons in this stage can benefit from the rewards that participation in several "worlds" can offer.

In Stage 5, *multi-ethnicity and reflective nationalism,* the individual at this stage is able to function effectively in several ethnic groups within his or her own nation. He or she can understand and appreciate as well as share the values of several groups. While identifying with one's own group on a basic level these individuals may also have a strong commitment to the pluralistic nation and its values of human rights and dignity for all persons. Banks cautions, however, that many never reach this stage and often those who do participate on a superficial level, such as eating at ethnic restaurants or listening to music from other cultures. Few ever fully understand the values, symbols and traditions of other cultural groups.

Finally in Stage 6, *globalism and global competency,* the individual has developed the skills necessary to function in groups on a global level, not just within his or her own nation. These individuals have internalized universal values and principles and have the skills and commitment needed to function in a truly global context.

It must be obvious that the further one develops from Stage 1 to Stage 6 the greater the capacity to live and act in terms of true racial, social and gender equality.

EXERCISES:

1. Answer the question, I am _____. Use as many descriptive terms as possible. Look at the terms you have selected; how well do you feel they describe or reflect your identification with your own ethnic group?

2. Like many Americans, your background may consist of more than one ethnic group. How do the terms you have selected in #1 reflect each of these backgrounds?

3. If you could be reborn into a different racial or ethnic group than your own, which would you choose? Why?

Banks, J.A. "Multicultural Education: Its Effects on Students' Racial and Gender Role Attitudes," in James Shaver (ed), *Handbook of Research of Social Studies Teaching and Learning.* New York: Macmillan, 1990.

Montagu, A. *Man's Most Dangerous Myth: The Fallacy of Race.* New York: Meridan, 1965.

Chapter 9

Stereotypes

We human beings like to use convenient shortcuts in our thinking and decision making. One of the most common of these shortcuts, is the use of *stereotypes*. The term originally referred to a metal printer's plate, which would faithfully print thousands of copies of a picture, all exactly alike. Later, the famous author Walter Lippman used it to mean "pictures in our heads" about various racial, national or social groups — that is, perceptions of members of a given group as all being identical copies of each other, all having the same characteristics and traits.

For purposes of this text we will define stereotype as a mental image or set of beliefs which a person holds about most members of a particular social group. Of necessity such beliefs are highly simplified and they may be highly evaluative and rigidly resistant to change (e.g., "women are irrational," "Italians are musical.") Note that this definition does not specify that stereotypes must always be inaccurate, however, even when accurate they never apply to all members of any group and they deprive us of the opportunity of relating to a member of that group as an individual person. The stereotype becomes a psychological filter which will not allow the real person to get through to our consciousness.

Stereotypes develop and persist because they are useful. They reduce the tremendous complexity of the world around us into a few simple guidelines which we can use in our everyday thought and decisions. If we "know" that "all politicians are crooked," we can dismiss government scandals without having to think very hard about what should be done to prevent or control them. Similarly, if we believe that "women are irrational," we won't hire one to be our lawyer. Unfortunately, however, the simpler and more convenient the stereotype, the more likely it is to be inaccurate, at least in part.

Stereotyping is common to human beings in all places and in all times. Children in all parts of the world are most likely to describe a tiger as a male animal and a rabbit as a female animal. This also illustrates the fact that they are learned very early in life — a reality which adds to their resistance to change.

Stereotypes are learned in many ways, however two of the most common are:

1. *Explicit teaching.* Particularly when children are young, they are frequently given explicit stereotypic information by their parents as they are taught about life ("kitties are nice," "damn politicians," "dirty commies," "honest cops," or "police brutality"). Later on, peers and teachers may also pass on stereotypes directly. In addition, this explicit transmission of stereotypes is augmented by another process which occurs with much less conscious awareness.

2. *Incidental learning*, particularly from the mass media. This is typically a process of learning by association, in which members of a social group are repeatedly paired with particular personal characteristics. For instance, time after time, images in old movies have shown

blacks as lazy or stupid, American Indians as bloodthirsty or treacherous, women as subservient housewives, and so on. Though more recent movies and TV shows have included a wider range of behaviors for these groups, there are still subtle forms of racism in their portrayal of blacks (Pierce, 1980) and non-Americans and Chicanos are typically depicted on lower-status activities (Seggar & Wheeler, 1973). On children's TV programs, more than half the villains have accents, typically German or Russian. The repeated portrayal of such characteristics as being typical of particular social groups is a potent source of stereotypes among the mass media audience.